Writing Okinawa

Writing Okinawa is the first comprehensive study in English of Okinawan fiction, from its emergence in the early twentieth century through its most recent permutations. It provides readings of major authors and texts set against a carefully researched presentation of the region's political and social history; at the same time, it thoughtfully engages with current critical perspectives on subaltern identity, colonialism, and post-colonialism, and the nature of "regional," "minority," and "minor" literatures.

Is Okinawan fiction, replete with geographically specific themes such as language loss, identity, and war, a regional literature, distinct among Japanese letters for flourishes of local color that offer a reprieve for the urban-weary, or a minority literature that serves as a site for creative resistance and cultural renewal? This question drives the book's argument, making it interpretative rather than merely descriptive. Not only does the book provide a critical introduction to the major works of Okinawan literature, it also argues that Okinawa's writers consciously exploit, to good effect, the overlap that exists between regional and minority literature. In so doing, they produce a rich body of work, a great deal of which challenges the notion of a unified nation that seamlessly rises from a single language and culture.

Providing a much-needed critical understanding of how to read this important genre of literature, *Writing Okinawa* will be essential reading for anyone interested in Japanese literature, as well as Okinawan studies and wartime literature.

Davinder L. Bhowmik is Assistant Professor of Japanese Literature at the University of Washington, USA.

Asia's Transformations
Edited by Mark Selden, Binghamton and Cornell Universities, USA

The books in this series explore the political, social, economic, and cultural consequences of Asia's transformations in the twentieth and twenty-first centuries. The series emphasizes the tumultuous interplay of local, national, regional, and global forces as Asia bids to become the hub of the world economy. While focusing on the contemporary, it also looks back to analyze the antecedents of Asia's contested rise.

This series comprises several strands: *Asia's Transformations* aims to address the needs of students and teachers, and the titles will be published in hardback and paperback. Titles include:

Debating Human Rights
Critical essays from the United States and Asia
Edited by Peter Van Ness

Hong Kong's History
State and society under colonial rule
Edited by Tak-Wing Ngo

Japan's Comfort Women
Sexual slavery and prostitution during World War II and the US occupation
Yuki Tanaka

Opium, Empire and the Global Political Economy
Carl A. Trocki

Chinese Society
Change, conflict and resistance
Edited by Elizabeth J. Perry and Mark Selden

Mao's Children in the New China
Voices from the Red Guard generation
Yarong Jiang and David Ashley

Remaking the Chinese State
Strategies, society and security
Edited by Chien-min Chao and Bruce J. Dickson

Korean Society
Civil society, democracy and the state
Edited by Charles K. Armstrong

The Making of Modern Korea
Adrian Buzo

The Resurgence of East Asia
500, 150 and 50-year perspectives
Edited by Giovanni Arrighi, Takeshi Hamashita and Mark Selden

Chinese Society, second edition
Change, conflict and resistance
Edited by Elizabeth J. Perry and Mark Selden

Ethnicity in Asia
Edited by Colin Mackerras

The Battle for Asia
From decolonization to globalization
Mark T. Berger

State and Society in 21st Century China
Edited by Peter Hays Gries and Stanley Rosen

Japan's Quiet Transformation
Social change and civil society in the 21st century
Jeff Kingston

Confronting the Bush Doctrine
Critical views from the Asia-Pacific
Edited by Mel Gurtov and Peter Van Ness

China in War and Revolution, 1895–1949
Peter Zarrow

The Future of US–Korean Relations
The imbalance of power
Edited by John Feffer

Working in China
Ethnographies of labor and workplace transformations
Edited by Ching Kwan Lee

Korean Society, second edition
Civil society, democracy and the state
Edited by Charles K. Armstrong

Singapore
The state and the culture of excess
Souchou Yao

Pan-Asianism in Modern Japanese History
Colonialism, regionalism and borders
Edited by Sven Saaler and J. Victor Koschmann

The Making of Modern Korea, Second edition
Adrian Buzo

Asia's Great Cities

Each volume aims to capture the heartbeat of the contemporary city from multiple perspectives emblematic of the authors' own deep familiarity with the distinctive faces of the city, its history, society, culture, politics and economics, and its evolving position in national, regional and global frameworks. While most volumes emphasize urban developments since World War II, some pay close attention to the legacy of the *longue durée* in shaping the contemporary. Thematic and comparative volumes address such themes as urbanization, economic, and financial linkages, architecture and space, wealth and power, gendered relationships, planning and anarchy, and ethnographies in national and regional perspective. Titles include:

Bangkok
Place, practice and representation
Marc Askew

Shanghai
Global city
Jeff Wasserstrom

Hong Kong
Global city
Stephen Chiu and Tai-Lok Lui

Representing Calcutta
Modernity, nationalism and the colonial uncanny
Swati Chattopadhyay

Singapore
Wealth, power and the culture of control
Carl A. Trocki

The City in South Asia
James Heitzman

Asia.com

Asia.com is a series that focuses on the ways in which new information and communication technologies are influencing politics, society and culture in Asia. Titles include:

Japanese Cybercultures
Edited by Mark McLelland and Nanette Gottlieb

Asia.com
Asia encounters the Internet
Edited by K. C. Ho, Randolph Kluver and Kenneth C. C. Yang

The Internet in Indonesia's New Democracy
David T. Hill and Krishna Sen

Chinese Cyberspaces
Technological changes and political effects
Edited by Jens Damm and Simona Thomas

Literature and Society

Literature and Society is a series that seeks to demonstrate the ways in which Asian literature is influenced by the politics, society, and culture in which it is produced. Titles include:

The Body in Postwar Japanese Fiction
Edited by Douglas N. Slaymaker

Chinese Women Writers and the Feminist Imagination, 1905–1948
Haiping Yan

Routledge Studies in Asia's Transformations

Routledge Studies in Asia's Transformations is a forum for innovative new research intended for a high-level specialist readership, and the titles will be available in hardback only. Titles include:

The American Occupation of Japan and Okinawa*
Literature and memory
Michael Molasky

Koreans in Japan*
Critical voices from the margin
Edited by Sonia Ryang

Internationalizing the Pacific
The United States, Japan and the Institute of Pacific Relations in war and peace, 1919–1945
Tomoko Akami

Imperialism in Southeast Asia
'A fleeting, passing phase'
Nicholas Tarling

Chinese Media, Global Contexts
Edited by Chin-Chuan Lee

Remaking Citizenship in Hong Kong*
Community, nation and the global city
Edited by Agnes S. Ku and Ngai Pun

Japanese Industrial Governance
Protectionism and the licensing state
Yul Sohn

Developmental Dilemmas
Land reform and institutional change in China
Edited by Peter Ho

Genders, Transgenders and Sexualities in Japan*
Edited by Mark McLelland and Romit Dasgupta

Fertility, Family Planning and Population Policy in China
Edited by Dudley L. Poston, Che-Fu Lee, Chiung-Fang Chang, Sherry L. McKibben and Carol S. Walther

Japanese Diasporas
Unsung pasts, conflicting presents and uncertain futures
Edited by Nobuko Adachi

How China Works
Perspectives on the twentieth-century industrial workplace
Edited by Jacob Eyferth

Remolding and Resistance among Writers of the Chinese Prison Camp
Disciplined and published
Edited by Philip F. Williams and Yenna Wu

Popular Culture, Globalization and Japan*
Edited by Matthew Allen and Rumi Sakamoto

medi@sia
Global media/tion in and out of context
Edited by Todd Joseph Miles Holden and Timothy J. Scrase

Vientiane
Transformations of a Lao landscape
Marc Askew, William S. Logan and Colin Long

State Formation and Radical Democracy in India
Manali Desai

Democracy in Occupied Japan
The U.S. occupation and Japanese politics and society
Edited by Mark E. Caprio and Yoneyuki Sugita

Globalization, Culture and Society in Laos
Boike Rehbein

Transcultural Japan
At the borderlands of race, gender, and identity
Edited by David Blake Willis and Stephen Murphy-Shigematsu

Post-Conflict Heritage, Post-Colonial Tourism
Culture, politics and development at Angkor
Tim Winter

Education and Reform in China
Emily Hannum and Albert Park

Writing Okinawa
Narrative acts of identity and resistance
Davinder L. Bhowmik

* Now available in paperback

Critical Asian Scholarship

Critical Asian Scholarship is a series intended to showcase the most important individual contributions to scholarship in Asian Studies. Each of the volumes presents a leading Asian scholar addressing themes that are central to his or her most significant and lasting contribution to Asian studies. The series is committed to the rich variety of research and writing on Asia, and is not restricted to any particular discipline, theoretical approach or geographical expertise.

Southeast Asia
A testament
George McT. Kahin

Women and the Family in Chinese History
Patricia Buckley Ebrey

China Unbound
Evolving perspectives on the Chinese past
Paul A. Cohen

China's Past, China's Future
Energy, food, environment
Vaclav Smil

The Chinese State in Ming Society
Timothy Brook

China, East Asia and the Global Economy
Regional and historical perspectives
Takeshi Hamashita
Edited by Mark Selden and Linda Grove

Writing Okinawa
Narrative acts of identity and resistance

Davinder L. Bhowmik

Routledge
Taylor & Francis Group
LONDON AND NEW YORK

First published 2008
by Routledge
2 Park Square, Milton Park, Abingdon, Oxon OX14 4RN

Simultaneously published in the USA and Canada
by Routledge
711 Third Avenue Avenue, New York, NY 10017

Routledge is an imprint of the Taylor & Francis Group, an informa business

First issued in paperback 2012

© 2008 Davinder L. Bhowmik

Typeset in Times New Roman by
Taylor & Francis Books

All rights reserved. No part of this book may be reprinted or reproduced or utilized in any form or by any electronic, mechanical, or other means, now known or hereafter invented, including photocopying and recording, or in any information storage or retrieval system, without permission in writing from the publishers.

British Library Cataloguing in Publication Data
A catalogue record for this book is available from the British Library

Library of Congress Cataloging in Publication Data
A catalog record for this book has been requested

ISBN 978-0-415-77556-4 (hbk)
ISBN 978-0-415-54258-6 (pbk)

For Kinjō Toki

Contents

List of illustrations		xii
Acknowledgments		xiii
	Introduction	1
1	The color orange in Yamagusuku Seichū's Okinawan fiction	17
2	Subaltern identity in Taishō Japan	42
3	Marching forward, glancing backward: language and nostalgia in prewar Okinawan fiction	63
4	Ōshiro Tatsuhiro and constructions of a mythic Okinawa	89
5	Postreversion fiction and Medoruma Shun	124
6	Darkness visible in Sakiyama Tami's island stories	158
	Conclusion	179
	Notes	183
	Bibliography	216
	Index	229

Illustrations

1 Okinawa's first nationally endorsed textbook,
  Conversations in Okinawa 22
2 Book cover of Ikemiyagi Sekihō's collected works 47
3 The opening pages of Kushi Fusako's *Memoirs of a
  Declining Ryukyuan Woman* 70
4 Cover of *New Okinawa Literature*, Okinawa's premier
  postwar journal 94
5 Book cover of "Droplets," Medoruma Shun's Akutagawa
  Prize-winning story 143
6 Sakiyama Tami's beloved coffee shop, Origin (Genten),
  located in Koza 173

Acknowledgments

I am indebted to a great many people for helping me to write this book. First, I thank John Whittier Treat. His incandescent teaching of modern Japanese literature when I was still an undergraduate led me to pursue graduate studies. His encouragement of my interest in writing from Okinawa since then has never wavered. I hope I can be the model to students that he was and is to me. Jay Rubin, too, has been there from the beginning. I am humbled still by his shrewd questions and comments about my work. For his continued friendship and his generosity I am particularly grateful. That he read through another draft of the manuscript even while on a much deserved vacation to Switzerland only increases my debt to him. Early on in the project, Marilyn Ivy helped me formulate the broader questions that gave shape to my research. I could not have asked for a more congenial group of fellow graduate students to share ideas with at the University of Washington where I began this work. Rachel Dinitto, Jim Dorsey, Christine Marran, and Doug Slaymaker remain the finest of friends.

During periods of research in Japan, I was fortunate to make the connections necessary to accomplish my research goals. Instrumental in this regard was Kuroko Kazuo, a scholar of Japanese literature at Tsukuba University. His letters of introduction to colleagues, writers, and activists in Okinawa opened many doors for me. Kawamura Minato of Hōsei University has shared with me his expertise on Japanese colonial literature in and outside the classroom. He also made the necessary arrangements for me to freely access material in the Institute of Okinawan Studies, housed at Hōsei. While in Okinawa I received extraordinary kindness, guidance, and support from colleagues who teach modern Japanese literature at the University of the Ryukuyus, particularly from Nakahodo Masanori, Okamoto Keitoku, and Shinjō Ikuo. I am in awe of the tremendous work this small group of three has done to include Okinawan literature in Japanese literary studies. Sadly, Okamoto Keitoku passed away while I was still preparing this manuscript. In his quiet way, I know he would have been pleased to see its completion. Ōshiro Tatsuhiro graciously permitted me an interview in his home in Shuri where he endured my endless questions. Many others provided help in countless ways during my stays in Japan. Among them I thank, in particular, Tomoko and Ryutarō Hayashi, Kanai Keiko and Kōno Kensuke, Yōko and Yasuo Tateoka, and Tish Robinson and Jun Yokokawa.

A number of friends and colleagues have read all or part of the manuscript at different points in its development. For their invaluable comments and support, I thank Ted Mack, Scott Swaner, Chris Hamm, Ravi Singh, Jim Dorsey, and Christine Marran. I am saddened that Scott's untimely death prevented him from seeing how his comments strengthened sections of the book.

Various institutions helped to defray the cost of research and writing. At the University of Washington, I am indebted to the College of Arts and Sciences for junior faculty development awards, and to the Japan Studies Program for its continued support. I am also grateful to the Japan Foundation. At Routledge, Stephanie Rogers, Leanne Hinves and Ulrike Swientek have shown great patience and professionalism in guiding this manuscript to its completion. Mark Selden has been the kindest and most efficient of editors. I owe him much.

The motivation to write this book grew out of the great attachment I formed to Okinawa in my childhood. For providing me such an intriguing home, I thank my parents Owater and Dilawer Purhar. Since their retirement, my parents and in-laws, P. K. and Geeta Bhowmik, have been unstinting in their support of my work. Happily, much of this support came in the form of home-cooked meals. Finally, I thank Raj, Robi, and Maya Bhowmik, who made it all worthwhile.

Introduction

My initial impression of Japanese literature, hastily made in my teens after I finished Kawabata Yasunari's *Snow Country* in Okinawa, where I was born and lived for twenty years, was that it was exotic. This response to the novel is by no means unique; yet, unlike those for whom the allure of the geisha Komako makes the work linger on in the mind, it was the snow, unheard of in Okinawa, which beguiled me. Accustomed as I was to a subtropical island, far removed from the urban centers of Japan that serve as the setting for so much of the nation's imaginative fiction, the Japanese literature that I, a Cold War spy kid, first read in Okinawa struck me as doubly foreign. That is, the foreignness of *Snow Country* stemmed both from its being a Japanese novel and from the fact that it diverged so radically from the landscape of Okinawa, my childhood home and the only Japan I knew.

Donald Keene writes,

> [t]he opening paragraph of *Snow Country* is perhaps the most celebrated of any work of modern Japanese literature: "When the train emerged from the long tunnel at the provincial boundary, they were in snow country. The depths of the night had turned white. The train stopped at a signaling station."[1]

For me, these famous lines only begged the question of how Okinawa, possessing neither the snow nor the trains so ubiquitous on Japan's main islands, figured in Japan, particularly within its literary fiction. Given the images reified in Kawabata's novel, it would seem Okinawa does not figure at all, whether in the nation or in its cultural representations. On one hand, the absence in Okinawa of canonical poetic objects such as snow, persimmon, and deer severs this peripheral region from the nation's past. On the other, the prefecture's lack of trains, clear symbols of modernization, suggests that Okinawa is stuck in the past. Neither here nor there, Okinawa eludes even temporal apprehension.

If the ontological ground of Okinawa is itself slippery, then what of the literature this region yields? Does it similarly defy critical grasp? Despite the striking dissimilarities that exist between the opening scene of *Snow Country* and the landscape of Okinawa—differences that suggest Okinawa's fiction is not modern, not Japanese, and, thus, suspect as national literature—there is an important connection between this most famous Japanese novel and the representative fiction from Okinawa that my book introduces. What links the two seemingly disparate kinds of fiction—the former, which came to represent Japan to an international audience after Kawabata received the Nobel Prize in 1968, and the latter, which reached a wider audience and came to represent Okinawa to a Japanese audience in 1967, when Ōshiro Tatsuhiro, Okinawa's preeminent postwar author, received the prefecture's first Akutagawa Prize—is their function. In essence, both Kawabata's tale of the snow country and its polar opposite, stories that feature balmy Okinawa, serve as sites of healing to which the urban-weary turn for revitalization. Just as Shimamura leaves Tokyo for the hot springs of Niigata, countless readers of Okinawan fiction seek refuge in the local color it offers. Although the immediate goal of this book is to show that fiction by Okinawa's authors offers readers far more than a dash of color or a touch of verisimilitude, there is no denying the hold that vibrant southern island landscapes have had on readers who consume Okinawan fiction to revel in the pleasures of escape. The island prefecture provokes a mix of desire and disavowal in mainland Japan, just as does Canton for China, Italy for Great Britain, and the Deep South for the USA.

In this book, I examine the development of Japanese prose fiction from Okinawa, beginning with its emergence in the late Meiji period (1868–1912) and continuing to the present day. My aim is to reveal the ways in which writing in the genre differs over time, yet still remains graspable as the fiction of Okinawa. To be precise, what I am writing about is a category of literature in the genre of Japanese fiction. As it shares certain conventions, which I enumerate in the following chapters, I call this body of writing whose constitution I am investigating a "genre," although I am aware that my use of the term departs from the grand division of writing Aristotle maps in his *Poetics*. In the study that follows, I present a series of central thematics—such as history, identity, language, nostalgia, and culture—by which to understand the region's major writers and works of prose fiction. Given the comprehensive nature of this study, which examines key texts from a century of fiction from Okinawa, I necessarily focus on aspects of the writing that best answer the question that drives this book: is prose from Okinawa regional fiction or is it minority fiction? In other words, does this body of fiction affirm or challenge the prevailing narrative of Japan that holds that Japanese national identity is equivalent to race, language, and culture?[2] While I begin this investigation with a consideration of two broad ways to read prose fiction from Okinawa—as regional literature or as minority literature—I conclude the book with clear evidence, drawn from the contemporary works of Sakiyama Tami, of a third framework by which to read this fiction: as minor literature.[3] The central argument of this book is that authors of the genre consciously exploit, to good effect, the overlap that exists between regional and minority literature. In so doing, these authors produce rich works, a great many of which contest the notion of a unified nation that seamlessly rises from a single language, culture, and identity. What this book examines is *how* prose fiction from Okinawa resists naturalized ideas of national identity through creative expressions of historical, linguistic, and cultural difference.

Even as it meets the needs of readers who turn to regional fiction for solace, fiction from Okinawa, I argue, also serves the expressive needs of its authors to present a fuller picture of life in the region. Okinawa's prose fiction is replete with the history, language, culture, and identity of its denizens. Indeed, in small places like Okinawa, long caught between powerful nations, history continually insinuates itself. As a result, the region's imaginative writing reveals tensions not seen elsewhere, certainly not in popular media, which continues to fuel the "Okinawa boom" by averting the nation's gaze from the region's colonial past and neo-colonial present and directing it instead toward affirmations of Okinawans' food, music, dance, and lifestyle. This latest type of colonization is cultural rather than material in form. Once it is internalized and reproduced by Okinawans themselves, a curious thing happens: the countercolonization of Japanese cultural space. It is precisely because the production and consumption of cultural forms is such a muddy exercise that Okinawan fiction cannot be neatly characterized. It is not simply writing that serves as a site for mainland Japanese to heal, nor is it only a means by which Okinawans can protest their lot: it is both.

While the literary texts I discuss underscore key distinctions of prose from Okinawa, particularly with regard to history, language, culture, and identity, the differences to which I point are ones of degree, not kind. I raise these differences less to celebrate alterity than to provide a nuanced view of Okinawa, and, by extension, its fiction. Thus, this study speaks both to the sunny depictions of the island endlessly produced by mass media and to the decidedly negative cast of much scholarship that concerns Okinawa.[4] Of course, as I will show, it is the region's tumultuous history that accounts for much of this negativity: its centuries of oppression, from the time of colonial rule of Okinawa by the Shimazu clan of Satsuma in the early seventeenth century to decades of prewar imperial subjectification, wartime annihilation, a protracted American occupation, and Okinawa's present neocolonial incarnation as Japan's most heavily militarized prefecture. To be sure, this unkind history provides Okinawa's authors with plenty of material for their fiction, but I maintain that there are other matters with which this fiction is concerned. Language, culture, and identity are as inextricably linked to Okinawa's prose fiction as is the region's tumultuous history. If it is the weight of Okinawa's history that casts a shadow over the region's prose, then it is its authors' creative expressions of identity and culture that fill Okinawan fiction with unexpected light.

Since my interest is in the literary and historical significance of Okinawan fiction, I focus on matters of style, form, and narrative while making clear the relation between the texts and the times. From my first chapter on Yamagusuku Seichū, Okinawa's pioneering author of fiction, to my concluding chapter on Okinawa's most intrepid author, Sakiyama Tami, I aim to provide a measured analysis of the genre, much needed in a field beset with identity politics. In my readings of Okinawan fiction I do not attempt to resolve a complex history; rather, I map contradictions inherent in the genre: the constancy of its traditions and the rapidity of change in the wake of both external forces and internal needs.

The issue of Okinawa

In his 1903 essay "The Souls of Black People," W. E. B. DuBois wrote,

> Between me and the other world there is ever an unasked question: unasked by some through feelings of delicacy; by others through the difficulty of rightly framing it. All, nevertheless flutter around it. [...] To the real question, How does it feel to be a problem? I answer seldom a word.[5]

As the title of DuBois's essay indicates, his characterization of black souls as "problems" arises from a particular American context. Nevertheless, he might well have been discussing the case of Okinawa, itself long viewed as a problem by others.

Why a problem? In particular, the "Okinawa problem" refers to the burden Okinawa continues to bear today as Japan's most heavily militarized prefecture, more than a quarter century after its twenty-seven-year American occupation.[6] More broadly, the "Okinawa problem," as Ōshiro Tatsuhiro explains, relates to the region's culture, one which he steadfastly believes lies somewhere between assimilation with Japan and independence from it.[7] The issue of culture in Okinawa predates the twentieth century by several hundred years. Okinawans who decry the prefecture's current plight as Japan's "war prefecture" typically wax nostalgic for the distant past, as early as the fifteenth century, when Okinawa was the center of the seafaring, independent kingdom of Ryukyu. This averting of the eye, from the unsightly bases that occupy much of Okinawa's prime land, to a pristine, irenic past, is a familiar trope in the rhetoric of authenticity. A strategic move, it is made by those who, resisting their present lot, lay claim to cultural distinctiveness through a valorization of the past. As irresistible as it may be for Okinawans to define themselves as Ryukyuan—or Japan's cultural other—doing so only fuels racist discourse, which, ironically, operates in a similar fashion. Though motivated by a different political position, in its emphasis on difference, this racist discourse merges with the rhetoric of authenticity. In the end, differences raised in racist discourse do not affirm the distinctiveness of the individual so much as they suggest deviation from a normative (Japanese) subject. This putative deviation, in turn, then neatly serves as the basis for discrimination.[8]

When the Shimazu clan from Satsuma invaded Ryukyu in 1609, the kingdom initially enjoyed a cultural efflorescence, benefiting from continued trade with China and Japan, countries to which it paid dual tribute. During this time, it was the powerful Shuri kingdom that ruled weaker neighboring islands such as Amami Ōshima and Miyako in a heavy-handed manner. Thus, center–periphery tensions are by no means limited to Tokyo and Okinawa, but exist, as they have for centuries, within the Ryukyu island chain. One only need visit the remains of castles in the central town of Nakagusuku or the northern city of Nago on the main island of Okinawa to realize that the Ryukyu kingdom, centered in the southern city of Shuri, was by no means free of power struggles. The stark contrast Okinawan nationalists draw between the region's presumed innocent past and tainted present is as simplistic as it is essentialist. To avoid such reductionist thinking, I believe it is critical to distinguish between essentialism and historical circumstances. Despite what travel brochures proclaim, there is no distinctive Okinawan spirit; however, there has been, at least since the seventeenth century colonization of Ryukyu by the Shimazu clan, an Okinawan predicament.

The Satsuma invasion in the early seventeenth century foreshadows a series of encroachments of Okinawa and its people made by the nation-state of Japan, soon after its formation in 1868. Despite the abolition of the clan system in 1871, Ryukyu was designated a clan (*han*) in 1872 and remained in this anomalous state until 1879 when Japan formally incorporated the territory as a prefecture. The last king, Shō Tai, whom the state had named a marquis in 1871, was then taken against his will to Tokyo, where he remained imprisoned for five years. Japan forcibly annexed the Ryukyu kingdom precisely when Okinawans were living in poverty due to the Shimazu clan's increasing exploitation of them.

That Okinawa became a de-facto colony even as it was formally designated a prefecture in 1879 is not difficult to argue. Not only were all prewar governors and educational administrators mainland appointees but also most police officers in Okinawa came from Kagoshima, clearly suggesting a continuation of Satsuma authority. Military conscription, one of the primary means by which to unify the nation-state, was made "universal" in 1873; in Okinawa it began a quarter of a century later, in 1898. The region's financial health did not improve after annexation. Rather, Okinawa, which was then and still remains Japan's poorest prefecture, spent more on taxes as a percentage of income than any other region in the prewar period.[9] While there are compelling cases for viewing this series of events in terms of the modernization of Okinawa rather than in terms of its colonization, it seems to me that what tips the balance in these arguments is the degree to which the nation-state acted according to its own needs.[10] The 1879 annexation of Okinawa furthered the reach and strength of the nation, just as the formal colonization of Taiwan and Korea did, in 1895 and 1910 respectively.

6 Introduction

The same year DuBois published "The Souls of Black People" (1903), Okinawans railed at their inclusion in an exhibition at the Fifth Domestic Exposition for the Promotion of Industry, held in Osaka's Tennōji Park. The ostensibly scientific exhibit, titled the "House of Peoples" (*Jinruikan*) consisted of a primitive hut in which two prostitutes brought from Okinawa were displayed as "Ryukyuan noblewomen." Joining these women were other human specimens such as Ainu from Hokkaido, Taiwanese aboriginals, Indians, a Turk, and an African. Okinawans' anger at the patently discriminatory racial hierarchy the exhibit reinforced led organizers to return the two prostitutes to Okinawa. This quieted the controversy but did little to lessen the humiliation Okinawans experienced as a result of the incident. The event remains a flashpoint in prefectural history and resonates more than a century later as the indeterminate status of Okinawa persists in the national imaginary. Out of this ambiguity come the most powerful works of Okinawan fiction.[11]

Writing Okinawa

Even after its incorporation into the nation-state, loyalties in Okinawa remained divided between Japan and China until the former's victory in the Sino-Japanese war in 1895. Previously, Okinawa was neither fully integrated into the nation-state, nor was it completely absent from the Chinese world order. Yamagusuku Seichū depicts the prefecture's ongoing negotiation of its place in "Mandarin Oranges" ("Kunenbo," 1911), a pioneering work of Okinawan fiction, which I discuss in Chapter 1. Okinawa's fluctuation between the territory of China and Japan proper came to an end in 1895, when Okinawans recognized that despite cultural ties with China, their ultimate success rested in the hands of Japan, now the more powerful nation.

Of course, Okinawan identity did not simply cohere overnight. Identification and disidentification with others remains central to Okinawa's ongoing construction of its identity. In Chapter 2, I focus on the issue of identity in Okinawa during the Taishō period (1912–26) by analyzing Ikemiyagi Sekihō's finely crafted story, "Officer Ukuma" ("Ukuma Junsa," 1922) through the postcolonial concept of the subaltern. In tandem with Ikemiyagi's story, I discuss mainland critic and writer Hirotsu Kazuo's "phantom novella," *The Wandering Ryukyuan* (*Samayoeru Ryūkyūjin*, 1924), since Hirotsu's work, as its title asserts, well illustrates that Okinawan identity, far from being fixed, is in constant flux.

Though 1880, the year following Okinawa's annexation, marked the inauguration of Japanese language education in the prefecture, the state's effort to fashion Japanese subjects out of Okinawa's citizens escalated after the proclamation of the Imperial Rescript on Education in 1890 and Japan's victory in the Sino-Japanese war, five years later.[12] Imperial subject education took place throughout Japan, but the degree to which educators enforced standard language was most acute in the nation's extremes. Coercive measures were taken in Tōhoku, to the north, and Kagoshima and Okinawa in the south, where students who lapsed into dialect at school were made to wear dialect-tags (*hōgen fuda*). The most extensive use of these tags occurred in Okinawa prefecture, where the local language was prohibited not only in public but also in private.

Okinawa's prewar authors, beginning with Yamagusuku Seichū, freely used dialect to varying degrees in order to infuse their works with local color and thereby make them realistic. However, after forty years of imperial subject education through the medium of standard Japanese, Okinawa's residents acquired the facility in Japanese they would need to succeed as subjects of the nation-state; what they lost in the process was the language of felt life. Chapter 3 focuses on the effect national language policies had on Okinawan prose. In my readings of prewar fiction I show a conspicuous absence of any markers of Okinawan language, identity, and culture. Save for fleeting glimpses of a nostalgic past that emerge, I argue, as assertions of identity, this style of writing is virtually indistinguishable from mainland authors who, for much of the prewar period, wrote in an autobiographical vein. These forays into the past, brief as they are, call to mind the writing of the Japanese Romantic School (*Nihon rōman-ha*), also noted for its nostalgia for lost origins.

The devastation wrought by the Battle of Okinawa in the spring of 1945 forced authors to think anew about the direction Okinawan fiction would take in the postwar era. The leveling of Okinawa and subsequent defeat of Japan provided writers a blank slate upon which to create new possibilities, ones that were difficult to achieve in the preceding era, in no small part due to its strictures on language.[13] If 1880 marked the inaugural year of standard language education in the increasingly repressive prewar period of imperial subjectification, 1946 marked the beginning of a period of cultural recovery in Okinawa. More than any other writer from Okinawa, Ōshiro Tatsuhiro remains firm in his resolve to make the southern islands the cornerstone of his fiction. Indeed, Ōshiro's ambition knows no bounds. Going so far as to call himself Japan's Faulkner, he seeks to recreate, if only in myth, Okinawa's vibrant culture. What Ōshiro lacks in humility, he makes up through his sheer determination to inscribe Okinawa into fiction. Comprised of thirteen volumes, his collected works appeared in 2002 with much fanfare, particularly given the economic conditions of the time. A slump in Japan's publishing industry, created in part by the country's decade-old stagnant economy, resulted in far fewer publications of such collected works.

Ōshiro's works center on all the critical themes of Okinawan fiction: the island's history, language, identity, and indigenous culture. As attentive as Ōshiro is to the region's history, however, I view his works as curiously united by a singular concern to transcend the particulars of Okinawa. In this respect, Ōshiro heeds the recommendation of Iha Getsujō, who, as Okinawa's foremost literary critic in the Meiji period, looked beyond mainland Japan in search of literary models that Okinawa's writers might emulate. Iha urged writers in Okinawa to connect indigenous culture to universal truths, much as Yeats had done through English prose that captured the nuances of Irish culture. Thus, even as he focuses on Okinawa in his writing, Ōshiro's fiction conjures a mythic, alternative world for readers wishing to escape the region's harsh realities. In so doing, he unwittingly provides the fantasy world to which so many readers of Okinawan fiction are drawn. In Chapter 4, I examine the rediscovery of Okinawa's culture in Ōshiro's mid-to-late-1960s fiction and consider his vision of culture with that presented in a series of essays written from the 1950s to the 1970s by mainland author Shimao Toshio. In these essays, collectively known as the *Theory of Yaponesia* (*Yaponeshia-ron*), Shimao painstakingly records aspects of southern island culture, as does Ōshiro in his fictional work. I argue that while both authors' efforts to represent culture in their writing may well be sincere, these efforts are ultimately undermined by conflicting desires.

Okinawa's succeeding generation of writers shares with Ōshiro a deeply personal connection to the prefecture, despite their clear departure from Ōshiro's methods and a palpable resistance to his considerable influence. These younger writers' postreversion fiction bears few signs that the prefecture's return to Japan on May 15, 1972 has effected a complete homogenization of culture. Indeed, the finest writers among them, such as Medoruma Shun and Sakiyama Tami, whom I discuss in Chapters 5 and 6 respectively, succeed in writing stories that straddle the divide between the concerns of Okinawan prose and issues that run through a wide range of international fiction. Whereas Ōshiro's works target mainland readers eager to learn about Okinawa, as Sakiyama herself notes, Medoruma's differ in orientation.[14] The questions upon which his narratives uneasily rest are more likely directed to Okinawans themselves. Ōshiro may be content to teach outsiders certain lessons about Okinawa; Medoruma is not. In his fiction, he pointedly implicates fellow Okinawans, making his work far more polemical but nonetheless engaging. The appeal of Medoruma's fiction lies in his liberal mix of the magical with the real to pose questions of history, particularly the Battle of Okinawa. His fresh writing style destabilizes truth, unlike Oshiro's fiction, which, despite its focus on the particulars of Okinawa, ultimately upholds transcendental ideals.

Sakiyama Tami's own island stories appear, superficially, at least, firmly rooted in the terrain of Okinawa. However, as I argue in the final chapter of this book, the ironies of her fiction turn on their heads all the conventions of Okinawan fiction, making her writing verge on that which dismantles the genre. Sakiyama neither writes to teach mainland Japanese, as Ōshiro does, nor to instruct Okinawans, as Medoruma does. Rather, she perversely confounds all readers. Those daring enough to engage in her wild dance of standard Japanese and island language (*shima kotoba*) may glimpse traces of the links that tie her, albeit loosely, to fellow writers in the genre. Even as

Sakiyama labors to defamiliarize her writing, creating fiction difficult to place alongside representative works of the genre, in the final analysis, hers is writing in which Okinawa remains identifiable. The islands she depicts may not bear a direct resemblance to those that make up the prefecture, but that is Sakiyama's point: language is not a transparent medium by which to represent reality. Sakiyama's endlessly repeating island, which she likens to the act of writing, never completely reveals itself. To the trained eye, it is perceptible, however. To the trained ear, it may even be audible.

Framing Okinawan fiction

Having sketched the broad contours of the prose fiction from Okinawa I examine in this book, I turn now to discuss some of the ways to consider the genre. Standard histories of Japanese literature make scant mention of fiction from Okinawa despite the publications of local literary historians Okamoto Keitoku and Nakahodo Masanori. Long-established professors at the University of the Ryukyus, Okamoto and Nakahodo have introduced in their many works several important twentieth-century authors from Okinawa.[15] Outside of Okinawa, revisionist scholarship has begun to include the genre in discussions of Japanese literature but not without disquieting effects. For instance, Iwanami Press devotes one of seventeen volumes of its *Literary History of Japan*, published in 1996, to literature from Okinawa. A curious twist accompanies this welcome addition to the canon's purview, however. Rather than adopt the term most scholars from Okinawa use when referring to this body of writing—Okinawan literature—the Iwanami editors call it literature from Okinawa. The difference in Japanese, *Okinawa bungaku* (Okinawan literature) versus *Okinawa no bungaku* (literature of/from Okinawa), is slight, but telling. The metropolitan editors' emendation depoliticizes the fiction, which local literary historians have defined, in part, as containing within it antimainland sentiment.[16] By taking the subversive bite out of regional writing, the editors make it palatable for domestic consumption, like so many other commodified objects that market forces demand as they seek out the difference and diversity by which they grow. In short, if writing is regional, or from Okinawa, it is presumed to lie within the national frame, slightly different on account of its subtropical settings and quaint dialects but, at its core, essentially the same as prose from the main islands of Japan.

As I acknowledge in the first page of this book, given the confines of mainland Japan, particularly in its urban centers, readers may turn to prose fiction from Okinawa precisely because it is regional in nature. That is, readers seek writing in which the island prefecture becomes, in film critic Aaron Gerow's words, "a free play of space."[17] As seductive as is the idea of regional literature, which offers to authors the promise of their inclusion into the nation's fold, once regional literature gains entry into the canon of Japanese letters, the differential elements out of which regionalism is created vanish. The burden of modernity, Geoffrey Hartman explains, is what provokes in individuals a strong desire for "local romance," for stories that evoke a particular place, a home.[18] And as Stephen Dodd argues, it is in response to cries of alienation and despair that the native place (*furusato*) emerges as a tantalizing prospect, offering a cure for all that ails the writer.[19] To guard against the real danger of neutralizing prose fiction from Okinawa, it is vital to remain attentive to what makes this literature distinctive in the first place.

Since the late Meiji period when Japanese critics clamored for local color realism in fiction, Okinawa's authors have made it a prominent feature in their writing. Along with flora and fauna distinctive to the region, authors have, to varying degrees, incorporated local dialect within their works. In and of themselves, subtropical settings and language variations do not present much difficulty to readers who travel to Okinawa through its fiction. Rather, they provide the foreign atmosphere sought by those who embark on such journeys. It is when regional fiction goes beyond pedestrian local color realism that travel becomes much riskier. When lush settings give way to somber tombs where Okinawan civilians escape artillery fire, or to damp caves in which student nurses die by their own hands rather than suffer the indignity of capture by the enemy—not necessarily American—prose fiction from Okinawa demands pause. When expressions of intimacy are uttered in perfectly accented Japanese because to speak otherwise marked one as a wartime spy subject to immediate execution, readers become increasingly uneasy. What begins as purely escapist travel ends on a far different note. Drawn from the comfort of their armchairs, readers are pulled into Okinawa's history, which remains an insistent foreground to so much of its fiction.

To read prose from Okinawa as minority fiction requires that differences in language, history, culture, and identity remain in play rather than fade in significance, as is the case whenever a dominant culture subsumes regional prose. Critic David Lloyd confirms this point when he describes canonization as a "process of radical deculturalization."[20] While viewing Okinawan prose through the framework of minority fiction draws necessary attention to issues of difference, the framework itself is by no means free of problems. The danger in viewing Okinawan fiction as minority fiction in Japan lies in its minimizing the difference that exists between Okinawans and other minority groups in the nation. Those who feel they are "resident Okinawans" in Japan may indeed share similar experiences with resident Koreans, but the two groups have altogether distinct histories.[21] Conversely, in arguing for the distinctiveness of Okinawan fiction, there emerges the attendant risk of overemphasizing difference.

Neither regional literature nor minority literature is, by itself, a satisfying critical framework by which to understand prose fiction from Okinawa. Dominant culture subsumes regional literature, whose difference it views as innocuous; it also rejects minority literature, whose difference it views as threatening. Yet, these frameworks are not mutually exclusive. I have found that Okinawan fiction is best understood as writing in Japanese that reflects Okinawa variously—much like a kaleidoscope turns—through differing moments of the prefecture's tumultuous history. The radical historical transformation of Okinawa in the past century necessarily means that a single framework cannot be useful. The theme of identity that looms large for Taishō author Ikemiyagi Sekihō, to give one example, is not the central concern of authors who wrote in the more repressive 1930s. Prose fiction from Okinawa is nothing if not ambiguous, lying between the opposing frameworks of regional and minority literature.

The concept of minor literature, which philosophers Gilles Deleuze and Félix Guattari introduce, and by which I analyze Sakiyama Tami's prose in the final chapter of this book, resolves certain problems inherent in the frameworks of regional literature and minority literature. In their theory, Deleuze and Guattari argue that minor literature consists of three important characteristics: (1) a tendency to deterritorialize a dominant language, which is both an imposed and chosen medium; (2) a representation of the world as politicized; and (3) an articulation of a collective consciousness.[22] Like Kafka, upon whose writing Deleuze and Guattari base their concept of the genre, Sakiyama Tami, I argue, writes minor literature (Okinawan fiction) in a major language (Japanese). In its departure from the major, or canonical tradition, minor literature avoids the limitations of regional literature. And, through its intensive use of language, it achieves artistic liberation. Thus, to read Okinawan fiction as minor literature is to retain the political subversiveness of the writing and to recognize its artistic potency, something that neither the framework of regional literature nor minority literature permits.

While Sakiyama's writing presents the clearest case of minor literature in this book, the entire body of Okinawan fiction is fraught with the issue of language. From the inception of the genre, rather than discuss what subjects fiction would take up, intellectuals in the Meiji period focused instead on the language in which it would be written: Japanese. Given that Okinawan fiction is penned in a majority language in which writers consciously intersperse varying degrees of dialect, it is impossible to read this fiction without a consideration of power relations in the linguistic field. The incorporation of dialect, in particular, is a perennially thorny issue. For example, to circumvent the problem of valorizing one of Okinawa's many dialects over another, Ōshiro manufactures an artificial language for the dialogue portions of his story, "Turtleback Tombs" ("Kamekōbaka," 1966.) Taking another tack, fellow Akutagawa Prizewinner Higashi Mineo chooses the dialect of Koza to write his novella, *Child of Okinawa* (*Okinawa no shōnen*, 1971). These two authors' use of dialect has provoked much critical comparison. When set against the far more natural speech of Higashi's work, Ōshiro's constructed language fails to impress. Yet, if it is the case that writers use dialect to impart realism, then their attempts to do so are no more or less successful than any attempt to represent speech through written language.

Readers' expectations only exacerbate matters in that they encourage the infusion of dialect in contemporary writing today. Despite the fact that occupation policies, which transformed Okinawa from an agrarian to a service and wage-based economy centered in urban areas, and education and mass media, which became centralized following reversion, largely eroded the use of dialect in Okinawa, heterogeneous language remains a staple ingredient in postwar Okinawan fiction. Some writers are judicious in their use; others are justly condemned for self-exoticism. As if yielding to the performative aspect of writing Okinawan fiction, Sakiyama Tami saturates her stories with island language. In doing so, she appears to exceed readers' expectations, and yet, curiously, Sakiyama's hybrid style does not come from a desire to assert regional identity. Rather, she is fully cognizant of the ironies that attend the representation of speech in writing, employing heterogeneous language instead to lure the unsuspecting reader. As inventive as Sakiyama's stories are, they point to the dilemma every writer of Okinawan fiction faces. Whether one eschews dialect, uses it sparingly or more liberally, each decision involves a risk. The mixture of language in Okinawan fiction attests both to its authors' creativity and to their complicity with market forces. In the Meiji period authors used Japanese, a state-imposed linguistic medium; today, savvy authors who perform culture write fiction in dialect less to strike back at the metropole than to satiate the needs of mainland readers. Never an easy matter, language choice continues to fuse art with politics in Okinawan fiction.

The contingency of the genre

Contrary to my expectations that prose fiction from Okinawa would lose its distinctiveness following the island's return to Japanese sovereignty in 1972, fiction published during the past quarter-century continues to reflect concerns of history, language, culture, and identity, just as it did in the prewar and occupation period. Thus, even as I risk reproducing the ideology that gives rise to the genre of Okinawan fiction by proposing it as a unitary category in this book, I find that the concept still remains operative. On the subject of atomic-bomb fiction, another distinct genre of Japanese literature, John Whittier Treat writes, "Genre is an operation of confinement, privileging, and sometimes protest: but it always means."[23] By discussing fiction from Okinawa as a genre, I am insisting that this body of writing be read in certain ways. Whatever the surface appeal this fiction holds—with its dreamy island tableaus and folksy language and customs—the genre continues to function as a creative space in which Okinawa's authors express particular concerns that bear a relation to Okinawa's past, present, and future.

Today, much of the discourse on Okinawa, both academic and journalistic, focuses on protests against US military bases in Okinawa, violence inflicted on the nearby civilian population, and the degradation of local culture bordering the bases. While such acts of aggression took place throughout the postwar period, responses to them reached a feverish pitch in the mid-1950s, late 1960s, and mid-1990s. The earliest peak occurred in 1956 when landholders spearheaded a protest against land seizures by the US military, then shoring its resources to fight the Cold War. Following this, there came opposition to the US–Japan Security Treaty, which galvanized the vast majority of Okinawans to support efforts to return the cast-off prefecture to Japanese sovereignty. Since Okinawa's reversion to Japan in 1972, its residents' hopes for parity with the mainland and the easing of US military domination of the islands have remained unmet. The reason the disturbing 1995 schoolgirl rape became a signal event in global politics is because it, like the 1903 "House of Peoples" incident, painfully underscored Okinawa and its residents' liminal place in the nation. This act of sexual violence, which so quickly became a symbolic incident, calls for reflection.

On September 4, 1995, a twelve-year-old Okinawan schoolgirl was gang-raped by three American servicemen in a sugar cane field on the outskirts of Kin village in Okinawa prefecture.[24] The incident, horrific in itself, was compounded by the fact that it occurred during the closing days of a summer that marked the fiftieth-year ceremonies commemorating the end of World War II. The timing of the incident, the girl's young age, and the geopolitically entangled scene of the crime all contributed to capture the imagination of local, national, and international audiences. Six weeks later, on October 21, in one of the largest protests in the island's postwar history, 85,000 Okinawans gathered together to rally against the American presence. Governor Ōta Masahide, buoyed by this unprecedented show of support, refused to sign the renewal of base leases, confounding officials in both Tokyo and Washington. In large cities throughout Japan, thousands protested to show their sympathy for the plight of Okinawans unduly burdened by military bases. Abroad, the rape of a young girl was likened to the rape of the island prefecture, not only by Americans but also by Japanese who first invaded the region in 1609, annexed it in 1879, and sacrificed the island in 1945.[25]

Just as Governor Ōta used the shocking incident of adolescent rape as a basis for seeking a reduction in military installations on Okinawa, news analysts the world over insisted on relating the incident as a metaphor for the island, despite the dangers inherent in such an overlapping. At one level, the rape and the military presence are conjoined by the fact that both were unwanted penetrations of force. On another level, such linkages occur precisely because Okinawa's turbulent history makes it difficult to separate individuals and their personal stories from the collective consciousness so readily ascribed to the island prefecture. Despite the astute refutations by Aijaz Ahmad, and many others, of Fredric Jameson's theory that all Third World texts are national allegories, owing to a lack of division between the personal and political realms, there is, as even Ahmad recognizes, "a very tight fit between the Third World Theory, the overvalorization of the nationalist ideology, and the assertion that 'national allegory' is the primary, even exclusive, form of narrativity in the so-called Third World."[26] For better or worse, Jameson's pronouncement proves fitting for much Okinawan fiction.

In speaking of the American South, William Faulker once quipped, the past isn't dead; it isn't even past. He might well have been speaking of Okinawa, where just a year shy of the sixtieth anniversary commemorating the end of World War II, prefecture residents were again rudely reminded of Okinawa's ambivalent status within Japan. In the middle of the afternoon on August 13, 2004, a helicopter from Futenma Marine Corps Air Station crashed onto the nearby campus of Okinawa International University, strewing debris for miles. Members of the crew sustained injuries, but miraculously no civilians were injured because the crash occurred during summer holidays. Several houses and automobiles in the vicinity were damaged, however. Adding insult to injury, the US military denied Okinawa Prefectural Police permission to conduct its own investigation, despite the location of the crash site. Unlike the furor generated by the schoolgirl rape a decade prior, this accident drew little notice outside Okinawa, perhaps because the damage was largely limited to property and perhaps because it was just another in a long string of military-related accidents in the island's postwar era.[27] Had the university been in session, students certainly would have been hurt. Even so, the incident crystallized the contradictions of daily life in Okinawa. Like its sister prefectures, Hiroshima and Nagasaki, Okinawa has labored in recent years to reinvent itself through tourism as an oasis of peace.[28] However, the prefecture's massive US military presence is a daily affront to this image of peace. In spite of the constraints on human agency imposed by Okinawa's geopolitical position, or rather, perhaps because of them, Okinawa's authors reveal a secret history through their fiction, a heady mix of art and politics.

As Japan's virtual, internal, or military colony, Okinawa continues to experience the ill effects of war. Residents still endure discriminatory treatment, as evidenced by the aftermath of the helicopter-crash incident. The US–Japan Status of Forces Agreement, enacted in 1960 and heavily criticized by leftists in Japan ever since, allowed American military forces to cordon off the accident site and disallowed local police and residents from entering the area for six days, despite the accident's having occurred on prefectural territory.[29] If the 2003 helicopter crash did not confirm Faulkner's words about the hauntedness of the present, then the 2007 textbook controversy most certainly did. While screening textbooks in early spring of 2007, the national Education Ministry reached a decision to remove phrasing that indicated the Japanese military forced civilians in Okinawa to commit mass murder during the Battle of Okinawa. Okinawans' reaction to this whitewashing of history was fierce. On September 29, 2007, in the largest protest since reversion, 110,000 people staged a rally in Ginowan demanding a retraction of the Ministry's ruling. This show of resistance resulted in a rare move by the Ministry to permit requests from high-school textbook publishers to insert previously objectionable phrasing such as "forced by the military." Such events freight the stories writers from Okinawa tell and cannot but impact those who read them.[30] In the representative works of the genre I discuss in this book, few stories can be read without reference to such extraliterary issues as history, language, culture, and identity.

Take, for example, the first half of this book, in which I introduce major prewar writers and the themes with which they grappled. The nation-state's emphasis on cultural nationalism in the years leading to the Battle of Okinawa figures prominently in this writing. According to Okamoto Keitoku, the intensity of imperial subjectification, which took place from 1879 to 1945, cast a negative light on Okinawan fiction (*hi no bungaku*) as it strove toward, but always fell short of, the imagined heights of fiction issuing from Tokyo. Yet, this characterization is significant only so far as we equate modernity with Tokyo. The negativity of which Okamoto writes is, like the perceived marginality of Okinawa, nothing more than an ascribed trait. Therefore, it is crucial to consider the position from which he speaks. Might the statement not reflect the constraints placed on Okamoto, an Okinawan scholar of Japanese literature employed in a national university? Rather than characterize decades of prewar writing as negative, one might regard this fiction as ahead of its time, given the circumstances of Okinawa's history wherein the region experienced the shock of modernity as early as the seventeenth century.

A major theme of postwar Okinawan fiction, the subject of the second half of this book, is the decimation of the civilian population in the Battle of Okinawa, deaths that bear witness to Benedict Anderson's conclusion that whatever the ills of nationalism, "nations inspire profoundly self-sacrificing love."[31] The battle that raged in the spring of 1945 looms large even in the postreversion period when young writers such as Medoruma Shun began to write of war's trauma. Even without the lived wartime experience of predecessors like Ōshiro Tatsuhiro, Medoruma captures the psychology of the many walking wounded in Okinawa. And, though Sakiyama's fiction shows no overt signs of the kind of destruction that fills the pages of much postwar Okinawan fiction, she is waging a linguistic battle in which she spares no hostages. Bent on destroying standard Japanese by infusing it with the imperiled sounds of island language, she skirts dangerously close to exposing the contingency of the genre of prose fiction from Okinawa. By this, I mean that just as she destroys the Japanese language, so too does she dismantle the medium through which Okinawa's writers have composed prose fiction since the Meiji period. Yet, after years of dialect-eradication campaigns, both in the prewar period and during the occupation period, when Okinawan teachers once again encouraged the use of standard Japanese (this time because they overwhelmingly favored the island's return to Japan), today there remains no viable linguistic alternative to standard Japanese in the public sphere. In her fictional world, Sakiyama incorporates dialect to a larger degree than any other author in Okinawa, but, as I show, she is fully aware of the irony involved in searching for language that is irretrievably lost.

In a recent interview, Okamoto Keitoku alludes to the indeterminacy of the genre of prose fiction from Okinawa by offering a provisional definition. Currently, Okinawan literature, he states, is writing executed in standard Japanese by authors of Okinawan descent who, taking Okinawa as a theme, pursue the issue of identity.[32] This definition is not without its problems. Not only is its fixation on purity a nostalgic fiction but so too is its insistence on the narrow terrain of Okinawa. Too close a focus on blood and soil only raises the specter of ideology, occluding from view imaginative writing that might be penned by mainland Japanese authors or by individuals living in diasporic communities in South America, where ties to Okinawa remain strong.[33] To his credit, Okamoto does not set his definition in stone. He hastens to add that Okinawan literature reflects the peculiarity of Okinawa's history and culture, thus, as Okinawa becomes less distinctive a place, so too will its literature.[34] Caveats aside, if Okamoto is correct, it is only a matter of time before the genre I discuss in this book disappears. And yet, judging from the fiction that emerged at the start of the twentieth century, when Yamagusuku Seichū precipitated a boom in Okinawan fiction, to works written in the past decade during which I have undertaken this study, it seems clear that that day has not arrived, nor is it imminent. The genre of Okinawan fiction continues to *mean*.

1 The color orange in Yamagusuku Seichū's Okinawan fiction

How did Okinawan fiction come to mean? What made this writing something other than a regional variation on the themes explored by contemporary authors of mainland Japanese fiction? To answer these questions, I begin by outlining in this chapter the conditions under which authors in Okinawa pursued their craft at the beginning of the twentieth century. Despite obstacles presented by the prefecture's late entry into the nation-state, by the need to master standard Japanese, and by a shortage of venues for publication, authors in Okinawa duly impressed critics in Tokyo who prized local color. Yamagusuku Seichū, in particular, is noted for his skill in making Okinawa come alive through fiction. This he accomplishes through detailed descriptions of island life seasoned with dialogue inflected by local language. Yamagusuku's success resulted in a boom in fiction-writing in the prefecture, where it also served as a model for subsequent generations of authors who sought to follow his lead in making the region speak through their creative expression.

"Local color," a frequent topic in discussions of literary realism that took place in the USA at the turn of the century, was also a much-discussed phrase in Japan during the late Meiji period. In Japan, it referred less to the regional features of a work than it did to an assumption made by critics and readers of the (supposed) tie between author and birthplace. While some writers such as Tokuda Shūsei and Masamune Hakuchō disliked the hasty association readers often made between author and region, others welcomed it.[1] As authors vied for recognition in the literary marketplace, this element naturally grew in importance. Aware of the cultural cachet gained by writers who integrated local color into their work, Yamagusuku made this feature a prominent one in his stories. Through the act of inscribing the climate and culture of Okinawa into prose, then a nascent form of writing in the region, Yamagusuku established himself as a pioneering author of Okinawan fiction. His writing also underscored the importance of native place literature (*furusato bungaku*) during this time. The origins of this literature lay in homeland art (*heimatkunst*; *kyōdo geijutsu*) first introduced, by way of Germany, to Japan in 1906. While this form of art featured descriptions with strong ethnic characteristics, over time it was reinterpreted as a literature of nostalgia (*kyōshū*).² Bearing this reinterpretation in mind, I argue that Yamagusuku is important not only for creating a literary place by means of local color but also for throwing into sharp relief the idea of home as forever lost.

The color orange

In the Greek myth "Song of Philomela," King Pandion's daughter Philomela becomes the unwilling object of her brother-in-law King Tereus' desires. After raping her, Tereus imprisons Philomela and cuts her tongue out to silence her. Despite this, Philomela weaves a tapestry in which she conveys to her sister Procne the details of Tereus' crime. Seeking revenge, Procne kills Itys, her son by Tereus. She cooks and presents Itys to Tereus, who then eats his own son for dinner. When he discovers the sisters' machinations, Tereus tries to kill the pair but to no avail. Amid his pursuit the three are transformed into birds: Tereus becomes a hoopoe, Procne, a swallow, and Philomela, a nightingale.

Classical authors as varied as Ovid, Spencer, Chaucer, and Milton have drawn upon this myth in their own creations, and modern and contemporary writers ranging from T. S. Eliot to Alice Walker have also found inspiration in the transformation of Philomela. While later versions differ from the Greek myth, all have in common the theme of beauty (the song of the nightingale) arising from destruction (the severing of Philomela's tongue). For example, in *The Color Purple*, a contemporary twist of the classical myth, Walker alludes to Philomela as she tells the story of protagonist Celie's rape and subjugation. Like her Greek counterpart, Celie has "no power of speech / To help her tell her wrongs. [...] / She had a loom to work with, and with purple / On a white background, wove her story in, Her story in and out."³ In vibrant color, then, does Celie's story emerge against the quilt's monochrome background.

Little did mainland Japanese and Okinawan critics suspect that their desire for local color at the beginning of the twentieth century would result in the formation of Okinawan fiction, which was then and (I would maintain) now a distinct genre in Japanese letters. As we shall see throughout this book, stories written in response to cries for regional flourish *did* depict the flora, fauna, culture, and customs of Okinawa, in accordance with the critics' demands. However, in addition to meeting these desiderata, prose fiction from Okinawa bore seeds of resistance, which, in the course of the century, alternately either threatened to erupt or simply lay dormant. Whereas mainland critics delighted in the superficial peculiarities of the region, its flora and fauna for example, local critics sought writing that probed deeper into the characteristics and issues of Okinawa. Naturally, these critics' desire for authors to go beyond local color came into conflict with those who expected only a regional variation of a given literary theme in prose from Okinawa.

Well before debates on local color occurred in Okinawa, influential critics such as Tsubouchi Shōyō published literary criticism on how modern Japanese literature ought to be fashioned.[4] Although the pursuit of origins continues, generally speaking, many literary critics tell us that they consider modern fiction in Japan to have been established by 1890 with the publication of works such as Futabatei Shimei's *The Drifting Cloud* (*Ukigumo*, 1886–9) and Mori Ōgai's "The Dancing Girl" ("Maihime," 1890).[5] What made this literature new, in part, was the language in which it was written. Futabatei and Ōgai put into practice Shōyō's theory of modern fiction, which stated that a language different from the stilted classical style that had heretofore been used was more suitable for representing the new realities of the Meiji period. By the end of the Meiji era, naturalist (*shizenshugi*) writers Tayama Katai and Shimazaki Tōson were writing in a language closer to their everyday speech than they would have just two decades earlier.

The situation 1,000 miles southwest of Tokyo is a study in contrasts. Okamoto Keitoku and Nakahodo Masanori mark the appearance of fiction in Okinawa in 1908, some twenty years after it was established in the metropole.[6] The reasons they posit for this delay have to do with the history of Okinawa, a region many perceived as lagging behind in Japan's frenetic quest to modernize, beginning in the late nineteenth century.[7] Another mitigating circumstance pertains to language, a present-day issue that came to the fore among writers in Okinawa in the Meiji period just as it did for writers then in Tokyo. Below, I consider reasons for the belated appearance of Okinawan fiction, describe the literary scene in Okinawa during the Meiji period, and read closely the works of Yamagusuku Seichū (1884–1949), the author of Okinawa's first important work of fiction, "Mandarin Oranges" ("Kunenbo," 1911).[8] My aim is to identify what led critics to designate fiction written in Japanese as "Okinawan" in the first place. It is clear that demand for local color among the central literary establishment in the early 1900s[9] precipitated a wave of fiction that featured southern island landscapes, but did these stories set in lush, semi-tropical Okinawa satisfy senior writers and critics in Tokyo and in Okinawa alike? More importantly, what criteria did critics use to categorize a particular work as Okinawan fiction?

A tumultuous history

In his history of modern Okinawan literature, Okamoto Keitoku makes frequent mention of the difficulties faced by writers in Okinawa.[10] In the outline that follows, I will expound on the constraints Okamoto raises, and under which authors labored. To begin with, owing to its liminal status, the region underwent modernization later than the mainland. Although the Shimazu clan of Satsuma had been in control of the Ryukyus since their invasion of Okinawa in 1609, the Ryukyus remained an independent kingdom that paid tribute to both China and Japan (*Nitchū ryōzoku*). Overseas trade, generally forbidden in Japan under the Tokugawa regime, was permitted and even encouraged in the Ryukyus, affording the politically dominant Shimazu clan hefty profits. Economic exploitation took place in the agricultural sector as well, as the Shimazu rulers coerced islanders to produce sugar cane and submit to heavy taxes from the early seventeenth century.[11] Thrust suddenly into Japan's feudal society, Ryukyuans faced enormous contradictions. Once a prosperous seafaring people, the islanders now tilled soil. The kingdom, which had disallowed weapons since the rule of Shō Shin early in the sixteenth century, was overrun by sword-wielding samurai. I do not mean to assert here, as many entangled in contemporary identity politics do, the false notion that Ryukyu was Edenic prior to the Satsuma invasion. In fact, Ryukyu was divided into three separate areas, Hokuzan, Chūzan, and Nanzan, a situation that surely did not come about peacefully. Thus, given that the Shimazu clan was the de facto ruler of Ryukyu, "independence" was only nominal.

In 1879, Okinawa, the center of the Ryukyuan kingdom since the twelfth century, was incorporated into the Meiji state. The so-called Ryukyuan Disposition (*Ryūkyū shobun*) is a complex merger that has been construed variously. Some view it as an "invasive militaristic annexation" enacted as part of the Meiji Government's seemingly benign efforts to consolidate the nation, while others regard it as "a type of slave liberation" that freed the islanders from agricultural subjugation.[12] Considering the timing of the annexation and the Meiji Government's painstaking efforts to secure the region, one would be hard-pressed to consider the 1879 Disposition as anything other than the first of many similar encroachments made by a rapacious central government intent on consolidating a fledgling nation.[13] However one interprets it, the annexation of Okinawa, followed by decades of intense cultural nationalism, which all but erased from people's minds the region's long-held ties to China, pressed islanders to adapt quickly to the demands of a new leadership, much as the Satsuma invasion had two and a half centuries earlier.[14]

Elementary schools, key apparati for the inculcation of imperial worship, were quickly established in 1880, one year after Okinawa attained its prefectural status. The prime objective of *Conversations in Okinawa* (*Okinawa taiwa*), the first textbook in wide circulation, was to teach students how to speak in standard Japanese on a wide variety of subjects. Comprised of two volumes, each containing four chapters, the text covered the following topics: nouns, seasons, school, agriculture, business, pleasure, travel, and miscellany. Individual chapters presented "typical" phrases in the standard language to be mastered with local-language equivalents for comprehension. In childhood reminisces, Okinawa's first modern-day students often point to the oddities of the new curriculum. For instance, the section on seasons taught students how to converse on snowy weather (in balmy Okinawa, no less!) as follows:

SPEAKER A: The wind tonight is really cold.
Konban no kaze wa zuibun samou gozarimasu.
Chū nu kaze dotto himushi.

SPEAKER B: Yes, it is. It's snowing a little more than it was a while ago.
Sō de gozarimasu. Sakihodo yori sukoshi yuki ga furite orimasu.
Yaya gēsā. Andēbiru. Namasachikara uhē yuchinu futouyabīshi.[15]

Despite how alien much of the Japanese terminology was, in the span of two decades, most Okinawans were convinced of the necessity to master it. Particularly conscientious were those who joined the military and émigrés to Hawaii; without knowledge of Japanese, these individuals would be putting their livelihoods at risk.

Naturally there was some resistance to the state-imposed language, but compliance was high, especially as Japan grew in strength. The state's need to teach patriotism through emperor-centered and assimilationist education coalesced with the desires of Okinawans to better their lives, resulting in some 99.3 percent of the school-age population attending elementary school by 1902. When a fire razed Sashiki elementary school in 1910, burning with it the Emperor's photograph, the school principal and teachers on duty were summarily dismissed from their positions.[16] Education of the time held that Okinawa was Japan's eldest son, Taiwan, its second son, and Korea, its third. Accordingly, education measures implemented in Okinawa, beginning in 1880, became the blueprint for colonial education in 1895 and 1910 when Taiwan and Korea became formal colonies.

In 1888, two years after his tenure on the island, Governor Uesugi Mochinori generously donated 3,000 yen for scholarships that would allow select students to travel to Tokyo for higher education.[17] The first group of five students was particularly influential in shaping Okinawa's future. The achievements of Jahana Noboru, Kishimoto Gashō, Takamine Chōkyō, Ōta Chōfu, and Nakijin Chōhan fill histories of the prefecture.[18] The Iha brothers are two other well-known Okinawan enlightenment scholars whose contributions are impossible to ignore. Iha Fuyū, a linguist, is widely regarded as the father of Okinawan studies. His younger brother, Getsujō, a poet and literary critic, occupies an equally important role in the field of Okinawan literature. As these students began to return home, they disseminated newly acquired knowledge to others in Okinawa, thereby dramatically changing the social and intellectual landscape. From 1880 to 1907, the rate at which Okinawans were educated rose from 2 to nearly 100 percent, an indication of both the state's nationalistic impulse and the islanders' own desires to rid themselves of their perceived "backwardness."[19]

Assimilation was by no means achieved without dissent. After Okinawa's formal incorporation into the nation-state, vast numbers of residents resisted modernization. The emerging class of enlightenment thinkers who looked to Tokyo for models for modern art and science may have welcomed a uniform education system with an emphasis on standard Japanese, but others viewed this type of top-down modernization as a clear imposition and threat to Ryukyuan culture. Many, bewildered by the onslaught of new Japanese institutions, grew nostalgic for the old ways and aligned themselves with China

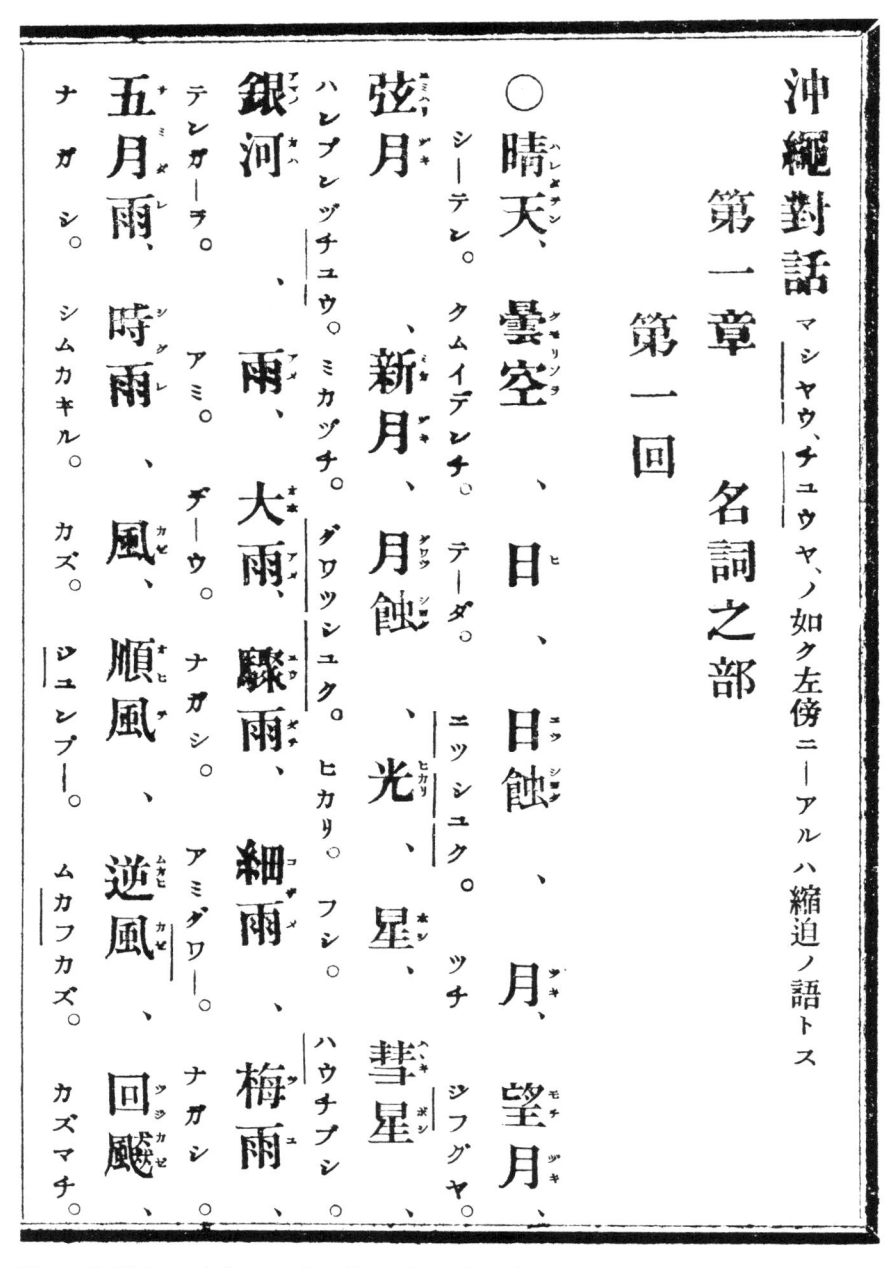

Figure 1 Okinawa's first nationally endorsed textbook, *Conversations in Okinawa*.

rather than Japan.[20] It was only after China's defeat in the Sino-Japanese war of 1894–5 that Okinawans demonstrated fuller support of the Meiji Government. Thus, although Okinawa became part of the modern nation-state in 1879, a decade later than the main islands, another fifteen years would pass before the central government secured the widespread loyalty of the Okinawan people.

As a result of Okinawa's late incorporation into the nation, military conscription and prefectural assembly elections were in turn instituted several years after other areas of Japan, further compounding the notion that Okinawans were "behind." Military conscription, particularly belated, was not established in Okinawa until 1898, more than two decades later than the rest of Japan. In fact, Okinawans were exempted from the 1873 Conscription Law because of residual doubts about their loyalty to the state.[21] Even after conscription was implemented, evasion of military duty in Okinawa remained high because of the language barrier many Okinawan men feared they would face.[22] Intellectual historian Kano Masanao traces the root of Okinawans' self-consciousness in the late Meiji period to the "House of Peoples," an exhibit in the Fifth Domestic Exhibition for the Promotion of Industry held in Osaka in 1903.[23] The display showcased a hut in which a man, presumably Japanese, stands with whip in hand over a motley group that included Ainu, Taiwanese aborigines, and Okinawan prostitutes. Far more shocked by their inclusion among ethnic groups at a major urban exhibition than by the display's inherent bias, Okinawans embraced Japanese systems with new fervor in order to rid themselves of social stigma.

In their desire to assimilate, Okinawans, particularly those in the nascent middle class, cast aside their local language, which, prior to the twentieth century was a central aspect of their identity. Of course, as we have seen, the state, too, played a role by suppressing the use of non-normative language. As the dramatic rise in numbers of students attending elementary school indicates, standard language education grew in importance, effectively squelching the use of local speech for literary expression. By the third decade of Meiji, conditions necessary for the production of modern prose appeared to be in place. Elite students had returned from Tokyo eager to enliven the antiquated literary scene in which the medium of expression remained some variety of Ryukyuan speech, rather than standard language.[24] In 1893, Okinawan writers in the Movement for Freedom and People's Rights (*jiyū minken undō*) who advocated cultural assimilation with Japan established the region's first newspaper, the *Ryukyu News* (*Ryūkyū shinpō*), which was integral for igniting political consciousness. For example, in the 1870s, some members of the movement bristled over the territorial dispute between Japan and Qing China over the Ryukyus.[25] Takahashi Ki'ichi, a member of the movement, believed Japanese control over the islands was needed to protect Ryukyuans from the feudalistic mentality of their ruling classes. In Okinawa the movement's elites advocated cultural assimilation with Japan by emphasizing comparisons with other parts of the country (*tafuken*).[26] The return home of a core group of scholars deemed enlightened on account of their metropolitan education, based on standard language, and the institution of newspapers were but two key factors critical for the emergence of modern literary forms. What writers in Okinawa lacked was a literary language through which new realities could be expressed. Modern prose did not appear immediately, simply because writers needed time to master the genre of fiction, not to mention the new language it employed.

The acquisition of a new literary language, a feat difficult in Tokyo at the end of the nineteenth century, was compounded in Okinawa by the fact that Ryukyuan dialects and Japanese, while related, are not mutually intelligible.[27] The Meiji Government, in its effort to consolidate the nation, encouraged the use of common language (*kyōtsūgo*) in Okinawan elementary schools beginning in the early 1870s. The fact that Okinawans had to learn a new language was not problematic; it was, after all, a necessity for artists as well as entrepreneurs in an era of rapid change. The *manner* in which local dialects were dismissed in favor of standard Japanese, however, was unsettling. Educational bureaucrats created a colonial atmosphere in Okinawa similar to that of the Japanese territories of Taiwan and Korea.[28]

Stiff resistance to these conditions led to Okinawa's first student strike, which revealed the intensity of educators who poured their energies into turning students into imperial subjects. The protest took place during the Sino-Japanese war when Kodama Kihachi, a nationalist middle-school administrator, dropped English from the curriculum. This was done ostensibly to ease the burden of Okinawan students whom he believed were saddled with the task of learning two foreign tongues—Japanese and English.[29] Kodama's paternalistic beneficence only exacerbated fears Okinawans already possessed regarding their purported difference from other Japanese.

Although officials in the Okinawa Bureau of Education, a majority of whom were Tokyo appointees, pressured teachers to eradicate local dialects and replace them with standard Japanese, it appears that most Okinawan people readily accepted these measures because they equated standard Japanese with what was modern. No doubt, mastery of standard Japanese was necessary for rapid success (*risshin shusse*) in the new era; thus, great effort was expended toward achieving this goal. Many local teachers, hypervigilant in their enforcement of the prohibition against dialect use in schools, humiliated offending students by forcing them to wear dialect placards around their necks, not unlike the metal plates reading "I am stupid" imposed on African students who lapsed into dialect in their classrooms, a world away.[30]

For pragmatic reasons, then, Okinawans widely accepted standard Japanese; still, many felt a discord between their native language and that imposed by the central government. Tension between the local languages spoken in the private sphere and the standard language spoken in the public sphere created difficulties for writers already laboring to express themselves in Japanese. It was no easy matter to use the new language to describe their homeland, its history, and its culture. Owing to the imposition of standard language, literary expression became ideological (*kannenteki*) and superficial.[31] Since modern literature—then a new concept—was something that could be acquired only vis-à-vis a modern language, namely, Japanese, what resulted in Okinawa was the preservation of native language for traditional sentiment and conceptions, above which lay a standard learned language used for new ideas. This practice created what Okamoto Keitoku calls "a dual structure of language" (*gengo no nijū kōzō*), similar to the notion of the African palimpsest that critic Chantal Zabus writes of in her descriptions of the tiered effect of language in anglophone and francophone areas of West Africa.[32] Conceptually, modern literature was readily grasped in Okinawa, but the practice of creating this literature took far longer since individuals had to accustom themselves to standard language before they could begin to use it freely and imaginatively.

In addition to Okinawa's late entry to the nation-state, and its wholly different dialects, there were few precursors to fiction in Ryukyuan literature for authors to reference in creating modern prose. At the end of the nineteenth century, verse dominated the Ryukyuan literary tradition, also rich in classical drama (*kumiodori*). Among all genres fiction was the last to emerge. To be sure, the problems encountered by writers in Okinawa were thorny, but not insurmountable. After the Sino-Japanese war, Okinawa, having entered its third decade of standard Japanese education, firmly aligned itself with the victorious modern nation-state of Japan. These historical and educational circumstances, coupled with the existence of a corps of elite enlightenment thinkers and a modern newspaper, constituted the minimal conditions necessary for the creation of modern literature in Okinawa.

The emergence of modern literature in Okinawa

From 1609, until immediately after the Meiji Restoration, the dominant literary genre in Okinawa was Ryukyuan verse (*ryūka*),[33] a poetic form that evolved from the *Anthology of Ancient Verses* (*Omoro sōshi*), Okinawa's most important classical literary work.[34] Japanese verse (*waka*), a competing form, became popular after the Shimazu clan began its administrative control of the Ryukyus in the early years of the Tokugawa period. There is little evidence to suggest that any major journals that might have contained modern literary forms existed in Okinawa during the Meiji period. Okinawa's first modern newspaper was, of course, an important vehicle for literature; yet, even after the establishment in 1893 of the *Ryukyu News*, it took time for new literary forms to appear. Moreover, given that only a small column of the paper was reserved for literary pursuits, the newspaper could not perform the function of encouraging and popularizing the arts as it would in later years. In general, former members of the Okinawan nobility or mainland officials and merchants posted to Okinawa wrote the Japanese, Chinese, and Ryukyuan verse that appeared in the paper as a form of diversion. It is not surprising that contemporary critics found these dilettantes' style and content decidedly old-fashioned.

In 1900, new style poetry (*shintaishi*) appeared. Said to be Okinawa's first modern literary genre, the published new verse was heavily influenced by the poetry of authors affiliated with the literary establishment in Tokyo. New style poetry written at this time was much like songs (*shōka*) and military verse (*gunka*) written in mainland Japan during the first two decades of the Meiji period. Prose fiction, if it appeared at all, came in the form of travelogues (*kikōbun*) and miscellany (*zuisō*) written in a pseudoclassical style. From the time of the Meiji Restoration until the third decade of the new era, a transitional period for Okinawan literature, few colloquial style prose works of note existed. Since newspaper articles of the day were still written in classical style, it was only natural that travelogues and such bore features of older writing.[35]

Modern literature began to make inroads in the last decade of the Meiji period when Okinawa became more socially and politically integrated with the rest of Japan. During these years, activities taking place in the literary establishment in Tokyo heavily influenced writers who began to experiment with new forms. A revolution of sorts took place as Okinawan poets absorbed the techniques of the New Poetry Society (*Shinshisha*) set forth by Yosano Tekkan in his coterie journal, *Morning Star* (*Myōjō*). European influence was present, too. Of particular interest is the fact that the prefecture's first dramatization of European literature was a 1906 production of Shakespeare's *Othello*. Given the Bard's focus on the Moor in *Othello*, the play likely struck a chord among local viewers who could readily identify with its socially maligned protagonist.[36]

A sudden burst of new energy in the genres of poetry, drama, and fiction took place during Okinawa's first decade of modern literature, roughly 1902–12. Of these genres, poetry—*tanka*, in particular—was the first to exhibit new modes of expression. This new poetry was highly influenced by mainland writers and, with few exceptions, seemed not to reflect any individual consciousness, at least not for critics who judged it by the standard of the day. The last modern genre to emerge—prose fiction—began appearing at the end of the Meiji period. Initially, it emerged in the form of fictionalized true stories (*shōsetsuteki jitsuwa*). "Troubled Heart" ("Mayoi kokoro," author unknown) is a representative example. After "Troubled Heart," short stories came to be included in the newspapers as part of the mechanism by which the *Ryukyu News*, together with *Okinawa News* (*Okinawa shinbun*) and *Okinawa Daily News* (*Okinawa mainichi shinbun*), the newspapers that followed it, competed for readership.[37] It was in this context that one of Okinawa's first fictional works, a short story entitled "Parting" ("Danen") was published in September 1908 by an author known only by the pseudonym Wakazō.[38]

"Parting," a story in which the mental state of a young man is roughly depicted, was soon followed by other stories such as "Twilight" ("Tasogare"),

"Little Haru" ("Haru chan"), and "A Record of Phantasm" ("Mugenki"), none of which contemporary critics regarded as any more sophisticated than "Parting." The distinguishing feature of these initial fictional works was that they were largely based on the lived experiences of students who had traveled to or studied in Tokyo. At this juncture, since the publishing industry was still in an embryonic stage, it was difficult for individuals to pursue writing as a profession. That is to say, the lack of appropriate venues hindered the rise of creative fiction.[39] Moreover, space limitations in the existing newspapers resulted in brief fictional stories that lacked depth. That so little of note was published by writers from Okinawa in these final years of the Meiji period makes Yamagusuku Seichū's "Mandarin Oranges" all the more remarkable.

Yamagusuku Seichū and the creation of modern Okinawan fiction

Before Yamagusuku Seichū wrote "Mandarin Oranges," there was little that differentiated fiction written in Okinawa from that produced in Tokyo. Critics considered the content of poetry and fiction up to this point to be largely derivative since Okinawan writers endeavored to master the form and content of writers popular in mainland Japan. For example, most stories published before 1911 had Tokyo as their setting. No significant modern prose that reflected the particular culture and landscape of Okinawa existed until the publication of "Mandarin Oranges." Given that Yamagusuku is considered the first author to write *Okinawan* fiction suggests that critics of the time regarded local color as an integral feature of the genre.

Born in Naha, Okinawa's capital city, on February 1, 1884, Yamagusuku Seichū was just five years old when the Meiji Government drew Okinawa into the nation's fold. In 1903, at the age of nineteen, Yamagusuku interrupted his studies in Tokyo to work at a hospital in Okinawa. During this year his essay "Thoughts about the Ill Poet Gorgy" was published. In 1905, Yamagusuku enlisted in the Aoyama Regiment of the Japanese Army. When he returned to Okinawa, he assumed duties for the prefectural government. Among his superiors was Noma Seiji, the man who would later establish Kōdansha, the well-known publishing house.[40] Yamagusuku left Okinawa for Tokyo in 1907, where he subsequently joined Yosano Tekkan's New Poetry Society. Through his membership in this group, he began to associate with fellow poet Ishikawa Takuboku, another of Japan's important regional voices.[41]

Yamagusuku's career ambitions abruptly changed from literary pursuits to dentistry, for practical reasons, no doubt. In 1911, he graduated from dentistry school but returned to Okinawa after failing his licensing exam. With others he founded two coterie journals, *Play* (*Asobi*) in 1912 and *We Five* (*Gonin*) in 1914. The publication of each journal was suspended after just three issues. In 1914, Yamagusuku worked as a newspaper reporter for the *Southern Daily News* (*Nankoku nippō*), and, in 1916, he became a member of the poetry selection committee for the *Okinawa Daily News*. The following year, after several failed attempts, Yamagusuku finally succeeded in obtaining his dentistry license and opened a dental practice. Much of his subsequent literary production consisted of *tanka* poetry.

In 1931, Yamagusuku became a member of Yosano Tekkan and Yosano Akiko's coterie and, with their support, published a collection of poetry, titled *Burning Money* (*Shisen o yaku*). Yosano Akiko describes Yamagusuku as "a pleasant, enthusiastic man of depth."[42] His enthusiasm reached an extreme in 1939 when he was strongly urged to curtail his heavy drinking, owing to illness.[43] As a result of his changed lifestyle, he seems to have become mentally unsettled, only gaining some semblance of peace by hand-copying *The Tale of Genji* and practicing an unspecified new religion (*shinkō shūkyō*). In 1941, Yamagusuku organized a division of the Okinawan Regional Cultural League, subsequently busying himself with the establishment of various literary organizations such as the Okinawa Arts Association (*Okinawa bungei kyōkai*), Okinawa Poets Association (*Okinawa kajin kyōkai*), and the Okinawa Calligraphy Association (*Okinawa shodō kyōkai*).[44] In July 1944, just three months before the fierce bombing of October 10 (*jūjū kūshū*) in which 1,500 Okinawans, both civilian and military, were killed, Yamagusuku was evacuated to Ōita prefecture in Kyushu. Safe in Ōita, he and his family were spared the devastating Battle of Okinawa that raged the following year. Yamagusuku returned to Okinawa in October 1946, residing there until stomach cancer claimed his life in 1949.

Clearly, Yamagusuku's interest in literature was broad and long-lasting. As the first writer of notable fiction from Okinawa, beginning in 1911 and continuing into the postwar, his literary output extends from the Meiji to the early Shōwa era.[45] Despite his eminent position as a leading author, however, he could not support himself solely through writing. Yamagusuku's juggling of two careers, one as writer, the other as dentist, points to a common difference between writers from Okinawa and Tokyo. Okinawan authors, generally speaking, did not have the financial wherewithal to pursue their writing as a vocation. This is not to say that all writers in Tokyo could or did single-mindedly and leisurely put pen to paper, but in the Meiji period, writing began to be conceived of as a respectable profession in the metropole. As is still true today, the vast majority of authors in Okinawa engaged in a second occupation by force of circumstance.

The year before the appearance of "Mandarin Oranges," Yamagusuku's best-known fictional work, the author wrote two other short stories. The first, "A Man Named Tsuruoka" (*Tsuruoka to iu otoko*) was published in *New Current* (*Shinchō*) in February 1910. This work told by a first-person narrator, *watakushi*, describes the plight of *watakushi*'s childhood friend, Tsuruoka, a young man who leaves the familiar surroundings of his home in Okinawa to look for work in Tokyo. *Watakushi*, a writer living in Tokyo, is surprised to see Tsuruoka turn up at his doorstep one day. Tsuruoka not only attempts to give his friend the impression that he belongs in Tokyo, he also feigns an intimate knowledge of the city. The narrator's description of Tsuruoka, however, leaves no doubt that he would stand out sorely in a crowd of urbanites:

> As for luggage, he had but a single small Chinese bag wrapped in a blue blanket. Strapped to a striped suit that was temporarily in vogue back home four or five years ago was a purple tie with red stripes. His hair was closely cropped, his complexion reddish-brown, a special feature of people from the South. The cheeks of his square face had lost some of their fullness. His eyes were red like a rabbit and clouded. And, whenever he talked his face was creased with deep wrinkles and his thick black hairy caterpillar-like eyebrows wiggled back and forth. One eyebrow nearly connected to the other. Back home we called this *kanabui*. I was told that a person with such features could see things like ghosts and other strange apparitions. He had a habit of staring at people with a strange penetrating gaze. From the time I met him this so unsettled me I couldn't bear it.[46]

In the course of their conversation, Tsuruoka tells *watakushi* that he, too, wishes to be a writer. *Watakushi* urges him to obtain some schooling in Tokyo. Tsuruoka casually mentions that he has plans to begin a literature course at Waseda University and that since his resignation from a menial job in Okinawa he has immersed himself in reading such books as Takizawa Bakin's *Biography of Eight Dogs* (*Hakkenden*, 1814–41).[47] A few days after arriving in Tokyo, Tsuruoka rents a room and settles into his new lifestyle.

One evening, *watakushi* goes out to eat at a Western restaurant with a group of other friends from Okinawa who have attained a modicum of success in education and publishing, as has he himself. Tsuruoka joins them only to be bewildered by the strange food. Yamagusuku again underscores how alien Tokyo is to a man fresh from the periphery. In the midst of their meal, Tsuruoka suddenly reveals that he would like to venture into the world of business. *Watakushi* is surprised at this change of heart, and though he suspects something is amiss, he remains silent. As the story progresses, Tsuruoka squanders his money on women and alcohol and is finally reduced to begging *watakushi* for financial assistance. *Watakushi* supports him for a short period, even allowing him, at times, to stay in his room. Peering at Tsuruoka in his alcohol-induced sleep, *watakushi* is reminded of his own fun-filled, peaceful childhood spent by the sea in Okinawa. Brief as this passage is, it clearly points to the demands placed on individuals by urban modernity and the attendant loss of youthful innocence and communal living.

However much nostalgia Tsuruoka evokes in him, *watakushi* realizes the only way Tsuruoka will survive is if he returns to Okinawa. *Watakushi* petitions the local Okinawa Friendship Association (*Okinawa kenjinkai*) for money for this purpose.[48] The story concludes as Tsuruoka leaves *watakushi*'s boarding house tearfully, return fare in hand. Yamagusuku captures the pathos of the scene through a final description of Tsuruoka stepping out into the rainy streets of Tokyo with only a broken umbrella to protect him. Beaten by the city he begins his journey home.

"A Man Named Tsuruoka" is a story similar to the earliest works of fiction published in Okinawa in that it is more about life as experienced in Tokyo than about Okinawa. Yamagusuku peppers this story about a writer in Tokyo, much like himself, with copious references to literary figures such as Kunikida Doppo, Nagai Kafū and Henrik Ibsen, ostensibly to offer a realistic depiction of the literary climate in Tokyo. Aside from the colorful—if stereotyped—description of Tsuruoka's Okinawan features, little distinguishes this work from countless other novel and stories—Natsume Sōseki's *Sanshirō* for example—that describe a naive person's encounter with Tokyo. Tsuruoka is a quirky and memorable character, but he does not live on in the reader's mind as Sanshirō does. The brevity of the piece makes him more a caricature than a fully developed character.

The second story written by Yamagusuku prior to "Mandarin Oranges" is "Stone Talisman," (*Ishigantō*), published in *New Art* (*Shin bungei*) in August 1910. Unlike "A Man Named Tsuruoka," this work is set in Okinawa. The title refers to round or angular stones still commonly found in Okinawan alleyways. Popular souvenir items today, the stones are one or two feet in length. On the stones is inscribed an historical name, consisting of three Chinese characters (石敢当).[49] The prevalence of the stone markers in Okinawa attests to the impact Chinese culture has had on the island. Given the rather abrupt erasure of Chinese culture in Okinawa following Japan's victory in the Sino-Japanese war in 1895, Yamagusuku's literary depiction of this form of Chinese exotica is telling. In fact, one of the ironies of the story is that it portrays "local" color, writ large.

The story employs a first-person narrator, *watakushi*, to describe an incident that occurs during a cholera outbreak that actually plagued Okinawa fifteen years prior to the start of the narrative. The narrator begins the story by explaining the misfortune that befalls a local family by the name of Shinagawa. A string of bad luck occurred when the family's grandfather, in a drunken stupor, had accidentally set a fire, which killed him and burned down more than half of the town's establishments, an act widely believed to have set in motion a seven-generation curse. Needless to say, no one in the town mourned the family patriarch. Seven or eight years later, the curse continued when a model son in the family became unhinged and committed suicide. Next, a young daughter took her life after being abandoned by her lover. In spite of these gloomy affairs, the bulk of "Stone Talisman" centers on a friendship that forms between *watakushi* and Tsuruju, the nephew of the family's last suicide victim, during the spring of his eleventh year.

Tsuruju, an only child, moves next door to *watakushi* at the age of nineteen. Due to past misfortune, his family maintains a low profile. A medical student, Tsuruju befriends *watakushi* by luring him to his house to look at graphic photographs of human anatomy. *Watakushi* visits Tsuruju's forlorn home often, and the two become fast friends. When a cholera epidemic rages through the town, *watakushi*'s parents, taking every precaution to keep their children free from the disease, forbid *watakushi* and his siblings from wandering about the town. This prohibition does not stop *watakushi* from immediately accepting Tsuruju's proposal to go into town one evening to view a slideshow pertaining to hygiene, a topic widely discussed in Meiji Japan as far-flung regions sought to sanitize and, thereby, modernize themselves.[50] The pair slip from their homes, arriving in town just as the moon is at its brightest.

Walking amid the deserted castle grounds of the town, Tsuruju stops suddenly and admits to *watakushi* that there is no slideshow to be seen. He then asks his young friend to act as a messenger and to deliver a letter to a certain girl who works at a paper shop nearby. Tsuruju is confident the boy will recognize her because, "being from the mainland, she has a white complexion."[51] When *watakushi* refuses, Tsuruju attempts to cajole him. Enraged by his failed sweet talk, Tsuruju pulls out a knife and threatens to kill *watakushi* unless he delivers the letter. In fear, *watakushi* runs to the shop and hands the letter to the girl who is working alone in the shop. Yamagusuku's description of the girl as seen through the eyes of an Okinawan child indicates how strikingly different she is from the local people: "To eyes only accustomed to seeing dark island girls, the lightly made up face of the mainland girl was pale, smooth, and beautiful."[52]

Upon the boy's return, Tsuruju asks him for the details of his secret delivery. When *watakushi* tells Tsuruju that the young girl only laughed after reading the letter, Tsuruju falls silent. Then, mustering his spirit, he thanks *watakushi* and the two return home. On their way Tsuruju tells the boy that the paper-shop owner had recently arrived from Osaka to start his business. His great success was largely due to his using his daughter Shizuko to draw in customers, mostly students walking by on their way to and from school. Another medical student had previously sent a letter to Shizuko, but his advances, too, met with failure.

One week later *watakushi* awakens in the middle of the night to find his family gathered together and speaking in hushed tones. He hears one of the servants relating suspicious acts he had witnessed next door. The following morning *watakushi* sees two policemen, the town doctor, and the head of the village come into his home and whisper something to his father. Later he learns that a doctor had visited Tsuruju, who was stricken with cholera, in the middle of the previous night. Under the cover of darkness he is taken to a hospital and quarantined. Soon after he succumbs to the illness and dies.

The story concludes as the narrator describes the lengths to which the community tries to rid itself of the contagion. Limestone is sprinkled before family gates, a policeman stands guard outside Tsuruju's house, and *watakushi*'s family refurbishes their long neglected stone talisman, placing it on the wall outside their home to ward off evil. The last scene occurs at dusk as a group of youngsters, huddled around the stone formation, light a straw fire. This ambiguous ending suggests that the misfortune experienced by Tsuruju's family will not end with his death.

In his reading of these two stories, Nakahodo Masanori calls attention to the theme of ignorance in "A Man Named Tsuruoka" and envy in "Stone Talisman."[53] He states further that while ignorance and envy may arise in any given situation, in these works they are inextricably tied to the mainland, and, thus, he concludes that Yamagusuku's subtle but broader theme is antimainland sentiment. "A Man Named Tsuruoka," a story set in Tokyo, describes an Okinawan man's ignorance of big-city ways. Nakahodo makes visible Yamagusuku's critique of the process by which life in Tokyo robs Tsuruoka of his innocence. Broken down and reduced to a shadow of his former self, he must beg for money to survive. Antimainland sentiment is present in "Stone Talisman" as well. The object of Tsuruju's love, Shizuko, is unattainable precisely because she is from Osaka. Yamagusuku's description of the fair-complexioned girl makes clear the envy and fascination that is triggered in local males who eagerly patronize the paper shop for a mere glimpse of the young girl's beauty. Nakahodo suggests that Tsuruju, smitten with Shizuko, experiences such a sense of despondency when she rejects him that he becomes vulnerable to the cholera strain that eventually kills him. In the first story, ignorance of life in Tokyo destroys Tsuruoka, and in the second, Tsuruju's envy and desire for a girl from Osaka hastens his death. While desire and envy of the mainland Other is plainly evident in the latter story, it is far-fetched to posit a causal relationship between heartbreak and cholera.

As interesting as Nakahodo's reading is, I am more intrigued by the motivation underlying his reading. Why must the cause of the victim's fate lie in the mainland Other? Might there not be a stronger link between the protagonist's illness and his heredity or environment? Given that the naturalist movement in Japanese literature was at its peak in the mid 1900s, this certainly seems plausible. It is only after reading "Mandarin Oranges," which probes deeper into the climate of Okinawa that the antimainland sentiment in Yamagusuku's earlier stories becomes conspicuous, as Nakahodo rightly points out.

In a 1910 review of "Stone Talisman," critic Uozumi Setsuro denounced the story for being merely a vehicle through which to explain the history of the stone markers so prevalent in Okinawa.[54] Incited by Uozumi's remarks, Yamagusuku proceeded to write and publish in 1911, at the tail end of the frenetic Meiji period, his most famous work, "Mandarin Oranges." While Yamagusuku's earlier stories "A Man Named Tsuruoka" and "Stone Talisman" contain themes that quietly suggest a reason for placing fiction from Okinawa in a thematic framework separate from mainstream fiction, "Mandarin Oranges" is a story in which Yamagusuku consciously articulates an antimainland stance, as evidenced by his insistent use of local color.

Yamagusuku's "Mandarin Oranges" and the issue of local color

In an effort to spur fellow Okinawan authors on, Iha Getsujō proclaimed 1909 as year one in a revival of arts (*bungei fukkō*). Although Iha had in mind invigorating Ryukyuan verse, the burst of creativity that resulted from his prodding came in a different genre—fiction—and in a different language—Japanese.[55] As I explained earlier, traditional literary forms such as Ryukyuan verse (*ryūka*), *tanka*, and traditional Japanese verse (*waka*) together with newer forms such as new-style poetry (*shintaishi*) and prose fiction (*shōsetsu*) underwent rapid changes at this time. Iha, a poet and critic, welcomed and feared these swift transformations. His main concern was that Okinawa's traditional arts would soon disappear under the onslaught of new thought. The tension he believed existed between old and new arts produced in his day led Iha to seek a new literary model that could somehow preserve those aspects of tradition he feared would be obliterated by modernization. It is no small irony that Iha discovered such a model in European literature, a subject in which he was well versed.[56]

Through his reading of European poetry and drama, especially that of William Butler Yeats, Iha became familiar with the realist technique of faithfully depicting the social and cultural climate (*fūdo*) of a particular region in modern literature. He was convinced that the adoption of this technique could resolve the tension between old and new forms that preoccupied him. Furthermore, Iha believed that if local writers would only write fiction set in Okinawa, worldwide acclaim would naturally follow. Iha longed for writers to create works that emphasized Okinawa's local color for he viewed this type of literature as the vehicle for Okinawa's modernization.[57] Whether critics in Tokyo agreed with Iha's grandiose designs or not, many petitioned for local color as well. For example, on March 10, 1909, Nobori Shomu, a critic of Russian literature, remarked in the *Okinawa Daily News*: "Today local color is all the rage in literary circles in Tokyo. In Japan, the color of the Ryukyus is something unique to Japan. I'd like to show the region's local color to our drab and gray literary establishment."[58] Here, Nobori echoes Iha's wish for an Okinawan Yeats, someone who, like the Irishman, livened the "pavements grey" of London with his pastoral fiction.[59] Decades later, Shimao Toshio would similarly prescribe an injection of local color into the lifeless landscape of mainland Japan, which he described as crammed with governmental buildings as bland and uninteresting as blocks of bean curd.[60] It is interesting to note how, time and again, local color is necessary to sate metropolitan needs to enliven the literary scene. Of all the European writers he knew, Iha found Yeats's writing particularly inspirational because of the Irishman's ability to describe beautifully the culture of his native land in the English language. Iha plainly desired a Yeats-type Okinawan writer who would, through the medium of standard Japanese, write modern fiction replete with local color in order to capture the beauty of Okinawa for all to see. Considering Iha's wishes, his dissatisfaction with early Okinawan short stories is not surprising since authors, in an effort to emulate mainland fiction, wrote about Tokyo. However, given Iha's opinion that the major problem with early Okinawan fiction works was its lack of local color, it is surprising that "Mandarin Oranges," the first piece of Okinawan fiction to be acclaimed precisely for its local color, also disappointed him.

A riot of color

"Mandarin Oranges" was published in the well-known haiku journal *Cuckoo* (*Hototogisu*) in June 1911, and appeared the following month in the *Okinawa Daily News*. The fact that Yamagusuku succeeded in publishing his story in a major mainland literary journal set off a "fiction boom" among fellow writers eager to find similarly distinguished venues for their writing. "Mandarin Oranges" itself is a historically accurate tragicomedy that describes in remarkable detail the social climate of Okinawa during the Sino-Japanese war. In the story, Yamagusuku depicts the ways in which the outbreak of the war in 1894 generates discord and fractures Okinawan society. Portrayed vividly are two opposing factions: the first, the "enlightenment party" (*kaikatō*), which is comprised of pro-Japanese Okinawans, and the "stubbornly conservative party" (*gankotō*), which is made up of pro-Chinese Ryukyuans. During this period a man from Kagoshima named Yamajō Ichi, pretending to be a secret envoy sent by Li Hung-chang, a Chinese politician, embezzled large amounts of money from Okinawans loyal to China.[61] This fraud, referred to as the "Yamajō affair," is the historical event upon which Yamagusuku's "Mandarin Oranges" is based.[62]

The story begins with a description of the landscape of Okinawa just after a typhoon has battered it. Boats at sea are heavily damaged and waterlogged; sandy beaches are strewn with sea-urchin fragments and broken crab shells. A crowd of shipwrecked fisher folk struggle ashore as the winter sun casts a faint glow over the entire bleak spectacle. Yamagusuku performs two functions with this opening. First, he presents the reader with a vivid scene that captures the typhoon-prone island, thereby fulfilling demands for local color. Second, and perhaps more important, by electing to depict a storm to begin his story of an island thrown into chaos after the outbreak of Japan's war with China, Yamagusuku foreshadows the ensuing confusion that pervades Okinawan society.[63]

Yamagusuku does not mention Okinawan place names explicitly, choosing instead to refer to the story's main settings as "Town N" and "Town S." Given the details he does provide, it is clear that "N" and "S" are the island's two most heavily populated areas, Naha and Shuri. After the opening scene, the story's setting shifts from the seaside to a mansion in the nearby town of Naha. This residence, which also houses a prosperous lacquerware business, belongs to a local family by the name of Matsuda. Ryōhei, the owner, and Tama, his wife, have succeeded in maintaining the generations-old business to such a degree that they have room to spare in their home. Upon the advice of a village elder, the Matsudas rent out a room to a man from Miyazaki named Hosokawa Shigeru, a schoolmaster at the neighboring junior high. Also joining the household is Ushi, an ex-geisha whose contract has been paid off by Hosokawa.[64]

Yamagusuku returns to his description of the storm-damaged landscape after explaining the various relationships that exist among the occupants of the mansion. Ryōhei, Tama, their three children, the family's four or five employed lacquerware artisans, the servants, and Ushi are gathered around the dozen or so orange trees that surround the residence. Ryōhei and a male servant climb the trees to pick the ripened fruit while the children run around excitedly collecting ripened and unbruised fruit hurled to the ground by the relentless storm. Each year, after distributing half of their harvest to relatives and neighbors, the family sells the remaining half to pay for the children's school expenses, New Year's clothes, and a supply of camellia oil. The story's picturesque beginning concludes as the narrator informs the reader that the family's storm-prompted harvest yielded 200 oranges. The subsequent scene in which two policemen and a detective come to the Matsuda home under cover of night to arrest Hosokawa contrasts utterly with the idyllic and pastoral scene that precedes it. Having returned from school, Hosokawa is eating and drinking with Ushi in a relaxed manner when the arrest takes place. Seeing the officers' unsheathed swords, Ushi lets out a cry, rousing the Matsudas. By the time they reach Hosokawa's room, he is being escorted to jail. The narrator caps this brief, shocking scene with a description of the disordered room where unconsumed food and drink glisten in the lamplight. The one link that ties the earlier rustic scene to this one is created by the author's final detail: "Near the sake was a lacquer tray upon which lay three oranges from this morning's distribution of fruit. Among them only one orange had its skin peeled in curls and was piled with sucked fruit."[65] In addition to consolidating the fruit motif suggested by the story's title the graphic nature of the scene contributes to the charged atmosphere set by Hosokawa's sudden arrest.

What follows in the story is a description of Okinawa at the time of Japan's declaration of war against China, which includes an explanation of the circumstances that led to schoolmaster Hosokawa's arrest. Yamagusuku marks a shift in the story by inserting a line of factual information: "The year was 1894. Because of the Tonghak Rebellion in southern Korea, rumors spread that troops from both Japan and China had begun to battle. On 1 August an edict declaring war was issued."[66]

Yamagusuku follows this historical aside with details on how Okinawan society is affected by the Sino-Japanese war. Now, for instance, Shuri Castle is occupied by troops dispatched from Kumamoto. The castle, an imprint of which caused a stir in Okinawa when it appeared on the new 2,000-yen note issued in Japan in July 2000, is an important landmark formerly inhabited by the Ryukyuan king (and currently preserved as a UNESCO World

Heritage site).[67] The declaration of war brings to the island new soldiers who drunkenly chase after women on Sundays, a day of reprieve from their military duties. Many of the women despise the troops as "Yamato beasts" (*Yamato no kedamono*).[68] With each battle, Japan's victories increase. Newspapers and magazines, chock full of battle details, arrive by shipload from the mainland. War posters plaster local storefronts. Yamagusuku's description of the Okinawans' reaction to increased militarization is slightly exaggerated, but, in retrospect, it is ironic considering how heavily militarized Okinawa is today: "The Ryukyuan people, being unarmed and unfamiliar with weapons since ancient times, greeted the soldiers with fear in their eyes."[69] The sudden onslaught of weaponry is one of the many burdens under which the islanders now struggle.

The story continues as the narrator states that the customs and manners of Okinawan society were nearly the same as they had been in the past. Men and women still wore their hair tied and fastened with traditional combs; males used two combs in the *katakashira* style; women used a single comb in the *karaji* style. The material from which their combs were made allowed one to distinguish between aristocrats and commoners alike. People still wore sleeveless wide-pocketed kimono with angular obi tied neatly in front. The narrator writes, "They were, finally, a peaceful people."[70] On occasion there appeared a student or a government official with disheveled hair whom the Ryukyuans despised and called "beggar monks." The narrator relates that the 80 percent of society that still adhered to customs of old outnumbered these few odd men.

The divisions in society go beyond hair and dress distinctions. In the realm of politics and philosophy, too, a wide chasm exists. On one hand, there are aristocrats and Confucian scholars who spent their childhood reading the Chinese classics, and, on the other hand, there are officials, intellectuals, and a mass of young people who had firsthand experience of the new educational system. The former group belongs to the conservative Chinese camp that remained indifferent to Japan's daily victories on the continent. The latter group supported Japan and predicted the total annihilation of China. Old and new styles collide in the personal and political lives of the islanders.

The story takes on added complications as the narrator relates the behavior of an eccentric man known only as "Old Okushima." The leader of the island's pro-Chinese faction, Old Okushima has long-standing ties to China that were formed during three study trips made to Beijing in his youth. Before the abolition of the clan system in 1879, he had occupied a high official position, which he lost when the island subsequently became a Japanese prefecture. After the changeover, Okushima used his earnings to establish a private Confucian-type school for young children. The old-fashioned school eventually encountered financial hardship and was forced to close its doors. Angered that the masses now dismissed his style of education, Old Okushima grew suspicious of—and actively opposed—all new trends and practices. He believed that Japanese-style education would lead people astray. Of Old Okushima, Yamagusuku writes, "he hated the so-called 'Yamato scholarship' as much as if it were a 'heretical religion.'"[71] Cursing his fellow man and present-day society, Old Okushima remained in seclusion until the outbreak of the Sino-Japanese war.

Once the war begins, Okushima seizes the opportunity to support his beloved China by marching through town spewing outlandish propaganda, a brazen act that ultimately alienates him from both the pro-Japan group and pro-China group. Rejected by both sides, he forms a one-man party, which, for unspecified reasons, he calls the "Stone Pillow Faction." As he walks in the scorching summer heat with his blue parasol the townspeople ridicule him as the "town hermit."

In the remaining pages of "Mandarin Oranges," Yamagusuku links the arrest of Hosokawa to the political confusion that pervades the island. Before his arrest, Hosokawa was active in promoting the war effort, as is evident by his having spent many an evening showing slides of various battles to the public. When rumors spread of an impending invasion by the Chinese, Hosokawa appeases the Matsudas' fears by assuring them of the superior might of the Yamato forces. While most households make wartime preparations, the Matsuda home remains calm. One night, Sei'ichi, the Matsudas' eldest son, awakens to use the toilet. On the way back to his room, he spies a hole in the wall through which he can peer into Hosokawa's study. Surreptitiously, he observes Hosokawa writing furtively in a notebook on his paper-strewn desk. After a few moments, Hosokawa picks up a blue vase in which he discovers a thick stack of bills. Assured that the money is safe, he puts the vase in the desk and leaves the room. Returning suddenly, he gathers up the notebook and papers and locks them in a satchel. Sei'ichi tells no one of the schoolmaster's suspicious behavior for fear his parents would punish him for spying. During the next few weeks, the Matsudas are visited by a man named Yokota Tsuneo who asks to see the family's lacquerware. As time passes, Yokota becomes friendly with the lacquerware artisans and begins asking pointed questions about Hosokawa. Yokota befriends Sei'ichi as well, inviting him out on the town one evening. They go to Tsuji, the infamous Naha red-light district filled with restaurants and teahouses.[72] Yokota induces reticent Sei'ichi to relax and enjoy himself, which, after a short time, he does. The morning after their gastronomic and sexual adventures, Yokota asks casually about Hosokawa, and Sei'ichi cannot help but blurt out to his new friend details of the "blue vase" episode. Telling Sei'ichi not to reveal the contents of their discussion to anyone, Yokota takes his leave.

Five days later, on the night after the storm described at the story's beginning, Hosokawa is arrested. The detective who accompanies the two policemen as they escort Hosokawa to jail is none other than Yokota. The following day a search of the house yields the blue vase and satchel. Yamagusuku explains that Hosokawa has been claiming to be a Chinese spy in order to embezzle money from eccentric Old Okushima in whom the narrator's sympathies appear to lie. The old man foolishly believed that the funds were being used to supply the Chinese army with weapons. At the end of the story, the schoolmaster appeals his sentence and is sent to Nagasaki; Ushi, the ex-geisha, is forced to return to her former occupation; and Old Okushima is rumored to be enticing beautiful young boys into his home with promises of mandarin oranges. Despised as a rebel and a traitor, the old man stays locked indoors, protecting himself from the slurs and rocks with which the townspeople assail him.

Ten days after "Mandarin Oranges" was published in the *Okinawa Daily News*, the paper printed a series of reviews of the story culled from *Waseda Literature* (*Waseda bungaku*), *Fiction* (*Sōsaku*), *White Birch* (*Shirakaba*), *Cuckoo*, and *Literary World* (*Bunshō sekai*). Most found the work "diffuse" (*sanman*), but many critics, including Takahama Kyoshi and Honma Hisao, praised its skillful depiction of the Ryukyuan region.[73] Iha Getsujō, the literary critic who had been eagerly awaiting a story replete with local color, wrote:

> People in other prefectures might think Yamagusuku's work is quite interesting, but we scholars who have researched classical Ryukyuan literature feel that the content is flat. Because it takes Naha as a setting, it is chock full of local color; however, it seems that Yamagusuku does not possess the fine sensibilities peculiar to Ryukyuans. He neglects to express human emotions through nature, other than as something perceived visually. For example, what is our mental state after a storm passes? Are our olfactory senses not able to detect a peculiar smell? In "Mandarin Oranges" the author's personality does not come through. A person who pursues a literary path must not forget to reveal his personality. What this means is that when a writer wholeheartedly concentrates his thoughts upon taking up the pen, something in the material must, as a matter of course, pass through his thoughts, emotions, and the fires of his imagination. That dual, broken language (*katakoto sōgo*), too, must be in that person's heart, a part of his blood, and in every last fiber (*yoreki*) of his interior life. Nietzsche railed, "Of all that is written, I love only what a person hath written with his blood. Write with blood, and thou wilt find that blood is spirit!" I believe this contains great import. Is individuality expressed in "Mandarin Oranges"? I'll leave that question to readers of the story.[74]

As this lengthy passage shows, Iha grudgingly acknowledges Yamagusuku's adept use of local color for depicting external landscapes but criticizes him for not going far enough to describe the interiority of the Ryukyuans that people his story. Here, he veers dangerously close to making a tautological argument whereby only a talented few, with Okinawan blood, can write Okinawan fiction. Of course, this aside, what Iha finds fault with hinges on the language issue that Okinawan authors encountered and (I argue) continue to face when writing fiction in standard Japanese. That is, given that writers in Okinawa began to write fiction with a foreign language and literature (Japanese) as their model, the shortcomings Iha points out in Yamagusuku's "Mandarin Oranges" are less serious than they might otherwise be.[75]

Local color is not the only feature of "Mandarin Oranges" that places it at the head of the list of early Okinawan fiction. The story's twin themes of fraud and deception linger in the reader's mind longer than do the plentiful images of subtropical flora and fauna. That the perpetrator of the embezzlement described in "Mandarin Oranges" hails from Miyazaki is telling for it underscores the antimainland element that runs through the story. Yamagusuku's work illustrates well conventional Okinawan thinking that holds that Okinawa's stability or lack thereof is ultimately connected to the mainland.[76] Not only is Hosokawa from the mainland, he is an educator who holds an administrative post. Since most educational bureaucrats of the time were national appointees, Hosokawa can be construed as a proxy for the emperor system. In fact, as we shall see, the untrustworthy educator is a stock character that appears frequently throughout modern Okinawan fiction.[77]

Yamagusuku's "Mandarin Oranges" is a story about deception at various levels. Hosokawa's deception of Old Okushima is central to the story's plot, but Sei'ichi, too, plays a part in moving the narrative forward as he is duped into telling Detective Yokota his secret about Hosokawa. Although it is not explicit or plot-related, the overarching act of deception in "Mandarin Oranges" occurs when Yamato culture begins to inveigle itself into Okinawan society at the start of the Sino-Japanese war. The armed troops steadily pour in like the storms that relentlessly pound the island. This grand deception brings to mind the Battle of Okinawa that raged in the spring of 1945, decimating the island's civilian population.

Yamagusuku's earlier stories, "A Man Named Tsuruoka" and "Stone Talisman" contain acts of Yamato-inspired deception, but in both cases the deception remains personal. Tsuruoka is the only one of a group of Okinawan "expatriates" in Tokyo who fails to attain success because, owing to his ignorance, he is deceived by the city. Tsuruju is the fourth victim of a curse that plagues his family, but a broken heart hastens his death by cholera. Deceived by the fair mainland beauty, Shizuko, he lacks the will to survive. On the other hand, "Mandarin Oranges" signifies Yamagusuku's enlarging the theme of deception perpetuated by Yamato culture from a single point perspective to that of an entire society. Mainland Japanese critics hailed the work for its local color but paid little heed to its attention to historical detail. Iha Getsujō, Okinawa's most important critic, took an opposing view by panning the work for its superficial depiction of regional terrain, but he also ignored the story's chronicle of discord wrought by the Sino-Japanese war. During a period when "local color" was a buzzword for critics of the day, Yamagusuku's island tableau, with its focus on a historically fraught moment, rose to the heights of Okinawan fiction, a lofty position it occupies to this day.

After the mixed praise for "Mandarin Oranges," Yamagusuku wrote fiction only sporadically, focusing instead on *tanka*. His abrupt return to poetry seems due to the unease he felt in using what was then virtually a foreign language to express ideas and to develop a narrative. His struggle to compose fiction in Japanese, however, was not unique among Meiji-period writers from Okinawa. What separates him from the others is not only an ability to conjure in the reader's mind a picture postcard of Okinawa but also the skill with which he created a historically and socially accurate portrait of the island and its people. Into the image of a sun-drenched and storm-battered island, Yamagusuku insinuates details of the chaos that pervaded society in Okinawa as old ways collided with new. In these descriptions of the contradictions that appear when two worlds clash, there emerges the increasingly discernible theme of identity, expressed here in terms of antimainland sentiment. Contrary to what Iha Getsujō asserts, I find that Yamagusuku's probing into the precarious lives of his characters gives his story depth. On the surface, he serves up local color in the form of a quaint story set in the rural countryside. Such a story would naturally appeal to large numbers of urban readers who yearn for homes left behind. And yet, as I have argued, the story coheres around the theme of shifting identities, paradoxically suggesting the gradual obliteration of the hometown. It is this complexity of theme that accounts for Yamagusuku's position as Okinawa's leading writer of the day and which best characterizes the genre of Okinawan prose fiction.

Through reading Yamagusuku's "Mandarin Oranges," a blend of portraiture and protest in short form, together with the criticism this inaugural piece of Okinawan fiction generated, we see clearly the contradictory nature of local and mainland critics' expectations regarding Okinawan fiction. The latter critics, eager for flourishes of color to liven up the drabness of urban life, praise the more superficial aspects of Yamagusuku's work; the former seek depictions of regional life, the complexity of which calls into question the very nature of the work. This raises the following questions: Is writing from Okinawa regional or minority fiction? Does this writing affirm Okinawa's position within the nation or does it contest that same nation? "Stone Talisman" and "A Man Named Tsuruoka" only obliquely suggest antimainland themes. "Mandarin Oranges," on the other hand, is bolder in its portrayal of the chaos that befalls Okinawa in the wake of Japanese-imposed modernity. It is far easier to dismiss Yamagusuku's early stories as benign works of local color realism than it is to apply this label to "Mandarin Oranges."

My readings of Yamagusuku's fiction underscore how, to varying degrees, contemporary critics sought local color in Okinawan fiction. These critics' expectations also coalesced in the topos of the lost home. Urban readers, for instance, reading for a sense of place, readily find it in quaint regional stories such as "Stone Talisman," which, as its title indicates, serves as a souvenir piece. Read it and the ills of modern life lessen. Or, so it would seem. As I show in my analysis of "Mandarin Oranges," an antiwar piece that critiques the propensity of mainland Japanese to engage in violence and fraud, home is already lost, with little hope of return. The fact that mainland readers "find" the same home "lost" by those who live in the region depicted by Yamagusuku is no small irony. This irony recurs in fiction from Okinawa, making it, from the outset, a contradictory and compelling body of writing.

2 Subaltern identity in Taishō Japan

Inspired by the example set by Leo Tolstoy, the utopian ideal of humanism took root in the minds of writers in Japan during the Taishō period (1912–26). For example, it is well known that Mushakōji Saneatsu, the acknowledged representative of the White Birch School, put into practice socialist ideals of freedom and equality in the "new village" he created in Kyushu in 1918.[1] Mushakōji's distinguished ancestry, his wealth, and the privileged education he received in the Peers' School leaves no doubt that he was a member of the elite, as were the members of his coterie. It is important to note that such power resided in the hands of but a few, despite the impression that it was equally shared. I focus, in this chapter, on the representation of ethnic minorities in literature of the period, underscoring relations of power to show who represents whom, and with what effects on the group's subjectivity. The readings of the stories that follow are informed by contemporary theories of subalternity, cultural hybridity, and colonial mimicry, all of which have led me to conclude that identity is the central theme of Okinawan fiction. As I will show, works by Ikemiyagi Sekihō and Hirotsu Kazuo provide an opportunity to illuminate how we understand the very term "subaltern" and its various interpretations among postcolonial critics. In turn, the literary texts I discuss show how identity is fractured along lines of gender, ethnicity, and class, and confirm the heterogeneous nature of the subaltern.

The brief Taishō era, falling as it does between the long, chaotic Meiji period that preceded it, and the increasingly militaristic early Shōwa era that followed, has led many historians to characterize these dozen-odd years as a time of democracy and liberalism. Indeed, politician Yoshino Sakuzō did popularize the idea of "people-centrism" (*minponshugi*) in the day's most prestigious journal, *Central Forum*, (*Chūō kōron*) which functioned as the "Dragon's Gate" through which aspiring authors entered the literary establishment.[2] And, while people-centrism is still lauded as an indigenous liberal ideal that developed in Taishō Japan, this notion, and other era slogans such as "Taishō democracy," are undergoing scrutiny as revisionist historians seek to understand the period less as a heyday for democratic ideals than as a segue to the Pacific War.[3] To be sure, politicians heeded growing calls for popular representation in the domestic sphere, but the era also witnessed the expansion of the Japanese Empire. The ink on colonial policies drafted in Korea, annexed in 1910, had already long dried when the nation embarked on a 70,000-troop expedition into Siberia in 1918 and subsequently made forays into former German territories in Manchuria, Inner Mongolia, and Micronesia.

In the years leading to the Pacific War, Japan suffered from severe rural poverty and depression-induced unemployment in urban areas. Nowhere was rural poverty more acute than in newly incorporated Okinawa, where residents continued to bear the heaviest tax burden of the Japanese citizenry, as they had since the Meiji period.[4] An outlying prefecture, Okinawa was plagued not only with inordinate taxes but also with natural disasters and social stigmas so relentless they effected large-scale emigration to the Kansai region in Japan and as far as Hawaii, South America, and a cluster of Pacific islands bordering the equator, collectively referred to in Japanese as the "South Seas" (*Nanyō*). Two literary works from this period, one by an Okinawan writer, the other by a prominent member of the literary establishment in Tokyo, show the difficulty with which Okinawans sought to construct a positive identity for themselves at the time. "Officer Ukuma" ("Ukuma Junsa," 1922) by the nomadic poet and short-fiction writer Ikemiyagi Sekihō is a quasicanonical story that describes differing levels of discrimination an Okinawan policeman encounters during the fabled period of Taishō "democracy."[5] Two years after the appearance of "Officer Ukuma," Hirotsu Kazuo, a literary critic noted for his espousal of humanism, published the novella *The Wandering Ryukyuan* (*Samayoeru Ryūkyūjin*, 1924), in which the protagonist is contrarily sympathetic toward and critical of a major Okinawan character who leaves poverty-stricken Okinawa to make a living on the main islands of Japan.

Following an overview of the conditions that prevailed in Okinawa during the Taishō period, and of the contours of Ikemiyagi's peripatetic life, I will analyze "Officer Ukuma," the crowning success of Ikemiyagi's many stories in which a police officer figures prominently. This work centers on a lowly officer from a disenfranchised segment of Okinawan society who yearns for sure footing and social acceptance despite his background. The figure of a policeman in a neocolonial locale makes it impossible to ignore the theoretical questions posed by Ikemiyagi's work. The novella I discuss at the close of this chapter is a remarkable historical document through which to further examine the question of Okinawan identity. Hirotsu's controversial work contains several unflattering depictions of Ryukyuans that provoked much discussion among critics at the time of its publication in 1926, and again in 1970 when it was republished. The work is notable not only for its inflammatory content but also because Hirotsu is reputed to be the first major Japanese writer since the Meiji period to depict Ryukyuans in his fiction.[6] Thus, just as some historians would maintain that political representation rested in the hands of an elite few in Taishō Japan, literary representation of ethnic minorities, too, fell under the purview of the elite. A writer such as Hirotsu, secure in his position as a leading critic and known to uphold ideals such as humanism, could not put into practice the notions of democracy and freedom he purportedly embraced. While "Officer Ukuma" and *The Wandering Ryukyuan* differ in authorial orientation, they cohere in their Okinawan characters' abject failure to rise above their socially prescribed station.

A state in ruins

In the Taishō period, ethnologists such as Yanagita Kunio and Orikuchi Shinobu were drawn, as if to a magnet, to scrutinize Okinawa. Encouraged by the lead of Iha Fuyū, the father of Okinawan studies (*Okinawa-gaku no chichi*), Yanagita first visited the prefecture in 1920 and soon discovered that without an intense examination of Okinawan cultural forms, there could be no understanding of "ancient" Japan.[7] In the following year, Orikuchi went to Okinawa to conduct fieldwork on Japanese language and religion because of evidence there of archaic Japanese words and extensive shamanism. From the mid- to late Taishō period, scholars cast Okinawa into the limelight eager to find commonalities between Okinawa and the mainland.

Ironically, during the same period that Okinawa was showered with long overdue attention, it was plagued by a series of famines and beset with a flagging economy. Owing to the intense gaze scholars focused on aspects of Okinawan culture that helped to reconstruct ancient Japanese culture, the actual state of affairs in Okinawa during the Taishō period has, until late, been largely forgotten. In fact, during the late Taishō period, if Okinawa was mentioned in the mainland newspapers at all, it was referred to either as "The Sago Palm Hell" (*sotetsu jigoku*) or "A State in Ruins" (*bōkoku*).[8] The use of these terms relates to the severe economic duress that Okinawa experienced in the early 1920s when the price of sugar cane, the mainstay of the island's economy, plummeted worldwide. The weakened economy left many Okinawans unemployed, precipitating a wave of emigration to the mainland and beyond the nation's borders. Okinawans who remained in the prefecture were subject to abject poverty and a hunger so great they risked their lives to eat the fruit of the sago palm, through a process that first required boiling the fruit to draw out its poison.

Richard Goldschmidt (1878–1958), a German geneticist, offers an insightful view of Okinawa during the Taishō period. While head of the Kaiser Wilhelm Biology Research Institute, Goldschmidt was invited to lecture at Tokyo Imperial University from 1924 to 1926. On his return to Germany in 1927, Goldschmidt traveled to the Japanese territories of Taiwan, the Ryukyu Islands, Ogasawara, Korea, and southern Manchuria. He recorded his impressions in a lengthy travelogue that included over 200 photographs and was subsequently published in Berlin under the title *The New Japan* (*Neu Japan*, 1927).[9]

Among the numerous anecdotes contained in the book, two are particularly noteworthy. The first involves an encounter Goldschmidt had on a ship from Kagoshima to Okinawa. Striking up a conversation with several young Okinawans on their return from Brazil and Hawaii, Goldschmidt was shocked to hear the islanders say proudly that, were Japan and Germany to go to war, Japan would surely win.[10] Given the dire straits Okinawa was then in, not to mention the exploitation of Okinawa since the Satsuma invasion in 1609, the fierce Japanese patriotism the Okinawans revealed took Goldschmidt by surprise.[11]

A second anecdote confirms how strongly the Okinawans Goldschmidt met during his travels wished to ally themselves with mainland Japan. Goldschmidt recounts how one day, wishing to see some local textiles, he paid a visit to a wealthy merchant who had employees attire themselves in richly dyed (*bingata*) kimono for Goldschmidt to peruse.[12] Impressed by the beautiful, vibrant colors of the cloth, Goldschmidt asked permission to snap some photographs. The owner flatly refused, explaining that if outsiders saw photographs of Okinawans dressed in traditional kimono they would think that the islanders were an uncivilized people who still clung to ancient customs.[13] Again, Goldschmidt was taken aback by the extent to which so many Okinawans felt compelled to erase any perceived differences between themselves and mainland Japanese.

These two episodes succinctly capture Okinawans' desire for inclusion in the nation and attest to Benedict Anderson's observation that, regardless of nationalism's "roots in fear and hatred of the Other, and its affinities with racism [...] nations inspire love, and often profoundly self-sacrificing love."[14] The situation in Okinawa is a textbook case. Despite rapid assimilation, which the vast majority of Okinawans apparently strove for in the Taishō period, objective factors, such as an economy that had nearly ground to a halt, and subjective factors, such as the pervasive fear of appearing to lag behind the times, thwarted the efforts of the Okinawans to identify themselves as Japanese.[15] Alan S. Christy explains the crux of this dilemma as follows: "[T]he analysis of a weak, insufficiently modernized Okinawan economy discursively constructed an Okinawan identity, which was correspondingly weak and undeveloped, to serve as the origin of the economic problem."[16] Known only through negative images as the "Sago Palm Hell" or "A State in Ruins," Okinawa is impossibly rutted in a perceived time lag by which it is denied contemporaneity with the rest of Japan, a condition Johannes Fabian calls "allochronism." In this state, the goal of constructing a positive identity for Okinawa and its people remained, at best, difficult in the Taishō period.[17] Ironically, the idea of "homogeneous empty time," a historical state in which there is no time lag, is one of the fundamental philosophical assumptions upon which Anderson posits the possibility of national identity. This is quite opposite from the notion of "allochronism." Whereas Anderson's rosy view of nationalism promises unity among the masses, Fabian's argument against the coevalness of time suggests a harsher reality, one that is perhaps closer to that experienced by residents of Okinawa.

Wandering poet, drifting Ryukyuan

The question of identity, the central theme of Okinawan literature, is taken up by Ikemiyagi Sekihō in "Officer Ukuma," the representative work of Okinawan fiction from the Taishō era. The police officer, a character that offered Ikemiyagi the chance to reflect on issues of power, recurs frequently in the author's oeuvre, as does Kume, his birthplace. Known by many as a "wandering poet" (*hōrō no shijin*) or "drifting Ryukyuan" (*samayoeru Ryūkyūjin*), Ikemiyagi Sekihō was born in 1883 in Kume, or Kuninda, as it is known locally, a historically noteworthy district in Naha, Okinawa's capital city. In 1392, King Satto of Chūzan, the island's central kingdom, had designated Kume as the village in which Chinese immigrants would reside. Famous as a center of Chinese studies in the early years of the Ryukyu kingdom, Kume later fell into decline and became "a lantern in the wind" when previously robust trade between it and China, particularly Fujian province, plummeted in the late 1500s.[18] The village's fortunes reversed in the seventeenth century, following the Satsuma invasion. Shimazu rulers, insisting that Ryukyuans preserve their customs and traditions (*Ryūkyū hozon*), encouraged the study of Chinese since it proved essential for continued trade between Ryukyu and China, which fattened the clan's coffers.[19]

Once he graduated from the Prefectural Middle School in Okinawa, Ikemiyagi traveled to Tokyo to attend Waseda University, following the approved route to success for elites. When Ikemiyagi returned to Okinawa in January 1916, he assumed a position as journalist for the *Okinawa Morning Sun News* (*Okinawa asahi shinbun*). In March 1917, Ikemiyagi became a Japanese teacher at the Prefectural Second Middle School. He resumed his career as a reporter, this time for the *Okinawa Daily News* (*Okinawa nichinichi shinbun*) in 1920.[20] "Officer Ukuma," the fictional story that established Ikemiyagi's reputation as a writer, appeared in 1922 in *Liberation* (*Kaihō*), a major Japanese journal founded in 1919 by Yoshino Sakuzō, the very same politician who promoted the idea of a Taishō democracy. Essays and stories published in the journal display a clear socialist bent and reflect well the historical moment.[21] A habitual wanderer, Ikemiyagi traveled from areas in the extreme south such as Yonaguni, the Ryukyuan island closest to Taiwan, to the northern island of Hokkaido.[22] Though he is remembered today for "Officer Ukuma," Ikemiyagi was also known for his excellent *tanka* and a gift for languages that enabled him to translate works by writers as varied as Maupassant, Dostoyevsky, and Longfellow, for which he earned the much-coveted praise of Kikuchi Kan, then dominant in Tokyo literary circles. In addition to publishing "Officer Ukuma" in 1922, Ikemiyagi married fellow writer Arakaki Mitoko, with whom he had two sons.[23] Arakaki and Ikemiyagi later divorced. Their elder son, a draftee, died in the war, and the younger disappeared in the chaos that followed. Ikemiyagi himself died accidentally in 1951; apparently intoxicated, he drowned while bathing.

Figure 2 Book cover of Ikemiyagi Sekihō's collected works.

The winning story

"Officer Ukuma," a work selected from among hundreds of manuscript submissions,[24] is the story of a young man named Ukuma Hyākū who hails from a "special hamlet" (*tokushu buraku*)[25] on the outskirts of Naha. The setting is critical in this story of ambivalent identity. As the narrator explains, the inhabitants of the community descend from Chinese immigrants who lived in the Ryukyus in prior times.[26] Shunned by Okinawans for their poverty and engagement in menial labor, the villagers eke out a living by catching frogs and carp to sell at the marketplace or by weaving straw sandals and caps. As a young boy, Hyākū shows much promise in his studies and is encouraged by his family to do his best. As a teen, he excels to such a degree that his family allows him to avoid working in the fields so that he can concentrate on his schoolwork. The young man becomes so motivated he attempts to take an examination required for entry to the police department. When he passes, he becomes the first person from his marginalized community to attain a position in the police force.

Needless to say, Hyākū is the pride of both his family and his village. A huge celebration is held to commemorate his success and soon afterward Hyākū begins his work as a policeman. Each day, when he dons his uniform and cap and fastens on his sword, Hyākū grows increasingly accustomed to his new life outside the village. Two or three months of relative peace ensue, whereupon Hyākū inexplicably becomes rankled by the squalid conditions in which his family lives. Displeased by the untidiness of his home, Hyākū vents his anger upon his family. Gradually he finds himself irritated by the relaxed lifestyle of his fellow villagers. One day, during a festival that draws the villagers to gather at the central square, Hyākū—apparently having waited for such an opportunity—begins to address the assembled crowd.

Given that I am reading Ikemiyagi's work to shed light on the question of subaltern identity and the theoretical bind Gayatri Chakravorty Spivak introduces when she questions whether subaltern speech is possible, Hyākū's utterances in this key passage are symbolic, perhaps even synecdochal. The crowd's anticipation is palpable. They listen, rapt, expecting their native son to deliver good news. Since Hyākū became a policeman despite his lowly background, they have been hoping the bureau might provide them with conveniences that would improve their abysmal living conditions. The villagers' hopes for such things as reduced taxes, free healthcare, and road repair are dashed when Hyākū lectures:

> From now on the sewers must be cleaned thoroughly every day. When it's hot in the summer, many of you go around without clothes. This is a crime punishable by law, so if a policeman sees you, expect to be fined. I'm a policeman, too, and from now on I won't let you get away with anything just because you say you're from this village. We public officials

value nothing more than impartiality. So we can't look the other way even if a member of our own families or a relative does something wrong or vulgar.[27]

Startled by Hyakū's decidedly imperious tone, the villagers slowly distance themselves from the man who has begun to view his own family and neighbors with disdain.

As Hyakū becomes estranged from his community, he begins to associate more frequently with his colleagues, the majority of whom are described as brawny (*takumashī*) men from Kagoshima, Saga, and Miyazaki in Kyushu, locales that most officers, unhappily appointed to serve in Okinawa, called home. Okinawans, for their part, keenly resented the central government's practice, begun in the Meiji period, of placing outsiders in positions of local leadership. As the decades wore on, the quality of these Tokyo appointees declined, particularly at the lower rungs, where a large percentage of the police force and lower-level bureaucrats happened to be men from Kagoshima unable to find ready employment after the failed Satsuma Rebellion of 1877. Many Okinawans particularly despised these appointees for they represented a none-too-subtle continuation of Satsuma authority in the prefecture.

Disregarding the rules he himself enforces while on the job, Hyakū invites his coworkers home at night, whiling away the hours in drink and song. Indifferent to the trouble his wild nights cause his family and neighbors, Hyakū persists in his efforts to become a well-liked and respected member of the police force. The story's ultimate irony is that Hyakū's career success and "impure" heritage result in his exclusion from both his community and his workplace. While his colleagues socialize with him, they never let Hyakū forget that he is somehow different. The narrator states that his peers regard Hyakū as a foreigner (*ikokujin*), and this cool reception leads Hyakū, who has endeavored to assimilate, to view his associates from a similar distance. In spite of the cruelty Hyakū inflicts on his family and neighbors, the narrator manages, through concise and well-crafted descriptions of Hyakū's mental state, to elicit the reader's sympathies for the young policeman as he struggles in vain to establish an identity for himself.

The setting and theme of "Officer Ukuma" immediately brings to mind Shimazaki Tōson's *The Broken Commandment* (*Hakai*, 1906), perhaps the groundbreaking work of modern Japanese literature. A naturalist novel, *The Broken Commandment* sympathetically portrays the mental anguish of Ushimatsu, a member of Japan's outcaste class (*burakumin*), as he struggles with the decision to reveal his origins. Tōson, like Ikemiyagi, devotes the bulk of his narrative to the protagonist's intense feelings of inferiority vis-á-vis the outside community, rather than to his feeble actions. In this regard, Ikemiyagi's work is also much like that of Natsume Sōseki, the author whose novels of alienated anti-heroes stand at the center of modern Japanese literary history.

Lost in transition

Not unlike fellow male protagonists in Japanese fiction, Hyākū seeks refuge from his problems in the pleasure quarters. Ostracized by his colleagues and those in his community, Hyākū spends his off-duty hours in Tsuji, the red-light district in Naha. There he meets a young woman, Kamarū, the daughter of a wealthy man who died. The woman's older brother, having squandered the family money, had no choice but to sell his sister into prostitution.[28] The story's two tragic characters, Hyākū and Kamarū, fall in love but have no chance of a life together as Hyākū cannot afford to ransom her contract.

The Tsuji interlude is an important part of "Officer Ukuma" for it suggests the possibility of a gendered reading of the story. A warren of teahouses bedecked with painted scrolls and elegant fans, and filled with the plaintive notes of the samisen and koto, Tsuji is charged with an air of femininity. Amid these surroundings, Kamarū, a hapless victim, occupies a place lower in the social hierarchy than does Hyākū. The fact that she is an economic outcast endears her to Hyākū, whose own feelings of loneliness and inferiority are assuaged in her presence. In Tsuji, Hyākū experiences freedom, albeit briefly, and only in the arms of his lover, a prostitute—and Okinawan—similarly ostracized by the outer world. It may be futile to measure the degree to which Ikemiyagi's characters are oppressed, but one might consider Hyākū and Kamarū as equals in that the former is an ethnic minority within Okinawa, and the latter is both Okinawan and female. Hyākū stands side by side with Kamarū in his shared lack of identification with mainland Japanese.

In one of the story's slight but telling details, Ikemiyagi includes a scene in which Hyākū changes out of his uniform and into street clothes before visiting his lover. The rush of power he experiences with his lover arises from his own masculinity not that derived from his state-issued sword, cap, and uniform.[29] Trapped and powerless, Kamarū serves as a convenient foil for Hyākū, a man whose acute feelings of inferiority disappear when in Tsuji. No longer constrained by his uniform, a symbol of the Japanese state and its authority, Hyākū, the narrator tells us, reverts to his "true self." This self, merging with the nation-state, is the very subject of Albert Memmi's writings on the nature of master–slave relations under conditions of colonialism. Memmi states:

> The first attempt of the colonized is to change his condition by changing his skin. There is a tempting model very close at hand—the colonizer. The latter suffers from none of his deficiencies, has all rights, enjoys every possession and benefits from every prestige. He is, moreover, the other part of the comparison, the one that crushes the colonized and keeps him in servitude. The first ambition of the colonized is to become equal to that splendid model and to resemble him to the point of disappearing into him.[30]

The critical attention Ikemiyagi pays to Hyākū's change of clothes, and the liberating effect this act has on the protagonist, affirms Memmi's point that those who are oppressed simply change their skin.[31] In Ikemiyagi's story, Hyākū's "true (native) self" is lost when he is in uniform and resurfaces when he is clad in civilian wear. A postcolonial critic, eager to find the slightest sign of resistance, might claim that Ukuma displays agency in this scene because he is effectively reversing, or negating Memmi's description of the process of colonial transformation. That is, Ukuma insistently removes the skin/uniform that makes him one with the nation, rather than allowing it to sublate him. However, this same critic would then, perforce, be confronted with the fallacy of an originary, true self.

After having spent the previous three days and nights with Kamarū in Tsuji, Hyākū is on his way home one morning. While he is brooding over his debauched love affair, a suspicious movement in an abandoned tomb catches his eye. Although he is out of uniform, Hyākū dashes inside the tomb, discovers a man crouched in hiding, and drags him out. Ikemiyagi writes: "In that moment Hyākū's languid mood vanished, and he became the consummate policeman."[32] Nakahodo Masanori cites this passage in arguing that Hyākū's transformation from a naive young village minority to a member of the police force is irreversible; however much he may try, Hyākū cannot shed his "uniform."[33] Dramatist Fujiki Hayato, whose performances in Nakagusuku today delve into the sacrifices Okinawans made for the nation in the prewar period, is careful to show that the soldiers who appear in his plays embrace militarization. Fujiki's insists that an Okinawan subject is not simply overwritten by Japanese military discipline; rather, he experiences an element of joy in the process of transformation. Fujiki's point is important to keep in mind here, for it is impossible to know whether Hyākū's actions are selfish or selfless. In other words, is his self-cultivation motivated by a desire to improve himself or to contribute to the nation to which he tenuously belongs?[34] In either case, the joy Hyākū experiences upon being recognized as a police officer functions as a crucial tool for identification and self-consciousness.

Excited by his single-handed capture, Hyākū arrests the suspect and takes him to police headquarters where he is charged after confessing to theft. The elation Hyākū experiences after making his first arrest dissipates the instant he learns that the man is none other than his lover's older brother. The story concludes as Hyākū's chief commands him to escort Kamarū to police headquarters for interrogation. In the memorable concluding lines, the narrator describes Hyākū's pained reaction: "Officer Ukuma felt all the blood in his body rush to his head. For a time he could only stare blankly at his chief. Then his eyes began smoldering with the fear and rage of a wild beast fallen into a trap."[35]

"Officer Ukuma" is the tragic story of a young man who exists in a state of limbo. As a second-class Japanese citizen of Chinese descent, Hyākū achieves outward success only to become doubly estranged: his background prevents him from becoming a full-fledged member of the police force, and his authoritative attitude ensures his ostracization from the villagers and family members who have encouraged him to succeed. Disillusioned, he escapes to Tsuji, a modern day "floating world" where he finds temporary solace. Even the pipe dreams he has of ransoming his lover are in the end quashed as he realizes the full import of his constrained position. Not only does the identity Hyākū strives for continue to elude him, but, as the story's final line reveals, he is reduced to a wild, frightened animal.

Officer Ukuma as subaltern

As well as bringing to mind the alienated antihero of Japanese and Western modern literature, Ikemiyagi's portrait of a native police officer whose position of authority ironically leads to feelings of powerlessness corresponds to contemporary debates on subalternity that inform postcolonial theory. It is Okinawa's position as a neocolonial area of Japan that compels me to go beyond a modern analysis of the story to examine it through a postcolonial framework. The main source of contention among theorists such as Gayatri Chakravorty Spivak and Homi K. Bhabha concerns agency and stems from the immense influence deconstruction has had on postcolonial theory. Because of the dissolution of the post-Enlightenment subject, it is difficult—if not impossible—to construct a speaking position for the subaltern.[36] While there is much disagreement about the theoretical legitimacy of the subaltern subject, postcolonial critics are united in their concern over how to effect agency for the (bracketed) subaltern subject.

One of the major problems that complicate the issue of subalternity is the unproblematic usage of the term "subaltern."[37] Notable exceptions to this practice occur in the writings of historians in the Subaltern Studies Collective as well as in essays by Spivak and Bhabha.[38] In the preface to *Selected Subaltern Studies*, Ranajit Guha clearly states that the word "subaltern" in the work's title has the meaning given in *The Concise Oxford Dictionary*, namely, "of inferior rank."[39] He explains that the term will be used throughout the studies as "a name for the general attribute of subordination in South Asian society whether this is expressed in terms of class, caste, age, gender and office or in any other way."[40] For further clarity, Guha appends to the preface a note that specifically defines the terms "elite," "people," and "subaltern." Briefly stated, the term elite signifies dominant groups, both foreign and native, with the native group further divided into regional and national levels. The terms "people" and "subaltern class" are synonymous, and the category is said to represent the difference between the total Indian population and the elite. Guha concludes his note by stating that the task of the collective is "to investigate, identify, and measure the specific nature and degree of the deviation of these elements from the ideal and situate it historically."[41]

While cognizant of the point that both dominant and subaltern groups are heterogeneous, Guha's fastidiousness is such that even Spivak, always specific, voices alarm over what she perceives as an overly taxonomic and essentialist program. In her well-known essay "Can the Subaltern Speak?," Spivak argues that the critique of the subject, as engaged in by Michel Foucault and Gilles Deleuze, unwittingly gives rise to a subject—in their cases, that of Europe. She further reveals that in the epistemic violence that attends the disclosing of the oppressed colonial subject, or subaltern as Other, the intellectual remains transparent. Contrary to Foucault, who believes that the oppressed can speak and know their condition if given the chance, Spivak concludes that, on the other side of the international division of labor, there is "no unrepresentable subaltern subject that can know and speak itself."[42] Spivak's negative response to the question of whether the subaltern can speak is not simply delivered. To support her views on the theoretical illegitimacy of any kind of authentic voice, or subaltern agency, Spivak painstakingly analyzes the discourse of Indian widow sacrifice (*sati*) to show how the gendered female subaltern is doubly shadowed by native patriarchy and foreign masculist-imperialist ideology, and thereby rendered historically mute.[43]

Spivak views the nature of the subaltern as "irretrievably heterogeneous" and cautions against regarding the relationship between colonizers and colonized as simply a binary or hierarchical one. Subaltern subjects, given the variegated types of colonial relationships in which they figure, cannot be homogenized. Although Spivak's complication of the term "subaltern" is necessary and productive, it makes the critic's task of recovering subaltern voices far more difficult. In the case of Ikemiyagi's story, neither Hyākū nor Kamarū can speak, precisely because their voices are always already lacking authority. This lack is less due to the dissolution of the Cartesian (bourgeois) subject than because of the subaltern's specific position within a historical nexus, in which power concentrates in an elite class, which oppresses the colonial subject.

Reading "Officer Ukuma" with Guha's definitions in mind, it is clear that Officer Ukuma is a character who occupies a place Spivak calls "the floating buffer zone of regional elite-subaltern."[44] Ukuma's position as a police officer marks him as a member of the regional elite, while his status as a second-class citizen from a discriminated village relegates him to the subaltern. The native police officer's authority is undermined precisely because of this ambiguity. Caught between the imperialist power structure, represented by the officer's Yamato or mainland Japanese colleagues and chief, and his emotions for the Tsuji prostitute, another member of the heterogeneous subaltern class that peoples Ikemiyagi's story, Ukuma stares vacantly, helpless as a trapped animal at the story's end. While his silence supports Spivak's thesis on subalternity, Ikemiyagi's depiction of the officer's mentality counters it.

Ikemiyagi's final description of Ukuma is not as negative and bleak as Spivak's portrait of the subaltern. The fact that the officer's eyes are smoldering with fear *and* indignation is critical since these contradictory elements are not only what constitute the subaltern, they are what make him a potential threat to dominant groups. Historian Gautam Bhadra singles out defiance and submissiveness as the two elements that together form the subaltern mentality.[45] He argues that the subaltern's collaboration with and resistance to the elite merge and coalesce to form a complex and contradictory consciousness.[46] Officer Ukuma cannot be reduced to an absolute negation for he is painfully cognizant of, and incensed by, his double bind. It is precisely the nature of the subaltern consciousness that makes the figure a compelling one. Just as the subaltern is complex and contradictory, so too is Okinawan fiction. That is, when read with an eye to its regional aspect the fiction affirms the idea of Japan as a nation, of which Okinawa is but a part. And, when read with an eye on its alterity, whether linguistic, cultural, or historical, the fiction contests the notion of a seamless nation.

The mimic man

While Spivak's writings on the subaltern come readily to mind in establishing the police officer's significance in Ikemiyagi's story, Homi K. Bhabha is, finally, of greater use for he offers a more hopeful view of the subaltern than does Spivak. As a consequence of his own heavy debt to deconstruction, Bhabha sees in the nature of language and the sign a split that produces polyphony and ambivalence. In his essay "DessimiNation: Time, Narrative, and the Margins of the Modern Nation," Bhabha argues that "people," the term which Guha uses interchangeably with "subaltern," are both objects of national pedagogy and subjects of a process of signification. He relates this doubleness to the idea of hybridity, which is defined in part as "the perplexity of the living as it interrupts the representation of the fullness of life."[47] For Bhabha, national narratives are disrupted by the presence of the subaltern whose identity-in-difference provokes a fundamental crisis. In his essay "Of Mimicry and Man: The Ambivalence of Colonial Discourse," Bhabha further elaborates that the identity of the true subaltern lies in his difference.[48] The processes by which colonizers groom native elites to serve as a buffer between them and the masses produce "a subject of difference that is almost the same, but not quite."[49] Hyākū, a local policeman in the employ of the Japanese state, thoroughly indoctrinated by state apparatuses of power such as schools and the police force, performs the duty of surveillance. What makes his gaze threatening is its doubleness. Observing through the eyes of a colonial representative *and* disenfranchised minority, Hyākū mimics the colonizer yet always retains his distance, precisely because of his identity-in-difference.

Because the mimic man, Hyākū, is constructed around the ambivalence of being both native and elite, Ikemiyagi must reveal the police officer's difference in order to maximize his potential to disrupt colonial authority. Hence, words such as "foreigner" are used to refer to Hyākū throughout the text. While the partial presence of the subaltern turns mimicry into menace, it does not signify that an essential identity, or "true" self, is anywhere concealed.[50] Hyakū's predicament is due to the fact that he is neither an ordinary citizen nor a respected official; his hybrid nature accounts for his utterly despondent state.

In Ikemiyagi's "Officer Ukuma," Hyakū is a subaltern who attempts to emulate his Yamato colleagues. The passage quoted above in which Hyakū instructs his village on proper deportment is perfectly illustrative of the type of colonial mimicry described by Bhabha. Positioning himself as an impartial public official, Hyakū addresses his neighbors in an imperious manner. The crowd's shock can be explained by the fact that they recognize in Hyakū their native son, not the colonial mimic he has become. Hyakū's transformation leads to his estrangement from the village and feelings of alienation. By the end of "Officer Ukuma," the protagonist's realization that he is powerless in both his civil and official capacities causes him to feel subhuman. Ikemiyagi's description of Hyakū as a vacantly staring trapped animal would lead one to agree with Spivak's pronouncement that the subaltern, by definition, cannot speak. However, considering the contradictory and ambiguous nature of the subaltern consciousness, what cannot be said becomes important. If Hyakū's fearful and indignant silence is measured, then the disturbing noise of the mimic insurgent is clearly audible.

A phantom novel

In 1926, four years after the publication of "Officer Ukuma," which concludes with a disturbing portrait of Hyakū's silent, bestial rage, Hirotsu Kazuo published his novella *The Wandering Ryukyuan*. The work provoked a loud and angry response from the Okinawa Youth Alliance[51] for its inclusion of unflattering depictions of Okinawans as animal-like creatures who only wreaked havoc. The alliance called for an immediate retraction, citing fears that such a portrayal would promote prejudice and would harm the chances of Okinawans who were already struggling to obtain employment in the Kansai area where job advertisements and even restaurants often explicitly excluded Koreans and Ryukyuans (*Chōsenjin, Ryūkyūjin O-kotowari*).[52] To his credit, Hirotsu promptly apologized, had the Alliance's protest published in the leading journal of the day, *Central Forum*, where *The Wandering Ryukyuan* had originally appeared, and forbade his publishers from ever including the work in hardback form or in any collected works. From 1926 until 1970, when members of the literary establishment in Okinawa obtained permission from Hirotsu's family to reprint the novella in the journal *New Okinawan Literature* (*Shin Okinawa bungaku*), *The Wandering Ryukyuan* remained a "phantom novel" (*maboroshi no shōsetsu*).[53]

Given the furor his novel unleashed, it is ironic to learn of Hirotsu's avowed humanism and stature in literary circles. Donald Keene writes that Hirotsu Kazuo (1891–1968), son of the important Ken'yūsha writer Hirotsu Ryūrō, was one of the three most important critics of the Taishō period.[54]

Like Ikemiyagi, Hirotsu attended Waseda University, working his way through school by translating various Russian and French authors through the use of English translations. Hirotsu began his career as a critic in 1916; during the same year he published a study of Tolstoy. He followed this work of criticism three years later with a study of Shiga Naoya, an author whose literary style was, and still remains, the envy of a host of Japanese writers and critics. These two admired pieces of Hirotsu's literary criticism are regarded as classics of the Taishō era.[55]

The fact that Hirotsu thought of himself as a humanist makes it all the more dismaying that *The Wandering Ryukyuan* is rife with negative images of Okinawans. Briefly told, this autobiographical novella relates the story of a curious relationship the protagonist, a writer known as H—undoubtedly Hirotsu's alter ego—has with an Okinawan unusually named Mikaeru Tamiyo.[56] The novella begins one day when H, one of the many "idle intelligentsia" that populate Japanese literary fiction, is disturbed by the intrusion of Mikaeru who has come to meet him after receiving an introduction from a mutual friend. Mikaeru is described in the following passage in which H reluctantly receives his uninvited guest:

> While frankly expressing my displeasure, I looked in the direction of the open screen doors and there appeared a man dressed in Western attire; his face was round, or rather square shaped, his jaw short. He had dark skin, a mustache, and a stubbled jaw. Laughing, "Eh heh heh," he poked his head in. I couldn't even begin to guess what variety of human being (*dō iu shurui no ningen*) he might be.[57]

Intensifying an already negative image, H later likens Mikaeru's distinctive laugh, "Eh heh heh," to the laughter of a bear.[58] Two other Okinawans appear briefly in the story. One, a character named O, is "bony, dark-skinned and has a habit of facing others with his shoulders squared."[59] H describes the second character, Mikaeru's wife, in the following way: "As you might expect, being Ryukyuan she gave me the impression that she was invisible. Even when I ran into her in the corridors, she wouldn't greet me."[60] All three of the Okinawans are clearly depicted in negative terms, and, since the mainland Japanese characters that appear in the work are given little or no description, the reader cannot help but notice the unflattering attention H pays the Okinawans.[61]

Critic Kuniyoshi Shintetsu refers to the depictions of the Okinawans in *The Wandering Ryukyuan* as an "unwelcome favor" (*arigata meiwaku*).[62] To have Okinawans appear in a work by a major author such as Hirotsu Kazuo, and published in a prestigious journal such as *Central Forum* was an encouraging rarity. However, the manner in which Hirotsu portrays Okinawans disturbs the Okinawan critic. Not only are the characters described unfavorably, their actions border on criminal. Mikaeru, ingratiating himself with H, proceeds to rob him of a gas stove he had convinced H to purchase during his stint as a peddler. Further, he cajoles H to buy his own fiancée a pair of gloves, sells ill-gotten new books from H's publisher to a used bookstore, and, in the novella's concluding scene, breaks out of his boarding house in the thick of night leaving H, his guarantor, to pay his delinquent rent. H, who is sympathetic to Mikaeru's struggle to survive and has all along been unable to hide his fondness for the Okinawan in spite of how many times Mikaeru dupes him, in the end admits that he should have been less indulgent and more cautious of Mikaeru's actions. Mikaeru's behavior certainly warrants concern, but time and again, H forgives the young Okinawan. O, the other Okinawan identified in the text, is not given the same leniency for similarly scandalous actions. When H compares Mikaeru with O, who, among other acts, brazenly writes H a curt letter stating he is keeping for himself a Maupassant novel H has generously loaned him (*senjitsu haishaku shita hon wa kinen no tame ni moratte okimasu*), he concludes that, while Mikaeru's behavior is somewhat pardonable, O's is not.

What makes Mikaeru an endearing figure for both reader and narrator is his tragicomical nature. During his frequent visits to H's boarding house, Mikaeru finds ways to turn a light-hearted conversation into a serious discussion of the economic plight of his native Okinawa. One moment he might be regaling H with an enumeration of the superior qualities of a ware he is peddling, the next he speaks in hushed tones of poverty in Okinawa. H clucks sympathetically as Mikaeru describes the deplorable situation:

> Middle-class Ryukyuans are in nothing but ruins right now, you know. Even if people grow sugar cane, it doesn't sell. No, because of wholesalers who are involved in mainland capitalism, these products—if they do sell—are dirt-cheap. Even if they are sold for a song, the money is not enough to live on. Young people resent this so they won't sell anything, but if they don't sell their sugar cane, they don't eat. And if they try to make a sale they become the helpless prey of the capitalists. On top of this, taxes are high, you know. (When he got excited, he had the habit of inserting "you know" in his speech.) You'd be shocked, wouldn't you, if I told you taxes in Naha are several times what they are in Tokyo. Okinawans are inordinately taxed. Naturally, if they remain quiet and do nothing, they are ruined, yet if they work they're still ruined. It's tragic. There's even a song, "To T, To T" [*T e, T e*] that young people in the Ryukyuan middle class sing among themselves. T stands for the coalmines in Kyushu. Think about it. For them, life in the coalmines seems like paradise compared to staying in the Ryukyus and going into ruin. It's utopia. The life of a *miner* seems ideal.[63]
>
> (Emphasis added)

Mikaeru's heated outburst softens H's attitude toward the young man, forcing him to reflect on the motivation for the actions of the Okinawans he knows. Through Mikaeru, H learns first-hand of Okinawans who along with some Koreans, work in miserable conditions in the coal pits of Kyushu, more commonly known as "Japan's Texas," a reflection of its rough nature.[64]

Throughout his text, Hirotsu liberally sprinkles references to prior instances of oppression in Okinawa, such as the 1609 Satsuma invasion, seemingly in order to establish the motivation that drives his Okinawan characters to behave as they do. In these passages, Ryukyuans and mainland Japanese are described as decidedly different. The former are long-suffering victims, the latter aggressors. Given the historical record of an unequal balance of power, H concludes that it is understandable for Ryukyuans to behave irresponsibly toward their mainland cousins since they have long been imbricated in an intensely fraught relationship.

Despite Hirotsu's outwardly sympathetic portrayal of Okinawa's prior and current historical predicament, the terms he uses in his narrative contribute to creating a further rift between center and periphery. Hirotsu's use of the terms "Ryukyu" (*Ryūkyū*) and "Ryukyuan" (*Ryūkyūjin*), in conjunction with "inner territory" (*naichi*) and "insiders" (*naichijin*), makes it difficult for one not to imagine a colonial situation in which the Ryukyus are but another of Japan's territories.[65] Judging from the gentlemanly response Hirotsu offered to vociferous protestors in the Okinawa Youth Alliance, it is likely his use of such charged terms was innocent but certainly unwise during a time when Okinawans were acutely aware of perceived differences between themselves and Japanese from other prefectures.[66]

Class divides

Just as Hirotsu's use of language divides the world of his text into victim and aggressor, so too do the clearly demarcated differences in class, a key criterion in Guha's definition of the subaltern. H is a writer living comfortably enough to spend money frivolously; for example, he admits early in the novella his weakness for acquiring useless gadgets. His is a life of leisure—days and nights spent looking outside his window when instead he should be writing. The writer's block that plagues him does not impact him financially since he is already somewhat established and can dash off translations for extra money. On the other hand, Mikaeru, his wife, and O inhabit a separate realm. They have left their blighted homeland in search of fame and fortune, but, in the case of Mikaeru, fortune is deferred as he works first as a peddler, then as a railroad employee, and finally a failed entrepreneur. Mikaeru's soliloquy on Okinawa's dreadful economic conditions makes clear the painful fact that the coalmines of Kyushu operate by the sweat of Okinawan workers. An early scene in which Mikaeru cajoles H into buying a pair of gloves for him so that he can present them to his girlfriend for Christmas also serves to underscore the different socioeconomic positions the two occupy.

Initially, *The Wandering Ryukyuan* appears to be about no more than a strange interlude in a writer's life. Like so many other works of modern

Japanese literature published in the heyday of personal fiction writing in the 1920s, it tells the story of an author's life. Yet, when one considers the terms "Ryukyuan" and "insider" that Hirotsu uses to demarcate the types of people in his text, and the stark contrast between those who labor and those who do not, the novella becomes far less personal than political. The fact that H is attempting in vain to write a novel over the course of the four years that occur between his first and presumed last encounter with Mikaeru is significant. H has, on several occasions, stayed awake to write, yet never produces anything. The story H/Hirotsu finally writes is *The Wandering Ryukyuan*, in which Mikaeru and, less significantly, his wife and O are vehicles around which the plot, such as it is, revolves. Given these characters' class differences, one would be hard-pressed not to view the content of the novella as exotic material for which the writer extracts compensation, if not prestige. Hirotsu inflates himself as a writer at the expense of the Okinawans he maligns in the text by summarily concluding that they are dangerous characters (*chūi jinbutsu*). Naturally, this pronouncement is made only after Hirotsu has finished enumerating the Okinawans' foibles.[67]

Visible markers of identity

In a particularly notable passage, it appears as if Mikaeru has concealed all outward signs of his difference from others on the mainland. After a disappearance lasting several months, the Okinawan abruptly shows up at H's boarding house one day, as is his habit, but this time Mikaeru's demeanor has changed completely: "Dressed in a dapper suit of the kind then in fashion, he had his hair combed back and his mustache neatly trimmed. He was wearing a pair of Harold Lloyd spectacles and carrying a folding briefcase."[68] H is stunned by Mikaeru's transformation until he witnesses the Okinawan pull a Golden Bat cigarette out of his pocket. H notes that "the tips of his flat nails were smeared with grease and thick black hair was growing around his knuckles, *it was the old Mikaeru after all*" [emphasis added].[69] With a mere phrase, H handily erases the positive image he has just given of Mikaeru as a dignified business man, attributing to him a physical characteristic that can only be construed negatively.[70] Even at this, his most successful juncture, Mikaeru is denied a flattering description, for the narrator shows cracks in his Japanese persona that reveal Okinawan traits beneath.

The transformation that Hirotsu's narrator effects is by no means unique. For instance, John MacKenzie, writing on Victorian popular theater, notes that the class tension characteristic of many early nineteenth-century melodramas dissipated by the century's end, resulting in a dark metamorphosis:

> By then, imperial subjects offered a perfect opportunity to externalize the villain, who increasingly became the corrupt rajah, the ludicrous Chinese or Japanese nobleman, the barbarous "fuzzy-wuzzy" or black, facing a cross-class brotherhood of heroism, British officer and ranker

60 *Subaltern identity in Taishō Japan*

together. Thus imperialism was depicted as a great struggle with dark and evil forces, in which white heroes and heroines could triumph over black barbarism, and the moral stereotyping of melodrama was given a powerful racial twist.[71]

Not only is class tension much in evidence, so too is the orientalizing maneuver that MacKenzie describes, wherein H must make plain the differences of Mikaeru and his fellow Okinawans in order for him to subsequently perform the judicious act of demarcating proper and improper deportment.

Interesting parallels can be drawn between Hirotsu Kazuo's *The Wandering Ryukyuan* and Ikemiyagi Sekihō's "Officer Ukuma." Like Hyākū, Mikaeru is trapped by pitiful circumstances. Forced to leave Okinawa because of its stalled economy, he struggles in vain to make a living in Tokyo. At one point in the novella, Mikaeru succinctly explains this predicament: "Now, if we are home in Okinawa we can't rest easy, and if we leave for the mainland we cannot relax. We Ryukyuans are an odd lot."[72] Uneasy both in his homeland and in Tokyo, Mikaeru will always be a wandering Ryukyuan.[73]

In Hirotsu's work, the wanderer is not the romantic figure one sees in Kunikida Doppo's "Musashi Plain" (*Musashino*, 1908), for instance. The animal imagery used to describe Mikaeru reduces him to a mere caricature; his bear-like laugh, his dark, hairy body and prowling nature turn him into a menacing presence. Not unlike Ukuma, Mikaeru is of inferior rank, a subaltern. H's explicit depiction of the Okinawan as an animal places him several notches below even Ukuma, himself a bestial character, as suggested by Ikemiyagi's concluding depiction. Further, Mikaeru's attempts to assume the demeanor of a well-heeled "Japanese" person calls to mind the performance of the colonial mimic man, one who closely resembles his colonizer while still maintaining his identity-in-difference. Absurdly, hairy knuckles are what separate colonizer from colonized in Hirotsu's novella.

Ikemiyagi Sekihō's "Officer Ukuma" and Hirotsu Kazuo's *The Wandering Ryukyuan* are two Taishō period works that show the lengths to which Okinawans of the time strove to assimilate into mainland Japanese culture. Officer Ukuma's success results only in hopeless feelings of inferiority vis-à-vis his stalwart Japanese colleagues. He painfully discovers that he belongs nowhere as he is doubly displaced from both home and nation. Well before colonial critics such as Fanon and Memmi or postcolonial critics such as Spivak and Bhabha articulated their theories on the psychology of the oppressed, W. E. B. DuBois, in his prescient 1898 essay, "The Souls of Black Folk," aptly describes the struggle in which Hyākū is engaged:

> After the Egyptian and Indian, the Greek and Roman the Teuton and Mongolian, the Negro is a sort of seventh son, born with a veil, and gifted with second-sight in this American world—a world which yields him no true self-consciousness, but only lets him see himself through

the revelation of the other world. It is a peculiar sensation, this double-consciousness, this sense of always looking at one's self through the eyes of others, of measuring one's soul by the tape of a world that looks on in amused contempt and pity. One ever feels his two-ness—an American, a Negro; two souls, two thoughts, two unreconciled strivings; two warring ideals in one dark body, whose dogged strength alone keeps it from being torn asunder.[74]

National allegories

Despite my own misgivings regarding Fredric Jameson's much-ballyhooed pronouncement that all "Third World" texts must necessarily be read as national allegories, I have found it remarkably easy to allegorize prose from Okinawa in this study, particularly given its links to the history of the prefecture. Among this prose, "Officer Ukuma" is perhaps the most finely drawn story, an emblem of the prefecture's own liminality. Hyākū is as clear a portrait of an individual possessed of a double consciousness as one can find in the body of fiction from Okinawa. And, yet, what finally makes Ikemiyagi's police officer linger in one's mind is not that he is torn between Okinawa and Japan; rather, his identity is fractured along yet another ethnic line: Chinese, confirming the "irretrievably heterogeneous" nature of the colonized subaltern of which Spivak writes. To construe Hyākū as divided between colonizer and colonized conceals his Chinese heritage and, with it, an entire history of a downtrodden community which once served as ambassadors, traders, navigators, and interpreters who facilitated trade relations between Ryukyu and other foreign countries. It is this dimension of the story that makes "Officer Ukuma" far more than a simple allegory of an Okinawan man whose loyalties are divided. The story, with its complex protagonist, not to mention his love interest, Kamarū, a young woman sold into prostitution, contains within it multiple pairs of victim and aggressor, suggesting that the relationship between Okinawa and Japan is often overdetermined and occludes internal levels of oppression, whether between Okinawans and ethnic Chinese, as in this case, or between fellow Okinawans from different islands in the prefecture. It is also a cautionary tale about the dangers that attend assimilation, which, as historian Niall Ferguson recently notes, exacerbates so many conflicts of the past bloody century.[75]

In *The Wandering Ryukyuan*, Mikaeru Tamiyo finds in H a benefactor who indulges him, but, as it turns out, this generosity stems from a desire to cull exotic material for his writing. H often states how fond he is of Mikaeru despite his "character flaws," yet his attitude remains, to the end, extremely patronizing. Mikaeru, an aspiring writer, is drawn to H, presumably due to the latter's professional success. Instead of imparting advice, or encouraging Mikaeru in his writerly ambition, H/Hirotsu depicts the Okinawan in an egregious manner, illustrating that orientalism is indeed an act of cultural strength. Hirotsu's bestial descriptions of Mikaeru diminish the Okinawan even as they affirm the superiority of H. I cannot claim that there exists a single type of Okinawan in the story, but Hirotsu does cast the novella's lot of Okinawans in a harshly negative light. Just as Ikemiyagi's work contains different types of Okinawans—literate, illiterate, male, female—so, too does Hirotsu's story. In addition to Mikaeru, there is O, described as a thief, and Mikaeru's wife, whom Hirotsu depicts, in stereotypical fashion, as invisible and silent, like all Ryukyuan women.

It is the characteristic silence of Okinawan women, as seen in the character of Mikaeru's wife, which permitted ethnologists in the 1920s to radically dehistoricize the experience of peripheral regions such as Okinawa. In their search for common prehistoric origins, Yanagita Kunio and Orikuchi Shinobu presented Okinawa as a fossilized shard of the Japanese past in which internal dynamism was minimized, as was local agency. Of course, the presumption of an eternal and absolute Japaneseness makes the work of these early scholars problematic today for their "fascist" bolstering of prewar nationalism.[76] Yet, as both Ikemiyagi's and Hirotsu's cast of mute characters confirms, in the Taishō period, the normative notion of a pure Japanese identity, in which one could just as easily be excluded as included, explains why Hyākū and Mikaeru diligently strive to overcome their ethnic identity through assimilation. Success for them is as elusive as the fabled Japanese identity they seek. As Hirotsu's title suggests, Mikaeru wanders. A drifter who fluctuates between the spheres of his village, workplace, and Tsuji, Mikaeru, like Hyākū, roams in search of an authentic identity. Captured in Hirotsu's prose as dark, hairy, and bestial, Mikaeru can never attain the identity he seeks. Even more disturbing, he is denied human qualities. Through characters clearly branded Okinawan and subhuman, Hirotsu and Ikemiyagi seriously call into question the vaunted notion of a "Taishō democracy."

3 Marching forward, glancing backward

Language and nostalgia in prewar Okinawan fiction

The immediate prewar period in Okinawan fiction is distinguished by the writings of three authors: Kushi Fusako, Yogi Seishō, and Miyagi Sō. Among them, Kushi, a rare female author, is the least well known, for her career ground to a halt almost as soon as it began. Her literary style, however, left a deep impression on those who continued to write prose long after she stopped. Critics dub the works of Yogi and Miyagi, two such authors whose biographies and literary output are remarkably similar, "intellectual fiction" (*interi shōsetsu*).[1] This stems from the fact that Yogi and Miyagi were prominent intellectuals of their age. Leaving Okinawa behind, they pursued and, for a time, acquired literary fame in Tokyo. With the encouragement of prominent New Sensationalist School (*Shinkankakuha*) writers Yokomitsu Ri'ichi and Kawabata Yasunari, each published his prose in major literary magazines. A more compelling reason for the "intellectual" appellation relates to the content of these writers' most famous works. Yogi and Miyagi's unrelenting depiction of artistic alienation grants their fiction a psychological depth missing in earlier narratives. In terms of content, this writing is indistinguishable from much prewar autobiographical fiction set in Tokyo. Stylistically, however, the authors inherit from Kushi Fusako a nostalgic mode by which the narrative takes a critical turn away from the constrained present to a largely imagined, freer past.

As is true of Ireland, where pastoral themes resurfaced when English became the dominant language under colonialism, nature becomes a site for nostalgia in prewar Okinawan fiction.[2] Writing in the 1930s and early 1940s, characterized by a longing for lost culture, reflects social realities of the time. In accordance with increasingly strict national and local enforcement of standard Japanese in place of local dialects in Okinawa prefecture, writers adeptly penned their works in a language other than their own. With few exceptions, the use of dialect, even to provide realistic dialogue, remained absent.[3] What emerged from this intersection of history and literature is a corpus of regional fiction that, on the level of language, betrays little if any hint of its origins. Notable for its authors' mastery of standard Japanese, prewar fiction compares favorably with contemporary texts written by Japanese authors on the main islands. Freed from the awkward ornamentation of dialect practiced by earlier writers such as Yamagusuku Seichū, it is far more accessible to readers of modern Japanese. What remains curious about the texts is the spatial and temporal backward leaps they contain.

The nation-state's particular attention to language education in its newest prefecture did not go without notice. In 1940, with nationalist fervor nearing its peak, folk scholar and social critic Yanagi Muneyoshi initiated a fierce debate on the issue of standard Japanese versus local dialects in Okinawa. The ensuing discussions among ordinary citizens and scholars in the prefecture and in Tokyo clearly pointed to fears that the encroachment of standard language was causing irreparable damage to once-flourishing local dialects. Interestingly, most Okinawans, eager to put an end to the rampant discrimination they faced outside their prefecture, took great pains to master Japanese, for it was the language which, for them, generated an imagined (national) community.[4] The intensity of government efforts to school Okinawans in Japanese was matched only by the islanders' desires to be part of Japan's social imaginary even at the expense of their own culture and identity. Never clearly resolved, the debate recurs often as Okinawan writers and critics grapple with the question of what it means to speak and write in an alien tongue.

In this chapter, I focus on the important year-long language debate and discuss its ramifications on the fiction of major prewar writers Kushi, Yogi, and Miyagi. I argue that the nostalgic mode these writers employ reveals the psychological costs that attend the act of a colonized people writing in the language of their masters. The theme of discrimination, so prevalent in Okinawan fiction, continues unabated in the writing of Kushi who concluded her sole work, and career as a writer, with an abrupt evocation of a distant Okinawan memory, spawning a trend evident in the subsequent fiction of Yogi and Miyagi. Yogi, the most consistent of the three authors, fills each of his narratives of ailing impoverished men with nostalgic glances in the direction of Okinawa. Miyagi offers some respite from the unrelieved gloom of Yogi's texts with similar flashbacks to a more innocent time, all the while meticulously recording his protagonist's rapid descent into poverty. Disjunctures in time and space characterize these prewar texts, necessitating a careful reading of them to show how the frequency of these literary occurrences relates to the vigorous but irresolvable language debate that raged during this period and, finally, to the issue of nostalgia.

Language enforcement and self-denial: the dialect eradication debate of 1940

As I will argue, the most significant element in the fiction of Kushi Fusako, Yogi Seishō, and Miyagi Sō is their use of the nostalgic. The similar style of these authors can be attributed to "literary influence," especially in the case of Yogi, whose writing is immeasurably enriched by the inclusion of a technique first associated with Kushi. Even so, I have found it productive to examine extraliterary events for insight into the conspicuous appearance of nostalgic literature during the prewar period. During the 1930s, the encouragement of the use of standard Japanese, initiated in the 1880s just after Okinawa became a prefecture not only continued unabated but also intensified as Japan began its military incursions into China.[5] By 1939, the Okinawa Bureau of Education, participating in the National Spiritual Mobilization Campaign, launched the "Standard Language Enforcement Movement" by plastering in classrooms and local buses such slogans as "In Every Place and Every Time, Standard Language" and "One Nation, One Family, One Language."[6] In 1940, as nationalist campaigns reached a feverish pitch, Yanagi Muneyoshi visited Okinawa and spoke publicly against the language policy, sparking a major debate.

On January 7, 1940, Yanagi, traveling in Okinawa with twenty-six members of the Japan Folk Craft Association, attended a discussion sponsored by the Okinawa Tourist Association during which he voiced his concerns about the suppression of local dialect. At the time of Yanagi's visit, the propagation of standard language was not limited to schoolchildren; elderly citizens were also "encouraged" to speak Japanese in the privacy of their own homes. Incensed by what he perceived to be an excess of nationalism, Yanagi asked:

> Is this not plainly a case of going overboard? Why, when families gather together, must they not use Okinawan? Why is language enforcement implemented only within Okinawa and not on the main islands? This seems to us to be an indication of Japan's special treatment of Okinawan citizens. What's more, will this not inflict insult to Okinawans? Is there not a tendency to regard their language as barbaric?[7]

Yanagi's motivations for defending Okinawa's dialects are surely related to his investment in Japanese arts. The dialects, retaining ancient "pure" Japanese words, were a veritable treasure trove, important to preserve. While Yanagi is often lauded as a defender of local speech, which he believed to be an essential component of broader Japanese culture, his own fierce nationalism is often overlooked. Indeed, Yanagi's wish to keep language in Okinawa "pure" issued from a desire to protect regional speech from the type of Western influence that had corrupted standard language in the main islands of Japan.[8] A more compassionate explanation for the folk scholar's critique is that his Buddhist faith compelled him to affirm human equality.[9] In any case, Yanagi's vocal attack reverberated throughout Okinawa, initiating the famous year-long "dialect eradication debate" (*hōgen bokumetsu ronsō*).[10]

The following day, local newspapers carried coverage of Yanagi's outburst, prompting a staggering number of responses by native educators, intellectuals, and journalists. The majority of people in Okinawa construed Yanagi's comments to be intrusive, if not meddlesome. Rather than valuing Yanagi for his support of local culture, they regarded him as a privileged member of the central Japanese intelligentsia whose dissemination of "dangerous ideas" beleaguered an already struggling island population.[11] On January 11, members of the Okinawa Bureau of Education wrote a strongly worded editorial that maintained that standard language education was vital for migrant laborers and military draftees.[12] Soon after, citizens began writing letters revealing their personal experiences. One émigré stated, "Outside the prefecture, standard language is second only to one's life in importance."[13]

As the debate continued, the outpouring of emotion elicited by Yanagi's comments forced the scholar to clarify his opinions on language use. He emphasized that it was necessary for Okinawans to learn Japanese—the language of the state—but not at the expense of local dialects. Yanagi's desire to preserve local dialects, which he believed were symbols of regional culture, ran counter to the views of many Okinawans who desperately needed expertise in Japanese for economic survival.[14] Though opinions were many and varied, the debate was essentially a clash between the cultural ideal Yanagi upheld and the more pragmatic nature of Okinawans during this time of fervent nationalism. Kim Brandt puts it more succinctly as a battle between "preservationism and assimilationism."[15] While proud of their local culture, many islanders feared that Yanagi's emphasis of it would lead to overexaggeration and thus further distinguish them from other Japanese.[16] I find it ironic that Yanagi asked publicly why, among Japanese, only Okinawans were subjected to a language policy, while in private, Okinawans viewed his attention to their dialects as precisely the type of privileging the scholar himself declared problematic.

Newspaper coverage of the debate moved to Tokyo where, among others, Yanagita Kunio, Hagiwara Sakutarō, and Yasuda Yojūrō joined the fray. Each raised his own concerns but all supported Yanagi's effort to save Okinawan dialects from extinction. Furiously discussed was the constructed nature of Japan's standard language and the critical need for further research of regional dialects from which a standard emerged.[17] In literary circles, Nakamura Murao and Aono Suekichi participated in a public forum in which both affirmed the value of local dialects.[18] Not all those involved in the debate agreed with Yanagi, however. Basing his opinion on prior travel to Okinawa, critic Sugiyama Heisuke stated that the government's policy of encouraging standard language and the concomitant pressure applied to local dialects were fully justified. Sugiyama feared a glorification of the island's ancient past would stall forward progress.[19]

Throughout 1940, the debate persisted without resolution. National authorities claimed that in promoting standard language it was not their intent to harm local dialects, yet, damage inevitably occurred. Eager to prove themselves as full citizens, Okinawans quickly memorized foreign sentences such as "The moon rises in the east, and sets in the west" (*Otsukisama wa higashi kara dete, nishi e hairu*). As Okinawans grew proficient in what was still, for them, a "textbook language," local dialects fell out of favor.[20] During Japan's fight for domination in the Pacific, language enforcement became all the more strict. In another of history's ironies, when American forces took over the management of Okinawa after Japan's surrender in 1945, they quickly embarked on a campaign to promote Ryukyuan culture so as to distance Okinawans from other Japanese. By this time, Okinawans were unable to comply with the American military's mandate that radio broadcasts be delivered in local dialects.[21] Having learned their (language) lessons well, there were few residents so skilled.[22]

As we have seen in several instances, most Okinawans in the prewar era believed proficiency in Japanese would not only afford them greater professional opportunities but would also assist in the effort to rid themselves of any markers of difference. The conversion from local dialect, used in the home from birth, to standard language, imposed from above in schools and workplaces, was not without its disquieting effects. Critics involved in the language debate worried that the suppression of once-flourishing local dialects was tantamount to killing the spirit of the people.[23] When language, a social phenomenon, died, so too, they argued, did the society from which the language emerged.[24] Okinawan writer Gima Susumu, echoing the ideas of Frantz Fanon, who wrote "to speak a language is to assume a world, a culture," claims that those who forsake dialect also abandon their Okinawan identity.[25] A highly charged relation between language and identity resulted as Okinawans negotiated uneasily between their own speech and a standard which they wished to emulate.

Okamoto Keitoku offers the clearest indication of the degree to which language choice has impacted writing by Okinawan authors when he states that modern Okinawan literature is a literature of self-denial.[26] Okamoto makes this bleak claim because, like Gima, he believes the decision to use Japanese reflects a fundamental change in a writer's consciousness. Earlier writers such as Yamagusuku Seichū, who produced fiction late in the Meiji period, and Ikemiyagi Sekihō, prolific during the Taishō era, created works in which there still existed a dual structure of language. This language consisted of standard Japanese, and, for traditional sentiment and conceptions, Ryukyuan dialect. As Okinawans gained greater fluency in Japanese during the modern period, however, the outward appearance of fiction changed. Major prewar writers such as Yogi and Miyagi wrote with growing confidence works of personal fiction. Reading their stories, so often set in Tokyo and narrated by a despairing protagonist, is not so different from reading the texts of contemporary Japanese writers Satō Haruo or Yokomitsu Ri'ichi, for example. The fluid style of Yogi and Miyagi's fiction immediately sets it apart from their predecessors' more stilted writing.

What does distinguish prewar Okinawan writers from mainland counterparts is the frequency with which their otherwise seamless narratives are interrupted with flashbacks to an idyllic past, or what I call the "nostalgic mode." It is hardly coincidental for Kushi, Yogi, and Miyagi to insert visual images of Okinawa precisely at the narrative point that their respective protagonists experience such intensity of emotion that language fails them. In "Memoirs of a Declining Ryukuyuan Woman" (*Horobiyuku Ryūkyū onna no shuki*), Kushi's melancholy narrator concludes her tale of a man desperate to hide his Okinawan identity with a poetic tableau of an island landscape etched into her mind from childhood. In Yogi's famed work "Banyan Tree" ("Yōju"), the protagonist recalls the protective banyan trees of his hometown during moments of existential crisis precipitated by the breakdown of his marriage and his growing alienation in Tokyo. Miyagi, the most hopeful of the three authors, is not free of writerly angst. When Heikichi, the protagonist of his text "The Birth of Life" ("Seikatsu no tanjō"), can no longer bear his family's impoverished state, Miyagi writes how he repeatedly draws strength from memories of the positive upbringing he enjoyed as a child in Okinawa. In the place of lengthy narration, these authors employ brief but conspicuous images of the past to convey deeply felt, inexpressible emotions.

I interpret the static wordless images prevalent in prewar Okinawan fiction to be an outward manifestation of the ambivalence writers experienced as standard language began to replace local dialects. Almost always unrelated to plot, these fleeting passages of island life become the site of struggle for linguistic expression. Kushi, Yogi, and Miyagi do not employ conventional methods of description to convey the intensity of their characters' emotions; instead, disorienting nostalgic scenes fill voids in the texts. The strategy these writers use to subvert an imposed language is one of avoidance. In places where standard Japanese will not fully express an emotion, and local dialect will not convey meaning to a larger Japanese audience, glimpses of local landscape appear. These spaces in otherwise ordinary Japanese texts signify a form of resistance practiced among postcolonial writers around the globe.

Writers' responses to an imposed language can vary from rejection to subversion. Since electing to retain a local language often severely limits readership, subversion of a dominant language is far more common than a rejection of it.[27] Indian-born writer Salman Rushdie is a prime example of an author whose irreverent use of English deterritorializes and decolonizes the language.[28] Irish poet Seamus Heaney, inspired by T. S. Eliot's notion of the "auditory imagination," writes English verse filled with shadows of days long gone, illuminating a polyphonic history in which the use of English is emancipatory as English becomes both English and Irish through linguistic disruption and assimilation.[29] Critic Michael Molino notes that Heaney's backward look "entails not a longing for a banished language but a calculated encounter with and intrusion of Irish words and dialect in the language which he cannot escape."[30] Prewar Okinawan writers, similarly bound to a rich linguistic tradition, may well have accepted rules on language use as they labored to publish in mainland art journals, but they resisted these at a deeper level. Writing in Japanese, they follow societal prescriptions; yet, their prose nonetheless captures the nuances and rhythms of their homeland through passages in which vestiges of the past are enshrined. On the topic of his use of English, Nigerian novelist Chinua Achebe, states, "Is it right that a man should abandon his mother tongue for someone else's? It looks like a dreadful betrayal and produces a guilty feeling. But for me there is no other choice. I have been given the language and I intend to use it."[31]

This matter-of-fact explanation applies as well to prewar Okinawan writers who similarly put to creative use a language other than their own. They had but little choice given that national efforts to promote standard language in Okinawa, initiated in the 1880s, and intensifying as Japan's military gained power during the 1930s, culminated in humiliating punishments, both verbal and corporal, for those who spoke in dialect when not on guard.[32] The 1940 dialect-eradication debate that erupted between Yanagi Muneyoshi and the Okinawa Bureau of Education clearly demonstrates that language choice was inextricably linked to identity for most Okinawans. By speaking Japanese, they assumed a different persona, one that would allow for greater economic advantage and less social stigma. Inhabiting another culture, however, necessitated a renunciation of one's own.

Prewar Okinawan prose, by virtue of the fact that it is written in polished Japanese and mimics the personal vein so prevalent in mainstream literary fiction, reflects the widespread self-denial that permeated Okinawan society at this critical juncture. It also resists linguistic strictures of the day by invoking an imagined, freer past. The works of authors Kushi Fusako, Yogi Seishō, and Miyagi Sō contain jarring reminders of their shared homeland, which I construe as assertions of identity. That prewar narratives, many of which are set in Tokyo and convey the despair of alienated individuals, contain frequent backward glances in the direction of Okinawa indicates the strain an imposed language placed on writers of the time. As I will show, the silent images of island life that echo loudly between the lines of these texts belie their surface smoothness.

The enduring imagery of Kushi Fusako's "Memoirs of a Declining Ryukyuan Woman"

Kushi Fusako, one of the few Okinawan women to publish fiction in the prewar period, had a short but memorable writing career.[33] When the first installment of her 1932 work entitled "Memoirs of a Declining Ryukyuan Woman" was published in the journal *Women's Forum* (*Fujin kōron*), the outcry that followed matched that of the response to Hirotsu Kazuo's *The Wandering Ryukyuan* nearly a decade earlier. Kushi's portrayal of a successful Tokyo merchant who takes great pains to conceal his Okinawan identity so as not to lose business infuriated members of the Okinawa Prefecture Student Association (*Okinawa kenjin gakusei kai*) residing in Tokyo. They objected to the story on the grounds that it would lead people to assume that all Okinawans who succeeded on the mainland similarly kept their past secret. The anticipation Okinawan critics had for this rare woman fiction writer came to an end when Kushi, forced by the harsh criticism of fellow Okinawan youth, published in the following issue of *Women's Forum* an eloquent defense of her story, together with a declaration never to write again.

In her spirited defense, Kushi comments on the association's criticism of her use of terminology as follows:

> It annoyed them, they said, to have Okinawans put in the same category as "the Ainu people" or "the Korean people," minorities with whom this word is often associated in Japan. Yet are we not living in modern times? I have no sympathy for their efforts to construct racial hierarchies of Ainu, Korean, and so-called "pure Japanese," or for their desire to feel some kind of superiority by placing themselves in the "highest" category.[34]

Kushi's progressiveness is matched only by her bravery. That her response alone did not generate an uproar for its clear opposition to prevailing hierarchical views is perhaps due to its appearing in a women's journal, likely overlooked by male intellectuals. After publicly admitting that she had made a serious slip of the pen (*hikka*), Kushi disappeared from the literary world leaving readers to puzzle over how her intriguing work would have concluded.[35]

In the prewar period, it was not unusual for persons of Okinawan descent to live cautiously on the mainland. Having left their home prefecture, these

Figure 3 The opening pages of Kushi Fusako's *Memoirs of a Declining Ryukyuan Woman.*

Okinawans would not only cease contact with relatives, they would also avoid the prying eyes of neighbors. Many had mail from Okinawa delivered to the homes of friends.[36] Some, feeling homesick, played recordings of Okinawan folk songs but with the rain shutters firmly closed, and, even then, only with their heads under a blanket thrown over the gramophone so as to muffle the distinctive rhythms of their native music.[37] Kushi's story, called a "true work" (*jitsumono*), revealed the existence of practices members of the Okinawa Prefecture Student Association wished to keep hidden.[38] While it appears that critics welcomed the truthfulness of Kushi's art, fellow Okinawans residing in Tokyo found the depiction of a man from Okinawa who denies his past too painful to withstand; hence their cries for the story's suspension.

Historian David Howell explains that in the prewar discourse of assimilation, the stock phrase "a dying race" (*horobiyuku minzoku*) came to be used to describe the Ainu.[39] Given that the phrase was clearly associated with an ethnically distinct group of Japanese from the north, it is difficult to accept that Kushi's use of this coded language in her title was as casual as she insists in her defense of the story. Despite her claims, the editors of *Women's Forum*, yielding to the protests of the Student Association, suspended the story's continuation. If the phrase "declining Ryukyuan" in the title "Memoirs of a Declining Ryukyuan Woman" did not indicate that Ryukyuans differ from other Japanese, surely, the subtitle, "Listen to the Sorrows of a People Thrust Away in a Corner of the Earth" (*chikyū no sumikko ni oshiyarareta minzoku no nageki o kite itadakitai*) does. Kushi's use of the term "race" (*minzoku*) angered members of the Student Association who believed that readers would consider Ryukyuans as racially different from the Japanese as were Koreans or the Ainu people.[40] Kushi's aborted writing career is all the more tragic considering that the story's objectionable title and subtitle were editorial choices rather than authorial ones.[41]

Though "Memoirs of a Declining Ryukyuan Woman" is Kushi's one and only piece of fiction, and unfinished at that, its importance in this study of modern Okinawan writers is twofold. First, like writers before her such as Yamagusuku Seichū and Ikemiyagi Sekihō, Kushi writes of the discrimination that Okinawans face when living on the mainland. Her work demonstrates that the theme of discrimination, closely linked to that of identity, is prominent in writing from Okinawa. Second, aside from the serious thematic content that places Kushi's story squarely within the genre of Okinawan literature, the work exhibits a style of writing which two more prolific writers, Miyagi Sō and Yogi Seishō, adopt in their fiction. The thematic and stylistic features of Kushi's work explain why a single incomplete story has generated such a disproportionate amount of criticism in the various cultural and literary histories of Okinawa.

"Memoirs of a Declining Ryukyuan Woman" is the story of a meeting that takes place between a young schoolteacher from Okinawa and her uncle, a businessman in Tokyo. The narrator, *watakushi*, briefly meets her uncle to receive from him a sum of money he wishes to have sent to his relatives in Okinawa. She relates that the encounter is the same as always. Impeccably dressed, he arrives at the usual coffee shop. After a few minutes of awkward small talk, he hands his niece a 10-yen note, then quickly takes his leave. The reader soon learns that the meetings are clandestine in nature and that *watakushi* has never been introduced to her uncle's wife or daughter. The reasons for this become evident as Kushi unfolds the story of the uncle's life through the eyes of his niece.

Thirty years before the narrative present, *watakushi*'s uncle disappeared after being discharged from military service in Kyushu. As the years passed, relatives in Okinawa began to doubt his survival, but twenty-five years after vanishing, the man suddenly returned to his home prefecture. A large section of Kushi's narrative is devoted to relating the events that transpire in the man's family during his long absence. At one time, the members of the household not only include the uncle's mother, father, and grandmother but also the father's mistress, a sympathetic woman who figures prominently in the story. When the uncle's younger brother died suddenly after toiling in the fields, his young wife and three children join a family already emotionally and financially taxed.

A number of other tragedies occurred in the past, reducing the family's size and leaving only the mistress to care for the remaining members, a nearly deaf, doddering ninety-year-old grandmother, the husband, and three grandchildren. The mistress, described as "the picture of trust and devotion," labored mightily to keep the children, whom she has grown to love, safe and healthy, but one by one they die of acute intestinal illnesses.[42] The narrator's lengthy description of this mistress' devotion to the family is one of the most unforgettable in the story:

> Though she worked to the very limits of her strength, it was like sprinkling drops of water on parched soil. With that tearful expression on her face, she made the rounds of every relative she knew, begging for help, but found them all in similar straits. Occasionally, they would give her twenty or thirty sen, which she spent on sweets for the boy or medicine for her [common-law] husband, never thinking of herself. All her clothes were threadbare hand-me-downs from relatives, and the hems and sleeves would soon be drooping like rags until a sympathetic family member gave her another piece of cast-off clothing. Having lost pride, she received anything they gave her with a childlike delight that had, pitifully, become second nature by now.
>
> She boiled foreign-grown rice into gruel for her mother-in-law, her sick husband, and the boy; but for herself she cooked only a few sweet potatoes that would serve as her meals over the next five or six days. She carried the boy on her back wherever she went. When he cried for a piece of brown sugar, pressing his head against her back, she felt her heart would break. "Poor thing. Please don't cry," she would say in her faltering voice, trying to comfort him, but she only ended up bursting

into tears herself. It hurt her even more to think that he had given up on real sweets and just asked for brown sugar. Yet only during the days she spent with the boy did her face, which always had that tearful look, recover the tiny trace of a smile.[43]

Amid this wretched poverty, the husband dies, and, soon after, the grandchildren follow, leaving the mistress beside herself in grief, with only the senile grandmother left to keep her company.

It is to this home, occupied now by his grandmother and his father's mistress, that the narrator's uncle returned years after his presumed death. The contrast between the well-heeled uncle who is driven to the house by a chauffeur and the two women dressed in tattered kimono sitting on shabby tatami is striking. The uncle is so distressed by the sad state of the house and its occupants he could not bear to stay there, opting instead to lodge at *watakushi*'s home. The narrator's mother took the gentleman around to all the relatives, but everywhere, Kushi writes, "stained, sagging tatami and chipped teacups" welcomed him.[44] Conversations, if one could call them that, were just the sorrowful cries of an oppressed people. All around were crumbled stone fences, overgrown grass and scores of elderly.

Rather than sympathize with the plight of those around him, the man could not contain his disgust. He left Okinawa abruptly once again, without letting his family know his whereabouts. Before going, the man explained the reason for his secretiveness:

"I've already transferred my family register to X Prefecture on the mainland," he explained to someone just before he left. In fact, nobody in Tokyo knows I'm from Ryukyu. I do a good business with prestigious companies and have lots of university graduates working for me. You have to understand that if people found out that I was Ryukyuan, it would cause me all kinds of trouble. To be honest, I even lied to my wife, telling her I was going to visit Beppu City in Kyushu.[45]

Of the story's many disturbing scenes, this last was certainly in the minds of the Student Association members who complained to the editors of *Women's Forum* about the negative light this work cast on their home prefecture.

In much Okinawan prose, writers indicate the differences that lie between Okinawans and other Japanese characters. For example, recall how Yamagusuku Seichū emphasized the hirsuteness of his Okinawan protagonist in "A Man Named Tsuruoka" offering a contrast to the fairness of a young Japanese girl from mainland Japan. Ikemiyagi Sekihō's "Officer Ukuma," too, was filled with real and perceived disparities, particularly among members of the police force. What is interesting about "Memoirs of a Declining Ryukyuan Woman" is that all the characters whose differences Kushi notes hail from Okinawa. The antimainland sentiment so prominent in Okinawan fiction has but a subtle presence in this story. The author's reaction to the fact that differences in wealth and class among Okinawans in Tokyo are largely predicated by how much such persons reveal of their pasts is stronger than her dismay over the discriminatory practices of mainland Japanese toward Okinawans.

In a roundtable discussion of Kushi's story, Ōshiro Tatsuhiro suggests that the work shares certain features with proletarian literature.[46] Indeed, there is, on one hand, a sharp rebuke of the uncle, a bourgeois merchant, and, on the other hand, a sympathetic portrayal of the mistress and other downtrodden characters. After describing how Ryukyuans in Tokyo avoid each other in the manner of "two cripples passing on the sidewalk"[47] to prevent others from knowing their origins, the narrator introduces the character of the uncle:

> He was another of our people who could not reveal the truth about himself for all the twenty years he had lived in the middle of Tokyo. He managed several branches of a company, supervised university and technical school graduates, and lived in a spacious apartment with a bossy wife and a daughter in her prime who was soon to be married. Yet he had never disclosed the slightest hint to any of them that he was Ryukyuan.[48]

While the story certainly contains undeniably proletarian elements, in my view, the reason it is so affecting is that the narrator, objective and dispassionate as she is, ultimately portrays *both* the rich uncle and his poor family in a sympathetic light. That the uncle is included in Kushi's catalog of victims complicates the work, making it more than a story of class inequalities, as Ōshiro would have it.

Kushi's provocative exploration of the theme of social injustice in "Memoirs of a Declining Ryukyuan Woman" ends in a startling fashion. The reader is offered no final words on the fate of the uncle or the bedraggled women in his home village. Instead, the narrator, having told the story of her uncle, leaves the reader with a poetic image of Okinawa she recollects while riding away in a carriage horse:

> The scenery all around me at dusk evoked poignantly the essence of these islands: sweet-potato vines trailing on the craggy soil, groves of lanky sugarcane plants, rows of red pine trees, clusters of fern palms, banyan trees with their aerial roots hanging down in thick strands like an old man's beard, and the sun setting radiantly in a shimmer of deep red behind the ridge of hills. It all flowed deep into my heart like the tide that rises to fill the bay.

The sounds of the horse trotting in choppy rhythms along the road and the coachman singing in a low, wailing voice seemed perfectly suited to our homeland's decline, as did the coachman's song in Ryukyuan dialect.

> Who are you blaming
> With your cries, oh plover?

My heart weeps, too,
When I hear your sad song.
The moon in the sky
is the same old moon as before.
What has changed
are the hearts of men and women.

The narrator adds, "Such music was probably born of the smoldering emotions in a people [*minzoku*] oppressed for hundreds of years. Yet I love this scenery at sunset and yearned for something in myself to compare with its declining beauty."[49] So the story ends, and, following the flurry of protests that the work incited, Kushi's writing career concluded as well.

The nostalgic image of Okinawa that appears in the closing scene of Kushi's work is memorable both for its beauty and the strangeness of its occurrence. In a story chock full of details about the secret past of a wealthy Okinawan businessman and the impoverished nature of his remaining family members, this lyrical passage stands in stark contrast to the realistic narrative that precedes it. Kushi manages to conclude her story with a romantic view of Okinawa that does not soften the harsh realities of life on the island depicted previously. The intensity with which the narrator describes the scene underscores her attachment to a place so difficult for many to live. Kushi's motives for the inclusion of this disorienting passage may never be known—perhaps she just hit upon a novel way to bring her work to an end. In any case, long after she put her pen down, writers who succeeded Kushi, in particular Yogi Seishō, adopted her technique of weaving inexplicable scenes of island life into their fiction.[50]

The persistence of memory: Yogi Seishō's quest for home, family, and village

After a brief period of time engaged as a poet in Okinawa, Yogi Seishō (b. 1905) left the island for Tokyo in 1927 in order to pursue a career as a fiction writer. One of many authors to do so, Yogi turned to the city because of the lack of venues for writers in Okinawa during this period of virtual bankruptcy. As an employee of the publishing house Kaizōsha, Yogi began writing stories and, in 1934, Yogi's best-known work, "The Banyan" was published in the magazine *Literary World*, upon the recommendation of Yokomitsu Ri'ichi. Kobayashi Hideo lauded his talent in an editorial postscript, writing that Yogi, a new disciple of Yokomitsu, had penned a commendable first work.[51] Yogi thus launched his career as a writer by garnering the patronage of a major novelist, attracting the favorable attention of an authoritative critic, and publishing his first major work in an esteemed journal.

"The Banyan" is a story fluid in style and rich in psychological realism. Yogi employs a first-person narrative to tell the story of a young man who leaves Okinawa for Tokyo in order to become a writer. In the capital, the man, *boku*, meets and marries a divorced woman from Okinawa, partly because she reminds him of his own mother, and partly in an effort to create in the vast, alien metropolis of Tokyo, a semblance of his own community. *Boku*'s torment begins with employment problems and escalates as his wife cuckolds him. The bulk of the narrative is a record of *boku*'s anguish and despondency over his failed marriage, financial ruin, and poor health.

Narrative passages referring to home and family appear immediately as *boku* explains how he came to marry Saeko. Unable to find work after arriving in Tokyo, Saeko calls on *boku* for financial assistance. Soon after *boku* lends her money, Saeko visits him in his lodgings to declare her intention to rent an adjoining room. Admitting he did not explore other living arrangements for Saeko, *boku* comments on the inevitability of their cohabitation:

> It goes without saying that, on top of the fact that the two of us met on a journey far from our homes in distant Ryukyu, there was also that Ryukyuan tendency of wishing to create our own village. We instantly began associating with each other in the manner of family.[52]

Boku and Saeko scarcely know one other, but their common birthplace unites the two.

The first nostalgic flashback in "The Banyan" occurs as *boku* explains that the real reason he married Saeko is because she frequently reminds him of his own mother who, like Saeko, was divorced and made to live apart from her child:

> My mother and father got divorced when I was three. I knew in my heart that my mother lost my father and me to my stepmother at the same time. For twenty years, from the time she was twenty-four until today, every time I think of her plight my heart has ached. Connected to these emotions is a memory from my childhood. Surrounded by old verdant banyan trees, my mother's small house stands at the far corner of a spacious lot. I adored my mother and loved to climb those banyans, peculiar to Ryukyu, and sing songs while gazing out over the sea. Escaping from my father's house, I played there everyday.[53]

The abruptness with which Yogi inserts this soothing, idyllic scene into his narrative is reminiscent of the technique Kushi Fusako used to conclude her work. While it is less clear why Kushi employs a startling nostalgic scene in her writing, in Yogi's case, the point at which nostalgic flashbacks occur is directly linked to his protagonist's mental state. In this, and in similar passages which follow, vivid scenes of Okinawa appear precisely when *boku* is experiencing intense emotion.[54]

In another important passage, in which *boku* expresses his sheer exhaustion at the effort it takes to succeed as a writer, the narrator again mentions

Okinawa, this time as a place of refuge. Whereas Tokyo appears as a forbidding city, Okinawa is described as a pastoral home to which one could "return to live the carefree life of a farmer."[55] Certainly, the narrator is romanticizing the work of farmers in a region as poor as Okinawa, but his aim seems to be to emphasize the trials of city life in contrast with more carefree days spent in Okinawa. Yogi writes:

> I was utterly exhausted from trying painfully for several years to establish a literary career for myself. Incompetence prevented me from embarking on this most cherished dream. I could see what lay beyond the precipice of my life—groveling on the ground for food, unable even to eat. How could I continue to lead my wife in this direction? I calmly determined that I would return to farming and started to discuss going back to Okinawa with my wife. She considered the complications she would have with her ex-husband after our return, but I persuaded her to go, and we decided to leave at once. Two days before we were to depart, I set out to say farewell to the teacher who had guided me for so long. Unexpectedly, he advised me to stick it out just a while longer. He was kind enough to say that if I could write a short story he would help me. This was so unexpected. At the time my eyes surely shone like stars. The winds of ambition came blowing over me once again. For the first time, I felt hopeful about my own talents. It was as if I had just made my literary debut.[56]

As the narrative develops, the reader finds that *boku* nurses this small kernel of hope despite great physical and financial adversity.

Saeko, elated that the couple will remain in Tokyo, assures *boku* she will look for work to support him in his writing, but weeks pass without any initiative on her part. On the contrary, Saeko acts as if the two were not unemployed. Compounding their financial distress, *boku*, arising daily in a cold sweat, has recently begun to feel acute chest pain. His medical expenses, together with Saeko's reckless spending, quickly deplete his savings of 300 yen. Haunted by their precarious living conditions, *boku* urges Saeko to work. At last, she does, but in a café, not a coffee shop as she intended.[57] Essentially a willing hostess to her male clientele, Saeko begins to spend more and more time away from her husband.

Boku's suspicions of Saeko's adultery lead him to pay frequent visits to the café to spy on his wife's male customers. Jealousy of one man in particular who lavishes Saeko with tips so anguishes *boku* he stalks her after she leaves the café at night, convinced that he will find the two together. Despite his persistence, *boku* never finds evidence of Saeko's affair and is disheartened to learn that her constant lies, flip behavior, and lack of regard for his welfare do not change the intensity of his feelings for her. Realizing the fragility of their relationship, *boku* pleads with Saeko to change jobs. In her characteristically nonchalant manner, Saeko ignores his concern, further wounding him by declaring her intention to stay at a lodging closer to her workplace, ostensibly to reduce transportation costs. Already wracked with doubts and mistrust of his wife, *boku* now sees her only once a week.

When Saeko does return home, it is to pick up clothes, ask for money, or even, to *boku*'s horror, to collect his books to sell. She makes no financial contribution, explaining that her meager salary only covers the purchases of clothing she needs for work. Weakened and unable to argue, *boku* can only stand by as his relationship deteriorates. Adding to the tension, the narrator punctuates the text with a detailed account of the couples' dwindling resources: 300 yen, 50 yen, 8 yen, 5 yen. Their lack of money forces *boku* to curtail his visits to the doctor even after his physician tells him he must follow a strict health regimen. Poignant depictions of *boku* waiting for Saeko, his sole companion in all of Tokyo, fill the story:

> From Hakusan to Meguro takes about fifty minutes and from Meguro it takes about ten minutes by private line, which means she usually returns around 1 A.M. or 1:30 at the latest. That night, however, even at 1:30 she still wasn't back. 2:00 A.M. The cold pierced my body. 2:30. 3:00. After I waited nervously, my tension eased, and finally I slipped into a state of melancholy. I went to the window and looked out to see the late autumn evening slowly advance. All I could see were dim street lamps lighting the deserted streets. Out of the depths of this solitude came the cacophony of dawn. My wife never returned.[58]

Boku's marital, medical, and financial worries leave him restless and unable to sleep. At the height of his indignation, he becomes aware of his own lunacy. One night, a train heading to Hibiya roars past. A description of *boku*'s recklessness follows: "In a daze I leaped on board. But then I realized I hadn't planned to take the train, so, in a fluster, I tried to get off. Just then, the conductor's hands shoved my shoulders. 'You idiot! That's dangerous.' His voice brought me back to myself."[59]

From this point on, *boku* dashes about on trains and 1-yen taxis roaming the city at night in an effort to still his growing agitation. *Boku* has moments of lucidity in which he is conscious of his crazed behavior, but these become fewer and fewer.

While pacing through the city one night, *boku* has a second flashback to his past in Okinawa. Beleaguered by his endless walking in streets filled with strangers staring at his Ryukyuan dress and unkempt appearance, *boku* can no longer even think. The narrator notes how, oddly, this state of sheer exhaustion triggers distant memories:

> As proof of the strange activity that takes place in the human head during an instance of madness, the distant memory of the day I saw my first girlfriend for the first time—a thought unrelated to the present— flashed through my mind. Her name was Shizuko; she was a sweet girl

who had just entered the second year of junior high. I discovered her beneath the village banyan trees. In our village, once a year, junior high students with excellent grades received a monetary prize that was given by the town hall. When I went to the hall to get my prize, she was there to receive hers also. Having arrived before me, she was sitting sideways on the green grass in the shade of the banyans thumbing through a magazine. From its hilltop location, the town hall had a beautiful view overlooking the sea. The scenery contributed to making Shizuko seem lovelier than anything. She captured my heart instantly and I experienced the first storm of my adolescence. This memory flitted by suddenly. Since it was vague and lasted only a moment I wasn't even aware when it happened. However, later, when I thought of it, I remembered it vividly.[60]

Both this and the first flashback in Yogi's story contain an image of the banyan. In the earlier scene the trees offer a place of refuge for *boku* as a young child separated from his mother by his parents' divorce. The banyan imagery in the second flashback, which occurs during *boku*'s frenzy over his wife's imagined adultery, is associated with pleasurable memories of his first love. Both flashbacks take place when *boku* is emotionally distraught and connect to visions of Okinawa in which protective banyan trees figure prominently. In the realm between *boku*'s madness and sanity lies the specter of home.

As *boku*'s sleepless nights continue, his emotions become uncontrollable. After waking from dreams of Saeko, *boku* is tormented by thoughts of his long-absent wife. Following on the heels of this torment, however, *boku*, "like a howling dog, becomes angry, then hateful, then sad, then uneasy, then bitter, then jealous, then regretful, then humiliated; most distressful of all was that intermingled feeling of fierce love which also lay knotted within him."[61] The only thing that remotely sustains *boku* during this time is his deeply held aspiration to be a writer. The thought of an impending publication offers a glimmer of hope for *boku* who has all but succumbed to overwhelming loneliness and despair.

In another fit of delirium, *boku* fantasizes about how he has written a lengthy autobiographical novel in which he exposes his wife's behavior. Just as it is published, he throws himself off a tall building, taking vengeance on his wife. *Boku* imagines the distress Saeko will feel when the newspapers cover the story of his suicide while simultaneously serializing his novel. The comfort *boku* draws from this implausible revenge fantasy dissipates that very day when he receives a polite letter from his teacher stating that his short story had been rejected for publication. Short of death, nothing could be more disastrous for *boku*, already plagued by misfortune.

In the remaining pages of the narrative, *boku* describes his ever-worsening health and deteriorating marriage. The story concludes as *boku*, crushed by personal and professional failures, reflects on his inevitable death:

> Pain came raging in from someplace trying to obliterate my existence. Like a criminal who couldn't die, I rolled around on the tatami, my entire body contorted. [...] After a while, I became a madman again. Stepping into my geta, I attempted to go out into the city. Just then, for no reason, a faint image of sunrays off the ocean, which pierced the verdant banyan trees of my hometown [...] flitted across my eyes.[62]

The faintness of this third and final flashback underscores the diminishing strength of Yogi's protagonist. *Boku*'s state of mind, his dream of success as a writer, and his hope of creating with Saeko a "village" in the forbidding landscape of Tokyo are all shattered.

"The Banyan" is a work of fiction in which Yogi adeptly reveals the consequences of *boku*'s alienation from all that is familiar to him. Hoping to ease the loneliness of life in Tokyo, a city so distant from his native Okinawa, Yogi's protagonist falls quickly into a relationship with Saeko simply because she is from his home. As various catastrophes befall *boku*, Yogi offers, through a series of flashbacks, a glimpse into *boku*'s fractured mind. Each return to the past involves a nostalgic image of Okinawa that serves to lessen *boku*'s suffering. That banyans, trees which provide island residences shelter from buffeting rains and wind, appear in every flashback further indicates *boku*'s desperate attempt to keep whole the image of home that sustains him. Scenes of Okinawa, distinct at the start of the narrative, fade as *boku* loses his mental acuity. Faint as it is, the insertion of a concluding island scene in this narrative of a struggling writer's alienation in the city suggests that, for Yogi, the pursuit of home, elusive as it may be, has its psychological rewards.

Yogi further articulates the importance of home in his next work "The Particulars," (*Tenmatsu*) published in *Literary World* in 1935 at the recommendation of Kawabata Yasunari. Set in Okinawa, this oddly moving story enumerates the details of a number of tragic events that take place in a fictitious Ryukyuan village shortly after the end of World War I. Abe, an adopted son-in-law, incites the anger of his father-in-law, a village elder, by allowing miners to excavate the hillsides of their village for ore. Financially pressed by a drastic drop in sugar prices, Abe, in his capacity as ward chief, invites the miners to town in hopes of improving the village's situation. This leads to a generational struggle between Abe and his father-in-law, a man who considers the mining of his ancestral village a desecration.

The plot of "The Particulars" is further complicated by the fact that Abe, an adopted son-in-law, must produce an heir for his wife's family. He eventually does gain a son, only to lose his wife in childbirth. He is further consumed by worries that her promiscuity may mean he is not the child's father. Even the thought that the child might indeed be his does not still Abe's fears, since he has recently discovered that he, himself, is experiencing the early stages of leprosy. Abe knows he must yield his son to his father-in-law as promised, but concerns about the child's origins, and the possibility that he might be burdened with an inherited disease, lead him to seek out another way to continue the family line.

In desperation, Abe impregnates his wife's mentally impaired elder sister, also a village shaman (*yuta*).[63] Demanding to know with whom she had the child, Abe's in-laws eventually believe their daughter when she tells them the child was immaculately conceived (*kamisama no ko*). The child is eventually welcomed into the family, and Abe is immeasurably relieved, for now the future of both his wife's family and his own is assured. Fears that his wrongdoing will be exposed are realized however, when, in a bizarre twist of plot, his wife's sister is bitten by a poisonous viper (*habu*). On her deathbed, she reveals that Abe is the father of her child. Her parents, not wishing to interfere with her happiness in the next life, considerately invite Abe to participate in their daughter's funeral, but Abe declines, only to be later discovered dead in a valley, the victim of suicide.

Yogi's narrative is heavily laden with bits of village lore, fragments of local dialect, and vignettes of rural life. While he convincingly portrays Abe as a sympathetic character who, in order to preserve his family, brings destruction to the village, Yogi's greater investment seems to be in capturing for posterity descriptions of prewar Okinawa. Given the staggering destruction wrought by the Battle of Okinawa just ten years following the publication of "Tenmatsu," it is fortunate Yogi wrote such a detailed chronicle of the region. In the following passage, for example, Yogi describes how news filters through a rural community:

> In summer, one of the pleasant scenes visitors traveling in the Ryukyuan countryside come across is that of farmers drinking tea on matting laid out near fences on dirt roads. To be indoors during the day is unbearable. In the crevices between fenced buildings surrounded by densely growing banyan and *fukugi* trees, the breeze caresses the farmers' skin, as if the wind survived only there. Outside, they strip to the waist and drink tea, half-naked. It isn't unusual to see among them, someone lying about in a loincloth. Women, their large breasts hanging like dried fish, spin banana fibers. Young girls, even if they were half-naked, tightly fasten the sleeves of their kimono above the chest so that only their shoulders are visible. Faces white with powder, the girls usually weave panama hats. Since this afternoon rest period by the fences is a daily ritual in almost every household, villagers who walk along the road at the time can't walk five hundred yards without stopping to chat. Often, some of them will sit and have tea the farmers offer them.[64]

Replete with scenes typical of village life in prewar Okinawa, "The Particulars" also contains numerous passages that show the widespread survival of folk beliefs. When the miners begin their work, for example, Abe's father-in-law summons his shaman daughter to make a divination:

> That night, at her parents' home, the slow shaman, dressed in white, sat upright before the family altar. [...] Sitting three feet away, her father prostrated himself before her. Following this, a number of men and women, while they did not prostrate themselves as much as her father, joined in by lowering their heads. Like the many mortuary tablets above the altar, they sat completely still. The scene was that of a princess and attendants waiting on an imperial court. With everything in place, the father stood and repeatedly implored his daughter for an oracle. At last the shaman spoke her prophecy: "Because the head of this village has been penetrated, he will incur divine punishment. Know that upon this village disaster will fall."[65]

Taking the prophecy as a confirmation of his fears, Abe's father-in-law rages against Abe, pleading in vain for him to put an end to the destruction. Later, as the mining progresses, a sacred boulder connected to the village's origins and believed to embody the spirits of departed relatives dislodges itself, prompting the old man to order another divination. This time, the shaman cries out, "Would a human survive with his head cut off?"[66] Likening the stone's removal to an act of dismemberment, the shaman voices the collective fears of the village elders. What finally deters Abe from his plan to modernize the village is a strain of influenza that decimates the village population. No longer able to ignore the anger of the gods, Abe arranges for the sacred stone to be returned to its original position. Calm is temporarily restored as the influenza reaches its peak and subsides.

Together with vivid descriptions of shaman practices, Yogi provides social commentary on the belief system of his fellow islanders:

> It may be due to the low level of culture, but Ryukyu is really an odd place. There is no religion to which one can give a name. All funerals and festivals are performed with Buddhist rituals, but even so, no one believes in Siddhartha Gautama, let alone even knows the name Nichiren or Shinran. The only thing Ryukyuans believe in is ancestors. It is rare to find such a high level of belief among a group of people of low intellect. Not only is their faith in ancestors absolute, the preponderance of rites for the dead is staggering.[67]

Yogi seems unaware that in underscoring the strength of the islanders' faith in ancestors he also maligns their general character. The offensiveness of Yogi's opinions is mitigated somewhat by his inclusiveness in the group about which he writes; however, his negative references to Ryukyuan culture and intellect remain puzzling in a work that celebrates the very culture the author slights in this passage.[68]

Yogi is at his best when he provides whole slices of island life free of such editorial remarks. In one of the story's many descriptive scenes, Abe, tormented by his declining health and his familial obligations, decides one evening to venture out and mingle with other young people who are thoroughly immersed in "night amusements" (*yoasobi*):

> Night amusement is another pleasant bustling southern spectacle. The entertainment usually takes place on a farm road on the outskirts of the village, or if not, to avoid the wind, behind rocks on the beach. First off, one or two people take their *sanshin* [string instrument] to a favorite spot and begin strumming. Enticed by the sounds of the instruments, and the singing voices, dozens of young people gather around. Surrounding the *sanshin* players, the group gradually increases in size, and people sing and dance in a mad frenzy. This is not all they do. Some kick sand and chase after girls; others lie around telling jokes; still others vigorously practice sumo on the beach. Mingled with the singing and dancing are laughs that erupt here and there giving rise to a wondrous commotion. At their feet, the full tide laps the water's edge as if blessing the time of these youths, then enters the East China Sea. Close by, the famed southern sun sets deep into the ocean.[69]

Here, as in the earlier scene describing tea-drinking farmers, Yogi breaks from his task of forwarding the plot to record a sight, capture its mood, and dwell for a time on a pleasurable vision of his home.

From the preceding string of quotations, it may appear that "The Particulars" is nothing but a well-written tourist brochure cataloguing island attractions. In fact, the work is a dense narrative in which Yogi pits two men against each other: Abe, a man compelled to bring modern technology into his village, and his elderly father-in-law, who clings fiercely to the traditions of his home, resisting any such modernization. That Yogi intersperses his tale with depictions of rural life in which groups gather to show their reverence of ancestors in the presence of the village shaman or to offer tidings together with tea on blazing hot days, or just to while away the evenings in song and merriment suggests his sympathies are divided. Certainly, Abe, alienated and estranged from his family is the object of pity, but Yogi laments, as well, a communal way of life in danger of passing.

Only glimpsed in "The Banyan" in moments of deep distress experienced by *boku*, Yogi's Tokyo-dwelling protagonist, Okinawa makes a grand appearance in "The Particulars." It is as if Yogi believed a faithful record of the particulars of his locale would keep his home safe from the kind of destruction Abe unwittingly invites. Though images of home are fleeting in "The Banyan," Yogi plumbs the depths of *boku*'s mental state, creating an indelible narrative. In "The Particulars," references to Okinawa are copious and detailed, perhaps at the expense of character development. What is noteworthy about the text, however, is Yogi's complete absorption with Okinawa's culture, history, and religious beliefs. The island is not merely a backdrop against which a story takes place; it *is* the story. Yogi's brief but intense flashbacks to Okinawa in "The Banyan," and his extensive descriptions of the island in

"The Particulars" are evidence both of his nostalgia for the past and of his confidence in treating Okinawa as the subject matter of serious fiction.

Toward a hopeful past: Miyagi Sō's "The Birth of Life"

A final example of the use of the nostalgic mode by a prewar Okinawan writer occurs in the fiction of Miyagi Sō, an author often paired with Yogi Seishō.[70] Like Yogi, Miyagi left Okinawa for Tokyo as a young man, worked at the left-wing publishing house Kaizōsha, and made his literary debut in 1934. If the similarity of their backgrounds is not striking enough, then the shared themes and stylistic features of their fiction certainly are. The same year that Yogi's story "The Banyan" appeared in *Literary World*, Miyagi saw the publication of his work "The Birth of A Life" in the journal *Mita Literature* (*Mita bungaku*). Heikichi, the protagonist of this work is nearly identical to *boku* in "The Banyan." Recently unemployed, Heikichi struggles to establish himself as a writer, suffers family illnesses, and falls deeply into poverty. Miyagi's narrator meticulously records his protagonist's pitiful descent, as did Yogi's in his debut work.

Thematic content aside, Miyagi's works are compared to Yogi's because his Tokyo-set narratives are interspersed with telling glimpses of Okinawa. "The Birth of Life" is a case in point. The work opens as Heikichi treks to Haneda, on the outskirts of Tokyo, to visit his friend Morikawa. Walking toward a lighthouse with Morikawa and another friend, Nishida, Heikichi reaches a point from which he can view Kawasaki, Tsurumi, and, further in the distance, the Miura Peninsula. A gentle ocean breeze wafts over Heikichi, carrying with it the smell of the shore. The narrator notes how the scent, at once strange and familiar, triggers in Heikichi memories of his past:

> The sweeping view and deeply pungent smell of the sea brought Heikichi back, suddenly, to his true home. What was this home? It was a poetic sentiment, a home where he spent his youth, comforted by nature. [...] Heikichi's father, abhorring his low-lying village, built a secluded home on top of a hill. Whether Heikichi liked it or not, ever since he could remember, he grew up with views of the village, rice fields, the extending coastline, a limitless sea, and islands dotting the vast ocean. Though he was accustomed to the multitude of ocean greens and cerulean blue skies, still, the brilliant colors so famous in the south never ceased to sparkle with blindingly fresh clarity. The beauty and power of this nature, together with the simple lifestyle of a self-reliant farmer who avoided the ravages of capitalism set his mind free.[71]

As this passage appears at the very start of the story, before the narrator has time to relate the travails of his protagonist, it does not seem, at first, to resemble Yogi's technique of punctuating moments of crisis with unexpected images of Okinawa. However, in the paragraph that follows, the narrator not only describes pleasing island scenes in further detail, he hints at a darker phase in the life of the protagonist:

> Heikichi's love of the south, its sea, sky, and verdant nature, was a source of great joy. But in the ten years that had passed since he left home, the hometown in his mind's eye had faded. Having experienced such happiness there, he could withstand whatever adversities he might face from this point onward.[72]

To be sure, Heikichi's flashback is instigated, in part, by the sights he observes while exploring a lighthouse in Haneda, but to a larger degree, his return to the past, in keeping with the pattern set by Kushi and perfected by Yogi, is connected to an, as-yet undescribed, emotional upheaval.

As the story unfolds, the narrator describes the adversities he earlier suggests the story's protagonist would face. Heikichi unexpectedly loses his job as a magazine editor and is left with no way to support his pregnant wife Masako and their three children. He decides to open a bookstore, spending weeks walking through Tokyo in search of a prime spot for his business. Unskilled in finance, Heikichi fails in this venture before it even starts. A brief moment of joy transpires when, while reading the newspaper one day, he discovers his name in an advertisement for a forthcoming journal issue. Heikichi's happiness is short-lived as the article's publication is cancelled. To add to this crushing defeat, two of his children fall ill, requiring lengthy stays at a nearby clinic. Much like in "The Banyan," the narrator devotes the bulk of his narrative to documenting his protagonist's spiraling descent into abject poverty.

Forced to move his family to a smaller, dilapidated house, Heikichi must endure his neighbors' stares as he unloads his tattered bedding and scanty belongings. Because of the family's poverty, housewives in the neighborhood cruelly taunt Masako. Heikichi visits all the acquaintances he has, accepting from them items of clothing, small loans, and endless advice on his fruitless job search. Matters worsen to the point that only a day's worth of rice remains. Heikichi staves off his family's hunger temporarily when he hits on the idea of asking different rice merchants for product samples. Having asked the same friends for loans three or four times each, Heikichi knows he cannot expect much more. With nothing left to sell in his home, and bills mounting, Heikichi becomes thoroughly despondent:

> Heikichi crept under his futon and buried his face, but soon he was roused by a vision of the aftermath of his own suicide. His eldest son would become a noodle shop boy who would get sopping wet delivering buckwheat noodles on rainy days. Or, Masako, with four children in tow, would return to their impoverished and isolated village back home, only to live in poverty. Unable to bear these thoughts any longer, Heikichi jumped up, went to the other room, and began pacing back and forth.[73]

Out of the depths of Heikichi's despair, the image of home appears once again, only this time, the narrator portrays the island's grinding poverty, not its grand scenery. Though cast in a negative light, the image of Okinawa is what flashes in Heikichi's mind at this moment of crisis.

As the story draws to a close, New Year's Day approaches, as does the birth of the couple's fourth child. Given their dire straits, Masako suggests to Heikichi that he wire his family in Okinawa for a loan. Incredibly, a small sum of money arrives, enabling him to buy a few trifles for Masako and the children. Shaking off his gloom, Heikichi busies himself by cleaning furiously for the holiday. The narrator leaves the family's fate unknown, but, considering how the work ends with the suggestion of a new beginning, it is unlikely that Heikichi will succumb to the suicidal thoughts that have recently begun to plague him. In the concluding lines of the work, the protagonist reflects on his wavering emotions and firm resolutions:

> On the embankment in Haneda, I felt uncoil within me a happiness I had not felt in so long, and I thought, "After this, I can face any adversity!" This was a fleeting moment of pleasure, however. Yes, it was a passing thought. I was wrong, but now I must, without hesitation, reflect once again on that contentment. I must never turn my gaze away from the error of my ways. There is nothing more fruitless than being frightened of killing my family [*ikka shinjū*] for want of food. There is nothing more critical than laboring assiduously for a long-held ambition. The gods will certainly spare my family. If I put forth all my efforts and still can't survive, well then, I'll have to cross that bridge when I come to it. Ignorance and idleness are what I must fear. The key is that I not cloud the spirit that was nurtured in me amid nature in the south. Then, [...] I must take one step toward the birth of a new life.[74]

This final passage illuminates the reason why Heikichi believes it is imperative he keep alive the sense of self-reliance and confidence instilled in him as a boy in Okinawa. More than anything, it is his upbringing on the island that sustains him whenever he experiences a crisis in faith. Memories drawn from a hopeful past become the life force with which Heikichi summons the strength to combat his despair.

As evidenced in "The Birth of Life," Miyagi's writing contains the clearest expression of the recuperative effects of nostalgia among prewar writers. Kushi, her career stalled by controversy, was unable to continue writing. While her career may have come to a premature end, Kushi's stylistic technique endures in the works of Yogi. His dark stories of diseased, beleaguered men, unhappy in life and love are infinitely lightened by sparkling passages that tell of an idyllic life in Okinawa, far removed from the alienating society his protagonists inhabit. Miyagi's writing is remarkably like Yogi's. He, too, creates a multilayered text by incorporating moments from the past into his gritty description of the trials faced by his impoverished cast of characters. One important difference between Yogi and Miyagi, and the works for which they are famous, "The Banyan" and "The Birth of a Life," respectively, is the degree to which the link between past and present is articulated. Yogi is far subtler in his use of the nostalgic past than is Miyagi, who divulges, through Heikichi's year-end resolutions, that the key to survival is to bolster oneself with memories of a literally sunnier past. For Kushi, Yogi, and Miyagi, this nostalgic past contains within it restorative powers that both enliven their fiction and embolden their characters.

Nature and nostalgia

The three authors I have discussed here wrote during a period when Japanese nationalism was on the rise. Educators and bureaucrats enforced standard language used to build a cohesive collectivity, one that would lead Asia in its fight against Western imperialism. The 1940 dialect-eradication debate revealed tensions that issue from the suppression of local languages. This strain, reflective of colonialism, itself a historical rupture, is visible in the texts of Kushi, Yogi, and Miyagi. Their writing bears the mark of this tension in scenes that contain a backward glance toward home. The nostalgic mode that prewar Okinawan authors employ is not merely a sentimental exercise; it is a rhetorical practice by which to recover wholeness.[75]

Certainly, many other Japanese authors wax nostalgic, too. Kobayashi Hideo's "Literature of the Lost Home," Tanizaki Jun'ichirō's *Some Prefer Nettles*, and Kawabata's *Snow Country* are but a few well-known examples. While these texts may be read as responses to modernity broadly construed, I believe that prewar authors from Okinawa are reacting to something more specific: colonial modernity.[76] By embedding urban texts with snatches of the past in the form of *nature* they are consciously engaged in the reclamation of usurped land and lost language. Center and periphery clash in pastoral scenes of Okinawa that disturb Tokyo-set narratives through temporal and spatial interruption.

While critics generally regard nostalgia as conservative in nature because it centers on preserving the past, there is, I believe, a radical potential in the nostalgic mode that prewar Okinawan authors use.[77] Through an imaginative reclamation of space, these authors provide a sense of continuity that has been ruptured by the nation-state's incorporation of Okinawa. The mapping or reterritorializing of Okinawa we see in prewar texts is thus part of an identity-forming process. Just as Emerson and Thoreau created an American identity, distinct from Great Britain, by turning to nature and the land, so, too, do Okinawan authors use the aesthetic modality of nostalgia as a pointed political tool.

The question of land is inextricably tied to Okinawan identity. Nostalgic texts by prewar authors from Okinawa show that an engagement with land, landscape, and place remains a powerful means by which to critique cultural upheaval. The backward glances these texts contain not only give them a modern tone, they also reinforce certain tropes of colonialism wherein land or nature is the female other (Okinawa) to the colonizing or usurping male (Japan). Nostalgia for the natural often bespeaks a longing for the feminine or maternal, and though one need not always conflate land and body, there is no denying the power of this equation.[78] In the space that is lost language, Kushi Fusako paints her final scene of Okinawa, one that takes place, notably, at dusk. The liminality of twilight is precisely when another world reveals itself. In this fleeting instance nature is all-powerful, the wellspring from which individuals draw strength. With the fall of darkness, the illusion of a purer past—uncontaminated by the harsh realities of a present in which language, culture, and identity—fades away.

4 Ōshiro Tatsuhiro and constructions of a mythic Okinawa

Ōshiro Tatsuhiro began his writing career in 1949, the very year historians of Okinawan literature mark as the start of Okinawa's postwar literary activity.[1] Moreover, he has continued to write fiction, drama, and essays for over fifty years, establishing for himself an incontestable position as the region's preeminent postwar author. From the beginning of his long career, Ōshiro has focused his attention on Okinawa and its people, creating a body of literature that departs radically from fiction written in the Meiji, Taishō, and prewar periods when authors looked to Tokyo for their models, and, save for a few notable exceptions, refrained from writing about what they presumably knew best: their lived experience in Okinawa. The energy with which Ōshiro scrutinizes Okinawa and interrogates its position within Japan is all the more striking given the lack of attention earlier generations of writers paid to the island. Whether he writes of modern Okinawa, the distant Satsuma/Ryukyu relation, or the island's entanglements with China, mainland Japan, and the Americas, Ōshiro's gaze upon his homeland is constant.

In this chapter I examine four of Ōshiro's most important works: "Turtleback Tombs" ("Kame kōbaka," 1966), *The Cocktail Party*, (*Kakuteru pātī*, 1967) *Island of the Gods* (*Kamishima*, 1968), and *Fantasy Island* (*Panarinusuma gensō*, 1969) to highlight the ways that Ōshiro focuses on Okinawan culture and identity all the while writing broad multidimensioned narratives. Written in the mid- to late 1960s, these works contain within them key problematics discussed in Okinawa and Japan as the island's reversion to its "fatherland" (*sokoku*) drew ever closer. Ōshiro's preoccupation with southern island culture is by no means limited to his fiction; several of his essay collections are devoted to further exploration in the form of cultural theory. In a similar vein, Shimao Toshio, a well-known mainland writer with ties to Amami Ōshima, takes up the theme of Okinawan culture to fashion a cultural theory he dubs *Theory of Yaponesia* (*Yaponesia ron*.)[2] In the final section of this chapter, I focus on this innovative extension of ideas of regional culture and identity in order to show both the possibilities and limitations inherent in such a reimagining of Okinawa's geographic position.

Ōshiro Tatsuhiro and the beginnings of postwar Okinawan fiction

American occupation forces, which maintained a presence twenty years longer than did their counterparts in Tokyo, strictly regulated Okinawa's postwar literary activity. From July 2, 1945, the official end of the Battle of Okinawa, to May 15, 1972, the date the prefecture formally returned to Japan (*hondo fukki*), the United States Civil Administration of the Ryukyus (USCAR), a paternalistic, colonial-style military government, strictly monitored civilian activities.[3] In the confusing months following the American victory, the island's literary climate stagnated as Okinawans lived in refugee camps where they depended entirely upon the USA for food and medical care. Prohibited from returning to their homes, some internees sought comfort by writing poetry in notebooks crudely constructed from rice-bag remnants; others fashioned traditional stringed instruments (*sanshin*) by attaching parachute strings to empty cans.[4] The first postwar newspaper, *Uruma News* (*Uruma shinpō*), began publication on July 25, 1945, but was used by USCAR primarily to transmit information to the local populace.[5] Far from being a means by which the people might convey any literary or otherwise creative expression, the paper functioned as an apparatus for social control.

In the fall of 1945, Okinawans were permitted to return to their home villages; the following year USCAR allowed residents the freedom to travel. Private enterprise began in 1948, spurring the publication of a number of newspapers, and, significantly, the management of *Uruma News* shifted from USCAR to local control. This important change unleashed an outpouring of literature, as *Uruma News* and other recently formed newspapers filled their literary columns with fresh works and writers to win readership. The publishing industry, which had only begun to thrive in 1949, immediately faced censorship as American forces, alerted to the China conflict, became consumed with stamping out any trace of communist elements found in the press. Okinawa, now a strategic location for the USA to launch its war against Communism, first in Korea, then in Vietnam, became the site of massive military base construction. Through the mid-1950s while the USA focused on making Okinawa its "Keystone of the Pacific," literary publications underwent a marked decline.[6]

In 1955, another dramatic shift occurred in Okinawa's postwar history when the *Asahi News* ran a series of articles on the American military's interference in the island's civil administration. News of the military's peremptory behavior in Okinawa spread internationally as well, forcing Washington to enact swift personnel changes in its occupation force, but to no avail. The damage wrought by the unfavorable news persisted through the late 1950s, and by 1960, groups whose aim it was to rid the island of foreign control and return it to Japan grew in number. The Vietnam War brought B-52 bombers to the island. The thundering presence of these weapons of war only confirmed Okinawans' (and my own childhood fears) of the risks posed by a continued American presence.

Through the mid- to late 1960s, plans for Okinawa's reunification with Japan were well under way; in 1967, discussions were held in Tokyo and Washington to determine a date for the return. On May 15, 1972, twenty-seven years after the American occupation began, Okinawa returned to Japan with much pomp and circumstance. However, well before the festivities began, and long after they came to an end, many Okinawans, disillusioned by their virtual exclusion from the reversion dialogue that took place between Tokyo and Washington, ruminated on the future of their homeland. Memories of rampant prewar discrimination, colossal wartime casualties, and the scarcely diminished postreversion presence of American forces still weigh heavily on the minds of Japan's newest citizens.

In 1925, Ōshiro Tatsuhiro, the most important literary figure to emerge in the postwar period, was born in the castle town of Nakagusuku. He received in 1943 a prefectural fellowship to attend Tōa Dōbun Shoin, a prestigious university in Shanghai that trained Japanese specialists of China. After his second year, the school closed as a result of the war between Japan and China. His academic ambitions crushed, Ōshiro then served as an interpreter in the Japanese Army. After Japan's defeat, he went to Kumamoto where his sister lived and, from there, several months later, returned to Okinawa. His experience in Shanghai of studying the ways in which China and Japan could achieve friendly relations despite the war that raged between them, followed by a stint in the Japanese Army where he served as a student-recruit, presented a myriad of ideological contradictions that only increased when Ōshiro finally reached Okinawa in 1946. Compounding the shock he experienced at seeing the devastation of his homeland was the fact that Okinawa, now cut adrift from Japan, was occupied by foreign troops. Ōshiro's struggle to make sense of Okinawa's changed position following the war unleashed within him an intense, creative energy, which led him to embark on a literary career that shows no sign of ebbing six decades later.[7]

When Ōshiro began writing in 1949, he was among the first wave of postwar writers from Okinawa. Some of his counterparts such as Yamagusuku Seichū were long established; others, most notably Ōshiro and Ōta Ryōhaku, were newcomers. In 1949, Ōta published in the journal *Monthly Times* (*Gekkan taimusu*) "Black Diamond" ("Kuro daiya"), a short story about a friendship that takes place between the protagonist, *watakushi*, and a young Indonesian boy during Indonesia's struggle for independence.[8] The popularity of this work, which obliquely suggested the possibility of Okinawa's own independence, paved the way for other fiction that soon followed in magazines such as *Monthly Times* and *Uruma Years* (*Uruma shunjū*). In 1951, writers such as Yogi Seishō and Arakaki Mitoko, active in the prewar years, began to serialize fiction in local newspapers. Whether new or veteran writers, authors of the time did not critique prewar literary trends or ruminate about Japan's defeat in their works. This presented a marked contrast with a number of contemporary mainland writers associated with the journals *Modern Literature* (*Kindai bungaku*) or *New Japanese*

Literature (*Shin Nihon bungaku*). Ōshiro's fictional debut, "Diary of an Old Man" (*Rōōki*, 1949), for example, tells the story of a father through the point of view of his son, the work's protagonist. As in Ōshiro's more mature work, the story does not focus on a single character. Rather, its emphasis is on the positions of several characters and their relations to one another.

In the 1950s, Okinawan writers formed several groups and magazines, raising to new heights discussions on issues of style and method. Though most journals were short-lived, one among them, *Ryūdai Literature* (*Ryūdai bungaku*) initiated in 1953 by Ryukyu University literature students, effected a literary revolution among writers.[9] Highly critical of specific acts such as the military appropriation of civilian land and of the oppressive American presence in general, the journal was subjected to several instances of suspension by USCAR forces. Also under attack by the journal for their adherence to "I-novel" techniques and their failure to depict the island's colonial social reality were writers who wrote immediately after the war, Ōshiro included.[10] Reprimanded by the military, the members of *Ryūdai Literature* gradually shifted from a hotbed of political activists to a group that urged writers to record their own experiences from an Okinawan perspective. Though the journal's largest impact was felt in the 1950s, it continues to provoke heated discussion today, particularly since Ōshiro remains adamant that art should come before politics in literature.

Ōshiro recounts that from the very start of his literary career, his primary interest has been in representing Okinawa. Among his early writings, he cites "Tale of a Horse Carriage" ("Basha monogatari," 1951) as the first of his works to deal with the issue of Okinawa, its history, and its people.[11] Thus, by his reckoning, he wrote about Okinawa before it became a literary imperative. Despite Ōshiro's early fixation on Okinawa, his major works on the theme did not appear until the mid- to late 1960s. One of the reasons for this is that it was not until the early 1960s when Okinawan authors formed ties with the literary establishment in Tokyo and began to write intently about Okinawan identity. This was part of a larger societal trend in which Okinawans sought to close their severed relation with Japan in order to reap the benefits of the country's miraculous economic growth. Politics, too, brought together citizens in Okinawa and the mainland as left-wing groups in both areas united to criticize the United States–Japan Joint Security Treaty (*Anpo jōyaku*). Earnest dialogue between Okinawa and Tokyo helped create the conditions under which Ōshiro was able to produce for local and mainland consumption the works that established him as the prefecture's leading postwar author.

The power of resistance in "Turtleback Tombs"

Ōshiro wrote the short story "Turtleback Tombs" in 1959, but due to a decline in the publishing industry, he was not able to see the work in print until 1966 when he helped establish the journal *New Okinawa Literature* (*Shin Okinawa bungaku*).[12] Appearing in the second issue of this important postwar literary journal, the story is an account of one Okinawan family's escape from the ravages of war to the precarious safety of their ancestral tomb. Like all such Okinawan tombs, theirs is built with a protective cowl that looks like the shell of a tortoise when viewed above ground. The turtleback tomb they inhabit becomes the locus of a generational struggle that takes place within the family. In the moist, cramped confines of the tomb, Zentoku, the family patriarch, struggles to preserve "family values." Stern and uncompromising, Zentoku remains a powerful figurehead, but it is his wife Ushi, who, in transmitting the Okinawan communal code to the rest of the family, figures as the story's central character. Through Zentoku and Ushi, the younger generation, daughter Take and lover Eitarō, in particular, witness the intensity of an ancient belief system.

The story's central and most concrete image, the family tomb, signifies life for Zentoku and Ushi. Fervently believing that the spirits (*mabui*) of their ancestors will keep them from harm, they regard the tomb as their haven. The irony of the work lies in the older generation's insistent adherence to the "valuation of life" despite the overwhelming presence of death inside and outside the tomb.[13] The weight Ōshiro attaches to the turtleback tomb cannot be understated; its importance in Okinawan culture serves to explain much of Zentoku and Ushi's behavior. Traditionally, Okinawan families visited their ancestral tombs to commune with the dead.[14] Folk beliefs associate the tombs with the female body and human regeneration since, from certain angles, the tombs resemble the lower half of a pregnant woman's body, legs curved around a small dark opening. Norma Field writes that the unique shape of the tomb makes it an "economical representation of death as a return to the origins of life."[15]

As grim as this story of war is, it begins quite humorously. Ōshiro opens the work with a pastoral scene in which Zentoku and Ushi are at home peacefully absorbed in family matters. The roar of naval guns shatters their domestic calm. To this rural couple who have never before experienced warfare, the booming sound, *dororon*, remains outside their ken.[16] A neighbor rushing by explains:

> "Old man! It's naval gun fire. Naval gun fire. [*kanpō shageki*] It's war!"
> Zentoku's hands, now motionless, had stopped weaving the straw mat he was holding.
> "Gum boats?" What the hell did gum have to do with that crazy noise, he wondered.
> Not gum. Gun. Gunboats."
> "What?"
> "Battleships with cannons. Firing shells. The war's coming!"[17]

Tragicomically, the couple fumble along, preparing for their escape from the artillery. Ushi hurries to feed the pigs and gather her grandchildren's belongings, while Zentoku pours rice into an oil can and places it in a straw basket.

Figure 4 Cover of *New Okinawa Literature*, Okinawa's premier postwar journal.

The tone of the story grows somber when Zentoku witnesses the mass exodus of his village. He realizes the bothersome firing that had disrupted his day has affected not only his family but also the entire community. As they leave the gate of their home, Ōshiro depicts the family's hierarchy: "Stepping from the wooden floor to the ground [Ushi] pulled out the crowbar, and Zentoku took it from her. Then Eitarō and Take, agreeing to leave for the tomb, walked through the front gate with the children following, eldest first."[18] Positions established, they join a procession of refugees. Nervous chatter ensues, and neighbors begin to ask about the family's destination. The narrator states: "When asked where they would go, most people answered 'To Yanbaru, up north' or 'South to Shimajiri.' The few old people amongst them replied 'To our tomb.'"[19] Here, the narrator makes an early distinction between the young Okinawans and their elders. The natural response of the older generation is to escape to their family tomb, while the younger generation seek more distant geographic remove from the artillery fire.

As Zentoku and his family make their way to the tomb, Ushi takes great care to keep the various family members together. Ushi worries that Take will not be able to rejoin them after she stops on the wayside for a brief respite. The decision to go to the ancestral tomb is the first indication of the importance of family relations to the elders. The anxiety expressed while Take is away from her family underscores the value that Ushi places on family solidarity. Here, and in several similar passages, Ōshiro clearly shows the unimaginable degree to which family and communal ties endured in prewar Okinawa.[20]

It is important to note that Ushi is Zentoku's second wife. After the death of his first wife, Zentoku, needing someone to perform family rituals, proposed to Ushi. Having been left by her first husband for a younger woman after their only child died, Ushi readily assented. She, too, was motivated to act in deference to her ancestors. Deserted by her husband, she would have had to endure the shame of living with her own family and of being interred with them in death. By marrying Zentoku, she was assured of a proper burial place. Zentoku and Ushi are joined not by mutual love but out of a deep sense of obligation to maintain the practice of ancestor worship.

While walking to the tomb, the family meets Zenga, a relative who asks how they are dealing with the outbreak of war. Ushi assures Zenga that all is well as they have Eitarō, Take's strong male companion, with them. Ushi concludes their brief exchange by saying, "Please come visit."[21] Utterly commonplace in conditions of peacetime, this expression (*asobi ni oide kudasare*) is a ludicrous one given the family's present situation. Ushi, however, cannot forget her role as family caretaker. Despite the raging battle, she follows the communal code in order to maintain social decorum.

At last the family reaches the tomb. The narrator's description of the site reflects both the reverence that Zentoku and Ushi have for the ancestral tomb and their belief that the spirits within will keep them from harm. The lengthy description is memorable not only for its detail but also because the tomb comes to life in the passage. The tortoiseshell structure with its feminine shape waits and welcomes the family. The use of personification at this critical point is telling. Ushi and Zentoku's belief in ancestor worship and communal ties is so intense that the physical structure actually manifests human behavior:[22]

> The tomb greeted the family as always, covered in a deep black coat of moisture. The three pines—in which of the family's generations had they been planted?—today reached a height of 30 feet, towering like guideposts at the cemetery entrance. Zentoku often spoke proudly of their majesty to all his relatives. Arriving on a hillside path, visitors to the family tomb entered the cemetery at the pine trees' roots and proceeded along a walkway 12 feet wide that resembled the front approach to a shrine. After walking 30 feet, they made a right-angle turn, then went another 18 feet to the tomb garden. The 450 square feet of lawn looked beautiful that day with its freshly cut grass. The large tomb within seemed to be leaning back against the hillside as it waited quietly for the family.[23]

The tomb is further personified as regenerative in the next paragraph: "This family's tomb, resembling a woman's supine body, her legs spread open, now looked out on an ocean where enemy warships floated in the distance. Yet it greeted the ancestors' descendants serenely, as if it knew the incantation that brings eternal life."[24] With some assistance, Zentoku removes the concrete slab, and the "offspring" enter the tomb. Ōshiro writes: "The deep spiritual exhilaration Zentoku felt in its presence even made the thundering stop for a moment."[25] The instant that Zentoku enters the tomb all his fears subside and the spirits that dwell there suffuse him with their energy. The irony of this passage is unsettling. Ōshiro appears to emphasize a constructed world in which ancestors proffer to their living kin the hope of eternal life. The passage may be read otherwise, however. The tomb, clearly depicted in feminine terms, symbolizes Okinawa—a victim who, legs open, is subject to (male) enemy assault. Here, Ōshiro's mythmaking obscures the prefecture's colonial history.

The younger members of the family have an entirely different experience than their elders. The children are terrified of the human bones arranged carefully in urns throughout the tomb. Zentoku urges the children to rest saying, "This is where we'll sleep. Just like our ancestors. You don't have to worry. They aren't ghosts, you know."[26] Ushi adds, "That's right. There's nothing scary about 'em. They're helping us."[27] Certain that the ancestors will not let any harm befall them, Ushi tries to instill this in her children and grandchildren. Take and Eitarō watch Ushi as she performs various rituals, obeying her requests for assistance. Although they participate in the ceremonies, it is clear the beliefs are those of the older generation, not the younger. Eitarō, Take, and the grandchildren join in the required rituals and obey despite their bewilderment over the necessity of these ancient rites. After seven days pass in the tomb, the family finds it increasingly difficult to maintain its religious values. Accustomed now to the roar of bombs, the family associates the war with "thunder, hunger, and shitting in the urn covers."[28] The gravity of the family's wartime predicament outweighs their fear that the gods would surely mete out punishment for the defilement of so sacred a place.[29] The family hierarchy begins to crumble as Zentoku passes the days scarcely uttering a word. Scorned by Zentoku in the first part of the story for his illicit affair with his daughter, Eitarō is the only member experienced in warfare. In China, where he served in the Japanese military, Eitarō lost a limb but returned armed with knowledge about war tactics. He attempts to relate information about the battle raging outside the tomb to the others but they cannot comprehend the alien terminology and standard dialect he employs to explain matters to them. Despite his failure to communicate, Eitarō's position begins to ascend. As the battle intensifies, Eitarō's wartime experience and tactical know-how commands Zentoku's attention and respect.

Eitarō beseeches the family to leave the tomb for safer shelter away from the bombings, and just as Zentoku is on the verge of capitulating, two terrible incidents occur. First, a Japanese soldier falls dead on the ground outside the tomb. Ushi is disturbed not only because the soldier's fall has harmed her grandchild, causing the child's spirit to dislodge, but also because the soldier's dead body defiles the ancestral tomb.[30] Ushi worries that either the family or the soldier will incur divine punishment. Ultimately, she determines the family must bury the soldier in a spot outside the tomb to appease the disturbed spirits.[31] The prayers she incants, then, are for the soldier, her grandchild, and the family. Ushi performs her rituals for specific reasons, but in the course of the rites, her prayers becomes so general that her actions are rendered virtually meaningless. Still, she persists in her duties as transmitter of the communal code.

The second incident that befalls the family occurs when Eitarō and Zentoku go to their field to gather food in preparation for their impending departure from the tomb. While digging for sweet potatoes, Zentoku spots a figure stealing potatoes from one of his own fields. He is shocked to recognize the thief as his own cousin Zenga. Enraged, Zentoku runs after Zenga in the heavy rain. He recalls having once witnessed a village council member fleeing the village with a pig under his arms. Zentoku had respected the council member because he was educated, but once he witnesses Zenga, a teacher, stealing, Zentoku realizes that education does not automatically command respect. Agitated by this realization, Zentoku pays no heed to the pounding rain and falling bombs and is killed in an explosion.

Naturally, Eitarō is distraught over his inability to save Zentoku, but as he struggles to carry Zentoku's dead body to the tomb, he feels a certain pride in the new responsibility that has fallen to him. With the family patriarch gone, Eitarō knows he must now guide the rest of the family. Up to this point, Eitarō has only outwardly accepted the value of communal ties. He understands that it is solely through Zentoku's death that he can finally appreciate the importance of family relations. Eitarō's pride is short-lived, for, upon his return to the tomb, not only does his new position of ascendancy remain unacknowledged but Ushi orders him and Take to inform Zenga and other relatives of Zentoku's death. Take and Eitarō are astounded at Ushi's insistence that it would be improper to cremate Zentoku without notifying the relatives. However, yielding to the authority of Ushi, now the eldest in the family, the young couple risk their lives to call on the very man whose act of theft led to Zentoku's grisly death.

Dodging artillery fire, Take and Eitarō soon lose sight of each other. Eitarō becomes trapped in the midst of heavy firing. As he lies in the mud, smeared with blood, he sees something moving towards the area where Ushi is quietly praying to the ancestors inside the tomb. Discerning the figures of soldiers, Eitarō resigns himself to the prospect that he might not be able to return to Ushi. Eitarō lies mired in mud knowing that he will have to pay for the sin of abandoning his family.

In the last paragraph of the story, the narrator turns his attention away from Eitarō, who, reaching a position of ascendancy in the family, loses it in an instant by obeying Ushi's conservative wishes. The narrator's final depiction is of this traditional old woman, Ushi, praying in the tomb: "Knowing nothing of Eitarō's ordeal, Ushi waited impatiently inside the tomb for her loyal relatives. Together with her grandchildren, she gazed at Zentoku's remains while outside, slowly, but surely, the firing line approached."[32] Here, Zentoku's demise and the probable death of Ushi and remaining family members represent but a few of the 100,000 civilian lives that would be lost in the Battle of Okinawa.

It is Ōshiro's emphasis on the theme of indigenous beliefs that makes "Turtleback Tombs" more than a war documentary. As well as recording a particularly tragic moment in Okinawa's history, the work is a testimony of Ushi's unshakable resolve to adhere to the ancient tradition of ancestor worship. Though Ōshiro presents the viewpoints of many family members, ultimately, it is with Ushi that authority lies. Of all the members in the tomb, it is she who is strongest. Ushi refuses to abandon her beliefs despite the realities of the war. By the end of the story, however, Ōshiro makes it clear that Ushi will die with the rest of the family, no matter how determinedly she clings to the beliefs that sustain her in life. What remains after all the death and destruction in "Turtleback Tombs" is a tomb filled with new and old spirits. This story about enduring communal ties does not end with the death of Zentoku and his family. The intensity of Ōshiro's portrayal of the Okinawan belief system relieves the story's dark ending for Ushi's devotion to the communal code will surely result in a tomb full of spirited ancestors at peace despite the raging battle and recent deaths in the family. At the level of historical description, then, Ōshiro writes about a battle that results in the destruction of traditional Okinawan culture. More important, however, is Ōshiro's mythic depiction of a tightly bound communal society in which death is viewed not with finality, but, far more hopefully, as the commencement of life with ancestors.

One of the ways in which Ōshiro stresses the weight of traditional Okinawan beliefs in "Turtleback Tombs" is to contrast it with the shallowness of Japan's prewar emperor-centered moral education (*kōminka kyōiku*). Critic Satohara Akira suggests that Zenga, an educator, represents Okinawa's assimilation of Yamato culture since he is one of the many school officials who play a major role in the eradication of local dialects.[33] Contributing to Zentoku's death is his shock at the realization that Zenga, an educated man, steals sweet potatoes from his own family. His recollection of the council member stealing a pig during his flight from the village only underscores the fact that the educated are dishonest men unwilling to place their trust in the indigenous belief system. Yamato culture and its system of education encroach heavily on conservative Okinawans such as Zentoku and Ushi. Satohara concludes that Ōshiro may be ruminating on future possibilities of the Okinawan valuation of life after a war that would destroy Yamato-assimilated Okinawa.[34]

Much of the power of "Turtleback Tombs" derives from its presentation of the Battle of Okinawa from the point of view of Okinawans. To lend authenticity to this focus on Okinawa, Ōshiro employs a local dialect for the dialogue portions of the story, and standard dialect for the descriptive passages. The story's subtitle, "A Gazeteer with Practical Dialect" (*jissen hōgen o motsu aru fūdoki*), indicates the importance language plays in telling this story of Okinawa. Local dialects are often used for dialogue in fiction to prevent any weakening of reality. In "Turtleback Tombs," Ōshiro creates an artificial language that has local flavor but is still comprehensible to readers of standard Japanese. Descriptive passages, difficult to render with conception-poor dialects, are written in standard Japanese. By using an experimental dialect in sections of dialogue Ōshiro is attempting to alleviate the dilemma of how to talk about Okinawans without displacing their voices. Critics' reception of his use of dialect has been mixed, however, with many expressing a preference for the more natural use of dialect evident in Higashi Mineo's 1971 novella, *Child of Okinawa*.

Ōshiro Tatsuhiro engages in the discourse of Okinawan culture by writing "Turtleback Tombs," a compelling portrait of a family that adheres to tradition in the face of modern warfare, written by means of an experimental dialect. His story is a valiant attempt to destroy the image of Okinawa prefecture as a place with no people, no history of exploitation, and no bloody battles set in place by nationally endorsed textbooks and media.[35] What undermines Ōshiro's efforts is his privileging of a largely mythic world. Still, the figure of Ushi silently praying in the confines of the family tomb as artillery fire draws near is unforgettable; the scene shows how resistance can come from the most oppressive and unlikely of places.

The bifurcated narrative of *The Cocktail Party*

Ōshiro is best known for winning the coveted Akutagawa Prize for his 1967 novella *The Cocktail Party*. Appearing in the February 1967 issue of *New Okinawa Literature*, the work describes the circumstances surrounding the rape of an Okinawan girl by an American serviceman. Although it appears that Ōshiro did not base his story on an actual crime, the work, set in Okinawa in the mid-1960s, does reflect a dramatic increase in violence that took place in Okinawa during the tumultuous years the island served as a refueling point for American B-52 bombers headed for Vietnam.[36] Considering the gravity of the crime portrayed, *The Cocktail Party* is remarkable for its lack of clear-cut victims or aggressors. Ōshiro maintains a clinical detachment from the painful events his characters reveal and throughout offers multiple perspectives on the tragedies.

The narrative structure of *The Cocktail Party* contributes to the overarching theme of the work: namely, the protagonist's growing self-awareness of his Okinawan identity. The work begins with a first-person account by a protagonist named *watakushi* (formal "I") then shifts dramatically midway to a second-person account by the same protagonist who refers to himself self-critically as *omae* (informal "you"). The rape of the protagonist's daughter effects this change in narrative, a brilliant show of how trauma can quickly lead to self-fragmentation. The narrative breakdown occurs just at the point that the protagonist can no longer deny what it means to be Okinawan in the Occupation period.

The Cocktail Party begins on a hot, muggy evening as the protagonist, *watakushi*, enters the gate to Base Housing in order to attend a cocktail party. After checking in at the guard station, he walks confidently through the gates, secure in the knowledge that even if he were stopped for trespassing, he would simply give the name of his host, Mr. Miller. An Okinawan civilian who spent part of his youth in China, *watakushi* has become acquainted with Mr. Miller through a Chinese-language group. Two others in the same group are Mr. Sun, a Chinese lawyer, and Mr. Ogawa, a Japanese reporter born in China. The protagonist's confidence stems from the fact that he believes himself an equal member of this international group. The narrator dwells on past insecurities he had experienced as a local entering base premises. Ten years prior to the narrative present, *watakushi* took an illegal shortcut through the base on his way home, only to become hopelessly disoriented by the maze of identical houses:

> None of the foreigners or Okinawan maids I passed seemed to notice I was a stranger. But when I realized I was lost, panic seized me. In my mind I tried desperately to cling to the notion that the housing area was, after all, in the very same township where I lived, but it was no use. Struggling to maintain my composure, I stopped one of the maids and asked her how to get to the east end. She showed me the way

impassively. Her placid, self-possessed air gave me the impression that she was someone who belonged here and made me feel a vast distance between us.[37]

A decade later, it is *watakushi* who walks through the compound with a self-possessed air, sure of his sense of belonging.

Once at the cocktail party, *watakushi* engages in stilted conversations about potentially provocative topics such as Okinawa's former relations with China, the island's "unique" culture, and its imminent return to Japan. He and the other non-Americans refrain from offering their frank opinions so as not to spoil the carefully orchestrated atmosphere of the party. Ōshiro uses the setting of a cocktail party as a backdrop for this polite exchange of words. The guests, in true form, steer clear of controversy by pausing to nibble on an hors d'oeuvre, or by refreshing their drinks. When an American asks Ogawa why Okinawa, with its distinctive culture, does not consider independence, the narrator relates: "Mr. Ogawa smiled. Then, excusing himself, he went over to the bar and poured himself another drink."[38] Such conflict avoidance strategies work beautifully until the mood of the party is shattered by news that the child of an American guest has disappeared, prompting an immediate search.

As *watakushi* and Mr. Sun, forming a pair, set off to hunt for the child in the vast military compound, *watakushi* is assailed by feelings of unease similar to what he felt a decade earlier when lost in the same area: "Countless stars sparkled overhead. But the warm air was heavy with humidity, and I wondered if a typhoon might be brewing somewhere to the south. The high wind above us seemed to be stirring restlessly; and the stars, lacking their usual tranquility, flickered in fitful patterns."[39]

As they walk, Mr. Sun painfully tells *watakushi* of a time twenty years prior, when his eldest son was missing in China. Living in an area secured by the Japanese Army, Sun at last discovered his son in protective custody at a Japanese military police station. *Watakushi* reflects on the similarities between Mr. Sun's past experience in occupied China and the island's present predicament when a passerby informs them that the missing American child has been safely found. According to the news, the child was in the care of a family maid who had unthinkingly taken the child home to her village on her day off. The guests of the cocktail party reassemble, clearly relieved, but the strain produced by this native appropriation of an occupation official's child suggests, as does the protagonist's recurring unease within the base, an unequal balance of power.

This suggestion of imbalance is confirmed in the second half of *The Cocktail Party*, which begins with a stunning shift in narrative voice:

> It happened on that same hot and humid night. Unable to locate Mr. Morgan's boy, *you* and Mr. Sun had stopped at the metal fence surrounding the family brigade. About the same time *you* were listening to

his recollections, your daughter was attacked at Cape M. [...] From the many rips and stains it was obvious that something terrible had happened to her, and the sight filled *you* with horror. She had been raped by Robert Harris, the American soldier renting your rear apartment. Three hours before her ordeal *you* had sauntered through the security gate into the family brigade feeling smug because *you* could walk around inside without the slightest worry.[40]

(Emphasis added)

The protagonist, upon learning of his daughter's attack, falls into a state of intense self-recrimination as evidenced by the switch from "I" to "you."

The distress *watakushi* feels is compounded when an official from the military's Criminal Investigation Division comes to take his daughter into custody for harming her attacker at the time of the assault. The protagonist learns from the local police department not only that his daughter's rape and her attacker's injuries would be treated as separate cases but also that the soldier's court martial would be conducted in English. Unable to believe his ears, the protagonist is further told that in a civil trial the attacker could not be questioned because the Okinawan judiciary system did not have the right to summon members of the US military. The protagonist's only recourse is to convince the assailant to testify. Realizing the impossibility of his task, he decides to enlist the help of his friend, Mr. Miller.

The American listens to the protagonist's request but is clearly unwilling to interfere. Citing the damage he might cause Okinawan–American relations, Mr. Miller strongly urges *watakushi* to proceed with the help of their mutual friend and attorney, Mr. Sun. As he takes his leave, *watakushi* catches sight of the soft skin above the neck of Mr. Miller's wife.[41] He remembers an ordinance from American occupation law in Okinawa which stated that anyone who raped or attempted to rape any female American personnel would face severe punishment or death. *Watakushi* imagines what kind of imbalance in relations would occur if he were to attack Mrs. Miller. The inequities of the military jurisdiction system force him next to turn to Mr. Sun for help.

It is in talking to Mr. Sun that *watakushi* realizes he must proceed with his case against Mr. Harris despite all odds. Strangely, what convinces him is not the injury his daughter has suffered so much as the personal tragedy Mr. Sun reveals to *watakushi* in the course of their discussion of the case. Upon ascertaining that both *watakushi* and Ogawa were in China in the spring of 1945, the former as a recruit in the Japanese Army, the latter as a student, Mr. Sun recounts the story of his son's disappearance, this time with more painful detail. After joyously finding him in protective custody, Mr. Sun returned home with his child only to find his wife had been raped by a Japanese soldier. Thinking it best to keep quiet, Mr. Sun suffered in silence for years. Ogawa and *watakushi*, enraged at Sun's story, question his failure to act. Visibly shaken, Mr. Sun, reminds them that they are all guilty:

he, for doing nothing about his wife, and Ogawa and *watakushi* for ignoring what was being done to the Chinese around them during the war. By retreating to the past, Ōshiro turns an Okinawan–American conflict into a Japanese–Chinese one. The protagonist's decision to act on his daughter's behalf stems from his indirect complicity in Mr. Sun's tragedy in China some twenty years earlier. He is determined to expose the social mask each member of the language group has donned. *Watakushi* must indict Robert Harris to expose the sham of the cocktail party. A month later, an investigation takes place at Cape M., the spot where the alleged attack occurred. Even the landscape is etched with pain:

> Cape M. was entirely too peaceful. The four or five tourists who usually came with their fishing rods were nowhere in sight that day. The area was deserted except for a single bonito fishing boat that drifted far out on the open sea. The melancholy splashing of the waves against the coral reef below the cliff was the only sound. To reconstruct in this landscape an event so peculiarly human seemed ludicrous.[42]

Watakushi tries to imagine what his daughter was feeling when made to reenact the rape before a group of men, himself included. Clothed in a one-piece dress, hair fluttering in the wind, she answers in full detail questions posed to her. As his daughter retells the act before the group, *watakushi* begins to feel that the entire episode is simply an illusion and questions what is real.

In the story's concluding scene, the protagonist's daughter strikes a curious, liberating pose which suggests that, she who has had no voice throughout, is at last telling her story:

> [T]he scenery at Cape M. seemed strangely vivid. Your daughter stretched one of her light-brown arms out over the cliff and held the other above her head. In the background was a sea so blue it seemed to soak into the pupils of your eyes. She might have been reenacting the moment of desperation when she pushed her tormentor over the cliff. In the ocean a white bank of wave crests glided toward a distant reef. You stared at your daughter and held your breath, praying that she would be able to fight her case openly and vigorously at a trial attended by Mr. Miller and Mr. Sun. In that courtroom there would be no illusions.[43]

This last scene, containing within it the powerful possibility of a young girl's resistance to the appropriation of her story, also reveals through its libidinal focus that victimhood requires a body. Both the feminine tomb vulnerable to enemy attack that appears in "Turtleback Tomb" and the protagonist's daughter in *The Cocktail Party* are problematic but powerful conflations of landscape and gender.

From the menacing security gate of the story's opening to the natural landscape of its conclusion, Ōshiro offers multiple perspectives on a personal tragedy, the rape of the protagonist's daughter. In conflating her rape with the rape of Mr. Sun's wife by Japanese soldiers in China during World War II, the author makes it difficult, if not impossible, to distinguish victims from aggressors. Ōshiro's cool logic and intellectual remove aids in the relativizing that occurs in the work. The abrupt shift that takes place midway through the narrative, however, is a clear indication that Ōshiro is not completely devoid of bias. The raw emotion of his protagonist's confession shows that Ōshiro's primary interest lies in Okinawa and its people.

Island of the Gods: guilt, atonement, and the recovery of faith

Island of the Gods is a novel based on a civilian group suicide (*shūdan jiketsu*) that occurred in late March 1945 when American troops landed on Tokashiki, an island of the Kerama chain, southwest of Okinawa.[44] In one of the worst cases of group suicides, Japanese Army Lieutenant Akamatsu Yoshitsugu ordered civilians to give up their lives, ostensibly to ensure the Army would have sufficient provisions to wage battle against the enemy.[45] Upon hearing Akamatsu's command, 329 people killed themselves. Some used hand grenades distributed to them; others, less fortunate, used razors, sickles, and hoes.[46] *Island of the Gods* explores the circumstances and repercussions of this group massacre.

The work boasts an interesting textual history. Originally appearing as fiction in *New Currents* (*Shinchō*), it was published as a play the following year in the journals *Theatre* (*Teatoru*) and *New Okinawa Literature*. It was also performed on stage in Tokyo. In 1974, the novel was reissued in hardback form with important revisions. Ōshiro, who has expressed how painful the work was to write, states that while his focus in *The Cocktail Party* was the different status accorded to Americans and Okinawans, in *Island of the Gods* he aimed to document the discord that persists between Okinawans and mainland Japanese.[47] Thus, he repeats throughout the work, "the twenty seventh parallel of one's mind" (*kokoro no nijūnanasen-do*), a phrase that refers to the dividing line used to separate Okinawa from mainland Japan after the war.[48]

Though the work's main theme is the division between Okinawans and other Japanese, numerous subthemes such as survivor guilt, war responsibility, reversion polemics, indigenous beliefs, and spurious folk scholarship appear throughout. Rather than explore each theme individually, I will give a brief description of the main characters to tease out the entanglements of this complicated novel. Ironically, Taminato Shinkō, the work's protagonist, is by far the least developed character. While he appears in the first and final sections of the novel, his presence is limited in the body of the work. Taminato, a teacher who evacuated with ten students during wartime, returns to his home after twenty-three years to attend memorial services for those of the group who have since died. Having entrusted his charges to a fellow teacher who safely saw them home, Taminato stayed on in Kyushu after marrying a woman from Miyazaki. For this he feels strangely guilty and senses some reserve on the part of the islanders despite their outwardly warm welcome. A familiar Ōshiro character who straddles two worlds—in this case, the mainland and Okinawa—Taminato may be best understood less as a fleshed-out character than as a device to propel the story line.[49]

The first person Taminato visits on the island is Futenma Zenshu, principal of the school at which Taminato once taught during wartime. Together with the village chief, Futenma relayed to his fellow islanders the order to commit suicide. Futenma himself survived the massacre when his hand grenade failed to explode. Burdened with enormous guilt for his indirect—yet major—role in the killings, this reticent old man spends his days combing the newspapers for articles related to the war. Reading and meticulously collecting these new items, he believes, will prevent him from reenacting the "animal-like obedience" (*dōbutsuteki chūseishin*) he displayed in the presence of imperial soldiers during the war.[50] Futenma, a school principal, is another in the long line of educational bureaucrats in Okinawan fiction who symbolize the shallowness of Japan's prewar emperor-centered moral education.

Futenma Zenshu's younger sister, Hamakawa Yae, is an island priestess (*noro*).[51] Invested with a sacred duty to worship the gods, she also mediates between the living and the dead. Yae, like Ushi in "Turtleback Tombs," is a powerful symbol of traditional Okinawan communality. To escape the group suicide, Yae violated ancient taboos by leading her husband and son into a sacred cave used only for the priestess's worship. Hidden in the hollow, the family managed to avoid the group suicide, but, to their horror, survivors of the massacre soon found their way to the cave and streamed in. Soon Japanese soldiers discovered the cave and also sought protection within. One day a soldier named Miyaguchi ordered Yae's husband, head of the town's agricultural division, to accompany him in gathering provisions. The two never returned. Yae herself left to hunt for food, but upon returning, spied American soldiers nearing the entrance of the cave. She found another place to hide, returning to the cave only when the war ended.

Assailed by the rotten stench of human flesh, Hae is filled with remorse for having defiled the sacred cave. Months later she returns to sweep the now bleached bones into a pile, and to seal off the cave's entry. From this point onward, Yae's mental life changes, for, though she does not dare to say so, she no longer believes the gods exist. Turning her back on island affairs, she has spent the past fifteen years searching for the prayer beads her husband clutched when he left the cave. While skeptical of the gods' existence, Hae firmly believes that were she to discover the beads, the remains of her husband would surely be found nearby.

Ōgaki Kiyohiko is a folk scholar from mainland Japan who has spent the past five summers on the island conducting research on indigenous beliefs. Greatly interested in Yae, he persistently asks her to show him the sacred priestess's cave, but each time she steadfastly refuses. Ōgaki is awed by Yae's devoted search for the religious beads and sees in her actions the beauty of ancient Okinawa. While tolerant of the scholar's presence, some islanders question his interest in Okinawa and wonder whether he is not in fact fetishizing the widow's tragedy. Ōgaki states his view of Yae and the island as follows: "She is what I call a beautiful person. Though tragic, she is beautiful. The original beauty of ancient Japan exists in this type of island."[52] By including the folk scholar Ōgaki among his cast of characters, Ōshiro seems intent in distinguishing his own balanced representations of culture from those made by many scholars like Ōgaki who have succumbed to an infatuation with Okinawa (*Okinawa byō no kanja*). Yonashiro Haruo is a young cameraman from mainland Okinawa who comes to the island in hopes of producing a documentary film on prereversion life on the island. In Naha, he casts doubts on the future of Okinawa after its return to Japan, and is perturbed by the inclusion of all war dead in the annual mourning ceremony.[53] Believing that the rites should be reserved for Okinawans only, he enlists the help of other youth to protest the participation of mainland Japanese. Like Ōgaki, Yonashiro is fascinated with Yae and discusses with town officials his desire to make her the focus of his film. The officials, not wishing to promote the island's suffering, implore Yonashiro to minimize the darker aspects of Kamishima's history and ask that he concentrate his efforts to produce a film which would increase tourism.

Kimura Hōshi is a young Japanese woman who met and married Yae's son in Tokyo, only to lose him shortly thereafter in a traffic accident. She makes a surprise visit to the island in order to present Yae with her husband's remains. Attractive and strong-willed, Kimura is disheartened by Yae's cold reception. The two are in constant conflict. Kimura does not understand the importance of Yae's role as priestess, nor the fact that she, as Yae's daughter-in-law, ought properly to carry on the tradition of worship; Yae, bitter because both husband and son have been taken from her by the Japanese, nonetheless believes it is Kimura's duty to help her with the monumental task of locating her missing husband.

Miyaguchi Tomoko is another young Japanese woman, from the city of Nagasaki. She has come to the island to learn how her father, a Japanese soldier, died during the battle. Welcomed by Futenma Zenshu to stay in his home, Miyaguchi helps the elder Okinawan collect news articles while waiting for the start of the ceremonies. Although Futenma and other islanders treat her kindly, she senses they are withholding from her information about her father's death. They tell her that since records indicate that there were two soldiers named Miyaguchi, it is not clear which one might have been her father, or what led to his death. It is Futenma, silent throughout, who finally reveals that he witnessed the gruesome sight of Miyaguchi's father plunging a sword into Yae's husband after the two left the priestess's hollow in search of provisions. Shaken by this news, Miyaguchi, in atonement for her father's crime, decides not to attend the ceremonies.

Instead, she accompanies Yae to the mountains to assist in the older woman's search.

Through the dialogue and internal thoughts of the novel's seven major characters, Taminato, Futenma, Yae, Ōgaki, Yonashiro, Kimura, and Miyaguchi, Ōshiro highlights the conflicts that separate Okinawans from mainland Japanese.[54] Yae, because of her double loss, is the most adamantly anti-Japanese character, but Yonashiro also shares some of her intensity. Kimura, a thoroughly modern woman from Tokyo, pits herself against Yae, an icon of island tradition, and Miyaguchi, also from mainland Japan, is treated ambiguously by islanders privy to the secret that her father was responsible for the death of Yae's husband. Taminato, married to a mainland Japanese, and Kimura, married to an Okinawan, are the only characters in this dark novel who offer some hope for an end to the division that exists between Okinawans and other Japanese. Ōgaki, a Japanese wedded to Okinawa through his scholarship, exacerbates tensions by singularly focusing on Kamishima as a distillation of ancient culture.

While most of the novel is devoted to dialogue, public and private, between the major characters, the latter section contains two notable dramatic scenes. In the first, Yae at last agrees to lead Ōgaki, Kimura, and Yonashiro to the sacred hollow. Each member of the group is variously motivated. Ōgaki is present because of his research; Yonashiro joins the tour to film the hollow for his movie. Yae hopes, by showing Kimura the priestess worship site, she will thaw the frosty relationship she has with her Japanese daughter-in-law. These hopes are shattered when, inside the hollow, Kimura sees the concealed pile of bones and questions why Yae did not properly dispose of the remains:

> "They shouldn't be left aside, unable to rest in peace. Why didn't you gather the bones and bury them?"
> "These people cannot be in peace. They are being punished for having defiled the gods."
> "So they will stay like this forever?"
> "It's sad, but there's no other way. [...] This is to atone for their crime against the gods. [...] We must all make up to the gods for violating the taboo. Please understand. [...] Know my pain and the anger of the gods."
> "It's egoism! You're so selfish."[55]

Thus ends Yae's earnest attempt to bridge the gap that separates her from Kimura. Though visibly moved by what she sees in the cave, Kimura refuses to accept the tradition-bound logic of her mother-in-law.

The novel's climax occurs when, at long last, the island's ceremony to mourn the dead begins. Yae, as is her habit, avoids the ceremony, choosing instead to continue her search for her husband. With pickax in hand she sets off for the mountains, joined at the last moment by Miyaguchi Tomoko, who wishes to atone for her father's war crime. Shortly afterward, the sound of an explosion startles those attending the ceremonies. They soon learn that just as Yae miraculously spotted the long-lost prayer beads, Miyaguchi, unpracticed at avoiding undetonated artillery, hits a shell with her shovel and is blown to pieces. The narrator conveys Yae's feelings of remorse:

> Just as Yae was about to crane her neck and say "Watch it!," the explosion occurred. Suddenly she felt as if the jewels in her hand increased 10,000 times in weight. With a guilty expression, she straightforwardly told Taminato that when the heat from the explosion cooled, she went right on searching for her husband's bones.[56]

It is only through the discovery of the beads and the attendant sacrifice of the innocent Miyaguchi that Yae is finally able to believe in the gods again. Yae's guilt-filled years of tireless atonement leave her in an instant; she can now assume her duties as island priestess, freed from the immense skepticism with which she has been so heavily burdened. In *Island of the Gods*, Ōshiro characteristically explores his themes by presenting a plethora of views, but, as in "Turtleback Tombs," the novel's strength lies in the resistant figure of the traditional matriarch. The work's weakness, too, lies in the portrait of Yae. The narrator's poignant depiction of Yae's renewed faith, signified by the dramatic discovery of the beads and her sudden perception of their weightedness suggests the possibility that something ineffable and new can arise out of the tragedy and destruction of a divisive war. However, as we have seen, this possibility only exists in an ideal world of Ōshiro's own creation.

The flight home in "Fantasy Island"

In 1967 Ōshiro's complex short story "Fantasy Island" appeared in *Literary World*. The first phrase of the work's title *panarinusuma* refers, in dialect, to an outlying island (*hanareshima* in standard Japanese) in the subtropics. Told in the third person by an omniscient narrator, the tale depicts the protagonist Yamatarō's sorrowful search to retrieve his lost identity. Tragic events lead Yamatarō to flee mainland Okinawa and hide on a small unnamed island where he stumbles upon the community's yearly celebration of the arrival of the harvest gods.[57] Drawn by the intensity of the sacred rites and customs he witnesses, Yamatarō attempts to penetrate the strangely familiar, tightly knit society, but his past deeds prevent his inclusion. Yamatarō's quest permits Ōshiro to explore the cultural practices of one of the dozens of smaller islands that make up Okinawa prefecture.

The story, told in seven sections, begins when Yamatarō arrives by boat on an island where "the wind never ceases to blow."[58] The boat's captain, Shinjō, tells Yamatarō that the population of the island, now around 100, will swell in the next few days to 300 as relatives and sightseers from other areas arrive for the festival. Because there are no inns available, Shinjō invites Yamatarō to lodge in his home together with three visiting folk scholars. At Shinjō's home, Yamatarō notices a well on one side of the dwelling. He finds it dry and littered with old fish bait and juice bottles:

> *Sasara, sasara,* Yamatarō whispered. He longed for water. From childhood he had been taught by his mother and father that "thirsty" was a forbidden word. They told him to say *sasara, sasara* whenever he wanted water. When he asked the word's meaning neither his mother nor his father knew. It was only after he started going to school that he realized these words were unintelligible to others. His mother said she was taught the words upon marrying his father. His father said he had learned them from his father. Since Yamatarō was born after his grandfather had already died he didn't know what went on beforehand. *Tsukuri, tsukuri* is what he said when hungry, and *hizuru, hizuru* is what he uttered when hot.[59]

As this passage indicates, Yamatarō's childhood was not idyllic. Yamatarō's grandfather, whose origins are known neither by his son nor his grandson, left his hometown for mysterious reasons; his father had repeatedly failed in his ventures. Raised strictly and in poverty, Yamatarō grew isolated not only from his family but from the larger society as well because he knew so little of his origins.

Shinjō warns Yamatarō to be sure to place a heavy object on anything he does want to have the wind blow away. This provides further insight into Yamatarō's past. Yamatarō recalls that placing heavy items on thin objects is something he had been instructed to do in childhood. He had thought the practice, taught to him by his parents, was born of poverty, but, suddenly, he wonders if there might not be a connection between him and the strange island. Yamatarō is not fully conscious of it, but his odd vocabulary and peculiar habits offer clues to his identity.

Although not much is clear, initially, about Yamatarō's origins, the narrator does provide much detail about his recent past as a laborer employed at a rubber-shoe factory. Yamatarō was a loner there as well, gaining notoriety only when the union decided to strike in protest against a number of layoffs. Yamatarō, along with two other employees, climbed to the factory chimney and refused to budge, thereby effecting a work stoppage. For nearly three weeks, the men maintained their positions until a death occurred, bringing them down from their perch atop the factory walls. One night, while the other two men are asleep nearby, Yamatarō heard the sound of footsteps climbing the ladder to the chimney. When Yamatarō realized it was a cameraman attempting to take a photograph of the three strikers, he pushed the man downward to his death. Not knowing what possessed him to act so violently, Yamatarō rushed away to escape capture.

Before he stowed away on Shinjō's boat, Yamatarō paid a visit to Saki, a fellow employee with whom he is infatuated. Saki, who has repeatedly been the target of undesired attention by another employee, Yutaka, was trying once again to ward Yutaka off, when she heard Yamatarō's voice outside her window. She and Yutaka were caught entirely off guard as the two of them believed Yamatarō is still atop the chimney. Nevertheless, the distraction drove Yutaka away and Saki found Yamatarō before her. The two, who had long desired each other, became intimate for the first time. It was only after their hurried, passionate lovemaking that Yamatarō revealed to Saki that he had just killed a man. Before Saki could fathom his words, Yamatarō escaped to a remote island, which coincidentally, was home to Saki and Yutaka.

The modern world of mainland Okinawa, as exemplified by the factory, labor dispute, and work stoppage is set in contrast to the mythic, primal world into which Yamatarō stumbles.[60] The narrator states, "To Yamatarō who had just climbed down the chimney and escaped the city, the island, seeming to possess an uncanny magic, greeted him."[61] The narrative then moves to describe a town meeting in which the elders discuss the festival and insist that no press coverage be allowed so as to keep the rites secret. When the ward chief suggested relaxing the rule, an elder named Akagi stubbornly retorted, "Secrets are secrets; customs inherited from ancestors are customs. If we in this generation destroy them, we will destroy them for our children and grandchildren."[62] The elders also discussed which three boys would undergo the rite of passage which, if successfully completed, allowed them entry into the island's sacred adult society (*yamaninju*). Saki's younger brother, Takejirō, was selected, prompting Saki to return for the ceremonies. To her dismay, Yutaka joined her, for it was determined that he would initiate Takejirō.

Because of his crime, Yamatarō cannot mingle freely with others on the island. From the top of Kaminohana Cliff he commands a bird's-eye view. He sees below him a group of adults seated by the shore on straw mats, gazing at the horizon, in anticipation of the gods' arrival. The narrator draws a parallel between Yamatarō's position in the city and on the island:

> The instant Yamatarō saw the group of people he was roused by the same emotion he had felt when he looked down over the town from above the factory chimney. It was a feeling of isolation. He himself could not recall what drew him to volunteer to block the chimney. He remembered feeling as if he were escaping from something. What that something was, he did not know. Was it that he was trying to escape from his bleak family life?[63]

Yamatarō's lofty position in both city and island, also points to the wide gulf that separates him from others. A newspaper reporter's sudden appearance disturbs Yamatarō's solitude on the cliff. The reporter has come to this vantage point to take photographs of the village below, an act expressly prohibited by the community. Yamatarō is assailed by an illusion of the cameraman he only recently pushed to his death and wonders if the two are one and the same. Yet another figure appears—a masked boy. His piercing glare convinces Yamatarō that the boy would, at any moment, angrily push either him or the reporter, or perhaps both, off the cliff, just as Yamatarō himself had pushed the cameraman off the chimney. Yamatarō returns the boy's stare, and the boy, saying nothing, turns his back and vanishes into the woods.

In the next section, the festival rules are clearly announced. In addition to the ban on photographs, the elders insist that no one trespass the sacred woods where the adults commune with the gods, and, without exception, everyone is instructed to participate in the dances following the gods' appearance. Yamatarō, hearing these pronouncements, knows he ought not involve himself, but suddenly he is unable to bear the cumulative weight of his experiences of isolation through childhood, at the factory, and now as an interloper on the island. He dons a mask and joins in the festivities. Just then, to his surprise, he spots Saki, whom he had no reason to believe was in any way connected to the island. Yamatarō then inexplicably loses consciousness.

On the third day of the festival, a news reporter is declared missing. Yamatarō immediately suspects the masked boy and now feels a connection between himself and the boy because, he assumes, they have both killed. The reasons behind the disappearance are not explicitly stated, but, given the ultraconservative nature of the island society, it is likely that the masked boy is Takejirō, who, as an initiate has enforced the elders' rule prohibiting photographs. Shinjō reveals to Yamatarō that, years earlier, when he chose not to enter the adult ranks, he and his wife were ostracized to such a degree that finally he relented and joined the others. Shinjō also tells him that those who cannot abide by adult rules are forced to leave the islands. The three folk scholars, also present, pontificate on the communal nature of the island. Listening to them, Yamatarō, who has an inkling that he is connected to this strange island, wonders if his grandfather might have been ousted from his home. Though he never knew his grandfather, thoughts of his possible banishment produce in Yamatarō hitherto unknown feelings of closeness.

Unable to comprehend—or perhaps bored by—the stodgy folk scholars' views, Yamatarō drifts off to sleep. Shinjō appears to him in a dream, revealing that Yamatarō's grandfather is one of the island's banished souls (*ishizō*). Having defiled a young girl, he was not permitted to become an adult formally. Leaving the island, he moved from town to town before his ignominious death at the hands of his coworkers. Yamatarō's grandfather, visiting a prostitute, skipped a labor-union meeting in the city, causing his coworkers to hunt for him. They threw him into the ocean where he drowned. Kuraji, the son he left behind—Yamatarō's father—knew nothing of his origins save for a few strange words and odd habits such as placing heavy objects upon lighter ones. Kuraji joined the military, but was unable to abide by its rules. One day he struck an officer, an act that resulted in his dishonorable discharge. These facts, presented in a dream, force Yamatarō to ask himself if it was not in his blood to kill the photographer. He wonders if the reason behind his rash action was that he could not bear to have anyone peer into the interior of his soul.

Yamatarō again ventures out to observe the festivities. He witnesses the arduous trials the three initiates are forced to endure. The narrator explains the origins of the rites:

> Originally the island was poor. There was scarcely any water and no way to escape the heat. [...] In order for the island's few residents to survive, each had to govern his desires. The gods Akanemoto and Kuronemoto came to the island once a year from the land of luxuriance beyond the seas to portend a bountiful harvest. To repay this kindness the gods stated that it was essential for the islanders to worship, without violation, the divine, and drive out from their lives any extravagant tendencies. When one complained of hunger, thirst, or heat, discord arose; therefore, they devised words without form to be used in lieu of expressions of desire. *Tsukuri*, a symbol for crops, replaced cries of hunger; *sasara*, a symbol for the flow of rivers, replaced cries of thirst; and *hizuru*, the word for cold, often replaced cries of heat exhaustion.[64]

Witnessing Yutaka's overly cruel tests of Takejirō's strength, Yamatarō experiences mixed feelings. He is drawn to Takejirō for they share in common past violence; yet, he also envies his earnest attempt to become an adult. Awed by his and other islanders' absolute devotion to the gods, Yamatarō speculates whether he, too, might one day become an adult. The section ends as Yamatarō visualizes success only with the support of Saki.

In the final, eventful section of the work, it is the last night of the festival during which the entire island stays awake to dance with the gods until they depart at dawn. The heavy weight of the gods' costumes necessitates that the adults take turns parading as the deities. In the melee, Saki receives a note "from the gods" asking to meet her at Kaminohana Cliff. Having previously spied Yamatarō in the crowd, Saki hopes the note is from him and not from her undesired suitor, Yutaka. Although it is a breach of custom to leave the festival and enter the woods, Saki does so with the sincere belief that the gods will forgive her. As she waits with bated breath for the arrival of new gods who will bring happiness to herself and Yamatarō, Yutaka arrives. Precisely when he begins to assault her, Yamatarō charges in, and the two struggle. Hearing a noise in the brush, Yutaka yells for Yamatarō to run, then takes his leave.

Worried that he might be spotted in the forbidden woods, Yutaka returns to the ceremonies and quickly dons the costume of a god. Meanwhile, Saki and Yamatarō enjoy a bittersweet reunion on the cliff. They lie awake at dawn after listening all night to the far-off songs and dances. When Yamatarō whispers, *sasara, sasara*, indicating his thirst, Saki is startled and asks him to repeat the words and reveal their meaning. Just as Saki realizes the truth of Yamatarō's origins, Takejirō abruptly appears to chase Yamatarō off the cliff, having been told by the gods that an interloper is present. Aware of Yutaka's betrayal, Saki looks searchingly at the expanse of ocean below the cliffs but she and Takejirō see only dawn's rays striking the waves. The work concludes with the lone figure of Saki at daybreak:

> A tinge of red trailed in the eastern sky. Out of the hazy redness, morning showed itself, making clear the undulations of the waves. From the sun a shadow like that of a crepe obi flowed in Saki's direction. Saki fancied this to be blood flowing from the gods. The wind, having blown all night, continued to blow towards day, giving no sign of abating. In its midst Saki lost consciousness. Facing the golden woods, her disheveled hair flowed in streams.[65]

"Fantasy Island" is an oddly moving tale of a young man's search for his origins. Straddling two worlds, a modern city in Okinawa and a mythic outlying island, Yamatarō ultimately fails in his attempts to reconcile these opposite extremes but recovers, in the process, his lost identity. Ōshiro depicts the very modern struggle his protagonist faces while simultaneously portraying the seriousness with which communality is viewed by the islanders. Like his father and grandfather before him, Yamatarō violates the rules of his society, resulting in his exclusion. In the restrictive world of the adults, individuals are dispensable for the greater good of the community. While Saki may rail at the unfairness of her fate, adult rules force Takejirō to drive out Yamatarō, the intruder.

Historian Takara Kurayoshi notes an important point about Yamatarō, namely, that Ōshiro's protagonist is given no physical description.[66] Considering the fact that Yamatarō also has no personal history, Takara concludes that Yamatarō is not human. Rather, he is a bundle of contradictions, mythic and modern. An abstract figure, rootless, and brimming with unease, Yamatarō brings to mind postwar Okinawan issues of confusion and homelessness.[67] The fantastic elements of the work—narrative shifts between dream and reality, Yamatarō's illusions upon seeing the newspaper reporter, Takejirō's dashing in and out of the woods like the wind that ceaselessly blows on the island, Saki's loss of consciousness—do lend credence to Takara's reading. In Yamatarō's character, Ōshiro expresses the multiple dimensions of Okinawa itself, from the largest most modern island to the smallest, most primal one, in the prefecture's chain. As instructive as Kurayoshi's observation of Yamatarō's formlessness is, however, it is also plain to see that Ōshiro merely uses the character of Yamatarō as a foil for an intellectual position. As with so many of the author's characters, Yamatarō is not fleshed out.

In his fiction, Ōshiro delves deeply into the question of Okinawan culture. Rather than focusing on the island exclusively, Ōshiro insistently presents other viewpoints by including in his cast of characters figures from China, America, mainland Japan, or one of the many remote islands in the Ryukyu chain. It is through this collision of Okinawans with other groups that Ōshiro is able to seize upon the distinctiveness of his own culture. To take just one example, in *Island of the Gods*, Ōshiro pits Okinawan characters against their Japanese counterparts. He does this not to further antagonize the two groups, but to bring about a mutual understanding of the importance of Okinawa's indigenous belief system. Ōshiro's postwar writings, exemplified by scenes such as Yae's recovery of her buried prayer beads, are instrumental in bringing to light facets of Okinawan culture long suppressed by the islanders as they endeavored to orient themselves to Japan through cultural assimilation from the Meiji period onward. By privileging culture over all else, however, Ōshiro fails to create believable characters or to address the complexities of Okinawan society. It is far easier to note this serious flaw of Ōshiro's fiction than it is to understand why the author invests so little in his characters and so much in mythmaking. I suspect the reason Okinawa is more fanciful than real is because Ōshiro uses a rhetorical strategy by which he mythologizes Okinawa to compensate for the suppression of culture in Okinawa during the prewar period. If this is so, the author's motivations are laudable. His stories, however, remain unsatisfying reads.[68]

While Ōshiro's fiction and essays, (in particular, "Becoming Japanese in Okinawa" and "The Okinawa Issue Is a Cultural Issue") mark the recovery of Okinawan culture after decades of neglect, Shimao Toshio's series of essays *Theory of Yaponesia*, written from the mid-1950s to the early 1970s, encapsulates that author's rediscovery of southern island culture.[69] In the concluding section of this chapter, I examine the best-known essays on Okinawa by a writer from outside the prefecture in order to include alternative representations in this discussion of culture and to demonstrate that mythic constructions of Okinawa are created by outsiders and insiders alike.

Colonial desire and ambiguity in Shimao Toshio's *Theory of Yaponesia*

In 1954, Shimao Toshio published "That Which Gives Okinawa Meaning," an essay in which he describes Okinawa as a paradisiacal "Shangrila" (*tōgenkyō*) that provided relief from the pervasive stagnation of the main islands of Japan. For the next twenty years, from the island of Amami Ōshima, Shimao continued to write about the therapeutic value of Okinawa and the Ryukyuan chain to which it belongs in a series of essays collectively titled *Yaponeshia ron*.[70] Coined by Shimao, the term "Yaponesia" first appeared in print in 1961 with the publication of "The Root of Yaponesia."[71] Simply put, Yaponesia is Shimao's reorienting of the Japanese islands towards their putative roots in the islands of the South Pacific and away from their subservience to the Chinese continent.[72] Intoxicated by the liberating power of this radical vision, Shimao embellished the geopolitical invention of Yaponesia in successive essays during the 1960s in order to show that Japan was a melding of three distinct cultures: Ainu, Yamato, and Ryukyuan. Associated with Yoshimoto Takaaki's essays "Theory of the South Seas" and "Theory of a Different Race," Shimao's *Theory of Yaponesia* captured the imagination of writers and critics throughout Japan during the politically turbulent mid- to late 1960s when the issue of Okinawa's return to the home islands was in the public eye.[73]

Theory of Yaponesia not only had an impact in Tokyo in the late 1960s, it also set in motion a flurry of scholarly activity in the Ryukyus that continues to the present day. Influenced by Shimao's incorporation of the fringe cultures of Hokkaido and the Ryukyus in the formation of Japan, historians specializing in both modern and ancient Japan have engaged in a revision of their national narratives. Inspired by *Theory of Yaponesia*, writers in the Ryukyus, particularly those from Amami Ōshima, have produced volumes of critical works either broadening or narrowing Shimao's ideas on what constitutes Japan.

Although Shimao's vision of Yaponesia begins with the northern regions of Tōhoku and Hokkaido and ends with the southern islands of Sakishima and Yonaguni, some writers have extended the scope of Shimao's cultural theory. Yamada Munechika challenges Shimao's borders in essays on "IndoYaponesia," a concept that he believes more fully encapsulates the breadth of Japanese cultural transmission.[74] Tsushima Katsuyoshi, a literary critic from Hokkaido, notes that although it is widely known that Yaponesia includes both Japan's northernmost and southernmost regions, Shimao's privileging of the Ryukyuan arc leaves northern Japan bereft of much critical attention.[75] Sekine Kenji, a researcher at the University of the Ryukyus, finds that Shimao's decided emphasis on the "unique" culture of the southern islands is at odds with a theory that aims to explore multi-centers of culture in Japan.[76] While acknowledging the contributions of Shimao's essays, Yamada, Tsushima, and Sekine are concerned that a Ryukyuan focus contradicts the search for diversity that lies at the heart of *Theory of Yaponesia*.

Whereas Shimao's essays on Yaponesia were received with enthusiasm in Okinawa, not a few writers voiced their concerns over the tendency of the essays to lapse into a new nationalism. Shimao's focus on Okinawa to the exclusion of other places in the south or the north, and his valuation of the identity of Okinawans over other Ryukyuans led Ōshiro Tatsuhiro to criticize the essays for their narrow focus and for the part they played in the rising tide of Okinawan nationalism during the 1970s.[77] Writer Miki Takeshi of Ishigaki and Okinawan poet Takara Ben have gone the opposite direction in their writings subsequent to the publication of Shimao's *Theory of Yaponesia*. Takara has expressed feelings of uneasiness with Shimao's ideas about Yaponesia because, despite the multiculturalism the essays espouse, it is still a Japanese nation-based theory. In an effort to distinguish the southern islands from the rest of Japan, Takara proclaimed in 1981 the creation of "Ryukyunesia."[78] Miki has similarly endeavored to concentrate on aspects of southern culture in his writings on "Okinesia."[79] While Ōshiro laments that *Theory of Yaponesia* has devolved into Okinawan nationalism, Takara and Miki, fearful of the nation subsuming its borders, redefine and bolster their home territory through their constructions of "Ryukyunesia" and "Okinesia."

That the reception of the Yaponesia essays was overwhelmingly positive, especially by writers living in Shimao's beloved Ryukyuan islands, is evident when one considers the sheer amount of scholarship the original essays have generated. If the essay's weaknesses—Shimao's insufficient attention to the northern islands, his abstract account of ancient Japanese history, or even his most often cited shortcoming, the absence of an explicit critique of the Japanese state—are mentioned, they are quickly dismissed or excused, in a rather familiar refrain, ostensibly because of the highly personal nature of his writings.[80] The fact that Shimao left Tokyo to live for twenty years in his wife's hometown of Amami Ōshima does explain why he pays so much attention to the Ryukyus in his *Theory of Yaponesia*, but the manner in which he depicts the islands reveals a deep ambivalence towards the south, an emotion that, while rooted in personal experience, took on a distinctly political tone as Shimao's views on Yaponesia were publicly disseminated and consumed over the course of two decades. In examining the image of the Ryukyus that Shimao presents in *Theory of Yaponesia*, I aim to show the unwitting effects of colonial desire.

Shimao begins his treatise by explaining his attraction to Okinawa, which resulted from his childhood reading of Takizawa Bakin's *Crescent Moon* (*Chinzetsu yumiharizuki*, 1807–11), a masterpiece that describes twelfth-century hero Minamoto Tametomo's adventures and eventual shipwreck in the Ryukyus. While in the islands, Bakin's Tametomo averts an uprising and saves a Ryukyuan princess whom he later marries. The popularity of the historical tale was in no way diminished by Bakin's embellishment of the facts of Tametomo's life. In actuality, the Minamoto hero never saw the Ryukyus.[81] The southern islands depicted in *Crescent Moon* are merely figments of Bakin's imagination, but Shimao never relinquished the excitement of this first exposure to Bakin's Ryukyuan Shangrila.

Shimao continued to exoticize the Ryukyus—and Okinawa in particular—gradually refashioning the area as an object of desire, a place that would allow him to escape the oppressiveness of the main islands. Shimao writes about this rediscovery:

> No matter where you walk in Japan, there are exactly the same facial expressions, and if you prick up your ears, all you hear is a readily understandable standard language. This causes everything to be stagnant and putrid. Its influence is felt only when meddling audaciously or in keeping people under control. Frightfully unhappy, self-complacent,

Ōshiro Tatsuhiro and mythic Okinawa   117

and exclusive, we have given up on coming into contact with different things that would enrich us and bring about mutual expansion—until the rediscovery of Okinawa.[82]

Shimao further describes the Satsuma "discovery" of the Ryukyus in terms of an art connoisseur stumbling upon a valuable gem: "One day Okinawa was looked at again with eyes skilled in art appreciation. The Yamato people longingly set out on a sightseeing trip to Okinawa."[83] Once there, the outsiders visit Okinawan art exhibitions, certain that truths about the island can be readily perceived there. Shimao believes otherwise: "There is no 'Okinawa' there—only a cast-off skin."[84]

Shimao's discussion of the exhibition as an embodiment of truth is notable for its relation to Orientalism. Writing of the role world exhibitions played in constructing the non-Western world, Timothy Mitchell explains how Arab writers coming to the West found not only exhibitions and representations of the world, but the world itself functioning as an endless exhibition:

> This world-as-exhibition was a place where the artificial, the model, and the plan were employed to generate an unprecedented effect of order and certainty. It is not the artificiality of the exhibitionary order that matters, however so much as the contrasting effect of an external reality that the artificial and the model create—a reality characterized, like Orientalism's Orient, by essentialism, otherness, and absence.[85]

In *Theory of Yaponesia*, Okinawa becomes, despite Shimao's efforts to portray the island's complexity, the object of his desires. As such, the island is rendered meaningless.

Shimao's femininization of Okinawa contributes to the objectification of the island. Repulsed by the rigidity in mainland speech and manners Shimao welcomes the kinder, gentler lifestyle of the Ryukyus:

> I have noticed that in the culture of these islands there does not exist the strain and stiffness that I could feel in the mainland. [...] It's not easy to put it in a word, but, hidden in the lifestyle of the Ryukyuan islands is something akin to a naive life force (*seimeiryoku*). I have been able to detect, in people's conduct, a "gentleness" that is all but forgotten in Japan proper. To say it without the fear of misunderstanding, in these islands that are unspoiled by modern enlightenment, I have sensed a lifestyle utterly like that of people in the middle ages or antiquity.[86]

Given the context, it is clear that Shimao is lauding the Ryukyus, but his praise is not only guilty of stereotyping, it is demeaning. The islands, naive but filled with vitality are imbued with "gentleness," a feminine attribute, while the islanders, robbed of history, remain unchanged by time. Ryukyuans are further defined as "proto-Japanese." As Alan Christy explains, the problem with using historical precedents in formulating Okinawan identity vis-à-vis Japan is that "the historical precedent is frozen at an originary moment."[87] The islanders, who Shimao claims resemble ancient ancestors are not modern beings, rather they are archeological relics denied any existence that produces history.[88]

Critics have made much of Shimao's characterization of the islands as "gentle." Shimao himself, bolsters his impressions of relaxed island life by pointing out that, unlike mainland Japan, the Ryukyus did not develop feudalism or a warrior code such as *bushido*. Ōshiro Tatsuhiro, calling the absence of such developments a "delay of history," offers it as one of the underpinnings of Okinawan history and culture:

> Historically speaking, Okinawan society, which emerged in the twelfth-century, did not give rise to a feudal society in any complete form until the nineteenth-century. I think, to this day, this remains a great problem for Okinawan culture. From the perspective of historical interpretation, I believe that feudal society is an important preparatory period that forms a bridge from the ancient period to the modern, and this feudal period is virtually absent. There has been a drastic, unavoidable leap from an ancient society to a modern one. In a feudal period, various classes, production, and vocations develop. [...] A specialist's consciousness manifests itself as well. We had to plunge into modern society with these things not well evolved.[89]

Since Okinawa did not have a distinctive feudal period, or a warrior class, feudal "loyalty" was in short supply; hence, Ōshiro concludes Okinawan society's hierarchical consciousness became "soft."[90] The gentleness that Shimao so admires is clearly construed here as a deficiency.

Given the Ryukyus' history of Yamato oppression instigated by the Satsuma invasion of 1609 and continuing through the devastation of the Battle of Okinawa, it is difficult not to regard Shimao's feminization of the southern islands as anything other than a trope of colonialism. Murai Osamu describes the relation between the Ryukyus and the Japanese state as gendered, the former playing the feminine partner with whom, in 1879, the year of the Ryukyu Disposition, the (male) state joined in "marriage." A similar gendered relationship developed in Taiwan in 1895 and Korea in 1910.[91] Rhetorically, as well as literally, marriage lies at the heart of Shimao's essays. The South Pacific islands that Shimao links to Japan through the construction of Yaponesia were embroiled in a relationship with Japan during its prewar imperial period, and prior to this, the "nesias" were engaged in a different set of relations with the European power blocs. Shimao's actual marriage to his wife Miho becomes the literal reason for his lengthy stay in the Ryukyus. Said to be mentally unstable as a result of her husband's affair with another woman, Shimao's wife Miho, together with

Shimao and their two children, left Tokyo in 1955 for Amami Ōshima, where she lived until her death in 2007. For the last several years she has wielded considerable influence in Kyushu literary circles by publishing essays and fiction and serving as a judge for literary prizes. Critics often note that Shimao's obsession with the southern islands relates to a personal desire to fully understand Miho and the reasons for her mental illness. Serizawa Shunsuke writes that, "for Shimao, visiting the southern islands is visiting his wife."[92] This connection between *Theory of Yaponesia* and Miho underscores the feminizing aspects of the essays.

As much as Shimao is drawn to the softness and gentleness of the Ryukyus, he is constantly aware of what separates him from the culture that so obsesses him. Throughout the essays, Shimao refers to the cold Tōhoku blood that courses through his veins, contrasting it with the island blood that runs through his wife and his children. He goes so far as to say that he regrets not having been born in Okinawa, taking great comfort in the fact that at least his children's blood is mixed with the blood of Amami Ōshima. Since the children are in part his, Shimao believes he is entitled to the status of partial victim, presumably, of Japanese oppression. During his second visit to Okinawa in 1966, Shimao, accompanied by his son Shinzō, experienced the island in a way he could not had he been alone. He writes of his difference as follows:

> Despite how difficult it was for me to engage with the Okinawans, my son, without effort, fit right in. This is because he has his mother's Okinawan blood in his veins. [...] No matter how much I think I have succeeded in losing myself in Okinawa, I am hit by the realization that I am an imposter, but, with my son, the circumstances are different. [...] In his company, wherever we walk in Okinawa, my alien disposition vanishes. I believe he has given me a pass to walk about freely.[93]

Shimao refers to Miho's blood as Okinawan because her ancestors, dating back ten generations, came to Amami Ōshima from Okinawa. This passage and others like it reveal Shimao's childhood obsession with his alien blood and the lure of Okinawan blood, however diluted. By repeatedly directing attention to the fundamental difference that lies between him and the Ryukyuans he writes of, Shimao indicates his utter isolation.[94] In "From the Perspective of the Ryukyu Arc," Shimao comments on the "strange feeling" he experiences when he views people from various regions in Japan speaking different dialects.[95] The fact that Shimao is both drawn to and disquieted by heterogeneity explains why Yaponesia remains a nation-based theory. Although much energy is expended in dismantling the Japanese state in *Theory of Yaponesia*, in the final analysis, the presence of the state remains undiminished. As much as Shimao wishes to rid himself of the rigidities of Japanese life, the fear that attends his fascination with the exoticized, dangerous Ryukyus never allows him to sever his (blood) ties to mainland Japan.[96]

In spite of the ambiguity of his desire for the Ryukyus, Shimao persists, as evidenced by his vast writings on the region, to search for a cure to his isolation. Born in Tōhoku, Shimao left before knowing the region. From childhood onward he moved from one city to another, none of which he could call his hometown. What he seeks in the Ryukyus is more a consolation for his rootless wandering than any evidence of Japan's diversity. The fact that his wife Miho returned to Amami Ōshima for therapeutic reasons after her mental collapse lends credence to the idea that the islands contained curative powers. In his essay "What I Think About the Southern Islands," Shimao explicitly acknowledges that the basis of the southern islands is its "power to heal" (*chiyuryoku*).[97] According to Hiyane Kaoru, the reason Shimao regards the Ryukyus as possessing this power is because he sees in the islands time as it was experienced in the ancient period (*kodai no jikan*).[98] Nakazata Isao states that if one were to ask what Okinawa represented for Shimao, the answer would be "the healing power of the southern islands."[99] Bereft of a locale that could evoke in him feelings of nostalgia, Shimao creates an image of an unchanging Ryukyus that serves to fill this particular void.

Considering the striking similarities between the discourse of Shimao and that of an earlier Ryukyuan "discoverer," Yanagita Kunio, it is puzzling why Yanagita remains unmentioned in *Theory of Yaponesia* (save for a brief reference to his well-known theory of Japanese cultural transmission via a sea route (*kaijō no michi*) through Micronesia.[100] Both Shimao and Yanagita privilege the Ryukyus in their respective theories on the roots of Japan and the Japanese character. The southern islands become the object of both men's intense gaze, yet their writings on the region ultimately serve to fortify Japan proper. And, most importantly, Yanagita and Shimao both turn to the Ryukyus for therapeutic reasons.

Turning his attention to the Ryukyus in 1921, Yanagita Kunio traveled to Okinawa, recording observations of the language and customs of the islanders in his *Record of the South Seas* (*Kainan shoki*, 1925). Yanagita was struck by what he perceived to be remnants of archaic linguistic and cultural forms, but what makes the findings of Yanagita and scholars of Okinawan Studies, particularly Iha Fuyū, problematic, is their persistent emphasis on commonalities with mainland Japan. Writing on Yanagita's memoirs of his journey through southern Japan, Alan Christy notes that as Yanagita went from Kyushu to Amami Ōshima and on to Okinawa, Miyako, and Yaeyama, references to the present vanish only to be replaced with a morbid fascination with an ancient past:

> In particular, Yanagita's tale of his trip is littered with the narrative bodies of the dead, as if to highlight a potential danger in the trip, as well as to suggest a descent into the past (the land of the dead). By the time he has reached the southern end of his journey, he has not only covered great distance, but also great time. Time itself has collapsed for

the people in the Yaeyama islands (in Yanagita's rendition) so that they "are just now beginning to forget what we forgot long ago."[101]

In an eerily similar passage of "The Root of Yaponesia," written forty years after Yanagita's travelogue, Shimao comments on how, in the "rhythm" of life in Amami Ōshima, defined by the melody of folk songs, the carriage of the islanders' bodies when dancing, their way of greeting, and their enunciation, he senses a certain drunkenness which completely intoxicates him.[102] Interestingly, he claims this rhythm is not that of a foreign land. Rather, it is what is difficult to detect any longer in the mainland—a rhythm that responds to and connects to distant memories.[103] What might be taken as evidence of a heterogeneous culture is dismissed as the ghostly shadows of Japan's past.

In addition to the fact that both Yanagita and Shimao waxed nostalgic when confronted with Ryukyuan culture, the two men share the same motive for turning their attention southward. Murai Osamu claims that Yanagita's discovery of the southern islands in the Taishō period was a direct result of the unease he felt about his involvement in the drafting of colonial policies on agriculture in Korea where he served as a bureaucrat in the Ministry of Agriculture. Murai writes convincingly of Yanagita's longing for therapeutic relief from the distress of his involvement in the Korean affair. Resigning his governmental post in 1919, Yanagita quickly retreated to the Ryukyus, concealing his past by rapidly absorbing himself in southern manners. Murai's repeated references to Yanagita's therapeutic use of the southern islands are echoed in Shimao critics who cite the curative properties of the Ryukyus as the basis for the author's desire.[104] Yanagita, in his search for elements of tradition in the southern islands that would explain Japanese character, forsook historical specificity, emphasizing only shared customs and habits. This ideological exercise could only help bolster the steadily growing Japanese empire. Ōshiro Tatsuhiro has suggested that decades later, when Shimao changed his original conception of the Ryukyus from the "tail" (*shippo*) to the "root" (*nekko*) of Japan, he was engaged in a similar imperialistic maneuver.[105]

In 1970, Shimao published the final installment of *Theory of Yaponesia* in which he expresses his fear of Okinawa's impending return to Japan. The final essay begins by describing the fate of Amami Ōshima, an island whose citizenry unanimously decided to return to Japan in 1953, nearly twenty years earlier than Okinawa would. Shimao writes of how administrative changes led to a rise in uniformly constructed, modern schools and governmental buildings throughout the island, as interchangeable as blocks of tofu.[106] Traditional thatched roof houses were gradually replaced with zinc and concrete.[107] It comes as no surprise that despite these outward changes, Shimao believed the essence of the islanders remained unchanged.[108]

Shimao's unease with Okinawa's reversion to Japan is clear by the conclusion of *Theory of Yaponesia*. In the remaining passages of the series' concluding essay, Shimao describes in painful detail three items indigenous to the Ryukyus: the samisen, pongee, and the indigenous viper (*habu*). The attention paid to these objects, so exotic and clichéd, is remarkable given the way Shimao began his discussion of Yaponesia. In the series' first essay, Shimao insists that the objects one sees at an exhibition of Okinawan products have little do with the reality of Okinawa, yet, at the end of *Theory of Yaponesia*, Shimao valorizes precisely the type of products he earlier claimed possessed no meaning. In fact, Shimao fetishizes the deadly viper, the indigo-dyed pongee, and the plaintive-sounding samisen just as he has obsessively clung to an image of the Ryukyus of his own making. The products Shimao sets up for display, in the manner of countless Okinawan tourist shopkeepers, are as meaningless as his vision of an unchanging Ryukyus. Shimao's longing to be part of the community he describes is as obvious as is his awareness of the impossibility of penetrating the walls of the museum he has himself created.

Shimao's profound despair over the state of modern Japanese society is what fuels his reluctance to allow Okinawa to step forward into an uncertain future. The haunting final words of *Theory of Yaponesia* underscore Shimao's intense longing for the islands to remain frozen in time. They also remind readers of the author's signature emotion, alienation:

> As I expected, isolated islands are lonely places. There are so many contradictions, matters of discord, and sorrowful conditions. Nevertheless, I cannot suppress my penchant for the islands of the Ryukyu arc. Because I am an outsider who possesses no native abilities, I am unable to use the local dialect or pass myself off as an islander. Even if I am faced with enmity, I wish to stay still firmly embracing the coral reef of the islands.[109]

Theory of Yaponesia is a travel narrative that recycles old stereotypes rather than denaturalizing them.[110] Shimao's repetition of hackneyed ideas such as the gentleness of island culture, the outward kindness and inward volatility of islanders, and the slowed-down time of the islands conceals the multifaceted reality of the Ryukyus.[111] It may seem insensitive to critique *Theory of Yaponesia* for Shimao's twenty-year-long stint of essay-writing represents an embarrassment of riches when one considers the lack of attention paid to the Ryukyus by scholars of mainland Japan. However, Shimao's vision of the southern islands remains, in the end, a libidinal illusion that robs the Ryukyus of a most certain existence.

I have shown that both Ōshiro and Shimao, each in his own way, create a mythic Okinawa. Though Ōshiro considers the islands from a number of viewpoints, often in the guise of characters that stand in for ideas he wishes to explore, it is the ineffable spiritual world, rooted in the culture of the islands, which reigns supreme in his works. Given the patent suppression of Okinawan culture in the prewar period, the privileging of culture evident in

Ōshiro's works is certainly not unwelcome, yet, when considering his fiction as a whole and together with Shimao's own romantic musings on southern island culture, one sees in both authors a desire to appropriate culture for particular ends. Ōshiro's career-long focus on the local moves so quickly to universal truths, one wonders which end of the spectrum is more important: local or universal? Shimao's obsession with island culture stems from a wish to reorient the Ryukyus away from subservience to the continent and toward other islands in the Pacific. The tropes he uses to describe culture, however, belie his original intention. Moreover, with the passage of time, his essays take on a more conservative tone. Despite these shortcomings, the energy that Ōshiro and Shimao pour into their writings on culture make them required reading for understanding how culture remains one of the fundamental bases for identity in Okinawa.

5 Postreversion fiction and Medoruma Shun

Immediately after Japan signed the San Francisco Peace Treaty in 1951 to conclude the American occupation of its country, Okinawans began to petition en masse for a reversion to Japanese sovereignty. The day that the treaty was signed is referred to as the "Day of Shame" by Okinawans, for, as John Dower has explained, "both the Japanese government and Imperial Household were willing from an early date to trade away true sovereignty for Okinawa in exchange for an early end to the Occupation in the rest of Japan."[1] The reversion movement in the 1950s and 1960s was extremely popular, with greater than 70 percent of the Okinawan electorate supporting a reunification with Japan. Protests mounted against the protracted occupation in Okinawa during the Vietnam War when the island served as a strategic staging ground. Calls for reversion became more strident in Okinawa, and great numbers of mainland Japanese, including public intellectuals such as Ōe Kenzaburō, who opposed the conflict in Vietnam, rallied in support of the reversion movement. In December 1969, Prime Minister Satō Eisaku and President Richard Nixon agreed to Okinawa's return to Japanese prefectural status, which took place, at last, on May 15, 1972.

While Okinawa did gain its long-sought prefectural status, its citizens' expectations for base closures, the departure of the American military, and new social and economic opportunities were not met. Japanese Diet deliberations that took place in 1971 over Okinawa's reversion betrayed the hopes of many Okinawans, for they revealed a Japan–US collusion to continue indefinitely the operation of American military bases. Legislation passed despite firecrackers set off by the Okinawa Youth League to protest the intractability of the US military and their own exclusion from policy-making.

Following reversion, the Japanese government established an agency for the development of the prefecture and poured in financial aid through the Okinawa Promotion and Development Plan. These measures sought to redress the economic gap between Okinawa, Japan's poorest prefecture, and the rest of the country, but the infusion of mainland capital has had unwonted effects. Julia Yonetani states that financial incentives have been utilized in Okinawa "as a means to placate opposition to U.S. military policy and the forced expropriation of private land for military use since the era of the U.S.

occupation."[2] As well, Japanese development in the decades since reversion has destroyed further the natural environment, already marred by unsightly military bases. The spiritual life of the people, impacted no less than the environment, suffers when, for example, taboos against cutting down sacred groves are disregarded by mainland construction companies whose cranes fell forests and clear communal lands.

In 1973, Shima Tsuyoshi's "Bones" won the first annual *Ryukyu News* Short Story Prize for its sobering view of the leveling of culture wrought by massive construction projects contracted on land in Okinawa where indigenous flora and fauna once thrived:

> Long, long ago the area had been covered in trees, and many tales had been told about the ghosts who resided in the dark, densely wooded area hills. But that was until the war. The heavy naval bombardment from offshore had leveled the *akagi* forests down to the last tree. And then came the postwar expansion of the city that had altered the way the land looked down below once and for all. It was as though the whole area had been painted over in colors that gave it a bright, gaudy look. The denuded slope was like a half peeled papaya. The top had been lopped off, and from there to the road a quarter of the way down the hill, the red clay was exposed to the elements. According to the notice posted at the construction site, the hilltop was slated to become the site of a twenty-story luxury hotel.[3]

Published just one year after reversion, this haunting work foretells the heavy environmental and social cost that attends the construction boom in Okinawa.

As discussed in the previous chapter, Ōshiro Tatsuhiro remained the dominant writer in Okinawa through the 1950s and 1960s, but in 1972, the year of Okinawa's reversion, Ōshiro's preeminence gave way when critics in Tokyo awarded the prefecture's second Akutagawa Prize to Higashi Mineo for his novella *Child of Okinawa* (*Okinawa no shōnen*), an event that heralded the arrival of a younger group of writers. Higashi's *Child of Okinawa*, set in the early 1950s, is a narrative of the sexual awakening of a young boy named Tsuneyoshi who lives in Koza, a hybrid town on the fringe of Kadena Air Base. Michael Molasky writes that the story "represents Tsuneyoshi's futile search for purity amidst the degradation of everyday life in Koza." In this sense it is akin to "Bones," which similarly juxtaposes an ideal state (a pristine Ryukyuan past in which traditions flourished as did indigenous flora) with grim reality (razed landscapes).[4]

Molasky astutely notes that the movement of Tsuneyoshi's family across space, from Saipan, to Misato, and the larger city of Koza, suggests an allegorical journey through history, with Saipan corresponding to Ryukyu, Misato representing prewar Okinawa, and condom-littered Koza signifying occupied Okinawa.[5] Upward mobility results only in estrangement and alienation for Tsuneyoshi who can no longer endure the sexploitation inherent in the modern capitalism represented by the ubiquitous brothels in Koza. Given that the novella's publication occurred on the eve of Okinawa's return to Japan, when it was common knowledge that military installations would remain undiminished, Tsuneyoshi's escape by boat from Okinawa at the story's end may well suggest the Okinawan population's disenchantment with the unchanging military presence in Okinawa even in the wake of reversion.

While it is difficult to deny that Higashi's work was awarded the Akutagawa Prize precisely because Okinawa was the object of intense media attention during the reversion movement, *Child of Okinawa* is nevertheless important both for its realistic description of occupied Okinawa and for the author's creative use of dialect.[6] While Ōshiro Tatsuhiro's "Turtleback Tombs" pioneered in incorporating an artificial dialect fashioned for the work, Higashi treads further in his use of dialect by employing it more fluidly than did Ōshiro in both the dialogue and descriptive passages of the novella.

The timing of Higashi's work and the recognition it received place *Child of Okinawa* at the head of a stream of writing in Okinawa's postreversion period that differs markedly from fiction written in the early postwar years. Just as every succeeding generation battles with its predecessors, or in the case of postwar Okinawan literature—predecessor—younger writers strive consciously to distinguish themselves from Ōshiro Tatsuhiro. While Ōshiro is certainly prolific and a central force in postwar Okinawan letters, the mythic world Ōshiro constructs lacks flesh and blood characters. An important difference between postwar Okinawan fiction, represented by Ōshiro, and postreversion writing is the attention later authors pay to creating characters from the inside out, rather than the kind of stock characters that stood for issues and ideas Ōshiro wished to interrogate.

An inward turn

One of the first literary voices to emerge in the postreversion era was that of Matayoshi Eiki, noted for early stories such as "The Wild Boar that George Shot" ("Jōji ga shasatsu shita inoshishi," 1978) and "The Ginnemu Mansion" ("Ginnemu yashiki," 1980) and lionized for his 1996 novella *Pig's Revenge* (*Buta no mukui*), which was awarded an Akutagawa Prize twenty-five years after that won by Higashi Mineo. Once again, politics bled into literature as Matayoshi, Okinawa's third Akutagawa Prize recipient, became nationally recognized only after the 1995 Okinawan schoolgirl rape by American servicemen, even though for over a decade he had been commanding the attention of critics for the unique perspective he injected into his stories of Okinawa. In "The Wild Boar," Matayoshi depicts the growing mental instability of an otherwise good-natured American soldier whose departure for the war in Vietnam is imminent. The story depicts in vivid prose the violence of American soldiers in Okinawa during the Vietnam

War and paints George, the work's rather timid protagonist, in a sympathetic light despite the fact that by killing an elderly Okinawan man hunting for scrap metal in the thick of night—all the while telling himself that he was shooting a boar—George exhibits the same capacity for violence as the aggressive American soldiers Matayoshi describes in the work. Based on an incident that took place in Okinawa in December 1960 when an American soldier shot and killed an Okinawan farmer, only later to claim that his target was a wild boar, Matayoshi boldly elects to narrate the tragic event through the eyes of a young American. As Molasky explains, the story "thus begins to break down the stereotypical image of the distant and invincible occupier, and by doing so it stakes out a new, confident stance toward the United States—a stance that may only have been possible after America's humiliating withdrawal from Vietnam."[7] Two years later, Matayoshi published "The Ginnemu Mansion," also distinctive for its depiction of Okinawans' discrimination toward Koreans.

Matayoshi's early short stories and *Pig's Revenge*, the novella for which he gained national attention in 1996, differ radically from a signature work by Ōshiro Tatsuhiro in that the narratives focus on the inner lives of their characters rather than contentious issues that lie beneath the surface of the texts. Had Ōshiro authored these works by Matayoshi, surely his interest would have been in the social issues of crimes perpetrated by US soldiers against Okinawan civilians (in the case of "The Wild Boar") internal discrimination (in "Ginnemu Mansion") and folk customs (in *Pig's Revenge*). The last-named is a light-hearted work that portrays the adventure its college-student protagonist, Shōkichi, takes with three bar hostesses to an offshore island where Shōkichi tends to the bones of his deceased father. Rather than dwell on these weighty but ultimately secondary ideas, Matayoshi chooses to delineate the mindscapes of his male protagonists in the early stories and the psychology of the female hostesses in *Pig's Revenge*.[8]

In addition to the fact that politics dominated literature in the reversion years, resulting in a faithful—if skewed—representation of reality in the works of Okinawans, the prefecture's geographical remove from the mainland resulted in a shortage of Okinawan stories published in central journals. The fact that those living in Okinawa required a passport for travel to Japan during the American occupation not only meant reduced educational opportunities (Okinawans applying for admission to mainland universities often missed deadlines owing to the time involved in procuring necessary travel documents), but the aspiration of writers could also be thwarted by onerous restrictions that prevented them from traveling to Tokyo with ease in search of literary patrons.

As in other remote regions, venues for publication are critical in Okinawa where there are few commercial publishers. Thus, the establishment of three major literary prizes in the 1970s was a great stimulus to aspiring writers in the prefecture. Okinawa's major local newspapers, *Ryukyu News* and *Okinawa Times* created two of these three prizes. In 1973, to commemorate its eightieth anniversary, *Ryukyu News* began awarding a prize (*Ryukyu shinpō tanpen shōsetsu shō,* or *Ryūtanshō*) for the best short story of the year. And, in 1975, *Okinawa Times* inaugurated an annual literary prize (*Shin Okinawa bungaku shō,* or *ShinOkishō*) to celebrate the thirtieth issue of its comprehensive arts journal *New Okinawa Literature* (*Shin Okinawa bungaku*), founded in 1966. In 1976, a third important prize emerged out of the Kyushu Okinawa Literature Prize begun in 1970 by the Kyushu Culture Association and the Kyushu Education Committee. This award was later renamed the Kyushu Art Festival Literary Prize (*Kyūshū geijutsusai bungakushō*). A common trajectory for successful writers from Okinawa is to win one or both of the local newspaper prizes, then the Kyushu regional prize, and for the very best, a national prize such as the Akutagawa. Medoruma Shun, Okinawa's leading writer of fiction, is a case in point. Literary output during the twenty-seven-year occupation of Okinawa tended to be political in nature, owing to inequalities in power between Okinawans and American forces. In an overview of occupation period literature, Medoruma Shun offers a host of reasons for the paucity of fiction from Okinawa beginning with Okinawa's late modernization and continuing with the devastation of the Battle of Okinawa and a protracted occupation characterized by censorship, the suppression of free speech, and the fostering of a cultural policy of Ryukyu–American "friendship."[9] The political frenzy and chaos surrounding Okinawa's reversion created a further vacuum as few literary works were published. While the 1970s is best represented by stories imbued with politics such as "The Wild Boar," set in occupied Okinawa during the Vietnam War, writing in the 1980s reflected newer subjective tendencies, also discernable in Matayoshi's early works.

After a general lull in the reversion period, when Ōshiro Tatsuhiro fell silent, Okinawa saw a surge in writing by women. For the first time in the history of fiction writing in the prefecture, several female authors were recognized for their talents, typically receiving one of the new literary prizes.[10] In Okinawa where most writers were otherwise employed full-time, producing fiction only as time allowed, women authors were particularly scarce in the pre-and postwar eras. The proliferation of female authors, as reflected in the number of women who received literary prizes since the mid-1970s, correlates to the lessening of an economic gap between Okinawa and other prefectures in Japan and the attendant increase in leisure time. Though a rise in writing by women is indisputable, most female authors (and plenty of males as well) have been one-hit wonders and have not enjoyed enduring success.

Given the dearth of fiction produced by women before reversion, the profusion of female writers that emerged from the mid-1970s is conspicuous. Relative to earlier periods, there was an undeniable boom in writing by women. Not all critics were necessarily pleased with the fiction that resulted, however. For example, Saegusa Kazuko, a noted mainland author who served on the selection committee for the Okinawa Literature Prize for nearly a decade before being replaced by Kōno Taeko in 2000, laments that her own high expectations for writing by women in Okinawa were betrayed during her tenure. Rather than finding women as subjects of writing, what she discovered, more often than not, was women as objects.[11]

Yonaha Keiko describes male author Nagadō Eikichi's fiction, typically set in Koza, as replete with prostitutes (*pan pan*s) and "honeys" who are derided for their profession but also cast in a sympathetic light through the author's portrayal of the women as victims sacrificed by economically distressed families.[12] Many stories in the years following reversion featured young women unmarried and pregnant or women unhappily married and taken in by their tough mothers who had survived the war. Initially, both male and female authors portrayed strong older women or women who served as pillars of communal life, but in the 1980s an increasing number of female authors published stories that featured single, divorced women. This no doubt reflected the high rate of divorce in Okinawa as well as the fact that divorce was less likely than in earlier decades to be perceived in negative terms.

Much of the fiction produced in the 1980s revealed the social engineering taking place in Okinawa to rectify the economic gap that existed between islanders and mainlanders. Works about the construction of the resort hotels that rim Okinawa illustrate the process undertaken by the Japanese government to align its newest prefecture with the mainland (*hondo namika*). Broadly speaking, fiction from the 1980s and 1990s was less likely to be about the war or the presence of the military bases, well-worn themes of the occupation period, than about a narrowing of the distance that separated Okinawa from other parts of Japan. Although the leveling of economic disparity was a desired goal of the populace, the sudden onslaught of capital from the mainland that effected this change may also have occasioned a resurgence of themes connected to indigenous culture, such as shamanism and ancestor worship. Ōshiro Tatsuhiro, who had written in this vein in the postwar period, wrote still more on the topic, along with younger writers such as Matayoshi Eiki, celebrated for his portrayal of folk culture in *Pig's Revenge*, and Ikegami Ei'ichi, a Saitama-based Okinawan writer whose 1994 novel, *Tale of Bagā Island* (*Bagājima panasu*), a local-color novel about folk beliefs, received the Grand Prize for Japanese Fantasy Novels. It is no small irony that indigenous culture became the purview of literature precisely when salient features of island life such as its distinct dialects, folk customs, and *dugong* were rapidly vanishing.[13]

There was a striking reversal in perceptions of the state of literature from Okinawa between the 1960s, just before Ōshiro Tatsuhiro's rise to national fame, and the mid-1990s when Okinawan literature experienced a boom. In April 1966, the inaugural issue of *New Okinawa Literature* posed as its theme the troubling question, "Is Okinawa a literary wasteland?" (*Okinawa wa bungaku fumō no chi ka*). Bemoaning the stagnation of fiction in the late 1950s and early 1960s, the founders of *New Okinawa Literature* hoped to stimulate aspiring writers into production through the new venue of their journal. The fourth issue, in which Ōshiro's novella, *The Cocktail Party* appeared, realized the founders' hopes. In 1967, as Okinawa's first recipient of the Akutagawa Prize, Ōshiro served instantly to inspire others in the prefecture. Soon the characterization of Okinawa as a literary wasteland was relegated to the past.

In contrast to the concerns raised about Okinawan literature in *New Okinawa Literature* in the 1960s, the success of Okinawan writers in the 1990s, particularly in the later years of the decade, prompted critics to proclaim that Okinawan literature was very much alive. Okamoto Keitoku cites four reasons for this positive assessment. He first mentions the significance of the Akutagawa Prize Matayoshi Eiki received in 1996, a quarter of a century after Higashi's award in 1971. Not only did a prolonged drought come to an end, but also national attention shifted away from the horrors of the schoolgirl rape to *Pig's Revenge*, a novella whose rather familiar theme of indigenous Okinawan folk culture Matayoshi revived. This he accomplished through a stock of vibrant, young characters who lighten the weight of traditional culture by engaging with it in idiosyncratic ways. In 1999, a film version of the novella, *Pig's Revenge*, directed by the Korean-Japanese film director Sai Yōichi appeared, furthering the work's public appeal.

Second, a symposium held in Naha in December 1996 generated scholarly and community interest in the subject of Okinawan literature. Titled *The Okinawa Literary Forum: From the Local to the Global—Okinawan Literature in the Age of Multiculturalism*, the two-day event was the brainchild of Ōshiro Tatsuhiro who had been alarmed at the sluggish state of literary activity in Okinawa during the years preceding the forum. Ihab Hassan, a professor of English from the University of Wisconsin specializing in postmodern literature and John Montague, an Irish poet, served as keynote speakers. The panel discussion and workshop, both devoted to the meaning of writing in Okinawa, brought together scholars, writers, and editors. These included Matayoshi Eiki, Ikezawa Natsuki, and Hino Keizō, writers and critics from Okinawa and the mainland. While the motivation for the symposium was to stimulate interest in Okinawan literature, more significant was the organizers' efforts to situate Okinawan fiction in a global framework. Hassan's work on postmodern literature and Montague's focus on global regionalism, together with discussion by vanguard Japanese writers succeeded in freeing Okinawan fiction from isolation, and curbed the tendency of many readers to essentialize writing from the region.[14]

The final reasons that Okamoto offers for the restored health of Okinawan literature witnessed in the 1990s relate to the growing recognition of younger writers by mainland critics. That Medoruma Shun won an Akutagawa Prize in 1997 on the heels of Matayoshi's award the previous year was an unprecedented success for Okinawa. Hino Keizō, a selection committee judge, acknowledged that many people would invariably ask, "Okinawa, again?" were Medoruma to receive the prize, but he nevertheless gave the author a hearty endorsement, as did several other judges, resulting in Medoruma's clinching the award.[15] While Medoruma is the Okinawan writer who presently commands the greatest critical attention, at least two others have produced work that places them in the ranks of Medoruma: Matayoshi Eiki and Sakiyama Tami. Sakiyama, the author most often paired with Medoruma, has written fiction steadily since the 1980s. In 1988 she won the Kyushu Arts Festival Literary Prize for her story, "Passage across the Sea" (*Suijō ōkan*), a work subsequently nominated for an Akutagawa Prize. Without question, Medoruma and Sakiyama are the prefecture's leading contemporary writers; their achievements and the efforts that Ōshiro expended in organizing the 1996 *Okinawa Literary Forum* have successfully spurred others onward, producing a critical mass.[16]

Given the dominance of Medoruma Shun, whom critic So Kyonshiku refers to as "Okinawa's Lu Xun," a close examination of his major works to date is in order. Not only does he best represent postreversion Okinawan literature, but his departure from the conventions of his predecessors also requires some reconsideration of the genre itself. If Medoruma is as unique as critics claim, is his place in Okinawan letters then not tenuous? Because he is a contemporary writer with a potentially long career ahead of him, only time will tell; however, as with other authors represented in this study, I analyze his major works bearing in mind what ties him to the genre of Okinawan fiction.

Medoruma Shun: language, memory, and degrees of realism

Medoruma Shun, a prominent Okinawan intellectual, was not widely known outside the prefecture until 1997 when he won the prestigious Akutagawa Prize. The recipient of several regional literary prizes since the early 1980s, Medoruma was born in Nakijin, a northern Okinawan town steeped in history. Located on Motobu peninsula, which juts northeasterly off the coast of the East China Sea, Nakijin abounds in various crops such as sugar cane, watermelon, leaf tobacco, greens, and, as Medoruma writes about in "Chronicle of a School of Fish" ("Gyogunki," 1984), pineapple. In Okinawa's three-mountain (*sanzan*) period, Nakijin was the residence of the Hokuzan king. Remains of the town's castle, awash every January in Japan's earliest-blooming cherry trees, demarcate what was once the center of the culture and economy of northern Okinawa. Geographically removed from Okinawa's capital city Naha, Nakijin was a world apart from the life Medoruma would live in the south where he studied literature at the University of the Ryukyus, under the tutelage of Okamoto Keitoku and Nakahodo Masanori.

The language of Medoruma's childhood and that of his entry into the adult world of the university are distinct and separable. Reminiscing on his grammar-school days, Medoruma relates that in 1969 he was ordered by his teacher not to use the local dialect. Instead, he was encouraged to replace a good part of his daily speech with standard equivalents. The memory of his teacher's strictness, the otherworldliness of the replacement phrases—common enough in such media as television or manga but not in Medoruma's everyday speech—left him suffused with shame. The self-loathing Medoruma experienced as a result of adhering to his teacher's commandment led him, perversely, to refrain from using standard language from the time of the incident to the point that he entered university.[17]

In an essay on Okinawa's peculiar linguistic quandary, published a year after he received the Akutagawa Prize, Medoruma notes that, from the mid-1980s onward, the boom in things Okinawan, striking to mainlanders and islanders alike, began with amateur theatre productions. One in particular was a 1986 production by the troupe Gekidan Sōzō.[18] What stays in Medoruma's mind long after the curtains went down on this particular performance was how playwright Chinen Seishin, noted author of the 1976 script *House of Peoples*, made conscious use of three types of language: local dialect, standard Japanese, and a hybrid of the two. Medoruma speculates that the rapidly changing face of Okinawa, postreversion, is the reason that dialect, suppressed in the prewar by state authorities keen on bringing Okinawa into the national fold and in the occupation period by local schoolteachers who advocated reversion, reemerged anachronistically in society.

In tandem with local theatre productions, Okinawan dialect captured the nation's and islands' imagination through the publication of the best-selling *Okinawa Keyword Column Book*; comedy groups that appeared regularly on television as well as stage; film director Takamine Go's dialect-rich movies *Paradise Views* (1985) and *Untamagiru* (1989);[19] the enduring success of older musicians such as Kina Shōkichi, who had emerged in the 1970s; and newer musical groups such as Rinken Band[20] and the Nenes. Further, on the literary front, from the mid-1980s, young writers from Okinawa began to publish their fiction in several mainland literary journals (i.e., *Kaien*, *Bungakukai*, *Subaru*, and *Shinchō*) and garnered literary prizes in rapid succession.[21]

As the proliferation of dialect in multiple forms of media in the 1980s shows, Medoruma's attentiveness to language, particularly the endangered dialects of the Ryukyus, is far from anomalous. "Unchanging dialect, changing Okinawa," he writes wistfully, though surely his is a romanticized view of local language as pristine and ideal, a stark contrast to the injurious effects of twentieth-century modernization on cultural formations.[22] Despite Medoruma's obvious penchant for dialect, which he has regularly used since his debut piece, "Chronicle of a School of Fish," his earlier works have a smaller percentage of glosses to supply the meaning of words in dialect than do his recent stories, a fact Michael Molasky attributes to the growth of Medoruma's readership beyond the reefs of Okinawa.[23]

For a decade or so after graduating with a degree in Japanese literature Medoruma took a number of jobs. At age thirty-four, a year shy of the deadline to do so, he applied for teaching credentials. Since receiving his teaching certificate, Medoruma has taught in various high schools in the prefecture. Thus, like his predecessors, Medoruma has worked full-time while pursuing his writing. Unlike most aspiring writers, however, for well over a decade, Medoruma has, to the best of his ability, consciously chosen to remove himself from local literary circles in a sincere effort to instill discipline into his life as a writer. Eschewing not only literary events, but even casual conversations about literature, Medoruma craves a "degree of severity" he believes will bolster his craft and keep it from getting soft.[24] The Henoko heliport controversy, in which residents in the northern city of Nago were made to choose between accepting an unwanted military installation in its jurisdiction or losing a huge incentive package, forced Medoruma out of hiding when he took a teaching position in Nago. However, his subsequent public appearances relate strictly to his concern for local politics and the rights of Okinawans rather than literary matters. Indeed, it is his disciplined nature that has kept Medoruma out of the limelight and from retracting his stated wish *not* to be categorized as a writer of Okinawan literature.[25] Baffling as Medoruma's position is, he has elected to distance himself from other authors in Okinawa and appears to view his writing separate from the genre of Okinawan fiction, even as he continues to produce work that clearly demonstrates deep ties to the island and (unwanted) connections to fellow Okinawan writers. Distant as he is from literary circles, in the last decade, Medoruma has become Okinawa's most commanding public intellectual by publishing hundreds of newspaper and magazine columns that address Okinawan issues.

Critics have cited a host of reasons for Medoruma's distinction among contemporary writers, from a literary style that "fuses earthiness with refinement, and brooding intensity with a gentle humor," to his continual experiments in narrative technique, and finally to what is surely the crux of Medoruma's success—the passion with which he assumes the role of writer of fiction and public intellectual.[26] Like fellow authors such as Ōe Kenzaburō and Nakagami Kenji who preceded Medoruma in their performance of similar dual roles in Japanese society, what best characterizes Medoruma is the doubling of his pen as a sword. This doubling explains why reading Medoruma's fiction can be such an exhausting endeavor.[27] It is not just that unfamiliar words impede the (mainland) reader; the cumulative weight of Medoruma's thorough probing of the psychology of his characters, his knack for guileless storytelling leavened with issues of contemporary concern, and the linguistic discord reflected in his writing all contribute to making his fiction serious reading despite the pleasures it affords and its contemporary appeal. What follows are analyses of Medoruma's most important works from his literary debut, "Chronicle of a School of Fish," to his recent novel, *Tree of Butterflies*. As well as discussing each work in relation to the genre of Okinawan fiction, I will examine the ways in which Medoruma transgresses generic boundaries.

"Chronicle of a School of Fish"

Medoruma first attracted public attention by winning the eleventh annual *Ryukyu News* Short Story Prize for "Chronicle of a School of Fish," published in 1984. This debut story contains several elements that recur in Medoruma's later works: rich metaphorical prose, an unmistakable social conscience, a concern for history and memory, and, last but not least, sex and violence. Rather than themes common to the genre, such as antimainland sentiment or the tragedy of the war, what emerges most clearly in the piece is the young protagonist Masashi's sexual awakening, a motif Higashi Mineo explored in *Child of Okinawa* a decade earlier.

The story is set in a northern farming village. Politics surface in the work but remain muted. A reader engrossed in Medoruma's finer depictions of Masashi's fantasies of sex and violence might overlook the comparatively prosaic fact that the story takes place during the reversion movement. Brief but significant references are made to the 1970 Koza riot, a rare show of violence by Okinawans toward American occupiers, and to the political involvement of Masashi's elder brother, a cannery employee who rouses others to join him in the fight for reversion. By electing to focus the narrative on a young boy, however, Medoruma is able to depict tensions among individuals without being heavy-handed. Had he instead chosen the elder son for his protagonist, the young man's strong political motivations might have robbed the story of its pleasing ambiguity. On Masashi's lack of awareness, the narrator states:

> My brother supported the reversion movement, and he was always getting into arguments about this with my father. Dad, who grew pineapple on a plot cleared from a narrow mountain, kept saying that if Okinawa returned to Japan he'd be forced to sell cheaply to mainlanders. When I heard that, I felt a vague sense of unease, but I couldn't really understand much more.[28]

Coupled with his political confusion is Masashi's ill-defined sense of his own sexuality. As he plays with other boys among the reeds that line a riverbank, male intimacy is as much a part of Masashi's interactions as is contact with the more obvious object of his desire, a Taiwanese woman who works with Masashi's elder brother in the pineapple cannery. What stays in one's mind long after reading "Chronicle of a School of Fish" is how Medoruma overlays the eyes of the "Taiwan woman" with the fish of the story's title and his own, creating both a bridge between humans and the animal world and dense, textured prose. The story's opening passage places the reader squarely in the realm of memory, but, unlike the fragrance of madeleines that gives rise to Proust's imaginings, it is the tactile feel of the pupil of a fish that transports Masashi:

> Even now I can recall clearly that touch at my fingertip. The pupil of the fish showed a vivid change in color from blue to indigo, and then to black, in the perilous depths of its taut, transparent membrane. By merely gazing at that pupil, brimming with deep unease, I was thrown into unknown territory.

I pierced the pupil with the pointed tip of a needle, from an arrow released from my bow. Removing the needle from the eyeball of the leaping fish, I put my small fingertip above the slight open wound. The cool touch and firm resilience of the fish, full of life, stirred, at once, my excitement, sent a shiver through the fine hairs above the nerves concentrated at my fingertip, and at last gave way to a quiet rapture.[29]

As the story progresses, the description of the fish's pupil, provoking in Masashi fear laced with desire, is applied to the "Taiwan woman" and to Masashi, uniting the helpless fish, the woman, and the boy as victims.

The fish's falling prey to the pranks of adolescent boys who let out their frustration by spearing tilapia is the story's most obvious display of aggression toward the weak. The female seasonal laborer's ethnicity casts her in a negative light, which explains why Masashi's father castigates his son for his repeated efforts to peep at the woman in her shabby barracks outside the factory. Naturally, the disparagement the female laborer experiences by adults filters down to the boys' world, particularly in one scene in which all the boys but Masashi throw away the woman's gift to them of canned pineapple before her shamed eyes. Medoruma subtly imbricates the boys in the more complex world of adults, as when Masashi states: "We called her 'Taiwan woman.' There was an echo of contempt and vulgarity in this label. We soon caught wind of the words' connotation by listening to the conversation of adults, imitating them by using the term with abandon."[30] Despite the sexual appeal of the woman to the males around her, the fact that she is an object of discrimination as well as desire *and* an easily dispensable cog in the cannery makes her as tragic a victim as the fish Masashi targets. For his part, Masashi joins the cast of victims through his junior status in the family. Tensions between father and elder son result in frequent disputes, and Masashi in turn suffers the wrath of his elder brother.

The woman's place in the hierarchy, with Masashi's father at one extreme, and the tilapia at the other, is not fixed securely. While the description of victims above would lead one to place the woman just above the fish, and below Masashi, on top of which would come his brother and father, the female laborer is, as Medoruma reveals in a startling conclusion, the woman whom all males in the family sexually desire, despite her foreignness. Midway through the story, in one of Masashi's rebellious forays to the woman's lodgings, he pieces together that the shadows he spied while loitering "like a fish" outside the windows of the barracks were none other than those of the woman and his brother. When Masashi is subsequently discovered hiding, his brother beats him soundly. The story concludes with a far more surprising discovery, one that calls to mind the twisted family narratives of William Faulkner or Nakagami Kenji.[31] Once again hoping for a taste of fruit forbidden to him, Masashi returns to the woman's lodgings only to find her room empty. In a scene reminiscent of Tayama Katai's *The Quilt* (*Futon*, 1907) Masashi savors her lingering scent—sweat mingled with the smell of pineapple—before burying his face in the curtains, his mind filled with fantasies about the woman:

> Motioning as if I were putting my body on top of her phantom, I lay down on my stomach in the middle of the room and closed my eyes. The figure of the tilapia that had disappeared to the bottom of the river, its pupil pierced, floated in the darkness. With the sun glimmering on its profile, the tilapia undulated quietly. [...] The feel of the fish's eyeball was revived in my fingertip, and the woman's deep pupils overlapped with the pupil of the fish. Like the fish at the time it neared its death, I rocked my body, and convulsed repeatedly. Then I softly faded away into the darkness.[32]

This masturbatory episode ends when a familiar voice outside the door calls for the woman. Receiving no answer, the intruder leaves, but not before casting one lingering look backward to the barracks. In the bright light of day, Masashi identifies the profile he could not distinguish indoors. Though the narrator hints earlier about the father's probable involvement, Masashi's discovery that his own father, who had repeatedly warned him to stay away from the woman, was, like his brother, having sex with her. This reveals to him the hypocrisy of adults, and, perhaps too, the realization that his childhood is now behind him and that he will tread a path similar to the older men in his family.

The loss of childhood innocence and reluctant assumption of adult roles evident in "Chronicle of a School of Fish" is a theme common in modern Japanese literature, from Higuchi Ichiyō's 1895 story "Child's Play" ("Takekurabe") to Ōe Kenzaburō's 1958 story "The Catch" ("Shīku"). Of these two well-known works, Medoruma clearly owes a debt to Ōe for several reasons.[33] In addition to the unity in theme, "Chronicle of a School of Fish," like "The Catch," is set in a remote village. Indeed, just as Ōe's story takes place in his native home, the northern village in "Chronicle of a School of Fish" is likely modeled after Medoruma's hometown, Nakijin, where men like Masashi's father farm pineapple. The story's content makes for a juicier comparison. In "The Catch," the villagers are thrust violently into a war that had remained distant—before a black soldier lands in their midst, that is. The narrative, told from a child's perspective, as in "Chronicle of a School of Fish," relates how the presence of a foreigner evokes in the child a myriad of emotions, including fear, awe, and desire. The "Taiwan woman," disdained by adults and children alike for her otherness, cannot but sexually excite them. In particular it is her skin "as white as to seem translucent," that intoxicates Masashi when he loiters in the nearby riverbed. There he kills time by masturbating and spearing tilapia in hopes of catching sight of the beautiful foreign woman.

While one might also cite a parallel between Ōe's depiction of a mythic world of the mountain village untainted by forces of modernization in "The

Catch" and a similarly unscathed village in "Chronicle of a School of Fish"—where fathers like Masashi's rear their children to abide strictly by communal rules that disallow fraternization with foreign women in an attempt to keep intact the family unit, so integral to preserving traditions of society—Medoruma's fictive world invites no such comparison. What is most interesting about "Chronicle of a School of Fish" is Medoruma's departure from Ōshiro Tatsuhiro's pained efforts to represent in his fiction, Okinawan culture and tradition, wherein the mythic realm, or community, is a force more powerful than any individual. Despite multiple warnings by his father, beatings by his brother, and the constant threat of detection by the panoptic security guard who roams the factory grounds, Masashi time and again transgresses the rules of home and society that impinge on his burgeoning sexuality by visiting the very woman with whom his father and brother have had sexual relations.

Contrary to the fact that depictions of strong women, be they survivors of the war or divorced daughters, increased in the 1980s, as Yonaha Keiko notes, the least conspicuous character of "Chronicle of a School of Fish" is Masashi's mother. Even more passive than the dying tilapia Masashi stabs, she remains mute as her husband and sons vie for the "Taiwan woman," who, though deemed socially inferior, reigns supreme as she draws the males ever toward her. In important ways, then, Medoruma diverges from both the traditional mountain village Ōe paints and the customs and culture that Ōshiro infuses in his fiction. In doing so, like Masashi who stubbornly betrays the expectations of his community, Medoruma quietly dismantles both the family as a cohesive unit, and the genre of Okinawan fiction, as predictable and unvariegated.

"Walking Through a Street Called 'Peace'"

Politics, a mere backdrop in "Chronicle of a School of Fish," nearly overwhelms "Peace Street," Medoruma's rich 1986 story of the effects of then Crown Prince Akihito and Princess Michiko's 1983 visit to Okinawa to inaugurate a blood-donation campaign. In this work, Medoruma shifts from the first-person retrospective he adopted in his debut to a more complex, omniscient narrative style. The work is told through multiple points of view, with no single character figuring as protagonist. While the story revolves generally around one ordinary family's reaction to the imperial visit, a range of thoughts and emotions held by a host of individuals in Okinawan society also surface, illustrating well that the prefecture is characterized by diverse opinion and experience.

The working-class Okinawan family that Medoruma incongruously juxtaposes with the royal couple contains three generations in its five members: husband and wife, Masayoshi and Hatsu, son and daughter, Kaju and Sachi, and their grandmother Uta. Tensions rise in the home when a local policeman charged with "cleansing" the city in preparation for the Crown

Prince and Princess's visit repeatedly intrudes on the family to ensure that it prevents senile, incontinent Uta from wandering the streets.

The policeman warns Masayoshi that a visit to his boss will follow if he does not restrain Uta, and so the roving narrative offers a glimpse of the family's economic vulnerability: Masayoshi had started working at the port as a stevedore for the past six months. The small construction company where he worked before had gone bankrupt because of bad business conditions, leaving him to depend upon day labor for nearly three years. Then, through the introduction of a friend, he was allowed to work in the port on a regular basis, and, with the salary that Hatsu received from her part-time job at the supermarket, they managed to keep their family of five fed. But there was never a day that was free of the anxiety of knowing that sickness could end it all.[34] Medoruma fills the story with internal views of other mentally, physically, or economically weak characters, which effectively widens the gulf between the local Okinawan populace and the imperial family. Kaju, for instance, is denied a place on the fourth-grade baseball team because of his poor physical condition, placing him in similar straits as his underemployed father and mentally deficient grandmother.

Between the shining royal couple and the feeble family of five looms the threatening presence of the police officer whose duty it is to keep the family at a safe distance. The policeman's faded khaki safari jacket and aggressive behavior recall to Uta soldiers from the distant past. Through key flashbacks, a hallmark of Medoruma's style, the author reveals Uta as a survivor of the Battle of Okinawa in which several members of her family, including her husband and eldest son, died. Heavy police surveillance seems to have triggered in Uta memories of past losses incurred in a battle that killed one-third of the island's population. That the war acts as a backdrop to the contemporary campaign to collect (more) blood from Okinawa makes the work exceedingly ironic, as does the story's title, with its reference to a certain area named "Peace Street."[35]

Though Kuroko Kazuo discusses "Peace Street" as a clear example of antiemperor writing, largely suppressed in contemporary Japanese literature owing to the Japanese right's occasionally lethal practice of invoking the "chrysanthemum taboo," Medoruma's use of a roving narration with no dominant point of view blunts the force of the work's critique of the emperor system.[36] Fumi, a central character, introduced as a fish peddler from Itoman, is completely devoted to Uta for having defended her years ago from thugs whose territory she encroached upon while selling fish. She vociferously resists attempts to sanitize the island for the ceremonial visit. When the policeman threatens to shut Fumi down if she does not close up shop (to prevent the unlikely scenario of a mad person's grabbing a fish knife to attack the royal couple), Fumi perversely brandishes her knife at the officer, yelling, "Why the hell do I have to stop working just for *their highnesses?*"[37] She also refuses to accept flags a male acquaintance distributes to the neighborhood to use in greeting the royal couple, asking pointedly why he wishes her to wave flags and welcome the pair when his own beloved sister had died in battle as a student recruit. Fumi's bond to Uta is so complete that when her friend reveals, in the story's most poignant scene, the circumstances in which Uta's eldest son had died outside a cave that sheltered them during the fierce battle, Fumi feels Uta's intense grief over losing her son as her own. Because Uta is largely voiceless in the story, it is her younger, feistier friend who must speak for her.

Hailing from Itoman, an area well-known in Okinawa for its fiercely independent fisher people, Fumi does not hesitate to show her anger over the imperial visit and, by extension, the state and all it represents, but, as Medoruma writes, the modernization of Okinawa's economy and attendant change of values marginalized and rendered powerless traditional segments of society, including the street vendor and the small company. In their place stand the franchise and corporation, both indicative of the changes that mainland capital has wrought, yet neither of which can accommodate the castoffs of Okinawa's economic transformation. Peace Street, where Uta and Fumi were fixtures for decades, mutually supporting one another, as did others in the warren of tightly knit fish peddlers and vegetable hawkers, is described as follows:

> "It had changed here, too," Fumi murmured as she had countless times in the past, walking, as if pushing away the crowd on Peace Street with her large body. The street used to echo with the raucous, sallying voices of women who sold underwear, dried bonito, and used twill US military uniforms, piled up on wall panels that lay atop empty wooden boxes. Fumi used to feel thrilled just walking among the women. The street was still full of life, only now all she could hear was the soft voices of young, part-time girls, obscured by the blare of foreign music. A roof had been built, no longer offering Fumi the pleasure of helping elderly women hurriedly remove displayed clothes when it rained. The street, covered in garish color tiles, no longer seemed like a place she wanted to walk along. Fumi stood still in front of a big supermarket banner that screamed, "BARGAIN! SEAFOOD SALE!" Customers, moved inside the store's glass windows like fish in a water tank.
> "Welcome! How about some crab from Hokkaido?" called out a smiling, fair-skinned girl of junior high school age.
> "I'm a fish vendor from Itoman," muttered Fumi, laughing to herself in response. Suddenly she was struck with an unbearable sense of solitude and went back the way she'd come. Up until two years ago, the area, now occupied by the supermarket, was where the women, Uta included, had set up their stalls ever since the war ended. They lined up their small shops like a coral reef that protects itself by banding together against waves dashing toward them from outside.[38]

Despite the general neutrality of Medoruma's narration that veers from one subjectivity toward another in quick succession, this portrait of Fumi, a lone figure amidst a sea of change, shows the narrator's pained efforts to give life to a dying generation, if only in prose.

Tensions mounted, the royal pair arrives in Okinawa to much (orchestrated) fanfare, and soon embark on the so-called "Peace Trail"—a string of war memorials and monuments concentrated in Mabuni, south of Naha. Having made the requisite visits, the imperial procession winds through the streets of the capital, which houses the civic hall in which the blood drive takes place. Forcing her way out of the locked room, Uta cuts through the assembled crowd, where Kaju, who has also maneuvered through several police barricades, joins her. Like the grandmother/grandson pair that appears often in Japanese folklore, the two rail against malign forces—here the imperial cavalcade. Not knowing what else to do to avenge the pain the couple's visit causes his grandmother, Kaju spits at the faces of the Crown Prince and Princess as they pass by in their motorcade. For her part, Uta smears excrement on the windshield that stands between her and the couple. In this patently scatological, climactic moment, saliva and feces emitted from the lowly pair sully the right wing's attempt to maintain the myth of purity in which the emperor system is shrouded.

Lest the irony of the Crown Prince's visit to Okinawa somehow escape the reader, the narrator caps the scene with two linked but contesting descriptions. The first tells how Kaju upon returning home, wounds himself with the jagged edge of the latch installed to cage his grandmother. The blood he draws is a visible reminder of the pain his grandmother suffers on account of the imperial family. Though Kaju's youth prevents him from knowing the nature of the relationship between his grandmother and the royal family in political terms, he nevertheless intuits the suffering caused her and deliberately injures himself out of a deep attachment for her. In this sense, the act is a bloody transmission of memory between those who have lived through the war and those who have not, a divide that Medoruma mines in subsequent fiction. The passage that immediately follows that of Kaju's bloodletting contains the Crown Prince's actual speech to the Okinawan people. The Prince first praises the audience by noting that Okinawa was above the national average in blood donation, then expresses his respect for their efforts. Placed as it is near the conclusion of a gripping story of suffering borne by an Okinawan family during a national blood campaign launched in a time of putative peace, one is hard pressed not to take the Crown Prince's words literally. Surely, Medoruma has in mind here the excessive blood "given" to the nation by Okinawans in, if not following, 1945.

Uta and Kaju's victory against the royal family is as intense as it is brief. In the story's final scene, Kaju, unable to withstand Uta's confinement, steals out of her bolted room promising to take her to idyllic Yanbaru in the far north where she lived as a child. The two walk through Peace Street to catch a bus that takes them away from Naha, through the central areas of Kadena and Moon Beach, and finally to Nago, close to their destination. As the bus leaves Naha with its recent flurry of right-wing activities surrounding the royal visit, it heads toward another vista that calls to mind civilian oppression: US military bases. In a work heavily laced with antiemperor/nation-state sentiment, this brief glimpse of the American presence seems incongruous unless one interprets the scene as cementing the author's antiwar theme. In linking Japanese soldiers to American ones, the narrator broadens the scope of the work to include Japan and America as objects of critique. The bus journey may also be read in terms of Kaju's efforts to understand who he is and where he is going.

When a fly alights on Uta's mouth and her body feels cold to the touch despite the sun streaming in through the bus windows, Kaju realizes Uta has died en route. Without his grandmother's presence, Kaju does not know how to reach Yanbaru, a distant place to which he is connected by blood, not lived experience. The bus presses onward without Kaju able to comprehend his surroundings. Despite knowing that she cannot respond, he asks, "Grandma, are we in Yanbaru yet?"[39] Where is Kaju venturing alone? As he is wont to do, Medoruma leaves this question that contains within it, like a Russian nesting doll, the more pressing question of Okinawa's future direction, unanswered. The dazzling greenery of the bases encircled by barbed-wire fences covered in a profusion of indigenous flowers suggests no end to the relationship between the island and its foreign "guests." More importantly, though, the uncertainty of Kaju's lone journey signifies an uncertain future for the younger generation in Okinawa that is rapidly losing its (war-) experienced guides.

Fractious memories in "Droplets"

The publication of "Droplets" ("Suiteki," 1997) marked a turning point for both Medoruma and for Okinawan literature. Ironically, Medoruma, who had long distanced himself from literary circles, found himself in the glare of national attention following his receipt of the Akutagawa Prize. Moreover, the consecutive prizes Okinawa garnered in 1996 and 1997 led increasing number of Japanese scholars to reflect on the subject of Okinawan literature, a topic largely dealt with previously by scholars in Okinawa. The theme of war in Medoruma's stories was hardly new. As the sole Japanese prefecture that experienced extensive land combat in World War II, Okinawa had long provided writers with gripping material for narratives of war. "Turtleback Tombs," written by Ōshiro Tatsuhiro in 1966 is perhaps the benchmark by which subsequent narratives of the Battle of Okinawa are most often compared. A grim tale of one family's survival in a cramped ancestral tomb, "Turtleback Tombs" conforms to conventions of war narratives in both its realist fiction form and its weighty content. "Droplets" and its sequel "Spirit Recalling" ("Mabuigumi," 1999), on the other hand, are fresh twists on the representation of war in Okinawan literature. Though by their very nature the content of these stories makes them a solemn tribute to Okinawa, which suffered devastating losses in the battle, the innovative and occasionally irreverent method Medoruma adopts to tell his tales of the walking wounded rightly place him at the cutting edge of fiction-writing in Okinawa today.

For a writer born in 1960, well after the end of the war, the obsessive war motif in Medoruma's fiction, from "Sound of the Wind" ("Fūon," 1985) to "Rainbow Bird" ("Niji no tori," 2006) would indeed be curious were it not for the fact that Okinawa is awash with war memorials, war widows, and military bases, instilling in its residents a greater degree of historical awareness than in the main islands of Japan. Not only do visible reminders of the war remain but there is also the depth of the impact of the battle and Okinawa's continued subordination to Japan and the USA. In contrast to the vast majority of Okinawan battle narratives, which, as Nakahodo Masanori points out, were first penned by soldier participants, then ordinary citizens, and finally authors, and which dealt blow by blow with the events of the battle, Medoruma's war writing focuses on the residual effects the battle has had on those who survived it.[40] While Ōshiro, too, depicts the war's intrusion on a particular family in "Turtleback Tombs," his narrative remains ensconced in the typhoon of steel that pummeled the island in April 1945. The appeal of Medoruma's work lies in his ability to delineate the shadows that war casts upon contemporary Okinawa.

Beginning with the story's Kafkaesque opening, "Droplets" departs wholly from the previous tradition of war narratives in Okinawa. In this allegory of a man who awakens to find his leg swollen to the size of a gourd and whose big toe emits water that phantom soldiers come nightly to imbibe, Medoruma injects large doses of humor. Some of the sources of this humor are the author's use of local dialect in the speech of his country bumpkin protagonist Tokushō and other villagers, and his employment of a comedic subtheme featuring a rascally character, Seiyū, who hits on the idea of marketing the toe water for its Viagra-like properties. While some might fault Medoruma's use of humor and a magic-realist mode to write about war, it is this wildly imaginative aspect of Medoruma's fiction that has made him one of Japan's most promising authors.[41]

In his discussion of public memory and modern experience, Geoffrey Hartman writes that books are the main bearers of public memory while nonverbal arts such as painting and memorials serve as cultural reference points. These arts, neither unified nor bounded, influence personal identity. Hartman argues that at present "information sickness" has left the individual wading through a sea of media representations which cleave rather than bridge public and personal experiences. Certainly technology alone is not to blame for this desensitizing trend. The passage of time also diminishes the reality of traumatic experiences such as war. How does one keep memories of the past alive when they are in constant jeopardy from both iconic media reiterations (e.g., repeated clips of World Trade Center attacks) and natural weathering? In the reversion period, war discourse in Okinawa became systematized. In part this was to present to the mainland a unified

Figure 5 Book cover of "Droplets," Medoruma Shun's Akutagawa Prize-winning story.

face, that of loyal prewar subjects who were victims of war.[42] The quintessential icon of such suffering was the Himeyuri, or Maiden Lily Student Nurse Corps, a group of 219 female student recruits, nearly all of whom died in the crossfire between Japanese and American soldiers. The subject of several film and narrative depictions, the Himeyuri have instilled in the minds of Okinawans and mainland Japanese alike the idea of Okinawa as victim. As Linda Angst puts it, the symbol of the female student nurses became the canonical narrative of postwar Okinawan identity.[43]

So seductive is Medoruma's yarn of a farmer whose bizarre bodily transformation throws an unnamed yet vaguely familiar northern village into confusion that one is tempted throughout to read the work as a quaint folk tale. Chock full of symbols such as gourds, water, and flowers, the work seems to emerge organically out of Okinawan soil, to which critics, since the story's publication, have tried to attach their various readings.[44] "Droplets," they would argue, like countless Japanese folk stories before it, is an Okinawan-inflected cautionary tale of the ruin that befalls the individual who lacks moral compunction. That is, Tokushō's illness is, as his wife Ushi reminds him not once, but twice, his "comeuppance for tryin' to profit off people's sufferin' in the war."[45] As the narrative unfolds Medoruma connects—through ghosts that serve as a bridge between past and present, and lime in water spouting from the big toe of Tokushō's leg that is shaped like a gourd—the protagonist's present ailment to his suppression of war memory and the embellished versions of battle experience with which he regales schoolchildren during yearly commemorations of the war's end.

The Battle of Okinawa, Medoruma refuses to forget, has left the island with many war victims at pains to put on a cheery front, all the while dying inside. Midway through the story, as Tokushō begins to have flashbacks of his experience in the caves, the story's theme of war becomes fairly obvious. Telltale signs come earlier, in the first page: "Tokushō's right leg, which had already ballooned to the size of a medium-sized wax gourd, was moist whitish green, and his toes fanned out like the heads of a family of tiny snakes."[46] The relationship between gourds and war is a subtle one, lost on many readers unaware that in the immediate postwar period, enormous gourds proliferated, seemingly nurtured by soil enriched by the corpses of war dead. Another hint of an intermingling of past and present comes in the scene in which Dr. Ōshiro, the local physician, reports that the liquid taken from Tokushō's leg for laboratory examination is simply water with a trace of lime. As in the story's fantastic beginning, the properties of the water contain an element linked to wartime, namely lime from the many natural limestone caves that provided refuge for fleeing Okinawans as well as hideouts for Japanese troops during the Battle of Okinawa.

In a telling comment, Hino Keizō, one of the Akutagawa Prize committee judges, describes such passages as the story's final image of a dazzling hibiscus attached by a long vine to an enormous gourd as "Okinawan" (*Okinawa teki*).[47] Kuroi Senji, another judge, similarly cites the spontaneous appearance of a crowd of villagers driven by curiosity to gather around Tokushō's home in hopes of learning more about his illness as the work's most striking feature. Such masses, Kuroi explains, have long been absent in Japanese fiction.[48] In Hino's comment, it is the oddity of "Droplets"—tropical flowers and vegetation redolent of the subtropics—that marks the work as "Okinawan." For Kuroi, presumably accustomed to stories of alienated city dwellers, the foreignness of crowd formation is what makes the work regional. Both judges' comments, patently Orientalist in their dismissive categorization of difference, nevertheless elucidate Medoruma's knack for creating a vibrant place where depending on one's point of view, strange things do happen. The burden of modernity, Hartman explains, is exacerbated by media artifice, provoking in individuals a strong desire for "local romance," stories that evoke particular places in the collective memory (e.g., *Winesburg, Ohio*).[49] Were such stories to feature traumatic events of the past, surely they would stubbornly resist the steady effacement of history outside the world of the text. For critics such as Hino and Kuroi, "Droplets" is a balm for weary metropolitan readers, a text that beckons the afflicted with the tantalizing promise of a cure, much as the postreversion marketing of Okinawa-as-resort welcomes tourists with open arms.

In one of many such essays, Medoruma rails against the portrayal of Okinawa—by mainlanders and Okinawans alike—as an island whose culture rejuvenates beleaguered spirits through its "gentleness" (*yasashisa*):

> Thanks to mainland subsidies the economy has developed, and Okinawa's "complex" is a story of the past. [...] Performances by poets who put on "Okinawan art" that caters to the expectations of mainland mass media by playing the samisen and doing the *kachāshī* in front of the elephant cage fill the television screen and newspaper pages. I think it's a poet's duty to destroy the image of "Okinawa" the mass media produces, and represent his own "Okinawa." Where's the "mainland criticism" in circulating images of Okinawa produced by prejudice—samisen and *kachāshī*, karate and Ryukyuan dance? [...] Words like *tēgē* and *chirudai* are praised to the skies, and catchy phrases such as "Okinawa's culture of gentleness" are thrown about. [...] I'm completely fed up.[50]

As Suzuki Tomoyuki explains, Medoruma abhors the idea of Okinawa as "cultural," and bemoans the fact that in recalling its cultural memory Okinawan society has become completely oblivious to what is politically important. For this reason, Medoruma administers his stories of Okinawa with a dose of what Suzuki terms "ill will" (*akui*), injecting a necessary corrective to the shopworn notion of "gentle Okinawa."[51]

It is Medoruma's "ill will," or spirit of contrariness, that prevents one from readily consuming "Droplets" as one might the bulk of cultural products by and about Okinawans. While judges like Hino and Kuroi may explain away the strange occurrences that take place in "Droplets" as conforming to

Okinawa's distinctly exotic culture in an effort to understand (before dispensing with) the story, Medoruma disallows such easy digestion of the work by embedding it with multiple traps. One pitfall occurs in the story within Tokushō's own story of the buried past, which features Seiyū, the protagonist's shiftless cousin who greedily capitalizes on the water from Tokushō's toe once he witnesses its magical power. Seiyū's "miracle water" marketing scheme succeeds to the point that his suitcase and bank account burst with money he envisions squandering in massage parlors from Kyushu to Tokyo. When the water loses its effectiveness, leaving Seiyū's customers disfigured rather than "healed," an angry mob forms to beat him senseless. Just as Tokushō dispenses lies to schoolchildren through his artfully constructed stories of war heroism, so too does Seiyū deceive his audience with sham water cleverly packaged in brown medicinal bottles affixed with gold seals and red lettering, surely a sly reference to the countless variety of similarly packaged vials ubiquitously sold in Japan to invigorate spent businessmen. Seiyū and Tokushō's moral lapses causes each much anguish; the former is beaten, while the latter suffers a debilitating illness that leaves him bedridden. Abiding by the conventions of fables, then, Medoruma rewards good and punishes evil—or does he?

In the story's most dramatic scene, Medoruma pits Tokushō against Ishimine, a phantom soldier whom Tokushō instantly recognizes as the close friend he abandoned in a cave during the battle. The story's very literal climactic scene, in which the physical sensation of Ishimine's tongue on Tokushō's foot causes him to ejaculate, not only showcases Medoruma's humorous, tongue-in-cheek wit, but it also underscores the work's complexity. The nightly phantom soldiers' visits stir up in Tokushō deeply repressed memories of his cowardice and force him to realize his own self-deception. When at last he understands this, Tokushō asks Ishimine for forgiveness. The narrator imbues the highly charged scene with an unmistakable trace of homoerotic desire:

> "Ishimine, forgive me!"
> The color had begun to return to Ishimine's pale face, and his lips regained their luster. Tokushō, despite his fear and self-hatred, grew aroused. Ishimine's tongue glided across the opening on his toe, and then Tokushō let out a small cry with his sexual release.
> The lips pulled away. Lightly wiping his mouth with his index finger, Ishimine stood up. He was still seventeen. A smile took shape—around those eyes that stared out beneath the long lashes, on the spare cheeks, on the vermillion lips.
> Tokushō burst into anger. "Don't you know how much I've suffered these past fifty years?" Ishimine merely continued to smile, nodding slightly at Tokushō, who flailed his arms in an effort to sit up.
> "Thank you. At last the thirst is gone." Speaking in well-accented, standard Japanese, Ishimine held back a smile, saluted, and bowed deeply.

He never turned to look back at Tokushō as he slowly vanished into the wall. A newt scampered across the wall's stained surface and caught an insect.

At dawn, Tokushō's wail echoed throughout the village.[52]

This critical passage raises several issues, none of which is easily reducible, and none of which aid in reading the story as a generic tale of a village temporarily disturbed by immorality.

First, Medoruma takes pains to differentiate Ishimine's speech in the passage. Even during a magical episode such as this one, Medoruma's attentiveness to language remains painstakingly accurate. While the speech of Tokushō, his wife Ushi, Seiyū and other older Okinawans is marked with a heavy local dialect throughout, the few words in the text voiced by Ishimine are carefully rendered into standard Japanese, conforming entirely to the reality of wartime, when prewar edicts prohibiting the use of local dialect were pushed to an extreme through the execution of those deemed spies for speaking in dialect.[53] Medoruma's language specificity brings the specter of wartime ideology into the text, making it clear that his writing is not generic, but geographically and temporally specific.

Another point to note in the scene is that Medoruma, who has posited Tokushō as an aggressor for his self-serving wartime (in)action rather than another in the cast of battle victims, shows that his protagonist has also suffered terribly from keeping secret his past behavior. Tokushō's decades of silence end in a wail heard throughout the village. The scene's final line underscores Medoruma's efforts to give voice to a dying generation long bound and gagged by painful secrets. This scene in particular, and the story as a whole, muddies the distinction between victim and aggressor, making it impossible to weigh in on whom to reward and whom to punish. It also explains why Tokushō, fond of drink, women, and song, indulges in escapist pleasures.

Through the discord wrought by idiosyncratic, private memories that Tokushō relives and standard communal memories of the Battle of Okinawa such as the Himeyuri trope, the story resists any pat reading. Even the conclusion offers no satisfying answer to questions raised in "Droplets." Most disturbing of these is why Tokushō remains fundamentally unchanged even after he has painfully relived his past and acknowledged his betrayal of Ishimine. The reader is by no means assured that Tokushō will rectify his errant ways; in fact, Medoruma suggests otherwise by having Tokushō return to his former vices of drinking, gambling, and womanizing. The story's formalistic ending—the picture-postcard image of vibrant hibiscus tethered by a vine to an enormous gourd that Tokushō beholds with moist eyes—may well satisfy critics seeking local color, but it does nothing to diminish the reality of Tokushō's unwillingness to reform. The order that settles upon the village after Seiyū's expulsion and Tokushō's "recovery" is superficial at best. Medoruma's rather bleak conclusion may simply indicate that the story has shifted from a fantastic to a realistic mode; however, given the author's predilection for critique, it is far more tempting to read the ending as an open rebuke of Tokushō's habits and perhaps even of Okinawans themselves, who, content in escapist pleasures such as playing the samisen and dancing the *kachāshī*, share his apathy.

Medoruma's focus on water, the element that Tokushō's story of repressed war memory and Seiyū's parallel tale share, represents one of the author's first attempts to incorporate indigenous culture in his fiction. Water figures prominently in the work as evidenced by its title and the contents therein, suggesting that Medoruma is probing folk beliefs of Okinawans, who according to Nakamatsu Yashu, highly revere and worship the spiritual power of water.[54] However, Kawamura Minato counters this view by pointing out that such beliefs in water are not unique to Okinawa: rather, they reflect a more universal faith in the sacredness of water.[55] Kawamura's quibble notwithstanding, by interjecting a nativist element in his writing, Medoruma is by no means paying homage to an ideal ancient state in which water imbibed by village elders courses through the blood of children. The story's emphasis on water naturally causes readers to place it in a long tradition of legends of sacred water, but, as is his tendency, Medoruma refuses to reduce his motif to a single symbolic meaning. Seiyū's discovery that what he sold customers eager to recapture their youth was simply plain water shows clearly Medoruma's fondness for contrivance, his deferral of absolutes, and penchant for illuminating hidden traces.

It is the story's smallest details—the trace of lime found in the water Dr. Ōshiro takes from Tokushō's toe, the echo of Ishimine's perfectly accented standard Japanese—that function like chinks in an armor, destabilizing the grand narratives of battle so well rehearsed and glibly repeated in classrooms, film, and text. The presence of lime in Tokushō's body, which utters through its grotesque transformation what Tokushō cannot voice about his past, is indisputable proof that he personally experienced war and that his particular hell is contained within the limestone walls of a cave in which he left for dead an intimate friend. Tokushō's story, eclipsed by public memories of the war, ultimately speaks itself through the body.

The lure of the distant shore in "Spirit Recalling"

"Spirit Recalling," published in 1998, can be read as a sequel of sorts to "Droplets" since the author's method and the story's content include many of the elements that contributed to Medoruma's Akutagawa Prize-winning text, yet it is eminently engaging even when read as an independent piece. Not only does Dr. Ōshiro reappear in "Spirit Recalling" as the village physician, but the setting—an unidentified, yet familiar (to readers of Medoruma) village—forms the larger textual space in which the author focuses again on the supine body of one villager whom he connects to the Battle of Okinawa through key flashbacks. As in "Droplets," Medoruma wages a battle between two forces. Rather than depict a clash between public and private memory, Medoruma pits the indomitable weight of tradition against those mechanized forces that have come to erode long-held communal values. "Spirit Recalling," which recounts the failed attempts of Uta, an elderly woman invested with spiritual power to summon back the "dropped" spirit of a middle-aged man named Kōtarō, whom she loves as dearly as a son, won Medoruma the Kawabata Prize for its skillful depiction of Okinawan beliefs.

Fond of sake and the *sanshin* like Tokushō, Kōtarō, married with two children, is a rather ordinary man, though uncommonly prone to the dislodging of his spirit that accounts for his lying inert on a sickbed through the narrative present. As she has so many times in the past, Uta, who serves as the village priestess, labors to summon his willful spirit back to Kōtarō's body. Up to this point, the plot outline is indistinguishable from earlier stories containing references to "dropped spirits," such as those written by Ōshiro Tatsuhiro. Medoruma tweaks the formulaic "dropped-then-recovered spirit" motif by colorfully filling the cavernous void left by Kōtarō's spirit with an enormous island crab (*āman*) that makes the male body its abode. A startling predator with its fierce pincers, the crusty crab figurally rends the outwardly smooth aspect of contemporary Okinawan society. As the story unfolds, the narrative retreats into the past where we learn that during the battle, Uta and Kōtarō's mother, Omito, stole away one night from the safety of the caves to hunt for food. Spying the eggs of a sea turtle, Omito began to collect them for sustenance just minutes before she was killed by artillery fire. Uta witnessed a sea turtle enter the ocean that tragic night in 1945, and it is a sea turtle she sees again when she follows Kōtarō's spirit to the ocean shore where it sits gazing at the vast beyond.

Though he does not use the Okinawan term, the great expanse that transfixes Kōtarō is surely the paradise for the dead known locally as *nirai kanai*.[56] One of the clearest tensions in "Spirit Recalling" is the struggle between the shred of life still remaining in Kōtarō's form and the cavern of death in which his mother, Omito, and thousands of other battle victims lie. In another of his bleak conclusions, Medoruma shows that the distant shore of death has a greater pull on Kōtarō's wandering spirit than Uta's well-attested powers. In Uta's failure to shield Kōtarō from the clutches of death—represented through the symbol of Omito, bifurcated into the twin forms of hermit crab and sea turtle—Medoruma's pessimism is unmistakable. Kōtarō's eventual death underscores a perennial point of Medoruma's that tradition cannot but crumble before the atrocities of the twentieth century. Unlike Ōshiro's "Turtleback Tombs," in which Ushi's dying prayers suggest that she and other victims of the battle will enjoy an afterlife together with their ancestors, Medoruma shows that war vitiates Okinawa's traditional belief system.

In the opening passage of "Spirit Recalling," which seems unrelated to the story's darker theme of war's impact on the psyche, the narrator dwells on a small detail—the waning tradition of morning tea-drinking—a custom that, like spirit recalling, has fallen by the wayside in the wake of modernization:

> Sitting on the veranda of a room left wide open, snorting at the radio exercise music that flowed from the civic hall, Uta put a lump of brown sugar in her mouth and sipped hot tea while watching the garden border, moist with morning dew, brighten vividly, infused with sunlight. Despite the fact that old folks had always boiled water and warmed their bodies with hot tea first thing in the morning, at the beginning of April, the village's education council members and officers of the Senior Citizens' Association started a joint radio exercise program for seniors and children in front of the civic hall, blathering that it would "promote interaction between kids and old folks" and "encourage people to keep early hours." For an entire month, Uta's friend from the Senior Citizens' Association would come by dressed in awful looking sports gear. No matter how many times her friend invited her along, Uta would say, "I won't go" and continued with her ritual of morning tea.[57]

Though the number of senior participants dipped after a retired friend of Uta's slumps to his death following a bout of "healthy" morning radio exercise, soon afterward, crowds of elderly return to the civic hall for more rousing national calisthenics. From this subtle aside on the rapid disappearance of morning tea under the onslaught of centralized culture, the narrator segues to the heart of story, which underscores another absence—that of faith in contemporary times.

In a dramatic showdown, the collective will of villagers who circle Kōtarō's bed to shield him from the intrusive lens of cameras held by two mainland filmmakers shooting on location in Okinawa locks horns with Uta, who belatedly arrives on the scene to help Kōtarō. Medoruma's farfetched, tragicomedic climax occurs when the island crab, startled by camera flashes, scurries inside Kōtarō's mouth and lodges itself in his throat causing Kōtarō's untimely death. In a fit of rage, Uta, who has cared for Kōtarō since Omito's death, lunges after the crab, but to no avail. Finally, a fellow villager is able to hack the elusive crab to pieces with a scoop and hoe just seconds after Uta realizes that the feisty crab must be a reincarnation of Omito, and that it, like the sea turtle, signals, through a reunion of mother and son in death, a restoration in the natural world.

The intensity with which the villagers who fight to kill the crab stems not from the kind of fierce loyalty to Kōtarō that Uta possesses, but rather from the fear that if the cameramen were to document the odd presence of a crab making its home in an Okinawan man, a lucrative hotel construction project would be shelved, leaving the village economically vulnerable. Medoruma uses strong language directly aimed at mainland readers to indicate Uta's wrath toward the cameramen after Kōtarō and the crab die, whereupon she proceeds to smash their cameras: "Keep what you saw here in your heart, do you hear? If not, you can bet that this old lady's coming all the way to the mainland to kill you."[58] These haunting words contain a pointed critique of mass media's infiltration of village life, alluded to in the story's opening radio exercise scene and driven home in the climax.

As in "Droplets," a semblance of order returns to the village following the expulsion of the predatory crab, yet the story delivers no moral victory. Medoruma's antihero, Kōtarō, dies; hotel construction will surely continue apace; formations of efficient groups of children, seniors, educators, and village officials will march lock step in time to precise instructions delivered nationally by an NHK radio broadcaster.[59] The story's poignant conclusion, in which Uta remains bereft on shore after Kōtarō's death, magnifies in its final line the full impact that mechanization has on indigenous beliefs, whether in the form of light morning exercise or heavy artillery fire:

> Uta stood on the shore and looked around her. The leaves of trees on shore swayed slightly, and she could hear the sound of hermit crabs clambering through the thickets. She was alone on shore, where a row of trees formed a black wall, guarding the village from the ocean. Assailed suddenly by a surge of unbearable loneliness, Uta stepped into the water and walked as waves lapped her ankles. Sea fireflies alighted and disappeared in the ripples. The ocean was gentle and warm. Coming to a stop, Uta looked out to sea, her hands clasped. However, her prayer reached nowhere.[60]

Yet again, the reader's expectations are betrayed as the logic of this fable-like story refuses to grant Uta the one wish that would permit her to continue in her role as the village priestess. Medoruma beguiles his readers with clever contrivances—a certified healer, a mythic sea turtle, a predatory hermit crab—yet Uta and the sea creatures are never securely attached to any convincing symbolic meaning, nor, in the end, are they any match for the war that engulfs them.

Considering that they are narratives of war, "Droplets" and "Spirit Recalling" make for surprisingly enjoyable reading, due in large part to Medoruma's irreverent ploys. To be sure, ingenious inventions such as drops of water trickling from the toe of an impossibly large, gourd-shaped leg, or a lusty crab staking its territory in a human body serve to entertain; they also force one out of conventional ways of thinking about war, memory, and identity. Deep beneath the surface comedy of the texts lies a tension Medoruma claims is the essence of literature, at least in the writing he most admires by Nakagami Kenji, Ōe Kenzaburō, and Murakami Ryū.[61] One is struck by the full force of unresolved tension in "Droplets" when Tokushō seethes with anger in a confrontation with his fallen comrade Ishimine, asking, "Don't you know how much I've suffered these past fifty years?"[62] Tension also comes to the fore in "Spirit Recalling" when Uta threatens to kill the cameramen who have come to document a village secret. In both stories, cultural memory, that suspect version of history which the island projects to others in its assertion of group identity, clashes with a different kind of memory, one that is contestatory, idiosyncratic, political. Uta destroys the cameramen's film because what for the men is a priceless shot that reveals to the mainland an unauthorized, hidden glimpse of Okinawa is for Uta her past. In short, the tension that lies at the heart of Medoruma's battle narratives rises from the question of who owns memory—Tokushō or the Himeyuri? Uta or NHK? While Medoruma gives voice to the former in each case, these stories show clearly tensions between and among local and national forces as they vie to narrate the past.

Circuits of memory in "Tree of Butterflies"

One of the longest and most harrowing of Medoruma's battle narratives is "Tree of Butterflies" ("Gunchō no ki"). Published in 2000, the story relates the deep and abiding love a dying old woman named Gozei has for a man named Shōsei, who, last seen in the midst of war, is presumed dead. After a long absence, Yoshiaki, the story's protagonist, finds himself in his hometown where his arrival coincides with the town's harvest celebration. As the annual festivities take place, Yoshiaki is slowly drawn toward traditions in which he had long been uninterested. These include music, dance, and the performance of melodramatic but beloved plays that depict rampant prewar discrimination toward Okinawans. The connection between Yoshiaki's quest for self and Gozei's love is faint, but it becomes more distinct as the work unfolds. Ultimately, it is Yoshiaki's ties to Gozei and Shōsei's generation that emerge as Medoruma's primary concern. The transmission of memory, ever problematic, particularly when related to war, was a raging issue among Okinawan intellectuals as the new millennium drew near, and one that clearly informs Medoruma's writing of "Tree of Butterflies."

Two separate but related debates that contribute to a fuller understanding of Medoruma's work filled the pages of local and national newspapers in 1999 and 2000. As both involve identity politics, they are naturally quite complex; here, I sketch only pertinent details to amplify tensions readers beguiled by Medoruma's absorbing story might easily miss. The first controversy, centering on proposed changes for Okinawa's new Prefectural Peace Memorial Museum, which opened in April 2000, bears heavily on the issue of cultural memory. In short, committee members who had since 1996 drawn up guidelines for the museum's designs and exhibit captions were treated to a shock when on August 11, 1999 *Ryukyu News* reported that the museum's content had been changed without the committee's knowledge.[63] LDP Governor Inamine Keiichi's defeat of Ōta Masahide in 1998 ushered in a far more conservative administration, which sought early on to tone down what it perceived as inflammatory content in the museum's exhibits. This whitewashing of material included the removal of a gun from a proposed exhibit on the daily lives of civilian refugees. The display was to have portrayed a Japanese soldier commanding a mother at gunpoint to stifle her child's cries. Also airbrushed out of the designs was a Japanese soldier who was to appear in a cave scene in which he handed an injured soldier cyanide-laced milk. Further changes were made in terminology. "Sacrifice" (*gisei*) replaced "massacre" (*gyakusatsu*); "war of attrition" (*jikyūsen*) replaced "sacrificed stone strategy" (*suteishi sakusen*); and "Asia-Pacific War" (*Ajia-Taiheiyō sensō*) replaced "The Fifteen Years War" (*jūgo-nen sensō*). Understandably, many Okinawans were outraged by the fact that a peace museum in Okinawa was itself now part and parcel of a national attempt (as noted in the 1982 school textbook controversy) to conceal the facts of Japanese wartime violence toward Okinawans.[64] Eventually the debate died down as Inamine bowed to public pressure and allowed the original displays with some compromise.[65]

The second debate concerned a joint proposal commonly referred to as the "Okinawa Initiative." This initiative was presented at a conference in March 2000 by three University of the Ryukyus professors—Takara Kurayoshi, Ōshiro Tsuneo, and Maeshiro Morisada—each a key player in Governor Inamine's administration. As Julie Yonetani states, the initiative "constituted an attempt to articulate an Okinawan historical and political position more in concert with the aims of the U.S.-Japan security partnership and Japanese government policy."[66] What angered so many about the professors' proposal was that underlying the steps they outlined for Okinawa's future economic success was an undeniable acquiescence to the national policy of accepting the bases that former Governor Ōta had vehemently opposed at least since the 1995 schoolgirl rape. Not only did the initiative accept the idea that Okinawa would shoulder the preponderance of bases in Japan, it also sanctioned the construction of a new base in Nago, which a majority of residents opposed in spite of massive financial compensation promised them.[67] The initiative, along with the government's continued national cash-for-bases policy and its selection of Nago as the site for the 2000 G-8 summit, was, Yonetani explains, a strategy to "'absorb' Okinawans' sense of identity and desire for political autonomy."[68]

Without a doubt, Medoruma emerged as the most prominent intellectual to voice his dismay before the conservative turn of tide that has swept Okinawa in recent years. The steady stream of political essays published by Medoruma since 1999 effectively quells any doubt as to his preeminence in matters of public concern. Like Ōe Kenzaburō and Nakagami Kenji, two authors whom Medoruma admires, he expends creative energy in writing compelling fiction, all the while fighting for deeply felt political causes. Given his longstanding disdain for the public eye, Medoruma's decision to abandon his reclusive life in remote Miyako Island to take a teaching position in Nago could not have been easy. His return to northern Okinawa, where he spent his childhood, marked a turning point in the author's life, one that has become increasingly decisive with every new essay that details his efforts to keep the idyllic north free of the US military presence that has bedeviled central islanders. While even the most neutral American reader might bristle at Medoruma's furious lashing out against US military bases, his and many other Okinawans' opposition to the bases reflects resentment toward the government in Tokyo as much as it does toward officials in Washington. Indeed, as savvy politicians have long recognized, cries over the "Okinawa (read base) problem" (*Okinawa mondai*) have generally resulted in outflows of cash and public works projects from Tokyo. This point was driven home by Inamine when he emerged victorious over Ōta largely because he pointed out how economically vulnerable Okinawa would be without the resources the national government had curtailed in their zeal to punish the former governor for refusing to sign leases that guaranteed the renewal of bases. It was into this political quagmire that Medoruma stepped when he left quiet Miyako for once quiet Nago.

Inamine employed a convincing argument to support his gubernatorial design choices for the new Peace Museum. His assertion that there existed multiple interpretations of the battle may not have been critical for winning the changes in exhibit content he sought, but the Governor's reasoning unwittingly served to support Medoruma's fictional enterprise. That is, as Medoruma fills in what Inamine strategically leaves out of representations of the past, he too is putting forth a different interpretation of the battle. Inamine's blatant censorship did not stop with attempts to remove indications of violence toward civilians by Japanese soldiers, or with changes in terminology. He also sought to sweep from memory less known atrocities that occurred in so called "comfort stations" by pressing for the removal of a map that indicated their placement throughout wartime Okinawa.[69]

It is precisely this aspect of the battle that Medoruma devotes his attention to in "Tree of Butterflies" through a gripping exploration of female psychology in the character of Gozei, who serves as a sex slave to Japanese military officers during the war and as a prostitute to American soldiers during the occupation. Lest one think that his is yet another portrayal of Okinawans as victims, Medoruma pointedly includes references to Korean sex slaves, below Gozei in hierarchy, given that their sexual services are restricted to lower-ranking enlisted men. While Gozei is a thoroughly developed character who gives voice to what politicians such as Inamine have tried to suppress, Medoruma characteristically leaves some stones unturned by placing side by side with Gozei's story the untold tragedies of unnamed Korean sex slaves. As in many of his other stories, Medoruma is careful to acknowledge internal discrimination in Okinawa, even as he writes more broadly of the wartime state's ill treatment of Okinawans, its second-class citizens.[70]

That Medoruma is attempting to write unwritten stories is clear once Yoshiaki begins to investigate his family lineage after Gozei mistakes him three times for Shōsei. As he learns, Shōsei is a distant relative of his, and it is Yoshiaki's resemblance to the older man that confuses Gozei, who, like Uta in "Peace Street," is slipping into senility. A broken but still coherent stream of scenes from the past jut violently into the narrative present, revealing the horrors of Gozei's life as a sex worker employed at the Morning

Sun (*Asahi*) "inn" where Japanese soldiers resided during the war. Shōsei, who was thought to be feeble-minded, nonetheless outwitted the authorities by falsifying an injury in order to avoid conscription. One of the few civilian men left in the village, he worked as a servant at the inn. In the course of their employment, Gozei and Shōsei became lovers. Their only relief from harsh servitude came in stolen moments savored under a tree clustered with masses of yellow blossoms that look like butterflies from a distance. Yoshiaki learns these particulars from a ninety-year-old gentleman named Uchima who had previously served as ward chief. In a telling line, Medoruma discloses that none of these details are recorded in the "Village History" that Uchima proudly shows Yoshiaki during their conversation. The perilous nature of these memories is underscored as one is made aware that even the orally transmitted history of the ostracized pair would have been lost had Yoshiaki not promptly queried Uchima about his ties to Shōsei. Well advanced in age, Uchima is, until Yoshiaki hears the tale, the sole repository of memories deliberately left unmentioned in village history. Just as Governor Inamine excises from public memory any disturbing hint of comfort stations in the exhibits of the Peace Museum, so too does Uchima leave for posterity only sanctioned memories secured in his prized "Village History."

In the story's final battle scene, the soldiers evacuate the inn to take up shelter in a nearby cave where they remain trapped with Shōsei and Japanese, Okinawan, and Korean sex slaves. As tensions heighten, the soldiers' already callous behavior worsens, resulting in one among them taking Shōsei who is suspected as a spy for speaking in dialect from the cave at gunpoint. Inside, Gozei lies in the mud, sexually degraded. She is unable to move, let alone rise to Shōsei's defense. Despite her repeated wish to die rather than survive, Gozei is treated infinitesimally better by Japanese soldiers than either the Korean sex workers or Shōsei. The guilt she suffers for this partiality remains with Gozei for decades. After the war ends, she makes the imprudent decision to remain in the village so that Shōsei, whereabouts unknown, would know where to find her. Disparaged for her sexual involvement with both Japanese and American soldiers, Gozei is a social pariah, yet she stubbornly refuses to start a new life elsewhere because of her deep feelings for Shōsei. She spends her remaining years living in a hut no bigger than a goat shed, eking out a living by collecting and selling aluminum cans. In a particularly haunting scene of Yoshiaki's recollections of childhood, he painfully recalls the harsh treatment meted out to Gozei after she returned Yoshiaki, who had been lost, to his family. Owing to her past, virtually all the adults suspected foul play and roundly censured her. For months afterward, Gozei avoided the accusing eyes of the villagers. Violence among fellow villagers, hinted at in many of Medoruma's early stories, such as "Chronicle of a School of Fish," lurks in the shadows of "Tree of Butterflies," surfacing most clearly in the villagers' open rebuke of Gozei based simply on her past.[71]

Gozei's declining mental state leads villagers to secure a room for her in a nursing facility where Yoshiaki is her sole visitor. In the three-week span of the narrative, Yoshiaki comes to a finer understanding of himself through encounters with Gozei, who awakens in him repressed memories and a desire to know more about his family and culture. In his first brush with Gozei at the harvest festival, Yoshiaki realizes that "the music of the island in which he had been born and raised flowed through his blood."[72] And, as Gozei lies bedridden in the story's conclusion, Yoshiaki painfully recalls that the reason he has always detested brown sugar, the traditional island sweet, is because of its association with Gozei who, after rescuing him as a child, had given him a lump of sugar to calm his fears. It is also as she lies dying that readers are presented with Gozei's heart-wrenching psychology, which shows that despite her imminent death, Shōsei, and by extension, Yoshiaki, remain etched in Gozei's mind:

> "Gozei! Gozei!" Shōsei called from far off. No, he was very close. Bathed in moonlight, the clusters of yellow butterflies on the hibiscus tree seemed on the verge of taking flight. When she went in the shade of the tree she was immediately drawn in by a strong force, and for an achingly short time, his hot tongue played at her throat, and his firm left hand pressed her back. She buried her face in his chest, and, choked with the scent of the forest and tide, she whispered in his ear, "I never thought a woman like me could feel this way being held by a man." She gently held his hands and stroked his hair. "Gozei! Gozei!," he said in a voice she could hear from the depths of the darkness. "It's ok," she said, recalling how Shōsei embraced her, coated in sweat down to the innermost folds of his body by the skin-clinging muggy night air. I had already oozed into the dirt. The Korean woman was saying something. She pressed something in my mouth. It was a piece of brown sugar. My saliva overflowed and I felt the thin shred of life inside me grow. "I'm ok now, thanks." The woman grasped my hand and stroked my fingers. Sensations throughout my body abated, and even the sharp pain in my pelvis went away. "Gozei! Gozei!" Kneeling down, beaten Shōsei raised his head to look at me. A shadow stood at the entrance to the cave, his back to the moonlight. "Ah. You know all about what kind of a person I am." I could see the figure of a girl walking along the road to a whorehouse, carrying a single bundle wrapped in cloth. "Go back. Don't take another step." I couldn't do it. No matter how narrow or twisted the path, even if it led to a dead-end, I just kept going. "Gozei! Gozei!" Pressing my forehead to Shōsei's chest, I stared at the hibiscus flowers that had just fallen to the ground, and laughed aloud. Opening the front of my kimono, I listened for the voice that sent blood rushing through my body and warmed it so. Turning my eyes away from the "I" that ridiculed me, I prayed that the special time would continue only under this tree. "He's got to be alive somewhere. How do you know that he's dead when you haven't seen it with your own eyes? Do you really believe he's dead? Is that the reason you've lived by the hibiscus tree?"

Waiting for him [...] pulling a cart, collecting empty cans and selling them to the brewery for a few coins to live on. [...] A road so glitteringly white from limestone dust I can't keep my eyes open. I'll never walk that road again. Wearing rubber sandals, my feet tainted white. The figure of a young boy crying at the roadside appears before me. For the first time ever I held a child who clung to me, crying. The feel of his thin arms around my neck. I never thought my own heart could hurt so much at hearing his cries in my ear. "Is this what children smell like?" I thought, pressing my nose against his thin chest. I felt awful that my washcloth was dirty, but that's all I had, so I used it to wipe his face and the back of his neck, then put a piece of brown sugar in his mouth. Thinking I mustn't frighten the child who had finally stopped crying, I put on an unfamiliar smile, seated him in the cart, and took him back to town. Afterward his parents gave me hell, but that brief time was the happiest I've had since I began living in the village. If only I could have had your child. [...] "Gozei! Gozei!" Do I have any cause for regret? In the end, my body and soul become viscous and murky, and, like the river near the hibiscus tree, they mingle with all the ephemera in this world to become one with the ocean. Trickling from my palm, seeping out my hair, coursing over my thighs, flowing from my eyes and ears, from my slack cells, one by one, matter dances in the air, like coral eggs. At last, a spirit emerges from my mouth as from a hollow tree, and, taking a butterfly shape, it flutters in the room, then escapes through the glass window, dancing toward the moonlit sky.[73]

Encapsulated in this remarkable stream of consciousness is no less than the life story of Gozei, into which the narrator also embeds the critical and formative experiences of Shōsei and Yoshiaki.

Just as deftly as the narrator weaves the life stories of Gozei, Shōsei, and Yoshiaki, culminating in poignant portraits of three individual selves, so too does he craftily suggest the impossibility of constructing an impenetrable self. Returning home from his visit to the nursing facility, Yoshiaki mentions in passing that his father might rewrite the faded characters inscribed on the memorial tablet dedicated to Shōsei. Yoshiaki's father, taciturn throughout the story, vehemently opposes Yoshiaki's suggestion, revealing in the story's final lines that "since there were no bones for Shōsei, ten years or so after the war, I went to the beach with my father, picked up several fragments of coral that resembled bones, put them in a new urn, and placed it in the family tomb."[74] Washed by the tide, the smooth coral fragments that lie one on top of the other at the bottom of the urn in the dark tomb, serve as a powerful yet contingent substitute for Shōsei, whose brutal wartime experiences, together with his lover Gozei's, would otherwise be expunged from history. It is precisely such perilous memories, which wash over fractured shards of identity, like tides over coral, that impel Medoruma to continue writing about a war he never experienced, but which he full well knows has not ended.

6 Darkness visible in Sakiyama Tami's island stories

Sakiyama Tami, frequently paired with, yet largely overshadowed by Medoruma Shun, is a remarkable author who has, in the past two decades, written fiction and essays with growing confidence and aplomb. Notwithstanding Medoruma Shun's stylistic likeness to China's revolutionary writer Lu Xun, today, it is Sakiyama's fiercely radical prose that most severely tests the genre of Okinawan fiction. Since her recent declaration to write fiction through a potent mixture of standard Japanese and regional dialect (*shimakotoba*), Sakiyama's writing has come to virtually defy description.[1] Critics certainly recognize considerable talent in the writer, twice nominated for the Akutagawa Prize; yet, even the most generous often fail to understand her opaque stories' content, or even summarize, with any confidence, their plots.[2] For her part, Sakiyama likens her chosen method of writing with dialect to being in hell, readily acknowledging that her modus operandi may well be impossible. She also seems aware that her project will, undoubtedly, limit her readership. Nevertheless, Sakiyama soldiers on in an effort to destroy the kind of smooth Japanese writing whereby dialect is used simply to supplement a central language.[3] Her undertaking, as ambitious as it is risky, when taken as a whole, invokes the fiction of authors as varied as Nakagami Kenji, Fukazawa Shichirō, Sakaguchi Ango, and Izumi Kyōka, all of whom unabashedly subvert writing conventions.

There are several reasons why Sakiyama does not fit easily within the body of prose-writing from Okinawa, among which, perhaps most conspicuous, is the scant attention she pays in her fiction to major themes of the genre, such as the Battle of Okinawa, the American occupation, or indigenous culture. Also, like Medoruma Shun, Sakiyama is herself averse to the idea of being read as an Okinawan writer, or, more precisely, as she puts it, a *female* Okinawan writer.[4] Whether or not one pays her disclaimer any mind, the absence of familiar thematic terrain in her works, which are not about Okinawa per se but center instead on an island the author refers to as "shima" in the syllabary reserved for foreign terms, does effectively distance Sakiyama from Okinawa and its writers. Tempting though it may be to regard Sakiyama's oeuvre as a geographic extension of prose fiction from Okinawa proper, one that neatly encompasses outlying islands such as

Iriomote, where the author was born and lived until the age of fourteen, a careful reading of the stories yields no such ontological ground upon which to argue for such territorial expansion.

Given Sakiyama's marked difference from others in the genre of Okinawan fiction, how then can one regard her as an Okinawan writer? The answer rests in her texts, spun from early memories of island sounds, now imperiled by large-scale postreversion development, commodification, and the passage of time. Sakiyama recalls, as one would a first love, the huge impact Higashi Mineo's dialect-rich *Child of Okinawa* made on her at the time of its publication in 1971. Sakiyama, then a high-school girl in the central Okinawan city of Koza where Higashi set his novella, describes the work as explosive both for its political edge and literary style. She notes in particular Higashi's gritty depiction of the volatile base town of Koza and his ability to make the local dialect "fly across the text as if it were poking fun at standard Japanese."[5] Though Sakiyama singles out Higashi's text for her personal bible, clearly inheriting from him a playful style, as I will show, her use of dialect, like other features of her style, is highly ironic, whereas Higashi's generally conforms to the social realism of much prereversion writing.[6]

Having established, albeit roughly, Sakiyama's uneasy place among her fellow writers, I will analyze her essays and fictional works, particularly, "Passage across the Sea" ("Suijō ōkan," 1988), "Tale of Wind and Water" ("Fūsuitan," 1997), and "The Origin of Muiani ("Muiani yuraiki," 1999) to demonstrate that, lineage aside, Sakiyama's writing occupies an important position in the genre of Okinawan fiction. Okamoto Keitoku, for example, groups Sakiyama and Medoruma together, praising both their work as a vital part of contemporary fiction from Okinawa, distinct from earlier works in the genre for their interiority. Either author certainly offers readers far more detailed description of the inner workings of the minds of protagonists who dwell in very particular narrative topoi: Medoruma reverts to the space of "the village," where repressed memories flood dark rooms and caves, and Sakiyama returns to the narrow, interior world of "the island," where her protagonists grapple with their surroundings. While Sakiyama's fictional space is extremely circumscribed, issuing from the dark recesses of the author's earliest memories in which she recalls sitting alone in the hollow of a banyan (*gajimaru*) tree from which she hears only the sounds of the ocean, the effects of her writing are such that any interiority or subjectivity this space might give rise to is perpetually deferred.[7]

My analysis of Sakiyama's fiction and essays stems partly from a desire to unyoke her from Medoruma, whose prose, like Sakiyama's stands very much on its own. I also wish to make clear the politico-ethical dimension of Sakiyama's prose. Okamoto rightly notes the interior turn prose fiction in Okinawa takes in the cases of Medoruma and Sakiyama, however, neither author produces merely navel-gazing writing. We have seen how Medoruma plumbs the psychology of his fictional characters. Sakiyama is a writer's writer, whose speakerly texts concern the issue of representation. The best support I have found for my contention that Sakiyama is not the apolitical author she appears to be comes from philosophers Gilles Deleuze and Félix Guattari's writing on the concept of minor literature, which illuminates the ways in which Sakiyama's prose, despite the relative depth of her characterization, very much resists the romance of the individual life and speaks, like much other writing in the genre of Okinawan prose, only in a different register, for a collective.

Mission impossible

Sakiyama Tami's 1988 debut story "Passage across the Sea" is deceptively simple in plot, yet replete with suggestions of the Sisyphean method of writing that characterizes her later works. Like Shiga Naoya's *A Dark Night's Passing* (*Anya kōro*, 1921–37) or Joseph Conrad's *Heart of Darkness*, Sakiyama's work involves a journey through darkness, in this case one precipitated by the death of a relative. Akiko, Sakiyama's protagonist, is a young woman, who, adrift in her mid-twenties, lives a self-imposed sequestered life with her parents in a city in Okinawa. When Akiko's grandmother dies, her father, Kinzō, charters a boat to his home island in order to retrieve from it his mother's memorial tablet, despite both her wishes to the contrary and his own failing health. Sakiyama's third-person narration maintains throughout the point of view of Akiko, who has embarked on the trip, it seems, in hopes of finding in her remote childhood home a foundation upon which to base her life. Not only does she fail, but so too does her father, who, after having successfully retrieved the memorial tablet, loses it on their return journey when Akiko inexplicably heaves the tablet out to sea, a bold act which marks the end of this tale of a futile journey across the sea.

The simplicity of the plot belies the tension that textures Sakiyama's story. Generational conflicts surface as one learns that Kinzō, much to his mother's displeasure, had been among the first to leave the island for better prospects on the mainland. In the narrative, Kinzō so fears the gaze of the islanders for having left them behind in poverty he charters a boat from an old man on a neighboring island who must ply the water in the thick of night to conceal Kinzō's presence. Akiko, too, is not free of the shame and guilt that impels Kinzō to take such extremes to avoid contact with others, presumably due to her familial connection with Kinzō and, by extension, the island. Sakiyama's work quietly suggests that the difficulty Akiko has in forming relationships on the main island stems from her physical displacement, at a young age, from the childhood island to which she is now drawn to for self-affirmation.

The prevalence in Okinawan studies of the discourse of "healing islands," (*iyashi no shima*) in which Okinawa is viewed solely for its curative properties even as less savory aspects of its history and culture are suppressed, leads one to expect that Sakiyama's protagonist will undergo a gradual, if not dramatic, recovery upon mere contact with the soil of her childhood home. This is not the case. Rather than portray an island where one merges with the landscape, drawing from it vitality and strength sapped by the drudgery of life in the much larger main islands—Okinawa included—Sakiyama depicts an island whose economy is ravaged, and community destroyed. For example, the author's description of a house belonging to Hatsu, a close friend of Akiko's grandmother in whose safekeeping the memorial tablet rests, shows the darker aspects of island life, not on view in the ubiquitous advertisements festooned with catchy slogans and vibrant color photographs that beckon travelers to sunbathe on sparkling sandy beaches:

> The deserted house was shrouded in cobwebs and littered with trash. The frame of the house was not warped, and its roof tiles, too, were attached so securely one might think the roof had been retiled. If one closed one's eyes to the pain caused by the sight of scattered trash and the siding stripped in several places, one might say a shadow of the house remained. Only the room off the entrance had been cleaned; here, where Hatsu had probably taken some extra care, the memorial tablet stood upright at the center of a Buddhist altar. The only light in the house came from several candles placed on all sides of the altar and room. A tray adorned with nested boxes of offerings of fruit and bread was placed on the tea table, and only here in this dilapidated house was there a strangely showy atmosphere.[8]

Unlike outlying islands such as Taketomi, with its fabled red tiles, or Ishigaki, known for its folk songs, the dilapidated state of the unidentified island of this passage suggests to critics Marukawa Tetsushi and Suzuki Tomoyuki a wholly different locale and tradition.[9] Piecing together textual clues with Sakiyama's personal history, they respectively argue that the physical descriptions in this work most closely resemble Sakiyama's home island of Iriomote, itself associated with the far from exotic, backbreaking coal-mining industry.[10] Oblique references to the island's stagnant economy, in fact, do correspond with the modern history of Iriomote, populated by coalminers who settled there from neighboring Ryukyuan islands and from Kyushu, Taiwan, and Korea.

A lengthy, but telling passage helps both to identify the island and present the historical circumstances that account for Kinzō's decision to leave his home twenty years prior to the narrative present, when, in the early 1970s, Japan experienced a "land boom," fueled by its postwar economic success:

> From the foothills of the island's center, the broad U river, which opened out into the northern sea, flowed as if cleaving the island. On the western side of the river, there still remained old villages that had escaped annihilation, thanks to the river having kept in check the transmission

of malaria some years back; on the eastern side there were new villages in which settlers from the abandoned towns had congregated.

    For decades the island had steadily languished. The main reason for the island's decline was that the tourist industry had great expectations of [Japan's] natural scenery, which incited a land boom. Then, with no show of resistance, island residents leapt at this opportunity, letting go of cultivated land available for privatization. With cash in their hands, these people left the island in droves, seeking another life elsewhere. The island was now engulfed in a reverse tide, having put on, for a short spell, a mere show of prosperity. Kinzō had been at the very head of that outward flow. Breaking free of the critical looks of his fellow islanders whom he had left behind in poverty, Kinzō set off for better prospects in the city twenty years ago, forcibly taking with him his mother, who to the end, hated leaving behind the island.[11]

The tension that pervades these lines explains why Kinzō is suffused with guilt and journeys home under the cover of night. Sakiyama's narrative lingers on the darker facets of island life, such as the communal rifts unchecked development incites, avoiding the dazzlingly sunny aspect of the islands portrayed by mass media. Even so, passages containing historically verifiable references to the hotbed of malaria that decimated villages on the island or to the land boom that led to an exodus of fortune seekers comprise a small portion of the text. In fact, the bulk of the narrative paints the island as unmoored in history, a free floating landmass to which Akiko returns for rest, solace, and healing.[12] Though Sakiyama does not bombard the reader with historical facts, or attempt to teach the island's history, her brief references underscore the decline in island economy.[13] Far from peaceful, the community Sakiyama portrays is riven by internal strife.

    When Kinzō's plans to retrieve the memorial tablet unobtrusively are thwarted by an episode of fainting, he is forced to spend the night in Hatsu's house. Leaving behind her bedridden father, Akiko seizes the opportunity to tour the island, employing the services of the boatman as guide. Since the tour takes place at night, Sakiyama's descriptions of the island landscape are, naturally, veiled. Akiko scrutinizes the dark landscape but discerns little. The further the boat circumnavigates the island, the less sure Akiko is of the contours of the terrain. As the landscape loses its form, Akiko begins to question her surroundings:

> When she paid attention to her own position moving over the water at night, gazing at the island, it struck her that the shape that appeared before her was the reverse of the island scenery that she had recalled in the city. Even in her life there, cooped up in a room, she always believed, somewhere in her heart, that if she could just go to the island, she'd find the island from her past, the one that was supposed to be there. But, when she took a good look around her, the shape of the

island, both in parts, and as a whole, was far less clear than the one she had drawn, as if tracing the contours of her memory, in her imaginings in the city.

Akiko continued to gaze at the faint island that shifted from one section to the next, together with the boat's movement. While she let her line of sight move across areas she could make out neither as land nor sea, the transformations of landscape inside Akiko came to a halt; all that remained was the boat's moving further and further east. Despite the fact that she continued to observe the hazy scenery, in the depths of her now accustomed eyes, she finally let the island remain unclear.[14]

Here, Sakiyama plainly shows Akiko's failure to find in her surroundings any solid ground or essence against which she can demarcate her own subjectivity. With nothing of substance to anchor her, she drifts like the boat, semiconscious in the predawn hours of night, self and landscape free-floating. The rich passage, in which the author portrays not the island itself, but something like the afterimage of the island Akiko remembers, captures perfectly the interstice that lies between darkness and light, or consciousness and unconsciousness, yet, in this space Sakiyama conceives of there lies no essential meaning.

Sakiyama's descriptions of the irreconcilable relationship between protagonist and island stand in stark contrast to notable encounters between self and other in Japanese prose, such as that found in Shiga's *A Dark Night's Passing*, a work which, like Sakiyama's, centers on the search for identity. Shiga's fusion of protagonist Tokitō Kensaku with Mt. Daisen offers a study in contrasts. Whereas Akiko fails to find that which she seeks in her island surroundings, Kensaku most certainly does, as is evident in the climax of Shiga's novel, which bears an uncanny resemblance to Sakiyama's description of her semi-conscious protagonist:

> He felt his exhaustion turn into a strange state of rapture. He could feel his mind and his body both gradually merging into this great nature that surrounded him. It was not nature that was visible to the eyes; rather, it was like a limitless body of air that wrapped itself around him, this tiny creature no larger than a poppy seed. *To be gently drawn into it, and there be restored, was a pleasure beyond the power of words to describe.* The sensation was a little like that of the moment when, tired and without a single worry, one was about to fall into a deep sleep. Indeed, a part of him already was in a state hardly distinguishable from sleep. He had experienced this feeling of being absorbed by nature before; but this was the first time that it was accompanied by such rapture. In previous instances, the feeling perhaps had been more that of being sucked in by nature than that of merging into it; and though there had been some pleasure attached to it, he had at the time always

tried instinctively to resist it, and on finding such resistance difficult, he had felt a distinct uneasiness. But this time, he had not the slightest will to resist; and contentedly, without a trace of the old uneasiness, he accepted nature's embrace.[15]

(Emphasis added)

Sakiyama's work lacks the epiphanic force of Shiga's fusion of man and mountain; in her story, self and island pass each other, (literally) like vessels passing in the night, never coalescing. Unlike Kensaku, Akiko remains unconsoled.

Hurriedly returning to Kinzō's bedside, Akiko learns from Hatsu how intensely her grandmother had wished for her remains to stay on the island. Despite Hatsu's entreaty, father and daughter leave the still dark island, memorial tablet in hand, venturing out to sea where Akiko tries yet again to penetrate the island with her gaze:

> When Akiko looked out, there was still no sign of the sun rising and the sea was a faint bluish white. At last the boat cut through an area between the deep sea and the coral reef. The surface of the sea ahead was starting to change into a leaden color. It was when the boat glided over that water. Akiko stood up, and peered overboard. Then, while swaying to and fro in the mist that began to shroud the signs of dawn, Akiko saw the sheer abyss of water that surrounded the island without end, like a black wall that continued to the depths of the earth. Suddenly, in Akiko's hands was the memorial tablet that she had wrenched away from Kinzō. Aiming the tablet at that abyss of water, Akiko hurled it forward. It made a high arc over the quiet water and disappeared in the waves.[16]

The story's final words come from Akiko who offers a reason for her inexplicable act: "This is what grandma wanted, more than any memorial service, this is what she wanted."[17]

Sakiyama marks with precision the moment in which Akiko, passive throughout the story, acts decisively. When Akiko sees the abyss of water that surrounds the island, she violently rejects Kinzo's attempts to fetishize the island by taking with him the tablet, his one remaining tie.[18] In an instant, Akiko experiences the twin realizations that just as she cannot return home, her grandmother cannot leave hers. Divided by the vast ocean, their worlds are irrevocably severed. In contrast to earlier stories in the genre of prose fiction from Okinawa, particularly in the prewar years by writers such as Yogi Seishō whose island gaze effects a nostalgic merging of protagonist with landscape, the gulf between self and other remains unbridgeable in Sakiyama's debut story. She debunks the romantic idea that persists in discourses of Okinawa of the individual drawing spiritual sustenance from the wellspring of nature, in this case, the island. In Sakiyama's story, those who break with the island or go to it in pursuit of a cure cannot but discover the irony of their attempt to return.

The island in "Passage across the Sea" bears some resemblance to Iriomote but ultimately resists identification. In her essays, Sakiyama suggests reasons why the island remains elusive despite her continued fascination with it. In the piece, "Writing the Island" ("Shima o kaku to iu koto", 1996), Sakiyama states that after having lived in Iriomote from birth to age fourteen, she returned only three times: once with family, again with a university club, and, finally, alone. She underscores the impact these few visits had on her decision to become a writer in her mid-twenties. Then, her choice of profession coincided with an awareness of the shadow the island had cast on her, perhaps, she writes, due to its sheer size among the various islands, small and large, which formed the Yaeyama chain.[19] Sakiyama frequently refers to this shadowy mass, or island, with the Japanese syllabary reserved for things foreign. Her explanation for this form of demarcation relates to the fact that Iriomote is no longer the home she knew for fourteen years. Sakiyama writes, "In my current life, I've lost the sense that the island belongs to me, so it has become, by necessity, an *island* beyond the real island."[20]

Thus compelled by the island's shadows, Sakiyama writes her island stories, which invariably involve a protagonist who returns home. Sakiyama asserts that, for her, the act of writing is tantamount to writing the island; yet, both her fiction and essays mutually reinforce the idea that island writing necessitates a return that is, finally, impossible. Despite this conundrum, Sakiyama does write, offering her readers a view of the constraints that keep her from penning anything more than the broad contours of the land, all of which lack substance. Akiko's journey imparts neither a sense of wholeness nor moves her from darkness to the rapturous light Kensaku experiences in nature. As with Conrad's protagonist Marlow in *Heart of Darkness*, which depicts an inner voyage that topples established hierarchies between "the far and the near, between the savage and the civilized, between the tropical and the urban," for Akiko, "child-of light," (another of Sakiyama's ironies) reality and its attendant truths lie outside her purview.[21]

"The Indistinct Island" ("Shimagomoru," 1991) and "Time and Again" ("Kurikaeshigaeshi," 1994) reinforce the theme of identity Sakiyama develops in "Passage across the Sea." The narrative in each advances and recedes as in a succession of waves created by an incoming tide, through which drift protagonists, who, like Akiko, sway between an attachment to, and repulsion from the island. In these island stories, Sakiyama performs the methodic, pacific labor of dismantling value-laden binary oppositions that regulate social codes, in particular, self and other. Her demolition work results in nonrepresentational writing that emphasizes form rather than content, which accounts for why baffled critics state that her stories are beyond description. Identity is never affirmed in the stories; rather, protagonists remain in perpetual flight, moving from one place to the next.

Deleuze and Guattari refer to this kind of motion, or style of writing as nomadic. They do not deem unsuccessful efforts to inhabit an identity as failure, focusing instead on the process of becoming. As they explain in *Kafka: Toward a Minor Literature*, the security of the subject is never problematic because there are no subjects, only collective assemblages of enunciation, or literary machines. These machines, which are comprised of a circuit of states, form a mutual becoming. Taking Kafka's "The Metamorphosis" as an example, they argue that Gregor Samsa is depicted neither in terms of man nor animal, but, rather, as becoming animal.[22] Evading either binary pole, Kafka's work frees itself from anything that smacks of meaning, particularly metaphor, focusing instead on metamorphosis. Because metaphor territorializes or inscribes meaning and its concomitant truths, Kafka's writing always moves in the opposite extreme, escaping old categories. Deleuze and Guattari describe this flight as "intensely going '*head over heels and away*,' no matter where, even without moving; it isn't a question of a line of escape or, rather a simple *way out*, 'right, left or in any direction,' as long as it is as little signifying as possible."[23]

The disequilibrium Sakiyama's writing effects arises from her persistent efforts to avoid the pitfalls of representational language. In her early island stories, the plainest example of Sakiyama's resistance to meaning can be seen in her phonetic rendering of "the island" (シマ). Less obvious to the casual reader is her reversal of geographical markers and constant refusal to allow the shadowy forms that appear in the stories to fully materialize.[24] While Sakiyama's protagonists' ever-receding memories may account for some of the haziness of the island stories, like the Kafka effect Deleuze and Guattari write of, the Sakiyama effect rests on her growing desire to undo, from within, prevailing discourses of the islands.

Soon after the events of 9/11, Sakiyama wrote a fiery essay, "A Wild Dance with Island Words" ("'Shimakotoba' de kachāshī," 2002) in which she describes her wish to write fiction through a method that destroys the framework wherein the languages of Okinawa are absorbed within standard Japanese. However, she does not envision island language as something that somehow asserts regional identity by sticking to Japanese, like the tailfin of a fish. Rather, Sakiyama conceives of the method of mixing languages as guerilla warfare. Showing herself as ever on guard for opportunities to set off explosions in which Japanese is booby-trapped by island language, Sakiyama writes:

> If my strategy succeeds, island language will detonate an explosion in the solid, high-rise building, steeped in history, we call Japanese. When it comes into contact with suicide bombing island language, this Japanese building will break into smithereens. To protests that will naturally arise, such as, "What will become of [Japanese] words that have lost their home because of the reckless, unforgivable, no-holds-barred act of barbarity just committed? Will they become refugees or orphans?" The

only thing I can say in response now is, "Either refugees or orphans is fine." But, unlike flesh and blood humans, words can live a long life, moving from place to place, even if they are scattered and in pieces, so long as there is open air. For a while they'll be nearly dea-ad (an example of my mixing, 死にがたがたー), having just been bombed, but then they'll strip off their scorched, heavy clothes underground and soar to the skies. Taking by the hand smashed up bits of island language, they'll commiserate over their wounds, and call it even. Even though they can't understand each other very well, together with the sound of the explosion, they'll somehow be carried away by the rhythm of the island language that begins to flow. If they manage to dance the *kachāshī* (an Okinawan style wild dance), my strategy will have been a smashing success.[25]

As the preceding scenario reveals, Sakiyama is not afraid of the potent mix of languages, since the prospect of mutual understanding outweighs all risks. Like Ōe Kenzaburō, who has also made known a similar wish to destroy the Japanese language, Sakiyama ravages words with pen and ink, committing acts of sabotage fueled by a strange optimism.

Noting in Kafka's works a similar tendency to make words tremble, as if, they, too, are victims of a bombing, Deleuze and Guattari write:

> What interests Kafka is a pure and intense sonorous material that is always connected to *its own abolition*—a deterritorialized musical sound, a cry that escapes signification, composition, song, words—a sonority that ruptures in order to break away from a chain that is still all too signifying. In sound, intensity alone matters, and such sound is generally monotone and always nonsignifying. ... In short, sound doesn't show up here as a form of expression, but rather an unformed material of expression, that will act on other terms.[26]

If Sakiyama's early island stories give emphasis to vision, with images of home that reside in the mind's eye, never quite matching up with reality to produce meaning or "the transcendence of the law," readers of her subsequent fiction are flooded by sound, which, not surprisingly, also lacks significance. Sakiyama's shift in orientation, from visual to auditory, roughly coincides with her declaration to destabilize Japanese, allowing one to see, or rather, hear, how she puts into practice her suicide-bombing fantasy, in which, as Deleuze and Guattari explain, sound is not expressive, but material, a force, which, like dynamite, impacts all that surrounds it.

Making sound visible

"A Tale between Wind and Water" serves as a neat transition between Sakiyama's first works, which involve a search for lost islands, to later ones that feature the pursuit of lost sounds. For Sakiyama, who considers herself a slow writer, the story was written hurriedly, dashed off between other assignments. The reason for its selection in an anthology of fiction by authors from Okinawa may be due to Sakiyama's realization upon publishing the work that this very story spawned the methodological consciousness that resulted in the radical extremes of her subsequent writing.[27]

The story depicts the plight of a man who comes to Okinawa from the mainland. His predicament is such that the longer he remains on the island, the more his sense of self diminishes. As he acclimates to island life, the man becomes aware of a shift in his position: "I have been completely seized by the island's eye," he muses.[28] His transformation is effected through a relationship he has with Sato, the young woman with whom he becomes entangled. The import of Sakiyama's story rests in its laying waste to the stereotype of the healing island girl, exotic and submissive, like her sister in Ipanema. Instead of affirming the protagonist's identity, Sato's presence calls it into question. This is not all. Sakiyama does far more in the story than reverse gender hierarchy; she creates a new figure that takes the guise of a siren. Whereas the traditional idea of the siren-seductress represents the metaphysical idea of woman as the site of truth, one who lures men with song only to destroy them, Sakiyama's siren is a site of absence. Free-floating in the fluid, untamed sea between the dry land of metaphysics, she represents the movement of the sign. Without woman to serve as anchor upon which all meaning is fixed, phallogocentric thought quickly becomes unmoored. Sakiyama's siren emerges out of the unfathomable depths where all notions of identity are distorted and where she remains free to signify as yet unknown possibilities.[29]

"Tale of Wind and Water" follows the wanderings of a forty-year-old man who is only identified by his place of origin: Yamato. The word suits the man. Lacking any will or sense of direction, the man is perhaps best defined by his absence of personality. A hollow thing set in motion by external forces, he resembles a jellyfish guided solely by ocean currents or a kite caught in the wind. Though he stays on the island well past his term as a reporter for a mainland daily newspaper, the man is repeatedly reminded that he is an outsider, the implication of which is that he return to the mainland. Because he is the filter through which Sakiyama depicts the island, the reader is left with an incomplete and fragmented understanding of character and events.

The man's island discoveries center on two female characters, one named, the other unnamed. The first is Sato, a twenty-six-year-old woman of racially mixed parentage with whom the man lives for three years on the island. He spends perhaps three hours of just a single night with the second, amorphous woman, who appears alternately as a prostitute or sea creature. While the man's interaction with this unnamed woman takes up the second half of the story, Sato remains the focus of the story as a whole. It is through Sato, native to the island, that the man comes to understand the place to the extent that he is able.

The man's tenuous tie to the island is best understood through Sato's connection with both wind and sea. The narrator vividly portrays the exchange between wind and sea alluded to in the story's title through descriptions of the natural environment, which segue to a deeper conflict that resides within Sato herself. Rather than to take the two elements of nature as metaphors through which the story of Sato/the island is told, I will show how they interact organically to form a complex field in which each element exceeds the limits of self-containment.

From the story's beginning, the narrator defines wind and sea as forces with opposite ends. Whereas the wind blows around midnight "in order to lull the people into a peaceful, deep sleep," the "tendrils of the sea reach out seemingly intent on waking people in the night."[30] The wind comforts, yet the sea is more powerful. It succeeds in waking the man and drawing him out into Sakiyama's beloved darkness, where he beholds its force: "The rolling motion of the ocean surface that is like intestines, shredded into a thousand pieces, arises from the undulation of waves buffeted by the wind."[31] The elements' descriptions fall into a distinct pattern in which the wind possesses attributes of warmth and good cheer, in contrast to the dark, black sea.

Having set in place these contradictory elements, the narrator proceeds to root the wind to Sato's childhood. Recounting to the man a particularly beloved memory, Sato explains how, when her grandmother sang the traditional island song called "The Windmill of Flowers" ("Hana nu kajimayā"), the wind would always start blowing, causing their windmill "to spin around and around."[32] Hearing Sato speak fondly of the wind as a benevolent, playful force, the man begins to believe "the wind is the root of a pureness that has remained in Sato."[33] This warm wind, which she holds inside her, is also reflected in Sato's voice, a natural conduit through which wind can find expression. Throughout, the narrator describes Sato's voice as cheerful, childlike, and innocent, making it a simple matter to link the wind with the innocence of Sato. In key passages, Sato even finds expression through the wind that blows around her, causing the man to "feel that the voice of the wind sometimes resembles the windmill song Sato hums."[34] Her intimate connection with the wind makes it difficult to distinguish where the wind begins and Sato ends.

If Sato is the wind, then who is the sea? When communication fails, the narrative wends its way to this menacing body, the seemingly insurmountable gulf that appears in many of Sakiyama's island stories. It is at sea, on a boat at night, that the man glimpses a woman leaning over a rail, as if intent on falling overboard. When he realizes it is Sato, the man observes her, "looking as if she were staring at endlessly flowing black water in a huge chasm inside her."[35] Here, and in subsequent descriptions of Sato, whose voice is cheerful, yet tinged with sorrow, the narrator discloses a darker aspect of the young woman's character. Eventually the man links the dark waters, which reflect an inexpressible sadness, to the cheerful, innocent aspect of Sato, carried in her voice. He forges this connection on another night at sea when he spies a pale figure that resembles Sato jump from a boat into the water and swim off like a creature of the sea. This spectacle calls to mind the man's first encounter with Sato the night she peered intently at the ocean, as if poised to dive in. Wondering whether what he saw before him was the spirit of Sato roaming the sea, while the flesh and blood Sato lay sleeping where he had only just left her, the man muses, "The body of Sato that I held so tightly that night was an empty shell. The real Sato was no doubt sinking into that dark sea."[36] As these passages indicate, Sato's connection to wind and sea is powerful indeed; it enables her body to metamorphize, to roam the ocean even as her voice is carried by the wind and she is nowhere to be seen. The unnamed woman appears to be a manifestation of Sato, the cheerful woman with a youthful voice, blue eyes, little makeup, and hair done up in a ponytail. As such she reflects a far darker, conflicted aspect of Sato than can be seen during her waking hours.

The second woman's conflicted nature is readily apparent in the physical description the man offers the reader. Initially, she "looks less like a woman than a prepubescent girl."[37] A moment later, he reconsiders, regarding her instead as closer to middle-aged on account of her full bosom and self-assured, languid stance. With an unskilled, child-like manner of speech and the plodding body movements of someone much older, she remains indeterminate in age. Even her large, child-like eyes are out of place on her tired, listless face. The mysterious second woman is a hybrid mix of young and old, sorrowful and carefree. Sakiyama's foreboding islands offer a marked contrast to the sunny isles depicted in tourist pamphlets. Her portrayal of island women, too, departs from media norms. Far from one-dimensional, the female characters in "Tale of Wind and Water," particularly this liminal creature of the sea, exhibit a broad spectrum of human characteristics.

Where other writers in the genre of Okinawan fiction might expound upon the reasons for these women's sorrow through details of the often difficult lives of Amerasian children abandoned by their parents, or through inserting scenes that would clarify the nature of the second woman's sex work, Sakiyama only gestures toward these possibilities.[38] Certainly, the narrator's conflicting descriptions of Sato, and virtual cleaving of character into flesh and spirit sound a note of alarm, forcing one to account for Sato's inexplicable trauma. The pain she must have endured—by not having had a father, by looking different from everyone around her, and by the mother who abandoned her—etch lines of sorrow in Sato's otherwise cheery face. Unable to communicate this in her daily life, she escapes the confines of her bedroom and slips into the ocean in another guise. Only through the murky water can she suggest the depths of her pain.

The man falls into a steady relationship with Sato, soon after which he finds himself wakening in the middle of the night. He wanders the town, where seduced by a prostitute, he is drawn into the water. Only at sea, does he begin to sense the siren's inner turmoil. What her words fail to communicate, the dark waters convey, "as if their actual fluid was comprised of the essence of sorrow."[39] In this grief-laden water he comes to understand concretely the "endlessly flowing black water" that Sato had been peering into on that night on the boat. As much as the sea may aid him, it is not a transparent medium by which he can "know" Sato. The sea is opaque, allowing the man partial glimpses, but it ultimately leaves obscure the woman whom the narrator describes through a series of conflicting images: young, old, innocent, resigned, human, animal. Curiously, the woman's mouth remains motionless, yet the man distinctly hears the song of the windmill. Sakiyama's siren song draws the story's cast of women together to form a powerful force that seeks to destroy the man by pulling him underwater. Despite its strength, the man resists, making his way back to safety, where to his surprise he finds the enigmatic woman he followed to sea.

The story concludes as the man is about to leave the unnamed woman after clumsily paying for their strange nocturnal interlude. The narrator tantalizes the reader by holding out, through the woman's parting words, the possibility of truth: "I trust you. There's something I want you to hear. Only one thing. From me."[40] As with earlier attempts to communicate, this one falls short. Incapable of even forming words with which to express herself, the woman's voice instead lets out a stream of sounds, which the narrator renders through a combination of odd symbols: "●△□◎."[41] The ineffable sorrow of Sato's life is encapsulated in this collection of symbols, which lie beyond comprehension. On this discordant note, the story ends, deferring even a single recognizable word, to say nothing of knowledge or truth.

As this passage shows, a cacophony of sound has come to characterize Sakiyama's recent fiction. In "Tale of Wind and Water" the sound the woman emits leads the man to conclude it is she who is destroyed. Critic Shinjō Ikuo argues otherwise. He notes that it is not the woman who is destroyed but rather the fixed position of the man who attempts to see, and thus master, the island.[42] The story's many reversals certainly lend credence to the conclusion Shinjō reaches, but, as I mentioned earlier, Sakiyama does more than reverse gender hierarchies in her story. Dismantling systems of oppression is one part of the story, the larger part of which constructs new possibilities. Sakiyama's siren is a composite of women whose complexity forever eludes grasp. Hers is a body that does not fuse with land but swims at a safe distance. While she bears traces of the femininity in Okinawa of which many speak, in no way does this femininity contain her.

As the suffix "tan" (譚) in the story's title indicates, the work also takes up the issue of speech and communication. Clearly, the characters in "A Tale of Wind and Water" are incapable of arriving at any concrete knowledge or state of mutual understanding, yet, in their failure lie the seeds of the methodological turn Sakiyama takes in her subsequent writing. Were these seeds—here, strange symbols—audible, they would amount to nothing more than static. Symbols with no meaning, they trail off, imparting to the reader only the incommensurability of language to adequately reflect experience, here, Sato's inner world. Given the story's setting, one might speculate that the symbols simply stand in for an island dialect that would be incomprehensible to an outsider such as the protagonist. If this were true, Sakiyama could attempt to render dialect through typographical means used by other authors in the genre, such as glossing or writing regional phrases in Chinese characters. That she chooses a wholly foreign, motley collection of symbols suggests she is pushing the limits of language to their very extreme, attempting a mode of writing that Deleuze and Guattari find prominent in minor literature. Their analysis of the literature focuses on Kafka, who writes against the grain from a linguistic space that is radically heterogeneous, thereby erasing "the tracks of an old topography of mind and thought."[43] In the concluding passage of "A Tale of Wind and Water," which demonstrates Sakiyama's transformation of sound into vision, not only are old categories of mind and thought dispensed with, so too is standard typography. The symbols she uses here in a last ditch effort to find a suitable medium of expression are, more likely than not, markers of speech impossible to apprehend, less owing to the protagonist's unfamiliarity with dialect than to the difficulty of arriving at anything close to certainty through any type of language, dialect or otherwise. By treating words as asignifying sounds, Sakiyama suspends sense.

Sakiyama's continued effort to make expression precede content through linguistic experimentation makes her prose a textbook example of minor literature. It is not the use of dialect, however, that allows one to categorize hers as minor writing. Rather, Sakiyama creates minor literature by writing in Japanese using linguistic elements that allow her to move language toward its extremes. In doing so, Sakiyama meets the first criterion Deleuze and Guattari state is characteristic of the mode: a high coefficient of deterritorialization. One of the means by which she avoids representative language is by frequently using sentence endings commonly found in folklore, particularly following speech (*toka, noda, sōda, toiukotoda*). This allows little to remain of the duality of a subject of enunciation and a subject of the statement, constituting instead "a single process, a unique method that replaces subjectivity."[44] Prevalent, too, is the use in dialogue of onomatopoeia whose meaning is difficult to understand (*muzumuzu, fugafuga, taputapu*). And, Sakiyama, like her beloved Higashi, extends her use of dialect to descriptive passages, making these sections far less intelligible to mainland Japanese readers. To make matters more difficult she renders dialect in a peculiar way, providing few glosses or Chinese characters to aid the reader. On the point of Sakiyama's stylistic excess, fellow author, Tsushima Yūko writes, "Of course, at first, readers are bewildered. But, there's a strange rhythm to the writing, so in no time, even readers unfamiliar with island language are somehow carried away, and come to understand it through the body. This leads to an odd feeling of ecstasy."[45] Indeed, if one surrenders to Sakiyama's style, as Tsushima does, the experience is rewarding. What her words lack in meaning they make up in intensity. This intensity is born of Sakiyama's desire to tear her writing away from the grips of Japanese, destabilizing, if only for the duration of her narrative, its dominance.

A curious aspect of Sakiyama's method is her insistence that the dance of words she enacts by bringing standard Japanese into contact with dialect is not motivated by a desire to revive regionalism. Sakiyama shows surprisingly little concern for issues of local color and identity in her essays, and takes great pain in her prose to do away with any notion of an originary essence.[46] Rather than perform a simple reversal of terms, between standard Japanese and dialect, or underscore the alienness of dialect vis-à-vis standard Japanese, Sakiyama's prose issues from a desire to expose the strangeness of language itself. Musing on Sakiyama's possible motivations, Marukawa Tetsushi asks whether Sakiyama's fiction is not a case of making one forget the Japan of Japanese, or rather, of rewriting the "origin" which sustains the fiction we call Japanese.[47] As Marukawa's question suggests, Sakiyama's interest is neither to assert regional identity or standard Japanese, but, rather, to defamiliarize language.

Migrating sounds

"The Origin of Muiani" exhibits a pronounced change in style. This style of writing, which Sakiyama began to recognize in "A Tale of Wind and Water,"

Figure 6 Sakiyama Tami's beloved coffee shop, Origin (Genten), located in Koza.

and acknowledges in full measure in the essay "A Wild Dance with Island Words" is a veritable cavalcade of words, standard and nonstandard, colliding together in wild abandon. "The Origin of Muiani" and the stories that follow it, such as "Rocking and Rolling" ("Yurateiku yuriteiku," 2000) are notable for a dramatic increase in the use of dialect and a clear departure from the social realism found in much Okinawan prose.[48] In these works, Sakiyama creates a mythic world by means of dialect but not without a certain irony. Where Ōshiro Tatsuhiro's artificial dialect in "Turtleback Tombs" aims for readability, Sakiyama's dialect in "The Origin of Muiani" does not, no doubt because the author recognizes the difficulty of representing ordinary speech, not to mention representing regional dialects in rapid decline. Nevertheless, adhering to her method, Sakiyama incorporates dialect, though her conception of the raw material of her writing is distinct in the genre of Okinawan prose. Sakiyama presents readers a view of island language, different from what they might imagine in the essay "The Landscape of Language" ("Kotoba no fūkei," 2004), a piece that provides a revealing glimpse of the linguistic diversity that surrounded her in Iriomote:

> In my case, language was more complex. I call it island language, but I was born and raised in a certain village on the western part of Iriomote where outsiders settled shortly after the war, on top of which, the village next to us was chock full of coalminers who had come before the war from the mainland, mostly Kyushu, so my memories of language are all jumbled up. There were lots of times when we'd laugh at one another's language and intonation. At home my parents spoke Miyako dialect; the neighbors next door spoke Hatoma dialect. From the back and to the side of the house we could hear high-pitched Sonai dialect. But, when we went to school, we'd very naturally switch into standard Japanese. Of these languages, I thought the neighbors' Hatoma dialect carried a certain exoticism. The foreignness of their words stirred my heart.[49]

Far from pristine, then, Sakiyama's island language is hybrid in nature, a cacophony of competing voices. Drawing from this tempest of sound, Sakiyama creates her fictional world, which, in recent years, has begun to bear far less relation to reality.

"The Origin of Muiani," as the story's title suggests, centers on unraveling the source of the word *muiani*, which the protagonist, *watashi*, only dimly recalls, but finds herself repeating twice daily upon waking. She knows neither its meaning nor whether it is even Japanese. In typical fashion, from the start, the work evades meaning and is set largely in the dark, where the protagonist, through the help of other women, sorts through imprecise memories. With minimal visual effects, and a heavy dose of aural and oral expression, the narrative wends its way to a surprising conclusion, buoyed by one voice after another in rapid and intensifying succession. Drawn by these voices, *watashi*, another in the cast of Sakiyama's female characters who lead a solitary existence, enters a journey of discovery. The beauty of the work lies in its seamless integration of *watashi*'s search for self with the recovery of memories of the child she once bore, a child whose name is Muiani.

The work begins as the protagonist's hermetic life is interrupted by a series of phone calls she receives from a woman who speaks in a mix of standard Japanese and dialect. The caller seems to have intimate knowledge of *watashi*'s reclusive habits and urges her, over the course of a few late night conversations, to come to her: "We've been waiting, all of us, for you to come. For days now, we've been waiting. You. What kind of person are you to make us wait?"[50] The plot thickens, as *watashi* has no idea who the woman is, despite the familiarity of her voice. The stream of words *watashi* does not comprehend wash over her gradually, wearing down her resistance. As she relaxes her guard, surrendering to this voice, and the unknown, *watashi* begins to recall memories, long forgotten, of birthing a child.

With its protagonist whisked away, midnarrative, in a car driven by a woman in sunglasses who takes her to a room in which she discovers evidence of having given birth to a child, "The Origin of Muiani" reads much more like a mystery than "A Passage across the Sea" or "A Tale of Wind and Water," though they too have elements of suspense. Lured by the voice on the phone, *watashi* leaves the confines of her room, only to find she has been trapped. Inside the car, she realizes the woman present is not the person to whom she spoke on the phone. In confirming the protagonist's suspicions, the second woman reveals another layer of intrigue:

> Yes. Of course, that wasn't my voice; I was summoned by it, too. These days there aren't so many people who can floor others with dialect so extreme it can shatter in an instant the mind of a person who is calmly whiling away the days. By and by, that type of language will end up in a museum—in the speech preservation section. But, it's still alive; it's just losing steam.[51]

The force that compels *watashi* to act is a language, which as this passage indicates, is on the brink of extinction. Almost already lost, this language nevertheless leads *watashi* by car through a dark tunnel that ends where she once lived. Guised as a familiar voice from the past, dialect assumes the form of a character, one that moves Sakiyama's inert protagonist.

The motif of darkness that fills the text, its references to a tunnel leading from the protagonist's room to a home temporally and spatially removed from the narrative present, and the profusion of voices audible there, all cry for a suspension of disbelief. Yet, despite its implausible series of events, Sakiyama's work succeeds in large part due to the power of its language. This is no small feat, considering that hers is decidedly not smooth Japanese but language violently usurped by dialect. In his attempt to describe the act of reading "The Origin of Muiani" Shinjō Ikuo writes:

> One doesn't feel the Okinawan language lends the story local color, instead what one experiences is the difficult to experience sensation of trying to grasp the freedom of language in the work, while blocking out any previous knowledge of "dialect." One shouldn't read this work in search of a theme for the work requires a flexible mind. Completely give in to the range of language that echoes in the text, lying between standard and local dialect. Forget, like the protagonist. Forget the standard way of reading.[52]

Here, Shinjō notes the importance of the text's language, confirming, too, how difficult it is to find meaning in the words; elsewhere, in the context of discussing what Okinawan literature is today, he asserts that Sakiyama's works are not directed at finding the self, but rather in losing the self. Indeed, Sakiyama perversely writes to evade certainty. While the dialect of "The Origin of Muiani" reveals little if anything, these words are part of *watashi*, the force that makes her otherwise flat character, and the story, come alive.

Deleuze and Guattari's definition of minor writing includes a second and third characteristic in addition to the first: a high coefficient of deterritorialization. These final characteristics are closely linked; the former holds that everything in minor writing is political, while the latter states that everything in the writing takes on a collective value. Sakiyama's fiction clearly exhibits the first tendency of deterritorialization, but how can her work, which incessantly draws her protagonists into inky nights, leaden water, and dark tunnels, where they ruminate on their respective existential plights, possibly contain within them a collective, political value? I believe this question is linked to a second one: namely, whom does Sakiyama intend her audience to be, given her deliberately impenetrable style of writing?

Take, for example, "The Origin of Muiani," a story centering on the loss of the protagonist's memory of bearing a child. If one construes this loss as analogous to the present state of dialect, also forgotten, or perhaps forsaken, then it is possible to read the work as another of Sakiyama's attempts to return to a specific place—the island—by borrowing a sound, *muiani*, the Miyako island word, rarely heard today, signifying a female charged with the care of a newborn. The fact that this story ends with the discovery of a child offers a glimmer of possibility that the protagonist will form social attachments through this child, thereby ending her confined existence. The world into which *watashi* enters in "The Origin of Muiani," peopled entirely by women, is a fragile community, but does this tenuous female network have a political cast?

Clearly, Sakiyama's method of writing in a mix of standard and nonstandard language is a head-on effort to tackle the thorny issue of language that has plagued writers from Okinawa, who from the inception of the genre, have used a language imposed upon them, which, when employed to depict the local, results in inevitable distortions. What Sakiyama gains in adhering to her method, though, she loses in readership as she clearly does not aim for readability by incorporating dialect. The indeterminacy of her works issues from its deterritorializing language, which seismically shifts Japanese, making it stutter, in the same way as Kafka's Prague German. This type of language does away with fixed categories in favor of becomings, a concept inseparable from minor writing. The reason critics fail to ascertain much in Sakiyama's works is because, by their nature, becomings defy precise description. Her writing relentlessly shifts and dodges meaning, breaking free of representational language's grips. The passages that fill her migratory texts, from island to island in "A Passage across the Sea," from land to water in "A Tale of Wind and Water," and from a solitary existence to a provisional community in "The Origin of Muiani," are part of the lines of escape Sakiyama takes to divest her works of all coded identity.

Needless to say, becomings, a prominent feature of Sakiyama's works, of necessity, call into question all identity formation; however, the writing which they inhabit does far more than dismantle and destroy old avenues of thought, such as the self. Minor writing, besides being a form of stuttering and a process of becoming is a kind of fabulation, and, as Deleuze and Guattari explain it, "[t]he fabulative function of literature is to invent a people."[53] By pushing language to an extreme, turning it on its head, minor writers invent a collective. In Sakiyama's prose, movement is the means by which fabulation creates a people. If minor literature is immediately political and collective, its most pressing problem is that the collectivity does not exist. In their discussion of a collective assemblage, Deleuze and Guattari zero in on the nature of the community for whom Sakiyama writes:

> When a statement is produced by a bachelor or an artistic singularity, it occurs necessarily as a function of a national, political, and social community, *even if the objective conditions of this community are not yet given to the moment except in literary enunciation.* [...] The most individual enunciation is a particular case of collective enunciation. This is even a definition: an statement is literary when it is 'taken up' by a bachelor who precedes the collective conditions of enunciation. This is not to say that this collectivity that is not yet constituted (for better or worse) will in turn become the true subject of enunciation or even that it will become the subject that one speaks about in the statement. [...] No more than the bachelor, the collectivity is not a subject of enunciation or the statement. But the actual bachelor and the virtual community—both of them real—are the components of a collective assemblage.[54]
>
> (Emphasis added)

Like fellow writers of minor literature, Sakiyama invents a collectivity through the process of becoming. The sounds that fill her pages are the voice of the minor people, whose collective enunciation finds expression only in and through the writer. In short, it is through linguistic experimentation that Sakiyama crosses the divide from the narrow world of the individual to the cacophonous sphere of the collective, wherein politics contaminates every statement. If writing in Japanese makes Okinawan authors political, as is often claimed, then Sakiyama's deadly mix of standard and nonstandard language, eviscerates interiority in a one-two punch, pulling out of its shambles, an audible, and perceptible collective. As Deleuze and Guattari's descriptions of minor writing suggest, "the romance of the individual life is exceeded, deterritorialized, escaped."[55] So, too, in Sakiyama's island stories is Okinawa itself, making hers an unsettled, and unsettling position in the genre of Okinawan prose fiction.

Conclusion

In this book, I have focused on the genre of Okinawan prose fiction, a category of writing that emerged in the early twentieth century and continues to thrive today. My research has shown that this body of writing constitutes a distinct countercanon with its own generic difference. While I submit that it is risky to speak of a unitary category of Okinawan prose without reproducing the polarizing ideology that gives rise to this category, I have found that stories in the genre share a number of striking features, making it a coherent and fascinating object of study, particularly in today's globalized world in which culture is all but flattened. By asserting the distinctiveness of Okinawan fiction, however, I do not mean to imply that the genre is cut from a single, vibrant cloth, while mainland fiction is spun from another, more muted one. Such a skewed division invariably minimizes the important differences that lie among Okinawan writers and fellow authors in the mainland. Okinawan fiction is a part of Japanese literature; the distinctions I have focused on are ones of degree, not kind.

The constituent features that recur in the genre of Okinawan fiction, and to which I have paid close attention in the preceding chapters, are issues of history, language, culture, and identity. I have shown that Okinawans remember history differently than do mainland Japanese. For example, Okinawans are far likelier to commemorate June 23, 1945, the day the Battle of Okinawa ended, than August 15, 1945, the day of Japan's surrender to the Allied Forces.[1] As for language, although Okinawa's return to Japan in 1972 and the influx of mass media that reunification precipitated have closed the language gap between those fluent in standard Japanese and those who are not, language remains a thorny obstacle for Okinawan authors who aim to represent both the language of the public sphere and that of felt life. And, as with history and language, one cannot assume Okinawans and mainland Japanese necessarily share the same culture. In traditional Japanese poetry, for example, the generic sounding "flower" (*hana*) could always be assumed to mean "the cherry blossom," but such an immediate association could not be assumed in semitropical Okinawa. The alterity of Okinawan prose arises from such differences in historical and lived experience, large and small. I have attempted in these pages to provide a critical framework for understanding

Okinawan prose from the early twentieth century to the beginning of the new millennium. In the Meiji period, Yamagusuku Seichū penned "Mandarin Oranges," a pioneering story in the genre. Its place at the head of this study stems from Yamagusuku's fulfilling the needs of Japanese readers for local color *and* for its marked resistance to a fraud perpetrated by a character from the mainland. It is this latter point—antimainland or oppositional sentiment—that has, in many stories, surpassed the first—local color—making Okinawan prose a conspicuous body of social protest.

Okinawa's geographical remove from Tokyo has much to do with the differences that abound in the prefecture's history, language, and culture. Caught since the seventeenth century between Japan and China, and since the end of World War II, between powers in Tokyo and Washington, Okinawans' agency has suffered under multiple constraints. A small player among larger forces, the prefecture is, more often than not, depicted as a victim of geopolitics. Indeed, the voices of Okinawans have had little impact on world affairs. A vivid reminder of Okinawans' lack of subjectivity came to the fore in 2000 when the Japanese government issued new currency to commemorate the G-8 summit held in Okinawa. The 2,000-yen note bore no Okinawan face, an erasure that understandably rankled many in the prefecture. In place of a subject, the note boasted an object: the gate to Shuri Castle, used as headquarters for the Japanese Army during the Battle of Okinawa. Not only did this Chinese style "gate of courtesy" (*shurei no mon*) point to Okinawa's difference from the rest of Japan, but it also reinforced the idea of Okinawa as a gracious host ever accepting multiple military bases and several thousand foreign troops. Arakawa Akira cites the note's creation as one of the most important events concerning Okinawa in the twentieth century, arguing that the newly minted bill contains within it the government's continued treatment of the prefecture as Japan's Other.[2]

The intensity of Okinawan prose, with its emphases on history, language, culture, and identity is not unconnected to the fact that the prefecture is politically constrained. Themes such as discrimination, of which Ikemiyagi Sekihō writes in "Officer Ukuma," or the Battle of Okinawa, a subject taken up by Ōshiro Tatsuhiro and Medoruma Shun, are the rule rather than the exception in Okinawan fiction—even today—decades after the rampant discrimination toward Okinawans that characterized the prewar period and led to the sacrifice of many civilian lives in the war. That the most influential contemporary authors, such as Medoruma Shun and Sakiyama Tami, born well after the war ended, insist on writing about the island's history and language speaks volumes about the thematic concerns of the genre. To date, themes such as love or adventure, more typical of affluent regions, have not gained much traction.[3] Okinawan writers' fixation on the prefecture as a setting for their works has provided both local color and a riot of themes connected to Okinawa's volatility in the modern period.

Owing to its recurring themes, I believe Okinawan prose demands a particular kind of reading. I have focused on reading stories in the genre in a mimetic, rather than aesthetic way, precisely because a vast amount of the literature deals with experiences of the prefecture. Questions of power have loomed larger than those of beauty not because the works are unrefined but because they are preoccupied with identity, the overarching theme in the genre. With its differing history, language, and culture, it is only natural that Okinawan authors have represented in their works the ambiguity of their identity in modern Japan. This ambiguity, put to strategic effect in the domain of identity politics, comes from the contradictions of daily life in which the region, long regarded as peaceful and courteous, exists today as Japan's most heavily militarized prefecture. Despite, or perhaps, because of these contradictions, Okinawans fluidly contest, create, and reconfigure themselves vis-à-vis others both inside and outside the prefecture. Demarcating themselves as "islanders" (*uchinanchū*), for example, allows Okinawans to assert their identity, using it as a weapon against outsiders who have largely sacrificed the interests of Okinawans in the modern period.

In the first half of this book, I introduced major prewar writers and the themes they struggled to express. Reflected in the works of these authors is the nation-state's emphasis on cultural nationalism during the years leading to the 1945 Battle of Okinawa. Language education, a central tenet of nationalism, began in Okinawa in 1880 when standard Japanese was adopted as the linguistic medium in schools. In Okinawan prose fiction, it would take several decades before the dual structure of writing in which local dialects mixed uneasily with standard Japanese gave way to a more homogenous type of writing. The works of prewar authors, particularly those by Yamagusuku Seichū and Ikemiyagi Sekihō, who wrote in the Meiji and Taishō periods respectively, reflects the fact that standard language had not yet taken root in Okinawa in the early part of the century. In the 1930s and 1940s, a noticeable shift occurs. Corresponding to increasing strictures on the use of standard Japanese, Okinawan fiction, as represented by authors Kushi Fusako, Yogi Seisho, and Miyagi Sō, becomes markedly free of dialect and is nearly indistinguishable from mainstream prose published in the mainland. The issue of language, never completely resolved in the prewar period, takes on new dimensions in postreversion Okinawa as several authors now use imperiled dialects to emphasize their ethnic roots. The tension between standard and nonstandard language, which has persisted during the entire span of the twentieth century, gives Okinawan fiction its distinctive shape as a minor literature. Though predominantly written in standard Japanese, owing to underlying linguistic tensions, this fiction retains its political subversiveness.

Since Okinawa's reversion to Japan, authors have taken the über-theme of identity in markedly different directions. Whereas much of the previous literature centered on tensions between Okinawan and non-Okinawan identities in works that verge on essentializing these identities, contemporary writers such as Medoruma Shun and Sakiyama Tami have taken another tack. Medoruma writes insistently about Okinawa, particularly its devastating history, but the pointed questions he directs to his readers include fellow Okinawans. This inclusion reveals a new confidence in the genre. Rather than writing exclusively for mainland audiences, an act that necessitates that Okinawan writers assume the burden of explaining their culture all the while creating imaginative stories, Medoruma has refused to perform his Okinawanness, choosing instead to explore a fictional world in all its depth.

United in their concern for Okinawa, Medoruma and Sakiyama nevertheless employ different methods to represent the issues they hold dear. For Medoruma, history is of utmost importance; his works delve deeply into the past to show the gulf that lies between personal and public memory. Moreover, the fact that his works depart from reality marks a break from the social realism of much of the genre. By employing the mode of magic realism, Medoruma takes the genre to new heights, liberating it from a tendency to document what goes on in the hearts and minds of people before and after the events that make history. While this history from the inside holds great appeal for those wishing to understand what Japan's textbooks have left out, it is Medoruma's imaginative narrative strategies that allow his works to stand on their own, alongside those of other internationally acclaimed authors.

Sakiyama Tami, too, straddles two poles. On one hand, her penchant for writing island stories makes her a vital part of contemporary Okinawan prose. Sakiyama's repeating island, one that proliferates endlessly, each copy different from the last, usually remains unnamed but bears a striking resemblance to the outlying island of Iriomote, where Sakiyama lived until age fourteen. What links Sakiyama to the genre, more than the physical setting of her works, however, is her attempt to write Japanese in which dialect fuses with standard language, rather than simply figuring as local color. Curiously, Sakiyama's efforts come from a desire to dismantle the system of Japanese language, rather than out of an interest in asserting regional identity. In this sense, Sakiyama's concerns go beyond the issue of identity and have allowed me to move from a discussion of whether Okinawan literature is regional literature or minority literature to how, in Sakiyama's case, surely, it is minor literature. Like Medoruma, then, Sakiyama can be understood both as a writer representative of the genre, and one who transcends it. Despite her seniority to Medoruma, I conclude this chronological study with Sakiyama's work precisely because it exhibits all the features Deleuze and Guattari ascribe to minor writing. Sakiyama's writing stays clear of the dangers inherent in overemphasizing regional identity even as it connects to a broader collective within which she, like fellow authors in the genre, engage in textual battles for social justice.

Notes

Introduction

1. Donald Keene (1984) *Dawn to the West: Japanese Literature in the Modern Era*, New York: Henry Holt & Company, Inc., p. 817.
2. While this equation continues to be debated in academic discussions, it remains largely intact in political discourse. As recently as October 15, 2005, in remarks delivered at the opening ceremony of the Kyushu National Museum, Aso Tarō, Japan's former Internal Affairs and Communications Minister, characterized Japan as having "one nation, one civilization, one language, one culture and one race." See, "Aso Says Japan Is Nation of One Race," *Japan Times*, October 18, 2005. Komori Yōichi discusses the formula's illogic in several of his works. See, in particular, Komori (1998) *Yuragi no Nihon bungaku*, Tokyo: NHK Bukkusu.
3. For an instructive series of essays on regional literature, see David Jordan (ed.) (1994) *Regionalism Reconsidered: New Approaches to the Field*, New York: Garland. Comparable collections of essays on minority literature are David Palumbo-Liu (ed.) (1995) *The Ethnic Canon: Histories, Institutions, and Interventions*, Minneapolis, Minn.: University of Minnesota Press and Abdul R. JanMohamed and David Lloyd (eds), (1990) *The Nature and Context of Minority Discourse*, New York: Oxford University Press.
4. I am referring here to much Japanese language scholarship, which tends to treat the terms "Okinawa" and "problem" as synonymous (*Okinawa mondai*), and the recent spate of English-language scholarship in Okinawan studies, which was, in large part, precipitated by the 1995 rape of an Okinawan schoolgirl. For example, see Tanaka Yasuhiro (1999) "'Okinawa mondai' to 'Okinawa no mondai'," in Jōkyō shuppan henshūbu (eds), *Okinawa o yomu*, Tokyo: Jōkyō shuppan, pp. 198–203.
5. W. E. B. DuBois (1998) "The Souls of Black Folk," in Julie Rivkin and Michael Ryan (eds), *Literary Theory: An Anthology*, Malden, Mass.: Blackwell Publishing, p. 868.
6. The main island of Okinawa prefecture comprises less than 1 percent of Japan's total land mass, yet houses 75 percent of all US military facilities and more than half of the 47,900 troops stationed in the country.
7. See Ōshiro's essays "Okinawa mondai wa bunka mondai de aru," and "Dōka to ika no hazama de" in his (2002) *Ōshiro Tatsuhiro zenshū*, Vol. XIII, Tokyo: Bensei shuppan, pp. 5–10 and 50–64.
8. Vincent J. Cheng examines the discourse of authenticity in his study (2004) *Inauthentic: The Anxiety over Culture and Identity*, London and New Brunswick, N.J.: Rutgers University Press, 2004.
9. Gregory Smits (1999) *Visions of Ryukyu: Identity and Ideology in Early-Modern Thought and Politics*, Honolulu, Hawaii: University of Hawai'i Press, p. 149.

10 For a useful overview on the competing versions of Okinawan history, see Richard Siddle (1998) "Colonialism and Identity in Okinawa before 1945," *Japanese Studies*, 18 (2): 117–33.
11 A case in point is Chinen Seishin's theatrical piece, *House of Peoples* (*Jinruikan*), published to much acclaim in 1976.
12 Patrick Heinrich provides an instructive analysis of standard language education and its effects on local language varieties in Okinawa in his essay (2005) "Language Loss and Revitalization in the Ryukyu Islands," in *Japan Focus*, November 14. Available online at http://japanfocus.org.
13 I do not wish to make here a clear-cut demarcation between Japanese oppressiveness in the prewar decades and American liberation in the postwar period. The absence of Okinawan subjectivity in prewar fiction, for instance, is due both to the Japanese state's intense efforts to inculcate Okinawans and the Okinawans' intense desire to rid themselves of markers of difference. After World War II, the USA promoted Okinawan culture in an effort to distance the island from Japan. Postwar fiction reflects the new found importance of regional culture. As the American occupation entered its third decade in Okinawa, however, the foreign military grew equally oppressive.
14 *Okinawa Times*, November 25, 2001, p. 22.
15 Nakahodo Masanori continues to teach at the University of the Ryukyus; Okamoto Keitoku retired in 2000, after which he taught at Okinawa University. His death in August 2006 was a blow to intellectual circles in Okinawa.
16 See my discussion of Yamagusuku Seichū's "Mandarin Oranges" in Chapter 1 for a fuller discussion of this central aspect of the genre.
17 Aaron Gerow (2003) "From the National Gaze to Multiple Gazes," in Laura Hein and Mark Selden (eds), *Islands of Discontent: Okinawan Responses to Japanese and American Power*, Lanham, Md.: Rowman & Littlefield, p. 293.
18 Geoffrey Hartman (1993) "Public Memory and Modern Experience," *The Yale Journal of Criticism*, 6 (2): 239.
19 Stephen Dodd (2004) *Writing Home: Representations of the Native Place in Modern Japanese Literature*, Cambridge, Mass.: Harvard University Press.
20 Quoted in Cheng, *Inauthentic*, p. 19.
21 Hayashi Kyōko uses the term "resident Okinawan" in a roundtable discussion: Hayashi Kyōko (2002) "Genbaku bungaku to Okinawa bungaku," *Subaru*, 24 (4): 207.
22 Gilles Deleuze and Félix Guattari (1986) *Kafka: Toward a Minor Literature*, trans. Dana Polan, Minneapolis, Minn.: University of Minnesota Press, pp. 16–17.
23 John Whittier Treat (1995) *Writing Ground Zero: Japanese Literature and the Atomic Bomb*, Chicago, Ill.: University of Chicago Press, p. 46.
24 I present facts of the 1995 rape not to further associate the rape to the island but rather to illustrate how intertwined personal stories are with historical ones in this region of Japan. For an excellent in-depth article on this incident, see Linda Angst (2003) "The Rape of a Schoolgirl: Discourses of Power and Women's Lives in Okinawa," in Laura Hein and Mark Selden (eds), *Islands of Discontent*, pp. 135–60.
25 See, for example, Dr. Antonia Levi (1995) "Okinawa: Thousand-Year Rape of an Entire People," *Seattle Times*, November 10, p. 11; Thomas Shapley (1995) "Child's Rape Echoes Rape of Okinawa Itself," *Seattle Post-Intelligencer*, November 14, p. 9.
26 Ahmad refutes Jameson's theory by disclosing the epistemological impossibility of Third World literature. He writes, "There is no such thing as a Third World Literature which can be constructed as an internally coherent object of theoretical knowledge." Aijaz Ahmad (1992) *In Theory: Classes, Nation, Literatures*, London and New York: Verso, p. 103. See Fredric Jameson (1986) "Third-World Literature in the Era of Multinational Capitalism," *Social Text* 15 (fall): 69.

Also of note, in a discussion of the Akutagawa Prize Selection Committee's insistence on separating art from politics in Ōshiro Tatsuhiro's 1967 novella *Cocktail Party*, Ikezawa Natsuki, a mainland writer and long-time resident of Okinawa, remarks how, given their circumstances, authors from Okinawa do not have the leisure (*zeitaku*) *not* to write in a political frame. See Ikezawa Natsuki (1992) *Okinawa iroiro jiten*, Tokyo: Shinchōsha, p. 21.

27 For a detailed account of these accidents, see Fukuchi Hiroaki (1992) *Beigun kichi hanzai: ima mo tsuzuku Okinawa no kanashimi to ikari*, Tokyo: Rōdō kyōiku sentā. On the 2003 helicopter crash, see Kurosawa Asako (ed.) (2005) *Okinawadai ga Amerika ni senryō sareta hi: 8/13 beigun heri suiraku jiken kara miete kita Okinawa*, Tokyo: Seidosha.

28 For an interesting discussion of Okinawa's tie-in to Hiroshima and Nagasaki, see the roundtable discussion with Hayashi Kyōko, Komori Yōichi, Inoue Yasushi, and Matsushita Hirobumi (2002) "Genbaku bungaku to Okinawa bungaku: 'chinmoku' o kataru kotoba," *Subaru*, 24 (4): 206–46.

29 Masamichi S. Inoue discusses the Status of Forces Agreement (SOFA) in his study (2007) *Okinawa and the US Military*, New York: Columbia University Press, pp. 33–4.

30 I am thinking here of the striking juxtaposition between fiction and contemporary history in Okinawa, particularly in the case of the prefecture's Akutagawa Prizewinning works. In 1967, just as reunification talks were in full swing, Ōshiro Tatsuhiro received the award for *The Cocktail Party*; in 1971, the eve of the year Okinawa reverted to Japan, Higashi Mineo's *Child of Okinawa* won the prize. Twenty-five years elapsed before another work from Okinawa was so richly awarded. However, following the 1995 rape case, undoubtedly the most sensational news from Okinawa since the late 1960s and early 1970s, Matayoshi Eiki was honored for his work *The Pig's Revenge* (*Buta no mukui*, 1996). Just a year later, Okinawa captured the limelight once more when Medoruma Shun's story "Droplets" won the prize. While I believe each of these four works is deserving of the prize, I stress here the timing of the awards in order to show that the prize is, unsurprisingly, not devoid of politics, as much as the selection committee members would disagree.

31 Benedict Anderson (1983) *Imagined Communities: Reflections on the Origin and Spread of Nationalism*, London: Verso, p. 139.

32 *Okinawa Times*, April 12, 2000, p. 17.

33 Shinjō Ikuo, a scholar at the University of the Ryukyus and successor to mentor Okamoto Keitoku, argues for a broader and more nuanced understanding of what Okinawan literature is in his provocative book (2003) *Okinawa bungaku to iu kuwadate*, Tokyo: Inpakuto shuppankai, pp. 231–4.

34 *Okinawa Times*, April 12, 2000, p. 17.

1 The color orange in Yamagusuku Seichū's Okinawan fiction

1 Richard Torrance refers to this in his insightful article on regional writing (1996) "Literacy and Modern Japanese Literature in the Izumo Region, 1880–1930," *Journal of Japanese Studies*, 22 (2): 327–62. Also instructive is Kären Wigen (1996) "Politics and Piety in Japanese Native-Place Studies: The Rhetoric of Solidarity in Shinano," *Positions: East Asia Critique*, 4 (3): 491–517.

2 See Mukubō Tetsuya (2006) "Kyōdo geijutsu, den'en, rōkaru karā," *Nihon kindai bungaku* 74 (5): 182–96. Stephen Dodd discusses native place literature in his study (2004) *Writing Home: Representations of the Native Place in Modern Japanese Literature*, Cambridge, Mass.: Harvard University Press.

3 Alice Walker (1982) *The Color Purple*, New York: Washington Square, p. 186. For an analysis of how Walker incorporates the Philomela myth into her novel,

see Martha J. Cutter (2000) "Philomela Speaks: Alice Walker's Revisioning of Rape Archetypes in *The Color Purple*," *MELUS* 25 (3/4): 161–80. See also, Komesu Okifumi (1991) *Piromera no uta: jōhōka jidai ni okeru Okinawa no aidentitī*, Naha: Taimusu senshō II, 8, pp. 199–209.
4 See Tsubouchi Shōyō (1983) *The Essence of the Novel*, trans. Nanette Twine, Brisbane: University of Queensland. First published as *Shōsetsu shinzui*, 1885.
5 On the establishment of modern Japanese literature, see Karatani Kōjin (1993) *The Origins of Modern Japanese Literature*, trans. Brett de Barry, Durham, N.C. and London: Duke University Press.
6 See Okamoto Keitoku (1981) *Okinawa bungaku no chihei*, Tokyo: San'ichi shobō, pp. 7–28, and Nakahodo Masanori (1991) "Okinawa kindai shōsetsu no dōtei," in *Okinawa kindai bungei sakuhinshū*, Naha: Okinawa taimususha, pp. 395–403.
7 For an incisive discussion on how Okinawans in the prewar period strove to become full-fledged citizens of the nation-state, see Alan Christy (1993) "The Making of Imperial Subjects in Okinawa," *Positions: East Asia Critique* 1 (3): 607–38. I might also note that calls for the advancement of Okinawa, which were strident and copious, presuppose the region and its people are behind the times.
8 In some publications, the author's surname is glossed "Yamashiro" rather than "Yamagusuku." I have opted for the latter rendering since it is the one given in the (projected) twenty-volume *Collected Works of Okinawan Literature* (*Okinawa bungaku zenshū*, 1990) and the one told to me by Nakahodo Masanori. The author may very well have referred to himself as "Yamashiro" to deemphasize his ethnic identity.

The *Kunenbo* plant, according to *Kōjien* (5th edn), is a short evergreen tree in the tangerine family. Indigenous to Indonesia, the plant bears fruit in autumn, which resemble tangerines but are quite larger. The skin of the fruit is thick, its flavor and scent strong. In the Okinawan dialect used in Yamagusuku's story, the fruit is referred to as *kunibu*.
9 See Nakahodo Masanori (1988) *Iha Getsujō: Ryūkyū no bungei fukkō o yume mita netsujōka*, Tokyo: Riburopōto, p. 240.
10 See "Kindai Okinawa bungakushi-ron" in Okamoto Keitoku (1981) *Gendai Okinawa bungaku to shisō*, Naha: Okinawa taimususha, pp. 3–83.
11 Gregory Smits explains that taxation before and after the incorporation of Ryukyu took the form of levies on villages. He writes:

> It was up to local officials to distribute land and tax burdens, and they rarely did so equitably. Particularly oppressive was the sugar levy. Although in 1882 it became permissible to pay salt and rice levies in cash, the sugar tax was not payable in cash until the general land reform of 1903 that did away with the former system. Individual sales of sugar were prohibited until the entire sugar tax had been paid, and all sales of sugar went to the government at a price set below that which the open market would bear.
> See Gregory Smits (1999) *Visions of Ryukyu*, Honolulu, Hawai'i: University of Hawai'i Press, pp. 147–8.

12 See Hokama Shuzen (1986) *Okinawa no rekishi to bunka*, Tokyo: Chūkō shinsho, pp. 76–84. Julia Yonetani notes, "postwar historians debated over whether events culminating in the *shobun* entailed a Japanese 'unification,' 'invasion' or 'invasion-type unification.'" See Julia Yonetani (2000) "Ambiguous Traces and the Politics of Sameness: Placing Okinawa in Meiji Japan," *Japanese Studies*, 20 (1): 16.
13 After the Meiji Restoration, the need to unify the country grew. In 1872, an international incident in which citizens of Miyako Island were killed in Taiwan

provoked the Japanese government to send troops in order to affirm that Ryukyuans were Japanese. To rid the region of any political ambiguity, Ryukyu nation (*koku*) became Ryukyu domain (*han*) in keeping with administrative divisions in other parts of Japan. Unable to erase all differences, the government classified the Ryukyu king as the Ryukyu domain king in 1873. Yonetani, "Ambiguous Traces," p. 16. See also Murai Osamu's essay "Nantō ideorogī no hassei," in which he focuses on Yanagita Kunio's "discovery" of the Ryukyus to elucidate the relation between the southern islands of Japan and Japanese nationalism. Murai Osamu (1992) *Nantō ideorogī no hassei: Yanagita Kunio to shokuminchishugi*, Tokyo: Fukubu shoten, pp. 7–58.

14 I am reminded here of Frantz Fanon's eerily accurate projection of cultural evolution and his emphasis on the national dimension of anticolonial consciousness rather than the racial emphasis of his peers. Fanon charts the following three distinct phases: the assimilationist phase, in which "the native intellectual gives proof that he has assimilated the culture of the occupying power"; the cultural nationalist phase, in which the native intellectual remembers his authentic identity and fights attempts to assimilate him; the nationalist phase in which the native man of culture "after having tried to lose himself in the people and with the people, will on the contrary shake the people." See Chidi Amuta (1995) "Fanon, Cabral and Ngugi on National Liberation," in Bill Ashcroft, Gareth Griffins, Helen Tiffin (eds), *The Post-Colonial Studies Reader*, London and New York: Routledge, pp. 158–9.
15 Okinawa kenchō hen (1975) *Okinawa taiwa*, Tokyo: Kokusho kankōkai, p. 27.
16 Asano Makoto (1991) *Okinawaken no kyōikushi*, Tokyo: Shibunkaku shuppan, pp. 211–22.
17 Uesugi, the second person appointed by the Meiji State to oversee Okinawa prefecture, was known for his benevolent rule, a contrast with that of his predecessor, Matsuda Michiyuki, the official responsible for ushering in the Ryukyuan Disposition. See Arazato Kinpuku and Ōshiro Tatsuhiro (1972) *Kindai Okinawa no ayumi*, Tokyo: Taihei shuppansha, pp. 90–6.
18 For biographical information on these individuals, see Okinawa taimususha (1983) *Okinawa daihyakka jiten*, Naha: Okinawa taimususha.
19 Hokama, *Okinawa no rekishi to bunka*, pp. 87–8.
20 Alan Christy describes the stubbornness of many in Okinawa who resisted the Japanese administration of the islands in his essay "The Making of Imperial Subjects in Okinawa." Before and after the disposition, Ryukyuan aristocrats petitioned the Qing Government to intercede on their behalf. Christy writes, "Memories and fears of an Okinawan inclination toward China were so strong among the military that even in 1940 Governor Fuchigami justified further intensification of the policy of 'imperial-subjectification'" (p. 615) The increase in severity was due to the presence of people in Okinawa who hoped to serve the Chinese during the Sino-Japanese war.
21 Medoruma Shun (1999) "An Okinawan Short Story," trans. Steve Rabson, *JPRI Critique*, 6 (12) p. 4. Available online at < http://www.jpri.org/publications/critiques/critique_VI_12.html > (accessed September 15, 2007).
22 Arazato and Ōshiro, *Kindai Okinawa no ayumi*, pp. 201–3.
23 Arazato and Ōshiro, *Kindai Okinawa no ayumi*, pp. 198–200. See also Gregory Smits, *Visions of Ryukyu*, pp. 149–50.
24 While most would cleanly divide modern Okinawan literature from preceding Ryukyuan letters based on the differing languages of these bodies of work, Sakiyama Tami, for one, blurs the distinction, showing how much Ryukyuan verse is indebted to the waka tradition. See Sakiyama Tami (2002) "'Shimakotoba' de kachāshī," in Imafuku Ryūta (ed.), *'Watashi' no tankyū*, Tokyo: Iwanami shoten, pp. 157–80.

25 Christy, "The Making of Imperial Subjects," p. 612.
26 Christy, "The Making of Imperial Subjects," p. 612.
27 The dialects of mainland Japan and the Ryukyus, while related structurally, became mutually unintelligible around 700 C.E. when they diverged from a single ancestral dialect. For a detailed history of a remote Ryukyuan dialect, see Leon Angelo Serafim (1984) "Shodon: The Prehistory of a Northern Ryukyuan Dialect of Japanese," Ph.D. dissertation, Yale University. For an analysis of Ryukyuan dialect and its use in modern Okinawan fiction, see Nakahodo Masanori (1981) "Kotoba to bungaku," in *Kindai Okinawa bungaku no tenkai*, Tokyo: San'ichi shobō, pp. 53–90. See also Nakahodo Masanori et al. (1998) in the roundtable discussion "Okinawa bungaku to hōgen katsuyō ni tsuite" in *Urasoe bungei*, 3, for further discussion of the topic.
28 For a discussion of language policy in the case of Taiwan see Patricia E. Tsurumi (1977), *Japanese Colonial Education in Taiwan, 1895–1945*, Cambridge, Mass.: Harvard University Press. See also Leo T. S. Ching (2001) *Becoming "Japanese": Colonial Taiwan and the Politics of Identity Formation*. Berkeley, Calif.: University of California Press.
29 Iha Fuyū, one of the students responsible for organizing the strike, gives a first-person account of this event in Arazato and Ōshiro, *Kindai Okinawa no ayumi*, pp. 204–14.
30 Hokama, *Okinawa no rekishi to bunka*, p. 88. See also Ngũgĩ wa Thiong'o, "The Language of African Literature," in Bill Ashcroft, Gareth Griffins, Helen Tiffin (eds), *The Post-Colonial Studies Reader*, London and New York: Routledge, p. 288. Ironically, dialect placards were used once again in the 1960s when the vast majority of educators in Okinawa gave their full support of the reversion movement in part by laboring to ensure that students had mastered Japanese and did not lapse into dialect. Placard use instilled the belief that Japanese language was integral to the formation of a national subject. See Oguma Eiji (1998) *Nihonjin no kyōkai*, Tokyo: Shinyōsha, pp. 564–9.
31 Okamoto Keitoku (1993) "Okinawa kindai shōsetsushi: seiritsuki," in *Okinawa bungaku zenshū*, 6, Tokyo: Kokusho kankōkai, p. 386.
32 Okamoto, "Okinawa kindai shōsetsushi," p. 386. See also, Chantal Zabus (1991) *The African Palimpsest: Indigenization of Language in the West African Europhone Novel*, Amsterdam and Atlanta, Ga.: Rodopi Press.
33 *Ryūka*, the indigenous short (thirty syllables) poetic form, is comprised of three lines of eight syllables and a final line of six syllables. Major themes of Ryukyuan poetry are the life and values of the commoner (*shomin*) class. This poetry is often accompanied by Ryukyuan string instrumental music (*sanshin*).
34 The *Omoro sōshi*, Okinawa's oldest collection of poetry is often compared to the *Collection of Myriad Leaves* (*Manyōshū*). Comprised of twenty-two volumes (1,248 pages), the *Omoro* was written between 1531 and 1623. It contains poems (*omoro*) that members of the Shuri Kingdom disseminated throughout the regions of Amami and Okinawa. *Omoro* is a Ryukyuan cognate of Japanese "omoi" (think, brood); *omoro* are poems to the gods. See Sakihara Mitsugu (1987) *A Brief History of Early Okinawa Based on the Omoro Sōshi*, Tokyo: Honpo shoseki shuppan.
35 Okamoto, *Okinawa bungaku no chihei*, p. 16.
36 Nakahodo, *Okinawa bungaku ron no hōhō: "Yamato yo" to "Amerika yo" no moto de*, p. 10.
37 In 1913, *Ryukyu News* established its New Writers Prize. This award played an important role in raising the quality of subsequent fiction.
38 Okamoto, *Okinawa bungaku no chihei*, pp. 19–20.
39 Okamoto, *Okinawa bungaku no chihei*, p. 20.

Notes 189

40 Having entered Tokyo University's education department in 1902, Noma was posted in Okinawa to teach at the prefectural middle school after obtaining his teaching credentials.
41 Ishikawa Takuboku writes of Yamagusuku in a similar vein in the April 4, 1909 entry to his *Diary of Roman Letters* (*Rōmaji nikki*): Yamashiro Seichū came in the evening. It seemed he was a bit drunk. Tonight, for the first time, I tried to deal with people firmly. With a look of despair, Yamashiro went back home. Quoted in *Okinawa kindai bungei sakuhinshū*, p. 22.
42 *Okinawa daihyakka jiten*, Vol. III, p. 747.
43 Yosano Tekkan memorializes Yamagusuku's fondness for drink in the following tanka:

> *Seichū wa medetaku Naha ni kaerikeri*
> *Ima wa you to mo nakazu ya aruran*
> Seichū has happily returned to Naha
> Though now drunk, I am teary-eyed.
> *Okinawa daihyakka jiten*, Vol. III, p. 747.

44 Yamagusuku and fellow calligraphers Jahana Unseki, a Nō playwright, and Shō Jun, son of the last Ryukyu king, Shō Tai, were known collectively as the "Three Okinawa Calligraphers" (*Okinawa sanpitsu*). See *Okinawa daihyakka jiten*, Vol. III, p. 747.
45 Because of its historical importance to Okinawan fiction, and this study's focus on the prose genre, I will concentrate on Yamagusuku's fiction rather than the poetry that earned him the honor of being the prefecture's representative *tanka* poet in the Taishō and early Shōwa period.
46 *Okinawa kindai bungei sakuhinshū*, pp. 24–25.
47 The incidental fact that Tsuruoka, who hopes to make it as a writer in the Meiji period, is reading Bakin's *Biography of Eight Dogs*, as so many others did at the time, makes one take Tsubouchi Shōyō's criticism of Bakin's Edo masterpiece far less seriously.
48 Due to the mass emigration of Okinawans in the pre- and postwar periods, Okinawa prefectural associations frequently sprang up in diasporic communities as far flung as Ponape and Bolivia. See *Okinawa daihyakka jiten*, Vol. I, pp. 485–6. See also Ronald Y. Nakasone (ed.) (2002) *Okinawan Diaspora*, Honolulu, Hawai'i: University of Hawai'i.
49 *Ishigantō* was the name of a legendary strong Chinese man who lived during the Five Dynasties Period (907–60). People in succeeding generations carved his name in stone to construct a guardian deity. Yamagusuku relates that *ishigantō* are mentioned in the works of Tokugawa scholars and that they can still be found in Nara and in the Ryukyus where Chinese influence is most pronounced. Today, *ishigantō* can be found at dead ends and various other spots where paths intersect in Okinawa. For further details, see Kodama Masatō's chapter on *ishigantō* (1993) in his *Shiryō ga kataru Ryukyu to Okinawa*, Tokyo: Mainichi shinbunsha, pp. 177–95.
50 The Department of Hygiene was established in Japan in 1873 as part of the Ministry of Education. In 1876, it was renamed the Sanitary Bureau and reassigned to the Ministry of Home Affairs, essentially the police. See Brigitte Steger (1994) "From Impurity to Hygiene: The Role of Midwives in the Modernisation of Japan," *Japan Forum*, 6 (2): 175–88. See also Michael K. Bourdaghs' chapter (2003) "The Disease of Nationalism, the Empire of Hygiene," in his study on Shimazaki Tōson, *The Dawn That Never Comes*, New York: Columbia University Press.
51 *Okinawa kindai bungei sakuhinshū*, p. 36.

52 *Okinawa kindai bungei sakuhinshū*, 37. For a discussion of the "quest for white flesh," a sexual myth perpetuated by alienated individuals, see Frantz Fanon (1967) "The Man of Color and the White Woman," in *Black Skin, White Masks*, trans. Charles Lam Markmann, New York: Grove Press.
53 Nakahodo Masanori, "Okinawa kindai shōsetsu no dōtei," in *Okinawa kindai bungei sakuhinshū*, p. 397.
54 *Okinawa kindai bungei sakuhinshū*, p. 398.
55 In an effort to spur fellow Okinawan writers on, Iha Getsujō proclaimed 1909 as year one in a revival of the arts. See Nakahodo Masanori, "Ryūkyū no bungei fukkō dai ichinen" in *Iha Getsujō*, pp. 53–80.
56 See Nakahodo, *Okinawa bungakuron no hōhō*, pp. 29–32.
57 Nakahodo, *Okinawa bungakuron no hōhō*, pp. 32–34. Whereas, Iha Fūyu, the father of Okinawan studies, believed that Okinawan writers could not easily cross the huge linguistic gulf that lay between Okinawa and the main islands of Japan, his younger brother, Getsujō, far more optimistically declared, "there is no reason that we Okinawans cannot write fiction." See Komesu, *Piromera no uta*, p. 203.
58 Nakahodo, *Okinawa bungakuron no hōhō*, p. 34. The term "local color" is romanized.
59 Oona Frawley (2005) *Irish Pastoral: Nostalgia and Twentieth-Century Irish Literature*, Dublin: Irish Academic Press, p. 67.
60 Shimao Toshio, "Kaiki no sōnen: Yaponeshia," *Okinawa bungaku zenshū*, Vol. XVIII, p. 302.
61 Li Hung-chang is the person who negotiated the Tientsin Convention with Itō Hirobumi in 1885. According to historian Peter Duus, this convention stipulated "a withdrawal of both Japanese and Chinese troops and military advisors from Korea and an agreement for each to give prior notice to the other in the event grave disturbances required a new dispatch of troops." See Peter Duus (1976) *The Rise of Modern Japan*, Boston, Mass.: Houghton Mifflin Company, p. 127.
62 A schoolteacher from Kagoshima, Yamajō Hajime, was executed for the fraud he perpetrated.
63 Ōshiro Tatsuhiro, author of the Akutagawa Prize-winning novella *The Cocktail Party* and Okinawa's best-known postwar writer, begins his short story "Turtleback Tombs" ("Kamekōbaka," 1957) in a similar fashion. The story, which describes the escape of civilian refugees to the confines of their ancestral tombs during the outbreak of the Battle of Okinawa, opens with a scene of tranquil village life. By focusing upon innocent Okinawan villagers, Ōshiro heightens the devastation wrought by the battle that follows. An analysis of this and other stories by Ōshiro follows in Chapter 4.
64 Ushi is one of several common names, like Nabi and Toki, given to females in prewar Okinawa. It is written in *katakana*, the script reserved for foreign terms, unlike many postwar female Okinawan names, which mimic mainland counterparts and include the female diminutive suffix -*ko* (i.e., Hanako, Momoko, Michiko).

The narrator's description of Ushi, whose name is quite traditional, erases the image of Ryukyuan women, then in circulation:

> Ushi sat quietly, her hands clasped. Her fingers, slim, fair, and smooth, were elegantly aligned. From ancient times, the local custom was to imprint a blackish-blue colored tattoo on the back of women's hand, on the rough skin; on this woman there was no such tattoo. These fair hands often caught the eyes of the young laborers.
> Yamagusuku, "Mandarin Oranges, p. 24.

65 *Okinawa kindai bungei sakuhinshū*, p. 43.

66 *Okinawa kindai bungei sakuhinshū*, p. 43.
67 In 1998, Ōta Masahide, who had governed Okinawa since 1990, lost a closely fought election to conservative candidate Inamine Kei'ichi. Inamine's LDP support, and his success in raising Okinawans' fears that Ōta's reelection would result in a reduction of the flow of money from Tokyo to Okinawa for publicworks projects, led to his victory. For a fascinating, if depressing account of the structural relationship between Okinawa and Tokyo, see Gavan McCormack (2003) "Okinawa and the Structure of Dependence," in Glenn D. Hook and Richard Siddle (eds), *Japan and Okinawa: Structure and Subjectivity*, London and New York: Curzon Press, pp. 93–113.

The new 2,000-yen note issued on July 19, 2000 commemorated a meeting of world leaders, including former President Clinton, at the G-8 summit held in Nago, Okinawa. The front of the bill bears an illustration of Shureinomon, the gate that leads to Shuri Castle in Naha, Okinawa. The back of the bill features a scene from the *Tale of Genji* and an image of Murasaki Shikibu, its author. The issue of the bill rankled the sensitivities of some Okinawans who felt that it, and the central government's decision to host the G-8 summit in Okinawa on the heels of the uproar over the schoolgirl rape and backlash against military bases, smacked of compensatory politics. Critic Arakawa Akira penned a scathing critique of Japan's incorporation of Okinawa by means of locating the G-8 summit in Okinawa and issuing the 2,000-yen note. See *Okinawa Times*, December 12, 1999, p. 13. Arakawa's recent memoir provides an in-depth analysis on the significance of the new currency, which he believes is the most significant event in the prefecture's postwar history. See Arakawa Akira (2000) *Okinawa: tōgō to hangyaku*, Tokyo: Chikuma shobō, pp. 17–58.

68 *Okinawa kindai bungei sakuhinshū*, p. 43. Okinawans use various expressions to denote non-Okinawan Japanese. The most common among these is *Yamatunchu*, a term far more neutral than *Yamato no kedamono*, but not free from negative connotations. Its counterpart, *Uchinanchu*, is the word Okinawans reserve for themselves.
69 *Okinawa kindai bungei sakuhinshū*, p. 43.
70 *Okinawa kindai bungei sakuhinshū*, p. 43.
71 *Okinawa kindai bungei sakuhinshū*, p. 44.
72 Tsuji, Okinawa's red-light district, was constructed in 1672, expanded in 1908, and laid to waste by the October 10 air raid in 1944, 270 years after it came into being. See *Okinawa daihyakka jiten*, Vol II, p. 818.
73 Nakahodo, *Okinawa bungakuron no hōhō*, p. 35.
74 Nakahodo, *Okinawa bungakuron no hōhō*, p. 37. Philosopher Friedrich Nietzsche's well-known lines appear in his essay (1974) "On Reading and Writing," in *Thus Spoke Zarathustra*, trans. Thomas Common, New York: Gordon Press, p. 48.
75 See Nakahodo, *Okinawa kindai bungei sakuhinshū*, p. 396.
76 See Nakahodo, *Okinawa kindai bungei sakuhinshū*, p. 398. On the subject of the close and often uncomfortable relation that exists between Japan's capital city and its southwesternmost prefecture, critic Kawamitsu Shin'ichi remarks, "When Tokyo sneezes, Okinawa catches a cold." Kawamitsu Shin'ichi (1987) *Okinawa, jiritsu to kyōsei no shisō: 'Mirai no jōmon' e kakeru hashi*, Osaka: Kaifūsha, p. 240.
77 In Ōshiro Tatsuhiro's "Turtleback Tombs," a character named Zenga is the counterpart to Yamagusuku's Hosokawa. Like Hosokawa, Zenga is a dishonest educator who can be read as an embodiment of Yamato culture.

2 Subaltern identity in Taishō Japan

1 See Donald Keene (1984) *Dawn to the West*, Vol. I, New York: Henry Holt & Company, pp. 446–57.

Notes

2 See Edward Mack (2002) "The Value of Literature," Ph.D. dissertation, Harvard University, p. 34.
3 See, for example, Jung-Sun N. Han (2007) "Envisioning a Liberal Empire in East Asia: Yoshino Sakuzō in Taisho Japan," *Journal of Japanese Studies*, 33 (2), pp. 357–82, and Peter Duus (1983) 'The Takeoff Point of Japanese Imperialism" in Harry Wray and Hilary Conroy (eds), *Japan Examined: Perspectives on Modern Japanese History*, Honolulu, Hawaii: University of Hawai'i Press, pp. 153–7.
4 Gregory Smits (1999) *Visions of Ryukyu: Identity and Ideology in Early-Modern Thought and Politics*, Honolulu, Hawaii: University of Hawai'i Press, p. 149.
5 I use the term "quasicanonical" as it is arguable whether literature from Okinawan is a part of the canon of Japanese letters. "Ukuma Junsa" is as canonical as a work from Okinawa can be. In an essay that follows the collected works of Ikemiyagi, Nakahodo Masanori suggests that the writer, a renowned wanderer, whose alter ego appears in Ukuma, is emblematic of Okinawa itself. See Nakahodo's essay (1988) "'Chairudohuddo' no tama," in *Ikemiyagi Sekihō sakuhinshū*, Naha: Niraisha, p. 192.
6 See linguist Kinjō Chōhei's essay (1992) "Ryūkyū ni shuzai shita bungaku," *Okinawa bungaku zenshū*, 17: 11.
7 In his study, *Nantō ideorogī no hassei*, Murai Osamu argues that Yanagita's discovery of the southern islands in the period was a direct result of the unease he felt about his involvement in the drafting of colonial policies on agriculture in Korea where he served as a bureaucrat in the Ministry of Agriculture. Murai writes convincingly of Yanagita's longing for therapeutic relief from the distress of his involvement in the Korean affair. Resigning his governmental post in 1919, Yanagita quickly retreated to the Ryukyus, concealing his past by rapidly absorbing himself in southern manners. See Murai Osamu (1992) *Nantō ideorogī no hassei: Yanagita Kunio to shokuminchishugi*, Tokyo: Fukutake shoten, pp. 7–58. See also Murai's (1995) "Iha Fuyū to Yanagita Kunio" in *Okinawa kara mita Nihon*, Tokyo: Kazama shobō, pp. 165–202. Of related interest is Kawamura Minato's chapter on the place of the South in modern Japanese literature (1994) *Nanyō/Karafuto no Nihon bungaku*, Tokyo: Chikuma shobō, pp. 59–82.
8 See Nakahodo Masanori's commentary in Hirotsu Kazuo (1994) *Samayoeru Ryūkyūjin*, Tokyo: Dōjidaisha, pp. 74–82.
9 R. Goldschmidt (1981) *Taishō jidai no Okinawa*, trans. Taira Ken'ichi and Nakamura Tetsumasa, Naha: Ryukyu shinpōsha, pp. 1–7. This publication is a translation of the Okinawa section of Goldschmidt's travelogue.
10 Goldschmidt, *Taishō jidai no Okinawa*, pp. 17–22.
11 Postwar writer Shimao Toshio devotes the "Amami: Nihon no nantō" section of his series of essays on the southern islands, collectively titled *Theory of Yaponeshia (Yaponeshia ron)*, to a fascinating and historically specific account of the Shimazu clan's economic exploitation of Amami Ōshima through forced sugarcane production from the beginning of the seventeenth century. The profits they garnered through colonial policies in the Ryukyus are convincingly related to the clan's key role in the formation of the modern Japanese state. See Shimao Toshio (1992) "Amami: Nihon no nantō," *Okinawa bungaku zenshū*, 18: 273–6.

The curious phenomenon of an oppressed group showing unflagging loyalty to its oppressors can also be seen in the case of Taiwanese aborigines, a group which displayed fervent loyalty to the Japanese, despite their position at the lowest rungs of the colonial hierarchy. See Leo Ching (2000) "'Give Me Japan and Nothing Else!': Postcoloniality, Identity, and the Traces of Colonialism," *The South Atlantic Quarterly* 99 (4): 781.
12 *Bingata* is the name of a dyeing technique developed in Okinawa. Various indigo-based colors are inserted onto a sewing pattern resulting in a complex

color tone. Flowers, birds, mountains, and rivers are used frequently in bingata designs. See Matsumura Akira (ed.) (1989) *Daijirin*, 15th edn, Tokyo: Sanseidō, p. 2079.
13 Hirotsu, *Samayoeru Ryūkyūjin*, pp. 72–3. Nakahodo Masanori relates Goldschmidt's account in the extended commentary appended to Hirotsu's book.
14 Benedict Anderson (1983) *Imagined Communities: Reflections on the Origin and Spread of Nationalism*, London and New York: Verso, p. 141.
15 Prior to Japan's success in the Sino-Japanese war of 1894–5, owing to a long history of Ryukyuan trade with China, there were segments of Okinawa's population that allied themselves with Qing China rather than with the Meiji government that had appropriated the Ryukyus in 1879. In light of the Japanese victory, loyalties quickly switched to Japan, the nation that was clearly emblematic of strength and modernity. The result of the Russo-Japanese war of 1904–5 only confirmed Japan's power, and, by the Taishō period, Okinawans redoubled their efforts to align themselves with the Japanese. See Okamoto Keitoku (1981) *Gendai Okinawa bungaku to shisō*, Naha: Okinawa taimususha 3–88.
16 Alan S. Christy (1993) "The Making of Imperial Subjects in Okinawa," *Positions: East Asia Critique* 1 (3): 607–38, p. 614.
17 Johannes Fabian (1983) *Time and the Other: How Anthropology Makes its Object*, New York: Columbia University Press.
18 Smits, *Visions of Ryukyu*, p. 40.
19 Smits, *Visions of Ryukyu*, p. 40.
20 *Okinawa kindai bungei sakuhinshū*, p. 111. See also Nakahodo Masanori and Tsunori Setsuko (eds) (1988) *Ikemiyagi Sekihō sakuhinshū*, Naha: Niraisha, for further biographical information on Ikemiyagi.
21 "Officer Ukuma" was the second piece of Okinawan fiction to appear in a major Japanese magazine, the first being Yamagusuku Seichū's "Mandarin Oranges," which was published in the well-known haiku journal *Cuckoo*.
22 For details regarding Ikemiyagi's years traveling throughout Japan, see Nakahodo Masanori's chapter (1994) "Hōrōsha no bungaku" in his book *Shinseinentachi no bungaku*, Naha: Niraisha, pp. 148–81.
23 Though divorced in life, Arakaki and Ikemiyagi remain united by the publication of their joint collections of literature (1988) *Ikemiyagi Sekihō sakuhinshū*, ed. by Nakahodo Masanori and Tsunori Setsuko, Naha: Niraisha, and (1988) *Arakaki Mitoko sakuhinshū*, ed. by Miki Takeshi, Naha: Niraisha.
24 In response to a contest for literary submissions, *Liberation* received 445 manuscripts. Of these, seven or eight won awards. In October 1922, two stories, one of which was "Officer Ukuma," were published from this smaller group. Ikemiyagi's story was selected as the top story. See Tsunori Setsuko's unpublished manuscript, "Taishō kōki no sakuhin: shōsetsu 'Ukuma Junsa' ni tsuite," p. 173.
25 Ikemiyagi's use of the term *tokushu buraku* indicates that the village in question is far from ordinary. Okinawan critics uniformly agree that the village Ukuma writes about is Kuninda, an area of Naha inhabited by many naturalized Japanese originally from China. See the roundtable discussion "Okinawa no kindai bungaku to sabetsu" featuring Kuniyoshi Shintetsu, Okamoto Keitoku, and Ōshiro Tatsuhiro (1973) *Aoi umi* 26 (fall): 88–99.
26 Although the story is no more specific about the group of Japanese of Chinese descent that live in certain quarters of Kume, critics have noted that the inhabitants of this special hamlet are people whose ancestors were once employed by the Chinese diplomats and traders who lived in the Ryukyus from the fourteenth century until the time of the Sino-Japanese war. After the defeat of the Chinese in 1895, Okinawans increasingly discriminated against these descendants from other villages. Having lost their means of income, they fell under the protection of Kume village, and, because they owned no land, the group could

not engage in agriculture and were therefore reduced to performing menial labor. See Horii Ken'ichi (1973) "Densetsu kara jijitsu e: Shōsetsu 'Ukuma Junsa' no koto," *Aoi umi* 26 (fall 1973): 100–2.
27 Ikemiyagi Sekihō (2000) "Officer Ukuma" in Michael Molasky and Steve Rabson (eds), *Southern Exposure: Modern Japanese Literature From Okinawa*, Honolulu, Hawaii: University of Hawai'i Press, p. 62.
28 Economic conditions being what they were at the time, many Okinawan families were forced to sell their daughters to brothels. See Nakahodo, *Shinseinentachi no bungaku*, pp. 148–65.
29 Nakahodo, *Shinseinentachi no bungaku*, pp. 166–79.
30 Albert Memmi (1965) *The Colonizer and the Colonized*, Boston, Mass: Beacon Press, p. 120.
31 It would be remiss to leave unacknowledged Memmi's intellectual debt to Frantz Fanon, whose *Black Skin, White Masks* is perhaps the *locus classicus* in postcolonial writing for the idea that the process of colonization effects changes in colonial subjects' very consciousness.
32 Ikemiyagi, "Officer Ukuma," p. 69.
33 Nakahodo, *Shinseinentachi no bungaku*, pp. 166–79.
34 See Christopher T. Nelson, "*Nuchi nu Sūji*: Comedy and Everyday Life in Postwar Okinawa," in Glen D. Hooks and Richard Siddle (eds), *Japan and Okinawa*, London and New York: RoutledgeCurzon, pp. 208–24, p. 218.
35 Ikemiyagi, "Officer Ukuma," p. 71.
36 I do not mean to imply that there is no theoretical possibility for subaltern speech. Whether or not the story's protagonist Ukuma "speaks" or not, the author Ikemiyagi Sekihō, a subaltern Japanese writer and noted representative of Okinawan fiction, clearly has little problem expressing himself.
37 To cite just one egregious example, in his article "The Subaltern Speaks," Alan Wald precedes a lengthy analysis of the ways in which American writer Guy Endore succeeds in allowing Carribean "others" to represent themselves in the 1934 novel *Babouk* with only the briefest mention of Gayatri Chakravorty Spivak's well-known essay "Can the Subaltern Speak?" Wald frames his own essay by stating that Spivak has questioned the ways in which Western scholars have given voice to "colonial subjects, the third world subalterns, of their first world societies" and asks whether there are techniques that would allow "subaltern subjects to represent themselves with maximum authenticity." Except for the apposition "colonial subjects" and the prefix "third world" nowhere does Wald define what he means by subaltern. See Alan Wald's (1992) "The Subaltern Speaks," *Monthly Review* 43 (11), p. 17.
38 Fredric Jameson is also scrupulous in his use of the term "subaltern." Influenced by Antonio Gramsci, Jameson refers to subalternity as "the feelings of mental inferiority and habits of subservience and obedience which necessarily and structurally develop in situations of domination—most dramatically in the experience of colonized peoples." See Fredric Jameson's (1986) "Third-World Literature in the Era of Multinational Capitalism," *Social Text* 15 (fall): 76. I should note, too, several critics have responded to Jameson's provocative essay. The most articulate of these remains Aijaz Ahmad, who notes that Jameson's "cognitive aesthetics" of Third World literature rests upon "a suppression of the multiplicity of significant difference among and with both the advanced capitalist countries on the one hand and the imperialized formations on the other." See Ahmad (1992) "Jameson's Rhetoric of Otherness and the 'National Allegory,'" *In Theory: Classes, Nations, Literatures*, London and New York: Verso, p. 376. For a spirited defense of Jameson, see Imre Szeman (2001) "Who's Afraid of National Allegory? Jameson, Literary Criticism, Globalization," *South Atlantic Quarterly*, 100 (3): 803–27.

Notes 195

39 Ranajit Guha and Gayatri Chakravorty Spivak (eds) (1988) *Selected Subaltern Studies*, New York and Oxford: Oxford University Press, p. 35.
40 Guha and Spivak, *Selected Subaltern Studies*, p. 35.
41 Guha and Spivak, *Selected Subaltern Studies*, p. 44.
42 See Gayatri Spivak's (1988) "Can the Subaltern Speak?" in Cary Nelson and Lawrence Grossberg (eds), *Marxism and the Interpretation of Culture*, Urbana, Ill.: University of Illinois Press, p. 285.
43 Spivak, "Can the Subaltern Speak," pp. 271–313.
44 Spivak, "Can the Subaltern Speak," p. 285.
45 See Gautam Bhadra (1989) "The Mentality of Subalternity: Kantanam or Rajdharma" in Ranajit Guha (ed.) *Subaltern Studies VI*, Delhi: Oxford University Press, p. 54.
46 Bhadra, "The Mentality of Subalternity," p. 91.
47 See Homi K. Bhabha's essay (1990) "DissemiNation: Time, Narrative, and the Margins of the Modern Nation," in *Nation and Narration*, London and New York: Routledge, p. 314.
48 Gayatri Chakravorty Spivak also identifies the true subaltern as one whose identity lies in difference. See Spivak, "Can the Subaltern Speak?" p. 285.
49 Homi K. Bhabha (1994) "Of Mimicry and Man," in *The Location of Culture*, London and New York: Routledge, p. 86.
50 Bhabha, "Of Mimicry and Man," p. 86.
51 The Okinawa Youth Alliance, formed in 1921, is considered one of Japan's earliest socialist organizations. See Kuniyoshi Shintetsu (1970), "*Samayoeru Ryūkyūjin* no shūhen," *Shin Okinawa bungaku*, 17 (summer): 45.
52 Kuniyoshi, "*Samayoeru Ryūkyūjin* no shūhen," p. 46.
53 Kuniyoshi, "*Samayoeru Ryūkyūjin* no shūhen," p. 45. By 1970, when Okinawa's identity was the subject of public discourse due to the island's impending reversion to Japan, it was argued that *Samayoeru Ryūkyūjin* should be regarded as a valuable historical document that ought to be more readily available to readers interested in past depictions of Okinawans.
54 According to Donald Keene, the other two important Taishō era critics were Masamune Hakuchō (1879–1962) and Satō Haruo (1892–1964). See Keene, *Dawn to the West*, Vol. I, p. 568.
55 Keene, *Dawn to the West*, p. 569.
56 Given Hirotsu's interest in Russian, I suspect Mikaeru is the Japanese equivalent of the name Mikhail.
57 Hirotsu Kazuo (1994), *Samayoeru Ryūkyūjin*, Tokyo: Dōjidaisha, pp. 9–10.
58 Quoted in Oshino Takeshi's informative essay (1993) "Nantō orientarizumu e no teikō: Hirotsu Kazuo no 'sanbun seishin,'" *Nihon kindai bungaku*, 49 (October): 33. Also helpful for understanding Hirotsu's oeuvre is Matsubara Shin'ichi (1998), *Taida no gyakusetsu: Hirotsu Kazuo no jinsei to bungaku*, Tokyo: Kōdansha.
59 Matsubara, *Taida no gyakusetsu*. Evidence in the text suggests that the character known as O is based on Ikemiyagi Sekihō, an author known for his habit of wandering.
60 Matsubara, *Taida no gyakusetsu*.
61 Kuniyoshi, "*Samayoeru Ryūkyūjin* no shūhen," p. 45.
62 Kuniyoshi, "*Samayoeru Ryūkyūjin* no shūhen," p. 45.
63 Hirotsu Kazuo, *Samayoeru Ryūkyūjin*, pp. 25–6.
64 For a history of coal-mining in Japan, see Matthew Allen (1994) *Undermining the Japanese Miracle*, Cambridge: Cambridge University Press.
65 Nakahodo Masanori discusses this in his commentary appended to the republication (1994) of *Samayoeru Ryūkyūjin*, Tokyo: Dōjidaisha, pp. 102–11.
66 During the Taishō period, Okinawans in Tokyo were highly sensitive to being called *Ryukyuan* because the word connotes a disassociation with the modern

196   *Notes*

Japanese state. Nakahodo Masanori discusses this in his analysis of Hirotsu Kazuo's *Samayoeru Ryūkyūjin* and Satō Haruo's *Hōrō sanmi: aru shijin no kaiwa*, in which he cites Okinawan poet Yamanoguchi Baku's "Conversation" ("Kaiwa," 1935), a poem that addresses the issue of what to call persons hailing from the Ryukyu Islands. See Nakahodo Masanori (1975) *Yamanoguchi Baku: shi to sono kiseki*, Tokyo: Hōsei daigaku shuppankyoku, pp. 53–72.
67 Kinjō Chōei (1902–55) uses this phrase in his reading of Hirotsu's novella. See commentary by Nakahodo Masanori (1994) *Samayoeru Ryūkyūjin*, Tokyo: Dōjidaisha, p. 115.
68 Nakahodo, *Samayoeru Ryūkyūjin*, p. 55.
69 Nakahodo, *Samayoeru Ryūkyūjin*, p. 56.
70 By negative attributes, I mean ones that are different from the majority of Japanese. In a far-from-neutral vein, anthropologist William P. Lebra describes Okinawans as follows:

> Relative to the Japanese, Okinawans are characterized by shorter stature, broader shoulders, darker skin, greater nasal breadth, wider eye opening, and less prognathism. The most notable phenotypic difference between the two peoples is in the relative degree of hairiness. Anyone who has used public baths in Okinawa is aware that a heavy mat of hair covering the back and buttocks of males is by no means a rarity.
> See William P. Lebra (1966) *Okinawan Religion: Belief, Religion, and Social Structure*, Honolulu, Hawaii: University of Hawai'i Press, p. 7.

71 Quoted by Patrick Brantlinger, "The Rule of Darkness," in Julie Rivkin and Michael Ryan (eds), *Literary Theory: An Anthology*, Malden, Mass.: Blackwell Publishing, pp. 856–67, p. 862.
72 Hirotsu, *Samayoeru Ryūkyūjin*, p. 30.
73 To educated readers of the Taishō period, the phrase "wandering Ryukyuans" would certainly connote the Jewish people and the diaspora with which they are associated. Several works published in Japanese include the phrase "wandering Jews" (*samayoeru yudayajin*) in their titles, an indication that Ryukyuans and Jews are similarly troped.
74 W. E. B. DuBois, "The Souls of Black Folk," in Julie Rivkin and Michael Ryan (eds), *Literary Theory: An Anthology*, Malden, Mass.: Blackwell Publishing, pp. 868–72, p. 868.
75 Simon Sebag Montefiore (2006) "Century of Rubble," *New York Times*, November 12.
76 See Murai Osamu (2002) "Japanese Ethnology, Fascism, Colonialism," in Uemura Tadao (ed.), *Okinawa no kioku/Nihon no rekishi*, Tokyo: Miraisha, pp. 33–73.

3 Marching forward, glancing backward: language and nostalgia in prewar Okinawan fiction

1 Nakahodo Masanori (1991) "Okinawa kindai shōsetsu no dōtei," in *Okinawa kindai bungei sakuhinshū, Shin Okinawa bungaku bessatsu*, pp. 395–403, p. 402.
2 See Oona Frawley (2005) *Irish Pastoral: Nostalgia and Twentieth-Century Irish Literature*, Dublin: Irish Academic Press, p. 34.
3 One notable exception is the story "The Particulars," ("Tenmatsu," 1935) by Yogi Seishō. In keeping with his apparent aim to depict Okinawa and its culture faithfully, Yogi employs local dialect to good effect in the dialogue portions of the work.
4 In his study of nationalism, Benedict Anderson explains that languages should not be treated as emblematic of the nation; rather, the important thing about

Notes   197

languages is their capacity for creating imagined communities or particular solidarities. See Benedict Anderson (1983) *Imagined Communities: Reflections on the Origin and Spread of Nationalism*, London and New York: Verso, p. 133.

5 Alan Christy discusses the increasing intensification of language education through modern Okinawan history in Alan Christy (1993) "The Making of Imperial Subjects in Okinawa," *Positions: East Asia Critique* 1 (3): 607–38, p. 628. According to Christy, the nation-state's initial encouragement of standard language use in late Meiji became an "absolutist imperative" by the prewar period.

6 Quoted in Higa Shunchō, Shimota Seiji, and Shinzato Keiji (eds) (1996) *Okinawa*, Tokyo: Iwanami shoten, p. 28.

7 Higa et al., *Okinawa*, p. 29.

8 See Gregory Smits (2006) "The Politics of Culture in Early Twentieth Century Okinawa," in Joseph Kreiner (ed.), *Japaneseness versus Ryukyuanism*, Bonn: Bier'sche Verlagsanstalt, p. 67.

9 The Buddhist philosophies that underlie Yanagi's theories of art are discussed in Arazato Kinpuku and Ōshiro Tatsuhiro (1966) *Okinawa mondai: Nijūnen*, Tokyo: Iwanami shoten, pp. 388–9. The authors argue that Yanagi's religious convictions prompted him to defend both Okinawans and Koreans against colonial oppression.

10 The dialect eradication debate is discussed in several histories of Okinawa and in various essays of literary criticism. Among histories, see Higa Shunchō et al., *Okinawa*, p. 27–30; Arazato Kinpuku and Ōshiro Tatsuhiro (1972) *Kindai Okinawa no ayumi*, Tokyo: Taihei shuppansha, pp. 385–91; Hokama Shuzen (1986) *Okinawa no rekishi to bunka*, Tokyo: Chūkō shinsho, pp. 88–9. For discussion in literary histories and miscellaneous essays, see Nakahodo Masanori (1981) "Bungaku sakuhin ni okeru Okinawa no kotoba: sono dōkō to hatten," *Kindai Okinawa bungaku no tenkai*, Tokyo: San'ichi shobō, pp. 56–90; Okamoto Keitoku, (1981a) *Gendai Okinawa bungaku to shisō*, Naha: Okinawa taimususha, p. 82. Ōshiro Tatsuhiro provides much detail in his essay "Dōka to kindaika no hazama de," *Taisoku no enerugī*, pp. 106–36 and, more recently, in "'Okinawa hōgen ronsō' o sōkatsu suru" collected in (1994) *Hāfu taimu Okinawa*, Naha: Niraisha, pp. 77–92.

11 Higa Shunchō, Shimota Seiji, and Shinzato Keiji use the phrase "dangerous thought" (*kiken shisō*) when writing about Yanagi's opinions on the promotion of standard language in Okinawa. See Higa et al., *Okinawa*, p. 29.

12 Three local newspapers, *Ryukyu News*, *Okinawa Daily* (*Okinawa mainichi shinbun*), and *Okinawa Daily News* covered the debate extensively. Of the three newspapers, only the most conservative, *Ryukyu News*, favored the use of local dialect over standard language. See Ōshiro, *Hāfu taimu Okinawa*, p. 82.

13 Quoted in Ōshiro, *Hāfu taimu Okinawa*, p. 82.

14 See *Okinawa daihyakka jiten*, 3, 444. Ōshiro Tatsuhiro includes the opinions of ordinary Okinawans, often absent in commentaries of the debate, in *Hāfu taimu Okinawa*, pp. 85–6.

15 Noting a discursive shift from linguistic controversy to social dilemma, Ōshiro Tatsuhiro states the larger issue the debate raised was where to place Okinawa, with its diverse culture, within Japan, a nation seeking to erase all difference in its inexorable drive to integrate and unify. See Ōshiro Tatsuhiro (1987) *Taisoku no enerugī: Ajia no naka no Okinawa*, Tokyo: Ningen sensho, p. 132.

See Kim Brandt (2007) *Kingdom of Beauty: Mingei and the Politics of Folk Art in Imperial Japan*, Durham, NC and London: Duke University Press, p. 176.

16 Higashionna Kanjun voiced the concerns of many in Okinawa when he stated that the language problem in Okinawa was due to the fact that Japanese bureaucrats viewed Okinawa in the same manner as they did Taiwan or Korea. Ōshiro, *Hāfu taimu Okinawa*, p. 88.

17 A special issue of the journal *Monthly Arts* (*Gekkan mingei*, 3, 1940) is devoted to the debate and, in particular, the issue of local dialect versus standard Japanese.
18 Interestingly, Aono is quite vocal on the overuse of regional dialect. Radio announcers who speak casually in local dialect distress him as do writers who overload fiction with dialect, robbing it of value. See Nakahodo Masanori (1981) "Kotoba to bungaku," *Kindai Okinawa bungaku no tenkai*, Tokyo: San'ichi shobō, p. 66.
19 Ōshiro, *Hāfu taimu Okinawa*, p. 89.
20 In the essay "Uchināguchi kara yutaka no gengo seikatsu o," writer Gima Susumu recalls his teachers' admonition to use textbook language (*kyōkasho no kotoba o tsukainasai*) whenever he inadvertently used local dialect. See Takara Ben (1995) *Hatsugen: Okinawa no sengo gojūnen*, Naha: Okinawa bunko, p. 112. Anthony Appiah, writing on Congolese writer Sony Labou Tansi, remarks that Tansi's mistakes in French led his colonial teachers to smear him with human feces. See Anthony Appiah (1998) "Topologies of Nativism," in Julie Rivkin and Michael Ryan (eds), *Literary Theory: An Anthology*, Oxford: Blackwell Publishing, p. 945.
21 This example of the extreme disuse of Ryukyuan dialects appears in Nakahodo, *Kindai Okinawa bungaku no tenkai*, p. 55.
22 This is not to say that no trace of local dialect remained; of course it did. However, those engaged in professions such as radio broadcasting did not perform their duties in dialect. Additionally, for all practical purposes, dialects, because they were conceptually limited, were deemed inadequate for relating modern day news. See Nakahodo, *Kindai Okinawa bungaku no tenkai*, p. 66.
23 See Ōshiro, *Hāfu taimu Okinawa*, p. 88. Similar fears are expressed in Ōshiro's *Taisoku no enerugī*, p. 58.
24 Nakahodo, *Kindai Okinawa bungaku no tenkai*, p. 58.
25 Gima Susumu capitalizes on Frantz Fanon's ideas on speaking the language of the empire in his essay "Gengo, bunka, sekai," in (1992) *Okinawa bungaku zenshū*, 18, Tokyo: Kokusho kankōkai, pp. 193–203. See also Frantz Fanon's chapter "The Negro and Language" in (1967) *Black Skin, White Masks*, New York: Grove Press, for a description of how mastery of a dominant language affords a colonized people power.
26 Nakahodo Masanori discusses Okamoto's bleak pronouncement in *Kindai Okinawa bungaku no tenkai*, p. 58.
27 One notable exception is the Irish poet Nuala Ní Dhomhnaill who, displeased by those who cannibalize Irish and peddle it as ethnic chic, writes Irish or dual-language works. (Ní Dhomhnaill prefers the term "Irish" over "Gaelic" which she views as marginalizing.) See Nuala Ní Dhomhnaill (1995) "Why I Choose to Write in Irish, The Corpse that Sits Up and Talks Back," *New York Times Book Review*, January 8, 27–8.
28 Salman Rushdie (1982) "The Empire Writes Back with a Vengeance," *The Times*, July 3, p. 8.
29 Michael Molino (1993) "Flying by the Nets of Language and Nationality: Seamus Heaney, the 'English' Language, and Ulster's Troubles," *Modern Philology*, 3 (2): 180–201.
30 Molino, "Flying by the Nets," p. 197.
31 Quoted in David T. Haberly (1974) "The Search for a National Language: A Problem in the Comparative History of Postcolonial Literatures," *Comparative Literature Studies*, 11: 95.
32 For an example of language enforcement in another colonial context, see Ngũgĩ wa Thiong'o, "The Language of African Literature," in Bill Ashcroft, Gareth Griffiths, and Helen Tiffin (eds), *The Post-Colonial Studies Reader*, London and New York: Routledge, p. 288. The author discusses how African students speaking

Gikuyu rather than English were caned by their teachers or forced to wear a metal plate inscribed with the words "I am stupid" around their neck. Both types of punishment were practiced in Okinawa prefecture from the 1880s to 1945; dialect placards resurfaced in Okinawa's classrooms in the 1960s when educators sought reunification with Japan.

33 Arakaki Mitoko, the wife of Ikemiyagi Sekihō, is perhaps the most prominent of the few women writers of the time. The daughter of a wealthy physician, Arakaki went to Nihon Women's University in Tokyo and there met Ikemiyagi, who was then studying at Waseda University. She fell in love with Ikemiyagi and married him in 1922. Their romance was shortlived as Arakaki was left to care for herself and her two sons while Ikemiyagi, an inveterate wanderer, traveled throughout Japan. To escape a life of poverty, Arakaki left Tokyo to return to her home in Okinawa. She began writing for educational journals while in Okinawa and subsequently published both poetry and fiction. Ikemiyagi tried throughout his life, albeit unsuccessfully, to reconcile with Arakaki. Arakaki's insistence in maintaining her distance from Ikemiyagi was thwarted recently when the couple's collected works appeared in a joint volume set. See Miki Takeshi (ed.) (1988) *Arakaki Mitoko sakuhinshū*, Naha: Niraisha. and Nakahodo Masanori and Tsunori Setsuko (eds), *Ikemiyagi Sekihō sakuhinshū*, Naha: Niraisha for more details on this well-known literary pair.

34 Kushi Fusako (2000) "In Defense of 'Memoirs of a Declining Ryukyuan Woman'," in Michael Molasky and Steve Rabson (eds), *Southern Exposure: Modern Japanese Literature from Okinawa*, Honolulu, Hawaii: University of Hawai'i Press, pp. 81–4, p. 81.

35 Kushi Fusako's slip of the pen incident (*hikka jiken*) is discussed in many works of Okinawan history and literature. See, for example, Arazato and Ōshiro, *Kindai Okinawa no ayumi*, pp. 392–7; Higa et al., *Okinawa*, p. 26; Okamoto, (1981b) *Okinawa bungaku no chihei*, Tokyo: San'ichi shobō, pp. 137–40. Keiko Katsukata-Inafuku considers the reasons for Kushi's capitulating to public opinion in a chapter on Kushi in her study (2006) *Okinawa joseigaku kotohajime*, Tokyo: Shinjuku shobō, pp. 101–56.

36 See Higa, "Toshitsuki to tomo ni," *Kindai Okinawa no ayumi*, p. 395.
37 Higa et al., *Okinawa*, p. 30.
38 Higa, *Kindai Okinawa no ayumi*, p. 395.
39 David L. Howell (2004) "Making 'Useful Citizens' of Ainu Subjects in Early Twentieth-Century Japan," *Journal of Asian Studies* 63 (1), p. 13. See also Howell's recent study (2005) *Geographies of Identity in Nineteenth-Century Japan*, Berkeley, Calif.: University of California Press.

Note that "dying" is how Howell glosses *horobiyuku*. The same word is glossed "declining" in the English translation of Kushi Fusako's story, thus my use of the word.

40 Kushi Fusako (1973) "'Horobiyuku Ryukyu onna no shuki' ni tsuite no kaimeibun," *Aoi Umi* 26 (fall): 110. For a concise summary of the concept of race as it applies to the Ainu people of Japan, see Richard Siddle (1996) *Race, Resistance and the Ainu of Japan*, London: Routledge, pp. 6–25.

41 Arazato and Ōshiro, *Kindai Okinawa no ayumi*, p. 396.
42 Kushi, "Memoirs of a Declining Ryukyan Woman," p. 76.
43 Kushi, "Memoirs of a Declining Ryukyan Woman," p. 78.
44 Kushi, "Memoirs of a Declining Ryukyan Woman," p. 79.
45 Kushi, "Memoirs of a Declining Ryukyan Woman," p. 79.
46 Ōshiro Tatsuhiro (1973) "Okinawa no kindai bungaku to sabetsu: 'Ukuma Junsa' to 'Horobiyuku Ryukyu onna no shuki' o megutte," *Aoi umi* 26 (fall): 89.
47 Kushi, "Memoirs of a Declining Ryukyan Woman," p. 74.
48 Kushi, "Memoirs of a Declining Ryukyan Woman," p. 74.

49 Kushi, "Memoirs of a Declining Ryukyan Woman," p. 80.
50 See Nakahodo Masanori (1991) *Okinawa no bungaku: 1927–1945*, Naha: Okinawa taimususha, p. 151.
51 Nakahondo, *Okinawa no bungaku*, p. 106.
52 Yogi Seishō (1993) "Yōju," in *Okinawa bungaku zenshū*, Vol. VI, Tokyo: Kokusho kankōkai, pp. 181–209, p. 182.
53 Yogi, "Yōju," p. 183.
54 Nakahodo Masanori, *Okinawa kindai bungei sakuhinshū*, 402–3.
55 Yogi, "Yōju," p. 184.
56 Yogi, "Yōju," p. 184.
57 For an informative description of café waitresses in the prewar period, see Miriam Silverberg (1998) "The Café Waitress Serving Modern Japan," in Stephen Vlastos (ed.), *Mirror of Modernity*, Berkeley, Calif.: University of California Press.
58 Yogi, "Yōju," p. 191.
59 Yogi, "Yōju," p. 196.
60 Yogi, "Yōju," p. 198.
61 Yogi, "Yōju," p. 202.
62 Yogi, "Yōju," p. 209.
63 *Yuta* is the designation Yogi uses to describe Abe's sister-in-law. Usually female, these shaman priestesses perform religious rites to assure tranquility among family members, living and dead. Individuals call upon *yuta* to interpret what are believed to be supernatural or more mundane human affairs such as illness or domestic unhappiness. For accounts of the role *yuta* play in Okinawan life, see William P. Lebra (1966) *Okinawan Religion: Belief, Ritual, and Social Structure*, Honolulu, Hawaii: University of Hawai'i Press, and Susan Sered's more recent, controversial study (1999) *Women of the Sacred Groves: Divine Priestesses of Okinawa*, Oxford: Oxford University Press. In his various essay collections, Ōshiro Tatsuhiro often writes about the role of *yuta* in Okinawan society. See, for example, (1994) "Yuta to kagaku to shukyō," *Hāfu taimu Okinawa*, Tokyo: Niraisha, pp. 16–26; (1993) "'Dakara yo' bunka no meian: Okinawa bunka no kanōsei," *Ryukyu no kisetsu ni*, Tokyo: Yomiuri shinbunsha, pp. 23–37; (1987) "Kami kara tōzakaru ningen: Noro no soshikika," in *Taisoku no enerugī: Ajia no naka no Okinawa*,Tokyo: Ningen sensho, pp. 35–44.
64 Yogi Seishō (1993) "Tenmatsu," in *Okinawa bungaku zenshū*, Vol. VI, Tokyo: Kokusho kankōkai, pp. 210–44, p. 221.
65 Yogi, "Tenmatsu," p. 220.
66 Yogi, "Tenmatsu," p. 225.
67 Yogi, "Tenmatsu," p. 231.
68 Ōshiro Tatsuhiro sheds some light on the topic of Okinawa's "low" culture in his essays "Okinawa mondai wa bunka mondai de aru" and "Hōken jidai ga nakatta koto." In both, Ōshiro explains how, in the Ryukyus, certain historical factors such as the absence of feudalism and the presence of Satsuma overlords after 1609, resulted in a society that lacked the concepts of hierarchy and allegiance as well as a sense of individual consciousness. The Ryukyus compared poorly to the rest of Japan, which Ōshiro argues, benefited from a rich feudal past in which monetary and other pre-capitalist systems matured and evolved into their modern counterparts. See Ōshiro Tatsuhiro, (1987) *Taisoku no enerugī: Ajia no naka no Okinawa*, Tokyo: Ningen sensho, pp. 5–18, 45–64.
69 Yogi, "Tenmatsu," p. 235.
70 Nakahodo Masanori discusses Yogi and Miyagi together in the afterword to (1991) *Okinawa kindai bungei sakuhinshū*, Naha: Okinawa taimususha, pp. 395–403, and in separate chapters of his study of prewar writers (1991) *Okinawa no bungaku 1927–45*, Naha: Okinawa taimususha. In both works, Yogi and Miyagi

are described as writers of *binbō shōsetsu* (tales of poverty), or alternately, *seikatsuku shōsetsu* (tales of a difficult life). While I am not aware of a separate category of Japanese fiction called *binbō shōsetsu*, the term first appears in connection to Yogi Seishō in a critique of "The Banyan" written by Kawabata Yasunari (1934) *Literary World* (p. 6). Quoted in Nakahodo Masanori (1990) *Ryūsho tankyū*, Tokyo: Shinsensha, p. 104.
71 Miyagi Sō (1993) "Seikatsu no tanjō," in *Okinawa bungaku zenshū*, Vol. VI, Tokyo: Kokusho kankōkai, pp. 104–42.
72 Miyagi, "Seikatsu no tanjō," p. 255.
73 Miyagi, "Seikatsu no tanjō," p. 277.
74 Miyagi, "Seikatsu no tanjō," p. 288.
75 Frawley, *Irish Pastoral*, p. 69.
76 Karatani Kōjin's also discusses trauma in relation to landscape in his *Origins of Modern Japanese Literature*, though his focus is not colonial landscape. For an informative essay on Karatani's theories, see Carl Cassegard (2007) "Exteriority and Transcritique: Karatani Kōjin and the Impact of the 1990s," *Japanese Studies*, 27 (1): 1–18.
77 In his (1979) *Yearning for Yesterday: A Sociology of Nostalgia*, New York: Free Press, Fred Davis explains that while the nostalgic reaction is distinctly conservative, it occasionally serves radical ends.
78 Jennifer Robertson writes of a "tenacious equation between females and native place" in her essay (1998) "It Takes a Village" in Stephen Vlastos (ed.), *Mirror of Modernity*, Berkeley, Calif.: University of California Press, p. 124.

4 Ōshiro Tatsuhiro and constructions of a mythic Okinawa

1 Okamoto Keitoku, "Sengo bungaku no tenkai," *Shin Okinawa bungaku*, 35 (1977): 31.
2 Three other mainland writers who have written extensively about Okinawan culture in the postwar period are Yoshimoto Takaaki, Okamoto Tarō, and Ōe Kenzaburō. See Yoshimoto Takaaki, "Nantō ron," *Bungei* (Fall 1989): 245–65; "'Nantō ron' to Okinawa" *Shin Okinawa bungaku* 79 (1989): 16–100; Okamoto Tarō, *Wasurerareta Nihon: Okinawa bunka ron*, Tokyo: Chūō kōron bunko; Ōe Kenzaburō, *Okinawa keiken*, Tokyo: Iwanami shoten, 1982.
3 From 1945 to 1950 the USA ruled solely; in 1950 each of the four major island groups (Amami, Okinawa, Miyako, and Yaeyama) were permitted to popularly elect a governor and legislature. The island group governments were abolished in 1952 in favor of a centralized Government of the Ryukyu Islands (GRI). USCAR appointed the chief executive of the GRI while allowing for the popular election of the legislature. Koji Taira describes the Washington controlled USCAR-GRI arrangement as reminiscent of "a conventional Western colonial system in which a metropolitan power's agency ruled an alien territory and population through a hand-picked native government." See Koji Taira (1997) "Troubled National Identity: The Ryukyuans/Okinawans," in Michael Weiner (ed.), *Japan's Minorities: The Illusion of Homogeneity*, London and New York: Routledge, p. 159.
4 Okamoto Keitoku (1981) *Gendai Okinawa no bungaku to shisō*, Naha: Okinawa taimususha, pp. 93, 103.
5 *Uruma* is an ancient designation for the Ryukyu Islands.
6 Okamoto, *Gendai Okinawa no bungaku to shisō*, pp. 89–128. For other discussions of postwar Okinawan literature see Okamoto, *Okinawa bungaku no chihei*, pp. 28–49; Nakahodo Masanori (1977) "Okinawa gendai shōsetsu shi: haisen kara fukki made," *Okinawa bungaku zenshū*, Vo. VII, pp. 344–60; (1977) *Shin Okinawa bungaku* 35: 31–196.

7 Like most authors from Okinawa, Ōshiro pursued his writing while employed outside the literary field. For forty years he worked as a local civil servant in the Trade Office of the GRI, and later in the Okinawa Institute of Historical Collections.
8 For further information on Ōta Ryōhaku, see the author's recently published collected works (2006) *Ōta Ryōhaku chōsakushū*, 4 vols, Tokyo: Bōdāinku.
9 Japanese intellectual historian Kano Masanao writes extensively on *Ryūdai Literature* in his study of postwar Okinawan thought (1987) *Sengo Okinawa no shisōzō*, Tokyo: Asahi shinbunsha, pp. 113–60. Archrivals Ōshiro Tatsuhiro and Arakawa Akira write at length of their involvement with the journal in *Kōgen o motomete*, Naha: Okinawa taimususha, 1997 and *Okinawa: tōgō to hangyaku*, Tokyo: Chikuma shobō, 2000, the authors' respective memoirs.
10 Although Ōshiro was the target of attacks by *Ryūdai Literature* members, he was regarded as a respected senior writer and enjoyed the journal's patronage in the form of commissions for his fiction. See Okamoto Keitoku (1978) "Ōshiro Tatsuhiro no bungaku to shisō: 'Ryūdai bungaku' to no kakawari no naka de," *Aoi umi* 69: 182–9.
11 Okamoto Keitoku (1969) "Sengo Okinawa bungaku no isshiten," *Okinawa bunka* 29: 15–25. "Basha monogatari" is a story in which the protagonist is forced to ask what Okinawa means upon witnessing the contradictions of postwar society. The event that triggers this introspection is the incongruous sight of a lone local farmer slowly leading his horse carriage along a newly paved road trafficked by huge American military trucks.
12 Okinawa's premier postwar literary journal, *New Okinawa Literature*, ceased publication in 1993. The vacuum created by the journal's suspension is filled in part by the comprehensive arts journal *Okinawa Literature Almanac* (*Okinawa bungaku nenkan*), published annually since 1993.
13 In her chapter "Okinawa," which focuses on Chibana Sōichi, an Okinawan supermarket owner prosecuted in 1987 for tearing down and burning the Japanese flag during a national sports event held in Yomitan village, Norma Field describes the interminable degree to which Okinawans persist in the reverence of ancestors. See Norma Field (1991) *In The Realm of the Dying Emperor*, New York: Pantheon Books, pp. 31–101.
14 Approximately 32,000 turtleback tombs existed in Okinawa after World War II. Today the numbers are dwindling as families sell their burial plots to make way for development. The destruction of turtleback tombs can be likened to the hundreds of Ryukyuan dialects that were eradicated after annexation and the war. See Gladys Zabilka (1973) *Customs and Culture of Okinawa*, Rutland, Vt. and Tokyo: Charles E. Tuttle Company, p. 123.
15 Field, *In the Realm of the Dying Emperor,* p. 83.
16 Hiyane Kaoru (1992) "*Dororon* no ekurichūru," *Shin Okinawa bungaku* 91: 47.
17 Ōshiro, "Turtleback Tombs," p. 113. Mishearing the neighbor, Zentoku thinks he is talking about combs (*sabachi*, in dialect) rather than firing (*shageki*).
18 Ōshiro, "Turtleback Tombs," p. 118.
19 Ōshiro, "Turtleback Tombs," p. 119.
20 These communal ties are not only intense, they are also restraining. See Field, *In the Realm of the Dying Emperor*, p. 83.
21 Ōshiro, "Turtleback Tombs," p. 115.
22 Anthropologist William Lebra notes that most Okinawans believe their ancestors remain in tombs close to their homes and that they are nearby observing the life of their descendants. He adds, (rather categorically) "All agree that the ancestors may cause endless misfortune for the living if proper ritual ties are not maintained." See William P. Lebra (1985) *Okinawan Religion: Belief, Ritual, and Social Structure*, Honolulu : University of Hawai'i Press, p. 25.

23 Ōshiro, "Turtleback Tombs," p. 122.
24 Ōshiro, "Turtleback Tombs," p. 123.
25 Ōshiro, "Turtleback Tombs," p. 123.
26 Ōshiro, "Turtleback Tombs," p. 127.
27 Ōshiro, "Turtleback Tombs," p. 127.
28 Ōshiro, "Turtleback Tombs," p. 133.
29 Lebra, *Okinawan Religion*, p. 34.
30 Lebra states that the location of life-sustaining spirits (*mabui*), is in the chest. These spirits can be dislodged with a sneeze or a fright of some kind (*mabui ochi*), Lebra, *Okinawan Religion*, p. 25.
31 Improper internment gives rise to ghosts who trouble the living (*majimun*). Lepra, *Okinawan Religion*, p. 29.
32 Ōshiro, "Turtleback Tombs," p. 154.
33 Satohara Akira (1991) *Ryūkyū-ko no bungaku: Ōshiro Tatsuhiro no sekai*, Tokyo: Hōsei daigaku shuppan kyoku, p. 3.
34 Satohara, *Ryūkyū-ko no bungaku*, p. 5.
35 A case in point is the former government's (Abe Shinzō, prime minister) position on war memory, which aims to present Japanese students a pride-inspiring version of Japan's history. To this end, textbook screeners eliminated unsavory references to comfort women and compulsory suicide (*shūdan jiketsu*) from school textbooks.

In contrast to folklorists such as Yanagita Kunio and Orikuchi Shinobu who argue that the Ryukyus are the essence of ancient Japanese culture, the mass media portrays the islands as being on the periphery—closer to nature than culture. Travel posters show stunning tropical isles that are characterized by a conspicuous absence of local people. For an interesting view on how both early folklorists and recent media have masked Okinawan culture see Ota Yoshinobu (1991) "Cultural Authenticity as Entropic Metanarrative: A Case from Ryukyuan Studies," *Central Issues of Anthropology* 9 (April): 87–95.
36 For a detailed account of the undesirable effects the Vietnam War had on Okinawa, see Watanabe Akio (1970) *The Okinawa Problem*, Victoria: Melbourne University Press, pp. 62–9.
37 Ōshiro Tatsuhiro (1989) *The Cocktail Party*, in *Okinawa: Two Postwar Novellas*, trans. Steve Rabson, Berkeley, Calif.: Institute of East Asian Studies, p. 36.
38 Ōshiro, *The Cocktail Party*, p. 39.
39 Ōshiro, *The Cocktail Party*, p. 48.
40 Ōshiro, *The Cocktail Party*, p. 52.
41 While much of the criticism of this story focuses on the body of the young Okinawan girl who is attacked, the protagonist's attraction to Mrs. Miller, an English teacher, is not commented upon. At the cocktail party Ōshiro describes Mrs. Miller's entrance into the room of guests as follows: "Turkey anyone? From the plunging neckline of a black one-piece dress, her white breasts billowed up full. The sight was dazzling." Ōshiro, *The Cocktail Party*, p. 39. In the last line of the first section of the text, the protagonist reflects on Mrs. Miller's allure: "I wonder if some of the men in her class felt guilty, excited by her voluptuous figure." Ōshiro, *The Cocktail Party*, p. 52. While it appears natural for critics to concentrate on a white man's gaze/desire for a native girl, the reverse seems to be a taboo.
42 Ōshiro, *The Cocktail Party*, p. 79.
43 Ōshiro, *The Cocktail Party*, p. 80.
44 Several other group suicides occurred throughout Okinawa prefecture during the Battle of Okinawa. Within days of the Tokashiki tragedy, 358 civilians died on Zamami, a neighboring island in the Kerama chain. The most well known civilian tragedy, involving the deaths of 210 teachers and teenage girls mobilized

to work as nurses during the war, is commemorated in Okinawa at the Princess Lily Memorial (*Himeyuri no tō*). Princess Lily is a name taken from songs and magazines associated with the girls' school. A lesser-known massacre took place in Chibichirigama, an Okinawan cave. Eighty-two people chose "honorable deaths" (*gyokusai*) rather than capture by Americans. See Field, *In the Realm of the Dying Emperor*, pp. 56–67. Unsurprisingly, since 2006 there has been severe opposition in Okinawa to the Abe government's efforts to sanitize Japan's textbooks. See Gavan McCormack (2007) "Fitting Okinawa into Japan the 'Beautiful Country,'" *Japan Focus*. Online. Available HTTP: < http://www.zmag.org/content/showarticle.cfm?SectionID=17&ItemID=129782 > (accessed on June 2, 2007).

45 Satohara Akira documents the statement of a group suicide survivor who stresses that Akamatsu ordered the suicide as a way to eliminate potential threats to the Japanese Army because he did not view the islanders as Japanese and feared they would become traitors if captured by the Americans. See Satohara Akira, "*Kamishima*: Okinawa no naka no Kamishima," *Ryūkyū-ko no bungaku*, pp. 13–22.

46 See Kano Masanao (1987) "Ika, dōka, jiritsu: Ōshiro Tatsuhiro no bungaku to shisō," *Sengo Okinawa no shisōzō*, Tokyo: Asahi shinbunsha, p. 385.

47 See Ōshiro's essay "Okinawa de Nihonjin ni naru koto: kokoro no jidenfū ni," *Okinawa bungaku zenshū*, Vol. XVIII, p. 54.

48 The actual dividing point is the twenty-ninth parallel, but after Amami Ōshima reverted to Kagoshima prefecture in 1953, the line moved two degrees further south.

49 Okamoto Keitoku likens Taminato to a *kyōgen mawashi*, the character in Nō drama who, while not the protagonist, functions to advance the story line. See "Shōsetsu Kamishima ron," in *Gendai Okinawa bungaku to shisō*, p. 149.

50 The phrase "animal-like obedience" is one of several objectionable characterizations of Okinawans uttered by critic Ōya Sōichi during his visit to the prefecture in June 1959 to obtain material for his essay series "Shin Nihon onna keizu" published in *Women's Forum*. See *Okinawa daihyakka jiten*, Vol. I, p. 414.

51 For more on Ōshiro's interest in representing female priestesses in his fiction, see Leith Morton (2004) "Shamans Make History in Okinawa: A Reading of Ōshiro Tatsuhiro's Novel *Noro* (Mantic Woman, 1985)," *JOSA* 36–7: 30–54.

52 Quoted in Satohara Akira, "Kamishima: Okinawa no naka no Kamishima," *Ryūkyū-ko no bungaku*, p. 29.

53 Because of the devastation Okinawa suffered in World War II, the prefecture is naturally committed to peace. However, as Ōshiro points out through Yonashiro, the all-embracing nature of Okinawa's commitment is not without controversy. In 1995, when the "Cornerstone of Peace" (*heiwa no ishizue*), a memorial inscribed with the names of Americans, Okinawans, Japanese, and Koreans who died in the Battle of Okinawa, was unveiled in Naha, there were many, who, like Yonashiro, opposed the inclusion of non-Okinawans. See Okamoto Keitoku (1995) "Sengo o yomu," *Ryukyu News*, June 29, p. 3. Also of note, Satohara Akira writes that in 1970, Lieutenant Akamatsu, the man who commanded the group suicide on Tokashiki, was invited by Okinawa prefecture to attend the twenty-fifth anniversary ceremony mourning the war dead. Not only did he accept, he also brought with him five surviving members of his unit. Needless to say, a mass of protesters awaited the men at Naha airport. See Satohara Akira, "Kamishima," *Ryūkyū-ko no bungaku*, pp. 17–19.

54 It is interesting to note that in Ōshiro's revised version of *Kamishima*, a new character, known only as Old Tobaru is included, apparently in an effort to take the sting out of the novel's indictment of Japanese. Appearing only briefly, Tobaru stumbles into a town meeting to express how grateful he is to the Japanese soldiers and states how "even among the Yamato, there are good

people." Quoted in Kano Masanao, "Ika, dōka, jiritsu," *Sengo Okinawa no shisōzō*, p. 387.
55 Ōshiro Tatsuhiro (1974) *Kamishima*, Tokyo: Nihon hōsō shuppan kyōkai, pp. 121–2.
56 Ōshiro, *Kamishima*, pp. 134–5.
57 Ōshiro calls the gods that appear in the story Akanemoto and Kuronemoto. These are fictional versions of the Akamata and Kuromata gods central to the harvest festival that takes place on the island of Iriomote in the Yaeyama chain. The three day ceremony Ōshiro describes appears to be based on rites which originated in Iriomote and later spread to neighboring islands. See *Okinawa daihyakka jiten*, Vol. I, p. 28.
58 Ōshiro Tatsuhiro (1974) *Panarinusuma gensō*, Tokyo: Kadokawa bunko, p. 6.
59 Ōshiro, *Panarinusuma gensō*, p. 7.
60 Historian Takara Kurayoshi ascribes economic terms to the two worlds of the story. He calls mainland Okinawa "society" (*gesselschaft*), and the remote island "community" (*gemeinschaft*). See Takara Kurayoshi, "Panarinusuma gensō," *Okinawa bungaku zenshū*, Vol. XVII, pp. 331–3.
61 Ōshiro, *Panarinusuma gensō*, p. 10.
62 Ōshiro, *Panarinusuma gensō*, pp. 14–15.
63 Ōshiro, *Panarinusuma gensō*, p. 32.
64 Ōshiro, *Panarinusuma gensō*, p. 61.
65 Ōshiro, *Panarinusuma gensō*, p. 74.
66 Takara Kurayoshi, "Panarinusuma gensō," in *Okinawa bungaku zenshū*, Vol. XVII, pp. 231–3.
67 Takara, "Panarinusuma gensō," pp. 231–3.
68 See Jane Campbell (1986) *Mythic Black Fiction: The Transformation of History*, Knoxville, Tenn.: University of Tennessee Press, p. 156.
69 To read a sampling of seminal essays by Ōshiro Tatsuhiro, see (2002) *Ōshiro Tatsuhiro zenshū*, Vol. XII, Tokyo: Bensei shuppan. Shimao Toshio's *Theory of Yaponesia* appears in *Okinawa bungaku zenshū*, Vol. XVIII, pp. 264–313.
70 The "Yaponesia" essays are filled with clinical terms such as "relief" (*ando*), "congestion" (*teitai*), and even "arteriosclerosis" (*dōmyaku kōka*) and "blood transfusion" (*yuketsu*). These last two appear as Shimao insists that the arteriosclerosis ridden Japanese people, language, and literature must receive a blood transfusion from the southern islands. See Shimao's "Okinawa o imi suru mono" in *Okinawa bungaku zenshū* Vol. XVIII, pp. 264–8.
71 According to Ōshiro Tatsuhiro, Shimao had originally wished to designate the Ryukyuan islands as "Yaponeshia no shippo," but changed from "shippo" to "nekko" because many islanders disliked the former word's association with animals. See Ōshiro's (1993) "Yaponeshia no shukudai: Toku ni hōgen no aidentitī o megutte," in *Ryūkyū no kisetsu ni*, Tokyo: Yomiuri shinbunsha, p. 40. Shimao's preference for "shippo" may be connected to both the lower geographical and societal position the Ryukyuan islands occupy in Japan. In a related matter, heeding the dismay of Amami Oshimans over his use of "Ryukyu" when referring to the southern islanders, Shimao adopted the more geographically neutral term "Ryukyu arc" (*Ryukyu-ko*). The former appellation, no doubt, brought to mind the days when the Ryukyuan kingdom, seated in Okinawa, reigned over the surrounding islands, which included Amami Ōshima. Tsushima Katsuyoshi discusses this change in terminology in his (1990) *Shimao Toshio ron: Nichijōteki hinichijōteki no bungaku*, Osaka: Kaifūsha, p. 288.
72 The island groups Shimao wishes to link to Japan are Indonesia, Melanesia, Micronesia, and Polynesia.
73 See the roundtable discussion (1987) "Yaponeshia ron to Okinawa: Shisōteki na imi o tou," *Shin Okinawa bungaku* 71 (spring): 14.

74 Miki Takeshi, "Okineshia bunka ron: seishin to kyōwakoku o motomete," in *Okinawa bungaku zenshū*, Vol. XVIII, p. 365.
75 Tsushima Katsuyoshi, "Yaponeshia no ichigu kara," *Shimao Toshio ron: nichijōteki hinichijō no bungaku*, pp. 273–311.
76 See Sekine Kenji's critique of *Theory of Yaponesia*, (1987) "Ryūkyū ko no naka no Yaponeshia ron," *Shin Okinawa bungaku* 71 (spring): pp. 40–6.
77 Ōshiro Tatsuhiro, "Yaponeshia ron no shukudai," *Ryūkyū no kisetsu ni*, p. 53.
78 See Hiyane Kaoru, "Yaponeshia ron to Okinawa," pp. 21–2.
79 Miki Takeshi seems aware of the dangers of nationalism, whether Japanese or Okinawan, for he writes:

> By capturing the Ryukyuan arc, from Yaeyama in the south to the Amami islands in the north, as the 'Okineshia Cultural Sphere' we will build a republic for the minds of people living in the Ryukyuan arc. This must be an unrestricted international philosophy unrelated to narrow minded nationalism or emperor system essentialism (*junketsu shugi*).
> See Miki Takeshi, "Okinawa bunka ron," p. 367.

80 Critics are divided about the extent to which Shimao actively engages in critiquing the Japanese state. Some, such as Tanikawa Ken'ichi believe that *Theory of Yaponesia* does not make much mention of Yamato centered society, while others, Takara Ben, for example, concedes that Shimao's censure of Japan since the Yayoi period constitutes a national critique. For an overview of Shimao's views on Jōmon and Yayoi culture as they pertain to Yaponesia, see Okamoto Keitoku (1990) "'Yamato' to 'Jōmon,'" "*Yaponeshia ron*" *no rinkaku: Shimao Toshio no manazashi*, Naha: Taimusu sensho.
81 Donald Keene (1978) *World Within Walls: Japanese Literature of the Pre-Modern Era 1600–1867*, New York: Grove Press, p. 425.
82 Shimao Toshio, "'Okinawa' no imi suru mono," *Okinawa bungaku zenshū*, Vol. XVIII, p. 265.
83 Shimao, "'Okinawa' no imi suru mono," p. 265.
84 Shimao, "'Okinawa' no imi suru mono," p. 265.
85 See Timothy Mitchell (1992) "Orientalism and the Exhibitionary Order," in Nicholas B. Dirks (ed.), *Colonialism and Culture*, Ann Arbor, Mich.: University of Michigan Press, p. 290.
86 Shimao Toshio, "Amami—Nihon no nantō," *Okinawa bungaku zenshū*, Vol. XVIII, p. 272.
87 Alan Christy (1993) "The Making of Imperial Subjects in Okinawa," *Positions: East Asia Critique* 1 (3): 607–38, p. 633.
88 For an account of "coevalness" or the control of the time of the Other, see Johannes Fabian (1983), *Time and the Other*, New York: Columbia University Press. The one notable exception to Shimao's collapsing of time in *Theory of Yaponesia* is in the "Amami: Nihon no nantō" essay, devoted largely to a fascinating and historically specific account of the Shimazu clan's economic exploitation of Amami Ōshima through forced sugar cane production from the beginning of the seventeenth century. The profits garnered by Satsuma through their colonial policies in the Ryukyus are convincingly related to the clan's key role in the formation of the modern Japanese state. See Shimao Toshio, "Amami: Nihon no nantō," *Okinawa bungaku zenshū*, Vol. XVIII, pp. 273–76.
89 Quoted in *Okinawa bungaku zenshū*, Vol. XVIII, pp. 360–1. For a fuller account of Okinawa's "gentleness" and lack of feudal mentality, see Ōshiro Tatsuhiro's essays "'Yasashisa bunka ron' no ne: jōsei no chikara to kyōdōtai" and "Hōken jidai ga nakatta koto: shakai chitsujō hattatsu to kōjin," in *Taisoku no enerugī: Ajia no naka no Okinawa*, pp. 19–34, 45–64.

Notes 207

90 Miki Takeshi, "Okineshia bunka ron," *Okinawa bungaku zenshū*, Vol. XVIII, p. 361.
91 Murai Osamu, (1992) *Nantō ideorogī no hassei: Yanagita Kunio to shokuminchishugi*, Tokyo: Fukutake shoten, pp. 44–9.
92 Cited by Nakazato Isao in *Shin Okinawa bungaku* 71, p. 19. See also Van C. Gessel (1989) *The Sting of Life: Four Contemporary Japanese Novelists*, New York: Columbia University Press, p. 151, for an account of the "spiritual battle" Shimao faced when Miho's mental attacks began in 1954. For a full-length treatment in English of Shimao Toshio's writing, see Philip Gabriel (1999) *Mad Wives and Island Dreams*, Honolulu, Hawaii: University of Hawai'i Press.
93 Okamoto, "'Yaponeshia ron' no rinkaku," p. 43.
94 For a short story that thematicizes the intense islolation that Shimao feels in the Ryukyus see "Kawa nite," *Okinawa bungaku zenshū*, Vol. VII, pp. 120–31. The work illustrates the alienation experienced when the protagonist, *watakushi*, an outsider, visits a remote Ryukyuan village. Relatedly, in "'Okinawa' no imi suru mono," Shimao points out that just as the people of Kagoshima exclude Amami Oshimans from among their close friends, the Amami Oshimans exclude people from Naha. The vicious circle continues as residents of Naha exclude those from Itoman or nearby Kudaka Island. See *Okinawa bungaku zenshū*, Vol. XVIII, p. 266.
95 Shimao Toshio, *Okinawa bungaku zenshū*, Vol. XVIII, p. 281.
96 The Ryukyus fill Shimao with a sense of danger and desire because it was there that he met Miho while commander of a suicide torpedo boat unit in Kakeroma, an island in the Amami chain.
97 Quoted in *Shin Okinawa bungaku* 71, p. 19.
98 Hiyane, "'Yaponeshia ron' to Okinawa," p. 23.
99 Nakazato Isao, "'Yaponeshia ron' to Okinawa," *Shin Okinawa bungaku* 71, 20.
100 Yanagita's theory of migration is discussed in Shimao Toshio, "Amami: Nihon no nantō," *Okinawa bungaku zenshū*, Vol. XVIII, p. 272.
101 Alan Christy, "The Making of Imperial Subjects in Okinawa," p. 626.
102 Shimao Toshio, "Yaponeshia no nekko," *Okinawa bungaku zenshū*, Vol. XVIII, 269.
103 Shimao, "Yaponeshia no nekko," p. 269.
104 The phrase Murai uses, "the southern islands as a site for healing," (*chiyu no ba toshite no Nantō*) is borrowed from Okaya Koji's study (1981) *Shima no seishinshi*, Tokyo: Shisakusha. See Murai Osamu, "Nantō ideorogī no hassei," pp. 27–30.
105 See Ōshiro Tatsuhiro, "Yaponeshia no shukudai," in *Ryūkyū no kisetsu ni*, p. 44.
106 Shimao Toshio, "Kaiki no sōnen: Yaponeshia," *Okinawa bungaku zenshū*, Vol. XVIII, p. 302.
107 Shimao, "Kaiki no sōnen: Yaponeshia," p. 302.
108 Shimao, "Kaiki no sōnen: Yaponeshia," p. 303.
109 Shimao, "Kaiki no sōnen: Yaponeshia," p. 312.
110 Philip Gabriel argues the reverse in his essay (1996) "Rethinking the Margins: Shimao Toshio and Yaponesia," *Japan Forum*, 8 (2): 205–20. Gabriel writes, "As he fills in details of the island lifestyle, one by one Shimao reverses the standard tropes of mainland discourse on the southern islands. [...] In his Yaponesia essays Shimao effectively rewrites each of these tropes and images of inferiority into a narrative of cultural distinctiveness and value" (p. 210). While I concede that Shimao attempts to denaturalize mainland stereotypes, he cannot himself escape from replicating them.
111 The terms Shimao uses to describe his perception of the islanders' disposition are gentleness and passionate (*yawarakasa, gekihatsu*).

5 Postreversion fiction and Medoruma Shun

1 John Dower (ed.) (1993) *Japan in War and Peace*, New York: New Press, p. 171. Yoshino Bunroku, the Foreign Ministry official who negotiated the reversion of Okinawa, recently acknowledged the existence of a secret pact between Tokyo and Washington that obliged Japanese taxpayers to bear the costs accrued by landowners in Okinawa during this volatile period. See "Secret Details of Sordid Okinawan Reversion Deal Revealed," *Kyodo News*, May 16, 2007.
2 Julia Yonetani, "Future 'Assets,' but at What Price? The Okinawa Initiative Debate," in Laura Hein and Mark Selden (eds), *Islands of Discontent*, Lanham, Md.: Rowman and Littlefield, p. 249.
3 Shima Tsuyoshi, "Bones," in Michael Molasky and Steve Rabson (eds), *Southern Exposure: Modern Japanese Literature from Okinawa*, Honolulu, Hawaii: University of Hawai'i Press, pp. 156–71, p. 156.
4 Michael S. Molasky (1999) *The American Occupation of Japan and Okinawa*, London and New York: Routledge, p. 56.
5 Molasky, *The American Occupation*, p. 58.
6 *Child of Okinawa* received the Gunzō New Writers' Prize, and the Akutagawa Prize in 1971.
7 Molasky, *The American Occupation*, p. 179.
8 While *Buta no mukui* is a Bildungsroman of protagonist Shōkichi's quest to discover his roots and self-identity, most critics of the novella emphasize the author's characterizations of the hostesses, who begin as a supporting cast and end up, through Matayoshi's fine ear for their lively conversation, and eye for their gaudy apparel, overshadowing Shōkichi.
9 See Medoruma Shun's commentary in (1996) *Nihon bungaku shi*, 15: *Ryūkyū bungaku, Okinawa bungaku,* Tokyo: Iwanami kōza, pp. 202–3.
10 Yonaha Keiko (1996) gives an overview of this burst of creativity by women in Okinawa, naming authors, sketching works, and detailing prizes received in *Nihon bungaku shi*, 15, 209–15.
11 Saegusa Kazuko (2001) "Okinawa no kakitetachi: 'Shin Okinawa bungaku-shō' no senkō o tsūjite," *Yurīka*, 8: 130.
12 Yonaha, *Nihon bungaku shi*, p. 210. See also Yonaha's article on prostitution and family sacrifice (1992) "Shōfu'sei no kaidoku," *Tōyō eiwa jogakuin tankidaigaku kenkyū kiyō*, p. 30. The term "honey" refers to mistresses of American GIs. Interestingly, this term appears to be a local variation of *onrī* ("only one"), the term favored for GI mistresses on Japan's main islands.
13 Writing on nostalgia for the past in Japan's modern period, Marilyn Ivy notes that "the very search to find authentic survivals of premodern, prewestern, Japanese authenticity is inescapably a *modern* endeavor, essentially enfolded within the historical condition that it would seek to escape." Marilyn Ivy (1995) *Discourses of the Vanishing: Modernity, Phantasm, Japan*, Chicago, Ill.: University of Chicago Press, p. 241. See Urashima Etsuko's article on the rapidly disappearing *dugong*, in *Kinyōbi*, October 25, 2002.
14 While I do not mean to diminish the impact of this symposium, I would be remiss not to mention that it was not universally well received. See Shinjō Ikuo (2005) "Okinawa bungakuron no (fu)kanōsei: Okinawa bungaku fōramu," *Nihon Tōyō bunkaron* 11 (3): 49–78; and Hanada Toshinori (2006) *Okinawa wa Gojira ka: han Orientarizumu nantō Yaponeshia*, Fukuoka: Hana shoin, for detailed discussions of the symposium's negative impact. Both authors regard keynote speaker Ihab Hassan's remarks, in which he emphasizes the nation-state, as reproducing colonial violence. Their dissatisfaction is by no means limited to Ihab, however. Shinjō and Hanada also interrogate inflammatory remarks made by mainland Japanese intellectuals such as Hino Keizō and Ikezawa Natsuki.

15 See the Akutagawa Selection Committee comments accompanying the publication of "Droplets" in (1997) *Bungei shunjū*, 9: 427–31. The commentary reveals that, in light of the times, many critics viewed the bestowal of consecutive awards as political correctness.
16 Another contemporary writer, Kohama Kiyoshi, has also attracted considerable notice by the literary establishment. Kohama, like Medoruma and Sakiyama, has published steadily in recent years.
17 Medoruma Shun (2001) "Yūshitai," *Gunzō*, 56 (11): 324.
18 Medoruma Shun (1998) "Uchināguchi to Yamatoguchi no aida de," *Bungei* 5 (37): 192–3. The name of the production Medoruma recalls so vividly is *Kozaban donzoko*.
19 See Aaron Gerow's essay (2003) "From the National Gaze to Multiple Gazes," in Laura Hein and Mark Selden (eds), *Islands of Discontent*, Lanham, Md.: Rowman and Littlefield, pp. 273–307.
20 In his analysis of Kina's "Shimagwa Song," anthropologist James Roberson explains that in both of Kina's versions of this song he implores his audience to remember their island spirit and never to forget the language of Okinawa. The song's second verse follows: "Don't throw away / Never throw away / The spirit of the islands / Don't throw away your heart / Don't forget our Okinawan language / We are the spirit of these islands." See Roberson's essay, (2003) "Uchinaa Pop: Place and Identity in Contemporary Okinawan Popular Music," in Laura Hein and Mark Selden (eds), *Islands of Discontent*, Lanham, Md.: Rowman & Littlefield, pp. 192–227.
21 The authors Medoruma cites as frequent prize-winners are Tabata Mitsuko, Eba Hideshi, Kohama Kiyoshi, Yamazato Teiko, and Nagadō Eikichi. He rounds out his list by including Sakiyama Tami and Nakawaka Naoko, distinguished, as is Medoruma himself, for receiving the critically important Kyushu Art Festival Literary Prize.
22 Medoruma, "Uchināguchi to Yamatoguchi no aida de," p. 192. Although Medoruma uses the phrase, "unchanging *uchinā*, changing Okinawa" (*kawaranai uchinā to kawatteiku Okinawa*), in which *uchinā* may best correspond to the ancient island kingdom, and Okinawa as the newly admitted modern prefecture, in the context of the essay, it is clear that Medoruma is using the term *uchinā* broadly to include forms attached to the island, namely, its dialect.
23 Michael S. Molasky (2003) "Medoruma Shun: The Writer as Public Intellectual in Okinawa Today," in Laura Hein and Mark Selden (eds), *Islands of Discontent*, Lanham, Md.: Rowman & Littlefield, pp. 164–5, p. 191.
24 Medoruma Shun and Ikezawa Natsuki (1997) "Zetsubō kara hajimaru," *Bungakukai* 9: 174–89, p. 179.
25 In this rare interview, Medoruma bluntly tells Ikezawa Natsuki, "I don't want my fiction to be categorized as Okinawan literature." Medoruma and Ikezawa, "Zetsubō kara hajimaru," p. 176.
26 Molasky (2003), p. 168.
27 Takeuchi Mitsuhiro describes the labor required of Medoruma's readers as stemming from, but not limited to his use of dialect:

> First dialect derails a reader, forcing a complete halt. At the same time the text puts a stop to one's thought, it demands new ways of thinking. The reader is forced to read, thinking all the while. It's on this account that one is wiped out each time one finishes a mere short story.
> (2000) "Bunka no mado," *Rekishi hyōron* 7 (603): 60.

28 Medoruma Shun, "Gyogunki," *Okinawa bungaku zenshū*, 9, 63.
29 Medoruma, "Gyogunki," p. 58.

30 Medoruma, "Gyogunki," p. 62.
31 Michael S. Molasky also draws a comparison between Medoruma and Nakagami and Faulkner in "Medoruma Shun: The Writer as Public Intellectual in Okinawa Today," p. 173. Shinjō Ikuo points out similarities between Medoruma and the early works of Ōe and Nakagami in (1998) "Kuwadate toshite no shōnen," *Shinchō* 95 (8): 181–7, p. 184.
32 Medoruma, "Gyogunki," pp. 72–3.
33 Kuroko Kazuo names Gabriel García Márquez, Ōe Kenzaburō, Nakagami Kenji, and Murakami Ryū as among Medoruma's most admired authors. *Ryukyu News*, October 13, 1997, p. 3.
34 Medoruma Shun, *Heiwa dōri*, *Okinawa bungaku zenshū*, 9, 89.
35 Peace Street (Heiwa dōri), an area frequented today by tourists and locals alike, is a thoroughfare that begins near the Mitsukoshi department store on Naha's International Street and ends at the pottery village, Tsuboya, 330 meters away. Lined with shops and food stalls, Peace Street also contains within it the Makishi fish market where all manner of marine island products are displayed, sold, and consumed. In the prewar period, the area was a marshy field near the Gābu river that occupation forces designated as forbidden territory in 1946 before erecting a cluster of barracks. Two years later, a black market called Shichamachigwā sprang up and thrived until heavy rains caused the adjoining river to flood, destroying the market. Together with embankment repair, the street was improved and renamed in 1948. See Okinawa taimususha (eds) *Okinawa daihyakka jiten*, Vol. III, pp. 416–17. Medoruma's selection of Peace Street as the story's setting creates an immediate sense of intimacy, for even a casual visitor to the island knows of the shopping street's existence, while longer-term guests might be familiar with the area's association with the war when widows began to make their living peddling fish and other wares at the black market.
36 Kuroko Kazuo, "Okinawa bungaku to Medoruma Shun," *Ryukyu News*, July 30, 1997. Kuroko discusses *Heiwa dōri* along with the following other anti-emperor works of fiction: Fukazawa Shichirō's *Fūryū mutan* (1960); Ōe Kenzaburō's *Sebuntīn* (*Seventeen*, 1961); Kiriyama Kasane's *Paruchizen densetsu* (*A Partisan Legend*, 1983). For an analysis of Fukazawa's work, see John Whittier Treat (1994) "Beheaded Emperors and the Absent Figure in Contemporary Japanese Literature," *PMLA* 109 (1): 100–15.
37 Medoruma, *Heiwa dōri*, p. 82. Emphasis in original. Throughout the text, the term for the royal pair is rendered in the syllabary reserved for foreign words (*katakana*), underscoring their remove from locals such as Uta and Fumi. Young Kaju, lacking a mature vocabulary, refers to the couple as "those two."
38 Medoruma, *Heiwa dōri*, pp. 84–5.
39 Medoruma, *Heiwa dōri*, p. 115.
40 Nakahodo Masanori (1982) *Okinawa no senki*, Tokyo: Asahi shinbunsha.
41 For a reading of "Droplets" through a magic realist frame, see Davinder L. Bhowmik (2003) "A 'Lite' Battle Narrative: Medoruma Shun's 'Suiteki'," *Proceedings of the Association for Japanese Literary Studies* 4 (summer): 311–18.
42 Suzuki Tomoyuki discusses this aspect of the reversion period in his lengthy but nuanced article (2001) "Gūwateki akui: Medoruma Shun to Okinawa sen no kioku," *Shakai shirin*, 48 (1): 1–52.
43 Linda Angst, "The Rape of a Schoolgirl," in Laura Hein and Mark Selden (eds), *Islands of Discontent*, Lanham, Md.: Rowman and Littlefield, pp. 135–57, p. 142.
44 For a sampling of such reviews, see the judge's comments upon the announcement of Medoruma's award in (1997) *Bungei shunjū*, 9: 426–31.
45 Medoruma Shun (2000) "Droplets," in Michael Molasky and Steve Rabson (eds), *Southern Exposure: Modern Japanese Literature from Okinawa*, Honolulu, Hawaii: University of Hawai'i Press, pp. 255–86, p. 272.

46 Medoruma, "Droplets," p. 255.
47 *Senpyō, Bungei shunjū*, 1997, 9, p. 427.
48 *Senpyō, Bungei shunjū*, p. 427.
49 Geoffrey Hartman (1993) "Public Memory and Modern Experience," *The Yale Journal of Criticism* 6 (2): 239–48, p. 244.
50 Medoruma Shun, "Okinawa no bunka jōkyō no genzai ni tsuite," *Kēshi kajī*, 13, 28–9.
51 Suzuki develops this idea in his essay (2001) "Gūwateki akui."
52 Medoruma, "Droplets," pp. 281–2.
53 Tomiyama Ichirō has explored the complexity of the Japanese state's treatment of Okinawans as both national subjects, and potential spies, owing to their occasional, and possibly rebellious use of dialects unintelligible to mainland soldiers. In English, see Tomiyama Ichirō (2000) "'Spy': Mobilization and Identity in Wartime Okinawa," *Japanese Civilization in the Modern World XVI Nation-State and Empire*, Senri Ethnological Studies, 51, Osaka: National Museum of Ethnology, pp. 121–32. In Japanese, see Tomiyama Ichirō (1990) *Kindai Nihon shakai to Okinawajin*, Tokyo: Nihon keizai hyōronsha; (1995) *Senjō no kioku*, Tokyo: Nihon keizai hyōronsha; and (2002) *Bōryoku no yokan: Iha Fuyū ni okeru kiki mondai*, Tokyo: Iwanami shoten.
54 Nakamura Yashu (1990) *Kami to mura*, Tokyo: Fukurosha.
55 Kawamura Minato (2000) *Kaze o yomu mizu ni kaku mainoritī bungaku ron*, Tokyo: Kōdansha, p. 75.
56 According to the *Kōjien* (5th edn), *nirai kanai* is a paradise believed by Okinawa and Amami islanders to exist far beyond the ocean. William Lebra defines the term, which he romanizes *Nīrē kanē*, or *Girē kanē*, based on local dialects, as follows: "A name found in early accounts, said to be an island in the eastern seas, the place of origin of the Okinawan people." See William P. Lebra (1966) *Okinawan Religion: Belief, Ritual, and Social Structure*, Honolulu, Hawaii: University of Hawai'i Press, p. 221.
57 Medoruma Shun (1999) *Mabuigumi*, Tokyo: Asahi shinbunsha, p. 7.
58 Medoruma, *Mabuigumi*, p. 42.
59 NHK, an abbreviation for Nihon Hōsō Kyōkai, or Japan Broadcasting Corporation, is Japan's quasi-national broadcaster.
60 Medoruma, *Mabuigumi*, p. 45.
61 Medoruma Shun and Ikezawa Natsuki (1997) "Zetsubō kara hajimaru," *Bungakukai*, 9: 185–6.
62 Medoruma, "Droplets," p. 281.
63 Gerald Figal discusses the Peace Memorial Museum controversy in the context of his overview of the peace movement in Okinawa. See Gerald Figal (2003) "Waging Peace on Okinawa," in Laura Hein and Mark Selden (eds), *Islands of Discontent*, Lanham, Md.: Rowman and Littlefield, pp. 65–98.
64 For details of the 1982 textbook controversy, see Ienaga Saburo (1993–4) "The Glorification of War in Japanese Education," *International Security*, 18 (3): 113–33.
65 Julia Yonetani, "Future 'Assets,' but at What Price?" p. 246.
66 For an analysis of both the initiative and the ongoing base problems, see Inoue Masamichi (2002) "Gurobaruka no naka no 'Okinawa inishiatibu' ronsō," *Shisō* 1 (933): 246–67. For an in-depth view of the military base issue, see Inoue's book (2006) *Okinawa and the US Military: Identity Making in the Age of Globalization*, New York: Columbia University Press.
67 Yonetani, "Future 'Assets,' but at What Price?" p. 251.
68 Figal, "Waging Peace on Okinawa," pp. 91–4.
69 In his essays, Medoruma has often referred to the extreme violence Okinawans displayed to other Okinawans during wartime. While this type of cruelty is less known than the ill-treatment of Okinawans by Japanese soldiers, it is not

212 *Notes*

unrelated in that Okinawans lashing out at their fellow islanders may have done so to show their loyalty to the state. Medoruma voices through Gozei his recognition of such cruelty in *Gunchō no ki*, and describes his own mother's negative experiences of being denied shelter by other Okinawans during the battle in his essays.

70 Recently, Medoruma has begun to write about the centrality of war in his family. His mother's experience, in particular, taught Medoruma that Okinawans were both victim *and* aggressor in the battle. See Medoruma Shun (2005) *Okinawa "sengo" zeronen*, Tokyo: Nihon hōsō shuppan kyōkai.
71 Medoruma Shun (2001) *Gunchō no ki*, Tokyo: Asahi shinbunsha, p. 182.
72 Medoruma, *Gunchō no ki*, pp. 223–5.
73 Medoruma, *Gunchō no ki*, p. 226.
74 Medoruma, *Gunchō no ki*, p. 226.

6 Darkness visible in Sakiyama Tami's island stories

1 I will use the word "dialect" since Sakiyama often alternates between the Japanese terms "dialect" (*hōgen*) and "island language" (*shimakotoba*) in her essays on writing. While the latter is more allusive, the former is less cumbersome. Frequent references to Sakiyama's decision to write against the grain appear in her essays and interviews. See, for example, her pointed reference to Ōshiro Tatsuhiro's problematic use of dialect in the essay (2002) "'Shimakotoba' de kachāshī," in Imafuku Ryūta (ed.), *'Watashi' no tankyū*, Tokyo: Iwanami shoten, pp. 157–80, p. 168 or (2000) "'Shōsetsu' no genjō kara," (dialogue with Medoruma Shun) *Kēshi kajī*, 27: 22–33.
2 Sakiyama's first Akutagawa Prize nomination was for "Passage across the Sea" in 1989; her second, in 1991, was for "Island Confines" (*Shimagomoru*)." Ōno Takayuki's response to Sakiyama's "Rocking and Rolling," (*Yurateiku yuriteiuku*) a story published in Gunzō in 2000, is typical of her critics:

> Since it was only just published, it's an extremely difficult work to assess. Sakiyama's insistence on using dialect to depict a community that is infused with excessive eroticism, yet declining on account of aging and low birthrates, is hard to figure even for younger Okinawans, and all the more so for mainland readers. Her story calls to mind the fantastic quality and narrative style of Izumi Kyōka; all one can say for certain is that it's a problematic work (*mondaisaku*).
>
> *Okinawa Times*, December 25, 2000, p. 17.

Even Shinjō Ikuo, a careful reader of Sakiyama, states in his overview of "Cradle on the Water" ("Suijō yōran," 2001), that it is pointless to describe the difficult-to-summarize work because movement and dance, rather than plot, carries it forward. *Okinawa Times*, September 5, 2001, p. 22.
3 Sakiyama, "'Shimakotoba' de kachāshī," p. 168.
4 Sakiyama discusses this issue in an interview with Medoruma Shun in which she describes reacting negatively when asked (rather stupidly) by a certain journalist, "You're an Okinawan woman, right?" Because of the prevailing discourse in Japan's mass media of Okinawa as a place of healing (*iyashi no ba*) where women function as guardians of the spirit, Sakiyama believed the journalist's underlying question was whether or not she was a shaman. See Sakiyama, "Shōsetsu no genjō kara," p. 29.
5 Sakiyama, "'Shimakotoba' de kachāshī," p. 173.
6 I do not mean here to dismiss Higashi's creative use of dialect by classifying it with others who wrote in a realistic vein in the postwar period; however, social

realism was an imperative among many Okinawan writers, Higashi included, who sought to correct the inaccuracies of past depictions. Remarking on this tendency, Patsy J. Daniels points out that, in the African case, myths and distortions of the vast colonialist literature on Africa made realism in the postcolonial context a historic and ideological necessity. She argues that social realism is not something one can point to as taking place in the past; rather, it is part of a revisionist and contemporary writing of that past. See (2001) *Voice of the Oppressed in the Language of the Oppressor*, New York: Routledge, p. 70.
7 See Sakiyama's essay (1996) "Shima no kubomi kara," in *Nantō shōkei*, Tokyo: Sunagoya shobō, pp. 109–15.
8 Sakiyama Tami (1994) *Suijō ōkan*, in *Kurikaeshigaeshi*, Tokyo: Sunagoya shobō, p. 159.
9 The island to which Akiko returns is not completely unidentified. Sakiyama alternately refers to it as "shima" or "O shima." This latter designation is interesting in that she pairs O shima with T shima, which, given the text's geographical markers, correspond to Iriomote and Ishigaki. If Sakiyama chose the letters O and T with Okinawa and Tokyo in mind, she may well be alerting readers to a center–periphery relationship between Ishigaki and Iriomote.
10 For sixty years, beginning in the mid-1880s, Japanese corporations operated coalmines in Iriomote. These mines, which ceased operation during World War II, resumed for three years in 1949, under the American occupation, and again briefly in 1954, before coming to a complete halt. For a pictographic history of the industry, see Miki Takeshi (ed.) (1986) *Iriomote tankō*, Naha: Niraisha. For a cultural history of Japan's coalmines, see Matthew Allen (1994) *Undermining the Japanese Miracle*, Melbourne: Cambridge University Press.
11 Sakiyama Tami, "Suijō ōkan," pp. 154–5.
12 The ahistorical thrust of Sakiyama's story suggests she is toying with the discourse of a pristine, romantic Ryukyu, free of weaponry and conflict. Historical records disprove the existence of such an ideal state. See Gregory Smits (2006) "Romantic Ryukyu in Okinawan Politics: The Myth of Ryukyuan Pacifism," paper presented at the Association for Asian Studies Annual Meeting, San Francisco, April 7, 2006 and (2003) "Iyashi no shima: gensō to nashonarizumu," an interview with Medoruma Shun, in *Yuibutsu kenkyū kyōkai*, 8 (October): 8–40.
13 Sakiyama pointedly remarks how she cannot write with the optimism that characterizes Ōshiro Tatsuhiro's corpus. This optimism comes from Ōshiro's hope that mainland readers will understand Okinawa and its culture through his writing. What underlies his optimism is his confidence and mastery in the subject of his writing. Sakiyama's work moves in a different direction, suggesting the impossibility of reaching such a point of certitude. *Okinawa Times*, November 25, 2005, p. 17.
14 Sakiyama, *Suijō ōkan*, p. 172.
15 Shiga Naoya (1976) *A Dark Night's Passing*, trans. Edwin McClellan, New York: Kodansha, p. 400.
16 Sakiyama Tami, "Suijō ōkan," p. 178.
17 Sakiyama, *Suijō ōkan*, p. 178.
18 Marukawa Tetsushi discusses island fetishization in (2004) "Shisha ni fureru meche," *Teikoku no bōrei: Nihon bungaku no seishin chizu*, Tokyo: Seidosha, p. 210.
19 Sakiyama, *Nantō shōkei*, pp. 106–8.
20 Sakiyama, *Nantō shōkei*, p. 107.
21 Daniels, *Voice of the Oppressed*, p. 52.
22 Deleuze and Guattari write,

> [t]o become animal is to participate in movement, to stake out the path of escape in all its positivity, to cross a threshold, to reach a continuum of intensities that are valuable only in themselves, to find a world of pure inten-

sities where all forms come undone, as do all the significations, signifiers, and signified, to the benefit of an unformed matter of deterritorialized flux, of nonsignifying signs.
See Gilles Deleuze and Félix Guattari (1986) *Kafka: Toward a Minor Literature*, trans. Dana Polan, Minneapolis, Minn.: University of Minnesota Press, p. 13.

23 Deleuze and Guatttari, *Kafka*, p. 6.
24 For a meticulous analysis of the reversals in geography in Sakiyama's debut piece, see Suzuki Tomoyuki (2002) "Hōi no tenkō: Sakiyama Tami *Suijō ōkan* ni okeru kioku no kūkan kōsei," *Shakai shirin*, 48 (3–4): 1–56.
25 Sakiyama, "'Shimakotoba' de kachāshī," pp. 170–1.
26 Deleuze and Guattari, *Kafka*, p. 6.
27 Sakiyama Tami (2003) "'Okinawa' to 'watakushi' no bungaku no aida," in Okamoto Keitoku and Takahashi Toshio (eds) *Okinawa bungakusen: Nihon no bungaku no eiji kara no koe*, Tokyo: Bensei shuppan, p. 401. Sakiyama, who has written a dozen works in the past two decades, partially accounts for her slow rate of production by stating that for every two hours of writing, she spends a full hour rewriting to achieve her desired rhythm. Of course, the time she devotes to raising her daughter and working full-time also has a huge impact on her output. See Sakiyama, "'Shōsetsu' no genjō kara," pp. 28–9.
28 Sakiyama Tami, *Fūsuitan*, in Okamoto Keitoku and Takahashi Toshio (eds) (2003) *Okinawa bungakusen: Nihon no bungaku no eiji kara no koe*, Tokyo: Bensei shuppan, p. 387.
29 Wendy O'Shea-Meddour (1999) "The Seduction of the Sirens: Derrida and Woman," *Textual Practice* 13 (3): 465–86.
30 Sakiyama, *Fūsuitan*, p. 384.
31 Sakiyama, *Fūsuitan*, p. 385.
32 Sakiyama, *Fūsuitan*, p. 390.
33 Sakiyama, *Fūsuitan*, p. 390.
34 Sakiyama, *Fūsuitan*, p. 384.
35 Sakiyama, *Fūsuitan*, p. 385.
36 Sakiyama, *Fūsuitan*, p. 388.
37 Sakiyama, *Fūsuitan*, p. 391.
38 I am thinking here of Ōshiro Tatsuhiro, through whose postwar works mainland readers have learned many aspects of Okinawa's culture, and Medoruma Shun, who writes of Okinawa's continuing war by employing to great effect flashbacks of war scenes.
39 Sakiyama, *Fūsuitan*, p. 395.
40 Sakiyama, *Fūsuitan*, p. 398.
41 Sakiyama, *Fūsuitan*, p. 398.
42 Shinjō Ikuo, "Sakuhin kaisetsu," in Okamoto Keitoku and Takahashi Toshio (eds), *Okinawa bungakusen: Nihon no bungaku no eiji kara no koe*, Tokyo: Bensei shuppan, p. 403.
43 Deleuze and Guatttari, *Kafka*, p. xiv.
44 Continuing this point, Deleuze and Guattari authors write,

> Furthermore, there is no longer the subject of the enunciation, nor a subject of the statement. It is no longer the subject of the statement who is a dog, with the subject of enunciation "like" a man; it is no longer the subject of the enunciation who is "like" a beetle, the subject of the statement remaining a man. Rather, there is a circuit of states that forms a mutual becoming, in the heart of a necessarily multiple or collective assemblage.
> Deleuze and Guatttari, *Kafka*, p. 22.

45 Quoted in Katō Hiroshi (2001) "Okinawa ni okeru gengo jōkyo to bungaku," *Meijigakuin daigaku shakaigakubu fuzoku kenkyūjo nenpō* 31 (3): 51–63, p. 60.
46 With fiction that all but eschews the notion of an essential origin, it is amusing to read of Sakiyama's fondness for her preferred venue for writing, a Koza coffee shop called Origin (Genten). See "Genten no kōhī, in *Nantō shōkei*, pp. 38–9.
47 Marukawa, "Shisha ni fureru meche," p. 215.
48 "Rocking and Rolling" tells the story of a fictive island, which, due to a declining birthrate, is now populated almost entirely by old men, ranging from seventy to 100 years in age. The dialect-heavy story is a free exchange of voices and songs, which, while admittedly baffling in places, does present a timely view on the contemporary issue of female barrenness. While Ōshiro Tatsuhiro has criticized the tendency among young Okinawan writers, Sakiyama included, to use dialect facilely. Critics reviewing "Rocking and Rolling" praise the work precisely for its rhythm, narration, and powerful writing.
49 Sakiyama Tami (2004) *Kotoba no umareru basho*, Tokyo: Sunagoya shobō, pp. 119–20.
50 Sakiyama Tami (1994) *Muiani yuraiki*, Tokyo: Sunagoya shobō, p. 11.
51 Sakiyama, *Muiani yuraiki*, p. 32.
52 Shinjō Ikuo (2003) *Okinawa bungaku to iu kuwadate*, Tokyo: Inpakuto shuppankai, p. 205.
53 Ronald Bogue (1999) "Minor Writing and Minor Literature," *Symplokē* 5 (1–2): 99–118, p. 110.
54 Deleuze and Guatttari, *Kafka*, pp. 83–4.
55 Dana Polan, Translator's Introduction, in Deleuze and Guatttari, *Kafka*, p. xxiii.

Conclusion

1 Significant dates in 1945 for those living in mainland Japan are December 8 (Pearl Harbor attack), August 6 (Hiroshima attack), August 9 (Nagasaki attack), and August 15 (Japan's surrender). For Okinawans, besides June 23, 1945, two other dates are greater in importance than the dates given above: April 28, 1952 ("Day of Shame"), and May 15, 1972 (return to Japanese sovereignty).
2 See Arakawa Akira's essay (2000) "Shinsatsu e no 'teikōkan' to wa nanika," in *Okinawa: tōgō to hangyaku*, Tokyo: Chikuma shobō.
3 Kuroko Kazuo raises this point in (1997) "Okinawa bungaku to Medoruma Shun," *Ryukyu News*, July 30.

Bibliography

Ahmad, Aijaz (1992) *In Theory: Classes, Nation, Literatures*, London and New York: Verso.
Allen, Matthew (1994) *Undermining the Japanese Miracle*, Cambridge: Cambridge University Press.
—— (2002) *Identity and Resistance in Okinawa*, Lanham, Md.: Rowman & Littlefield.
Amuta, Chidi (1995) "Fanon, Cabral and Ngugi on National Liberation," in Bill Ashcroft, Gareth Griffiths, and Helen Tiffin (eds), *The Post-Colonial Studies Reader*, London and New York: Routledge: 158–63.
Anderson, Benedict (1983) *Imagined Communities: Reflections on the Origin and Spread of Nationalism*, London and New York: Verso.
Angst, Linda (2001) "The Sacrifice of a Schoolgirl: The 1995 Rape Case, Discourses of Power and Women's Lives in Okinawa," *Critical Asian Studies* 33 (2): 243–66.
—— (2003) "The Rape of a Schoolgirl," in Laura Hein and Mark Selden (eds), *Islands of Discontent*, Lanham, Md.: Rowman and Littlefield: 135–57.
Anon. (1975) *Okinawa taiwa*, Tokyo: Kokusho kankōkai.
Appiah, Anthony (1998) "Topologies of Nativism," in Julie Rivkin and Michael Ryan (eds), *Literary Theory: An Anthology*, Oxford: Blackwell Publishing: 945–57.
Arakawa Akira (2000) *Okinawa: tōgō to hangyaku*, Tokyo: Chikuma shobō.
Arasaki Moriteru and Nakano Yoshio (1970) *Okinawa: 70-nen zengo*, Tokyo: Iwanami shoten.
—— (1990) *Okinawa sengo shi*, Tokyo: Iwanami shoten.
Arazato Kinpuku and Ōshiro Tatsuhiro (1966) *Okinawa mondai: Nijūnen*, Tokyo: Iwanami shoten.
—— (1972) *Kindai Okinawa no ayumi*, Tokyo: Taihei shuppansha.
Asahi shinbunsha (eds) (1972–96) *Okinawa hōkoku: fukkigo*, Tokyo: Asahi bunko, 1996.
Asano Makoto (1991) *Okinawaken no kyōikushi*, Tokyo: Shibunkaku shuppan.
Ashcroft, Bill, Gareth Griffiths, and Helen Tiffin (eds) (1989) *The Empire Writes Back: Theory and Practice in Post-Colonial Literatures*, London and New York: Routledge.
—— (1995) *The Post-colonial Studies Reader*, London and New York: Routledge.
Bhabha, Homi K. (1990) *Nation and Narration*, London and New York: Routledge.
—— (1994) *The Location of Culture*, London and New York: Routledge.
Bhaudra, Gautam (1982) "The Mentality of Subalternity: Kantanam or Rajdharma," in *Subaltern Studies: Writing on South Asian History and Society*, Delhi; New York: Oxford University Press, Vol. VI: 54–91.

Bhowmik, Davinder L. (2003) "A 'Lite' Battle Narrative: Medoruma Shun's 'Suiteki'," *Proceedings of the Association for Japanese Literary Studies* 4 (summer): 311–18.

—— (2006) "Literature as Public Memory in Contemporary Okinawan Fiction," in Josef Kreiner (ed.), *Japaneseness versus Ryūkyūanism*, Bonn: Bier'sche Verlagsanstalt: 111–18.

Bogue, Ronald (1999) "Minor Writing and Minor Literature," *Symplokē* 5 (1–2): 99–118.

Bourdaghs, Michael K. (2003) *The Dawn That Never Comes: Shimazaki Tōson and Japanese Nationalism*, New York: Columbia University Press.

Brandt, Kim (2007) *Kingdom of Beauty: Mingei and the Politics of Folk Art in Imperial Japan*, Durham, NC and London: Duke University Press.

Brantlinger, Patrick (1998) "The Rule of Darkness," in Julie Rivkin and Michael Ryan (eds), *Literary Theory: An Anthology*, Malden, Mass.: Blackwell Publishing: 856–67.

Campbell, Jane (1986) *Mythic Black Fiction: The Transformation of History*, Knoxville, Tenn.: University of Tennessee Press.

Cassegard, Carl (2007) "Exteriority and Transcritique: Karatani Kōjin and the Impact of the 1990s," *Japanese Studies*, 27 (1): 1–18.

Cheng, Vincent J. (2004) *Inauthentic: The Anxiety over Culture and Identity*, London and New Brunswick, Md.: Rutgers University Press.

Ching, Leo T. S. (2000) "'Give me Japan and Nothing Else!' Postcoloniality, Identity, and the Traces of Colonialism," *South Atlantic Quarterly* 99 (4): 763–88.

—— (2001) *Becoming "Japanese": Colonial Taiwan and the Politics of Identity Formation*, Berkeley, Calif.: University of California Press.

Christy, Alan (1993) "The Making of Imperial Subjects in Okinawa," *Positions: East Asia Critique* 1 (3): 607–38.

Creighton, Millie (2001) "Spinning Silk, Weaving Selves: Nostalgia, Gender, and Identity in Japanese Craft Vacations," *Japanese Studies* 21 (1): 5–29.

Cutter, Martha J. (2000) "Philomela Speaks: Alice Walker's Revisioning of Rape Archetypes in *The Color Purple*," *MELUS* 25 (3–4): 161–80.

Daniels, Patsy J. (2001) *Voice of the Oppressed in the Language of the Oppressor*, New York: Routledge.

Davis, Fred (1979) *Yearning for Yesterday: A Sociology of Nostalgia*, New York: Free Press.

Deleuze, Gilles and Félix Guattari (1986) *Kafka: Toward a Minor Literature*, trans. Dana Polan, Minneapolis, Minn.: University of Minnesota Press.

Dhomhnaill, Nuala Ní (1995) "Why I Choose to Write in Irish, The Corpse That Sits Up and Talk Back," *New York Times Book Review*, 8 January.

Dodd, Stephen (2004) *Writing Home: Representations of the Native Place in Modern Japanese Literature*, Cambridge, Mass.: Harvard University Press.

Dower, John (ed.) (1993) *Japan in War and Peace*, New York: New Press.

DuBois, W. E. B. (1998) "The Souls of Black Folk," in Julie Rivkin and Michael Ryan (eds), *Literary Theory: An Anthology*, Malden, Mass.: Blackwell Publishing: 868–72.

Duus, Peter (1976) *The Rise of Modern Japan*, Boston, Mass.: Houghton Mifflin Company.

—— (1983) "The Takeoff Point of Japanese Imperialism," in Harry Wray and Hilary Conroy (eds), *Japan Examined: Perspectives on Modern Japanese History*, Honolulu, Hawaii: University of Hawai'i Press: 153–7.

Fabian, Johannes (1983) *Time and the Other: How Anthropology Makes its Object*, New York: Columbia University Press.

Fanon, Frantz (1967) *Black Skin, White Masks*, trans. Charles Lam Markmann, New York: Grove Press.

Field, Norma (1991) *In the Realm of the Dying Emperor: A Portrait of Japan at Century's End*, New York: Pantheon Books.

Figal, Gerald (2003) "Waging Peace on Okinawa," in Laura Hein and Mark Selden (eds), *Islands of Discontent*, Lanham, Md.: Rowman and Littlefield: 65–98.

Frawley, Oona (2005) *Irish Pastoral: Nostalgia and Twentieth-Century Irish Literature*, Dublin: Irish Academic Press.

Fujii Rei'ichi, "Yaponeshia no shippo," in Okinawa bungaku zenshū henshū īnkai (eds), *Okinawa bungaku zenshū*, Vol. XVIII, Tokyo: Kokusho kankōkai: 317–25.

Fukuchi Hiroaki (1992) *Beigun kichi hanzai: ima mo tsuzuku Okinawa no kanashimi to ikari*, Tokyo: Rōdō kyōiku sentā.

Gabriel, Philip (1996) "Rethinking the Margins: Shimao Toshio and Yaponesia," *Japan Forum* 8 (2): 205–20.

—— (1999) *Mad Wives and Island Dreams*, Honolulu, University of Hawai'i Press.

Gerow, Aaron (2003) "From the National Gaze to Multiple Gazes," in Laura Hein and Mark Selden (eds), *Islands of Discontent*, Lanham, Md.: Rowman and Littlefield: 273–307.

Gessel, Van (1989) *The Sting of Life: Four Contemporary Japanese Novelists*, New York: Columbia University Press.

Gima Susumu, "Gengo, bunka, sekai," in Okinawa bungaku zenshū henshū īnkai (eds), *Okinawa bungaku zenshū*, Vol. XVIII, Tokyo: Kokusho kankōkai: 193–203.

Gohrisch, Jana (1996) "Mainstream or Margin? Ethnic Minority Literature in Britain," *Nature, Society, and Thought* 9 (4): 389–417.

Goldschmidt, Richard (1981) *Taishō jidai no Okinawa*, trans. Taira Ken'ichi and Nakamura Tetsumasa, Naha: Ryūkyū shinpōsha.

Gramsci, Antonio (1991) "Language, Linguistics and Folklore," trans. William Boelhower, in David Forgacs and Geoffrey Nowell-Smith (eds), *Selections from Cultural Writings*, Cambridge, Mass.: Harvard University Press: 164–95.

Guha, Ranajit (ed.) (1989) *Subaltern Studies VI*, Delhi: Oxford University Press.

Guha, Ranajit and Gayatri Chakravorty Spivak (eds) (1988) *Selected Subaltern Studies*, New York and Oxford: Oxford University Press.

Haberly, David T. (1974) "The Search for a National Language: A Problem in the Comparative History of Postcolonial Literatures," *Comparative Literature Studies* 11: 85–97.

Hall, Stuart (1991), "The Local and the Global: Globalization and Ethnicity," in Anthony D. King (ed.) *Culture, Globalization and the World System*, London: Basingstoke: 19–39.

Han, Jung-Sun N. (2007) "Envisioning a Liberal Empire in East Asia: Yoshino Sakuzō in Taisho Japan," *Journal of Japanese Studies* 33 (2): 357–82.

Hanada Toshinori (2006) *Okinawa wa Gojira ka: han Orientarizumu nantō Yaponeshia*, Fukuoka: Hana shoin.

Haring, Douglas (1969) *Okinawan Customs*, Tokyo: Charles E. Tuttle Book.

Hartman, Geoffrey (1993) "Public Memory and Modern Experience," *The Yale Journal of Criticism* 6 (2): 239–48.

Hayashi Kyōko, Komori Yōichi, Inoue Yasashi, and Matsushita Hirobumi (2002), "Genbaku bungaku to Okinawa bungaku: 'chinmoku' o kataru kotoba," *Subaru* 24 (4): 206–46.

Hein, Laura, and Mark Selden (eds) (2003) *Islands of Discontent: Okinawan Responses to Japanese and American Power*, Lanham, Md.: Rowman & Littlefield.

Heinrich, Patrick (2005) "Language Loss and Revitalization in the Ryuku Islands," *Japan Focus*. Online. Available HTTP < http://japanfocus.org/article.asp?id=444 > (accessed 14 November 2005).

Heshiki Bushō (2005) *Bungaku hihyō wa naritatsu ka*, Naha: Bōdāinku.

Higa Shunchō, Shimota Seiji, and Shinzato Keiji (eds) (1996) *Okinawa*, Tokyo: Iwanami shoten.

Higashi Mineo (1989) "Child of Okinawa," in *Okinawa: Two Postwar Novellas*, trans. Steve Rabson, Berkeley, Calif.: Institute of East Asian Studies, University of California.

Hirotsu Kazuo (1994) *Samayoeru Ryūkyūjin*, Tokyo: Dōjidaisha.

Hiyane Kaoru (1987) "'Yaponeshia ron' to Okinawa," *Shin Okinawa Bungaku* 71 (spring): 14–27.

—— (1992) "*Dororon* no ekurichūru," *Shin Okinawa bungaku* 91: 47.

Hokama Shuzen (1986) *Okinawa no rekishi to bunka*, Tokyo: Chūkō shinsho.

—— (2002) *Okinawagaku e no michi*, Tokyo: Iwanami shoten.

Hook, Glenn D., and Richard Siddle (eds) (2003) *Japan and Okinawa: Structure and Subjectivity*, London: Routledge Curzon.

Horii Ken'ichi (1973) "Densetsu kara jijitsu e: Shōsetsu 'Okuma Junsa' no koto," *Aoi umi* 26 (fall): 100–2.

Howell, David L. (2004) "Making 'Useful Citizens' of Ainu Subjects in Early Twentieth-Century Japan," *Journal of Asian Studies* 63 (1): 5–29.

—— (2005) *Geographies of Identity in Nineteenth-Century Japan*, Berkeley, Calif.: University of California Press.

Ienaga Saburo (1993–4) "The Glorification of War in Japanese Education," *International Security*, 18 (3): 113–33.

Inoue Masamichi S. (2002) "Gurobaruka no naka no 'Okinawa inishiatibu' ronsō," *Shisō* 1 (933): 246–67.

—— (2007) *Okinawa and the U. S. Military*, New York: Columbia University Press.

Ivy, Marilyn (1995) *Discourses of the Vanishing: Modernity, Phantasm, Japan*, Chicago, Ill.: University of Chicago Press.

Iwabuchi Kōichi, Tada Osamu, and Tanaka Yasuhiro (eds) (2004) *Okinawa ni tachisukumu: daigaku o koete shinka suru chi*, Tokyo: Serika shobō.

Jameson, Fredric (1986) "Third-World Literature in the Era of Multinational Capitalism," *Social Text* 15 (fall): 65–88.

JanMohamed, Abdul, R. and Lloyd, David (eds) (1990) *The Nature and Context of Minority Discourse*, New York: Oxford University Press.

Jordan, David (ed.) (1994) *Regionalism Reconsidered: New Approaches to the Field*, New York: Garland.

Kano Masanao (1987) *Sengo Okinawa no shisōzō*, Tokyo: Asahi shinbunsha.

Karatani Kōjin (1993) *Origins of Modern Japanese Literature*, trans. Brett de Bary, Durham, NC and London: Duke University Press.

Katō Hiroshi (2001) "Okinawa ni okeru gengo jōkyo to bungaku," *Meijigakuin daigaku shakaigakubu fuzoku kenkyūjo nenpō* 31 (3): 51–63.

Katsukata-Inafuku, Keiko (2006) *Okinawa joseigaku kotohajime*, Tokyo: Shinjuku shobō.

Kawamitsu Shin'ichi (1987) *Okinawa: Jiritsu to kyōsei no shisō: "Mirai no jōmon" e kakeru hashi*, Osaka: Kaifūsha.

—— (1990) "Okinawa bungaku no kadai," in Okinawa bungaku zenshū henshū īnkai (eds), *Okinawa bungaku zenshū*, Vol. XVII, Tokyo: Kokusho kankōkai: 106–20.

—— (1991) *Okinawa kindai bungei sakuhinshū (Shin Okinawa bungaku bessatsu)*, Naha: Okinawa taimususha.

Kawamura Minato (1994a) *Nanyō/Karafuto no Nihon bungaku*, Tokyo: Chikuma shobō.

—— (1994b) "Literature as a Myth of Resurrection: 'Hi no Hate Kara,'" *Japanese Literature Today*, (19): 81–7.

—— (2000) *Kaze o yomu mizu ni kaku mainoritī bungaku ron*, Tokyo: Kōdansha.

Keene, Donald (1976) *World Within Walls: Japanese Literature of the Pre-Modern Era 1600–1867*, New York: Grove Press.

—— (1984) *Dawn to the West: Japanese Literature in the Modern Era*, 2 vols, New York: Henry Holt & Company.

Kinjō Chōhei (1990) "Ryūkyū ni shuzai shita bungaku," in Okinawa bungaku zenshū henshū īnkai (eds), *Okinawa bungaku zenshū*, Vol. XVII, Tokyo: Kokusho kankōkai: 6–40.

Kinjō Minoru (1996) *Shitte imasu ka: Okinawa ichimon ittō*, Osaka: Kaihō shuppansha.

Kodama Masatō (1993) *Shiryō ga kataru Ryūkyū to Okinawa*, Tokyo: Mainichi shinbunsha.

Kohl, Stephen, W. McClain, Yoko Matsuoka, and Ryoko Toyama McClellan (1975) *The White Birch School (Shirakabaha) of Japanese Literature: Some Sketches and Commentary*, Occasional Paper No. 2, Asian Studies Committee, Eugene, Oreg.: University of Oregon.

Komesu Okifumi (1986) *Reda no matsuei: Airurando, Porineshia, Okinawa*, Naha: Okinawa bunko.

—— (1987) "Kotoba to bunka no aidentitī: Airurando no keiken," *Toshō*: 38–42.

—— (1990) "Bungaku ni okeru 'shinwa' no imi," in Okinawa bungaku zenshū henshū īnkai (eds), *Okinawa bungaku zenshū*, Vol. XVII, Tokyo: Kokusho kankōkai: 276–93.

—— (1991) *Piromera no uta: Jōhōka jidai ni okeru Okinawa no aidentitī*, Naha: Okinawa taimususha.

Komori Yōichi (1998) *Yuragi no Nihon bungaku*, Tokyo: NHK bukkusu.

Kreiner, Josef (ed.) (2006) *Japaneseness versus Ryukyuanism*, Bonn: Bier'sche Verlagsanstalt.

Kubota Jun (ed.) (1996) "Nihon bungaku shi," in *Ryūkyū bungaku/Okinawa no bungaku*, Tokyo: Iwanami kōza: 175–220.

Kuniyoshi Shintetsu (1970) "'Samayoeru Ryūkyūjin' no shūhen," *Shin Okinawa bungaku*, 17 (summer): 45–9.

Kuniyoshi Shintetsu, Okamoto Keitoku, and Ōshiro Tatsuhiro (1973) *Aoi umi* 26 (fall): 88–99.

—— (1997) "Okinawa bungaku to Medoruma Shun," *Ryūkyū shinpō*, July 30.

Kurosawa, Asako (ed.) (2005) *Okinawadai ga Amerika ni senryō sareta hi: beigun heri suiraku jiken kara miete kita Okinawa*, Tokyo: Seidosha.

Kushi Fusako (1993) "Horobiyuku Ryūkyū onna no shuki: Chikyū no sumikko ni oshiyarareta minzoku no nageki o kīte itadakitai," in Okinawa bungaku zenshū henshū īnkai (eds), *Okinawa bungaku zenshū*, Vol. 6, Tokyo: Kokusho kankōkai: 96–103.

—— (2000a) "In Defense of 'Memoirs of a Declining Ryukyuan Woman,'" in Michael Molasky and Steve Rabson (eds), *Southern Exposure: Modern Japanese Literature from Okinawa*, Honolulu, Hawaii: University of Hawai'i Press: 81–4.

—— (2000b) "Memoirs of a Declining Ryukyan Woman," in Michael Molasky and Steve Rabson (eds), *Southern Exposure: Modern Japanese Literature from Okinawa*, Honolulu, Hawaii: University of Hawai'i Press: 73–80.
Lebra, William P. (1966) *Okinawan Religion: Belief, Ritual, and Social Structure*, Honolulu, Hawaii: University of Hawai'i Press.
—— (1970) "The Ryukyu Islands," *Rice University Studies* 56 (4): 283–93.
Levi, Antonia (1995) "Okinawa: Thousand-Year Rape of an Entire People," *Seattle Times*, 10 November: 11.
Luhrmann, T. M. (1996) *The Good Parsi: The Fate of a Colonial Elite in a Postcolonial Society*, Cambridge, Mass.: Harvard University Press.
McCormack, Gavan (2003) "Okinawa and the Structure of Dependence," in Glen Hook and Richard Siddle (eds), *Japan and Okinawa: Structure and Subjectivity*, London and New York: RoutledgeCurzon: 93–113.
—— (2007) "Fitting Okinawa into Japan the 'Beautiful Country'," *Japan Focus*. Online. Available HTTP < http://www.zmag.org/content/showarticle.cfm?SectionID=17&ItemID=129782 > (accessed 2 June 2007).
Mack, Edward (2002) "The Value of Literature," Ph.D. dissertation, Harvard University.
Marukawa Tetsushi (2004) *Teikoku no bōrei: Nihon bungaku no seishin chizu*, Tokyo: Seidosha.
Matayoshi Eiki (1996) *Buta no mukui*, Tokyo: Bungei shunjū.
Matayoshi Seikyo (1990) *Nihon shokuminchika no Taiwan to Okinawa*, Ginowan: Okinawa aki shobō.
Matsubara Shin'ichi (1998) *Taida no gyakusetsu: Hirotsu Kazuo no jinsei to bungaku*, Tokyo: Kōdansha.
Matsumura Akira (ed.) (1989) *Daijirin*, 15th edn, Tokyo: Sanseidō.
Medoruma Shun (1996a) "Okinawa no bunka jōkyō no genzai ni tsuite," *Kēshi kajī*, 13: 28–9.
—— (1996b) "Okinawa no shōsetsu/engekishi," in *Nihon bungaku shi*, Tokyo: Iwanami kōza, Vol. XV: 175-220.
—— (1997) *Suiteki*, Tokyo: Bungei shunjū.
—— (1998) "Uchināguchi to Yamatoguchi no aida de," *Bungei* 5 (37): 192–3.
—— (1999a) *Mabuigumi*, Tokyo: Asahi shinbunsha.
—— (1999b) "An Okinawan Short Story," trans. Steve Rabson, *JPRI Critique*, 6 (12). Online. Available HTTP: < http://www.jpri.org/publications/critiques/critique_VI_12.html > (accessed 15 September 2007).
—— (2000) "Droplets," in Michael Molasky and Steve Rabson (eds), *Southern Exposure: Modern Japanese Literature from Okinawa*, Honolulu, Hawaii: University of Hawai'i Press: 255–86.
—— (2001a) *Gunchō no ki*, Tokyo: Asahi shinbunsha.
—— (2001b) *Okinawa kusa no koe ne no ishi*, Yokohama: Seori shobō.
—— (2001c) "Yūshitai," *Gunzō* 56 (11): 324.
—— (2003) *Heiwa dōri to nazukerareta machi o aruite*, Tokyo: Kage shobō.
—— (2004) *Fūon*, Tokyo: Ritoru moa.
—— (2005) *Okinawa "sengo" zeronen*, Tokyo: Seikatsujin shinshō.
—— (2006a) *Okinawa: chi o yomu toki o miru*, Tokyo: Seori shobō.
—— (2006b) *Niji no tori*, Tokyo: Kage shobō.
Medoruma Shun and Ikezawa Natsuki (1997) "Zetsubō kara hajimaru," *Bungakukai* 51 (9): 174–89.
Memmi, Albert (1965) *The Colonizer and the Colonized*, Boston, Mass.: Beacon Press.

Miki Takeshi (ed.) (1986) *Iriomote tankō*, Naha: Niraisha.
—— (ed.) (1988) *Arakaki Mitoko sakuhinshū*, Naha: Niraisha.
—— (1990) "Okineshia bunka ron: Seishin no kyōwakoku o motomete," in Okinawa bungaku zenshū henshū īnkai (eds), *Okinawa bungaku zenshū*, Vol. XVIII, Tokyo: Kokusho kankōkai: 353–67.
Mitchell, Timothy (1992) "Orientalism and the Exhibitionary Order," in Nicholas B. Dirks (ed.) *Colonialism and Culture*, Ann Arbor, Mich.: University of Michigan Press: 289–318.
Miyagi Etsujirō (1996) "Redressing the Okinawan Base Problem," *Japan Quarterly* 43 (1): 27–32.
Miyagi Sō (1993) "Seikatsu no tanjō," in Okinawa bungaku zenshū henshū īnkai (eds), *Okinawa bungaku zenshū*, Vol. VI, Tokyo: Kokusho kankōkai: 104–42.
Molasky, Michael S. (1999) *The American Occupation of Japan and Okinawa*, London: Routledge.
—— (2003) "Medoruma Shun: The Writer as Public Intellectual in Okinawa Today," in Laura Hein and Mark Selden (eds), *Islands of Discontent*, Lanham, Md.: Rowman & Littlefield: 164–5.
Molasky, Michael S. and Steve Rabson (eds) (2000) *Southern Exposure: Modern Japanese Literature from Okinawa*, Honolulu, Hawaii: University of Hawai'i Press.
Molino, Michael R. (1993) "Flying by the Nets of Language and Nationality: Seamus Heaney, The 'English' Language, and Ulster's Troubles," *Modern Philology* 3 (2): 180–201.
Morris-Suzuki, Tessa (1998) *Re-Inventing Japan: Time, Space, Nation*, New York: M. E. Sharpe.
—— (2001) "Northern Lights: The Making and Unmaking of Karafuto Identity," *Journal of Asian Studies* 60 (3): 645–71.
Morton, Leith (2004–5) "Shamans Make History in Okinawa: A Reading of Ōshiro Tatsuhiro's Novel *Noro* (Mantic Woman, 1985)," *Journal of Asian Studies* 36–7: 30–54.
Motohama, Hidehiko (2005) "Writing at the Edge: Narratives of Okinawan History and Cultural Identity in the Literary Texts of Oshiro Tatsuhiro," Ph.D. dissertation, University of Pennsylvania.
Mukubō Tetsuya (2006) "Kyōdo geijutsu, den'en, rōkaru karā," *Nihon kindai bungaku* 74 (5): 182–96.
Murai Osamu (1992) *Nantō ideorogī no hassei: Yanagita Kunio to shokuminchishugi*, Tokyo: Fukutake shoten.
—— (1994) "Iha Fuyū to Yanagita Kunio," in Okinawa bungaku zenshū henshū īnkai (eds), *Okinawa kara mita Nihon*, Tokyo: Fūma shobō: 165–202.
—— (2002) "Japanese Ethnology, Fascism, Colonialism," in Uemura Tadao (ed.), *Okinawa no kioku/Nihon no rekishi*, Tokyo: Miraisha: 33–73.
Nakahodo Masanori (1975) *Yamanoguchi Baku: Shi to sono kiseki*, Hōsei daigaku shuppankyokukan.
—— (1981) *Kindai Okinawa bungaku no tenkai*, Tokyo: San'ichi shobō.
—— (1982) *Okinawa no senki*, Tokyo: Asahi sensho.
—— (1987) *Okinawa bungakuron no hōhō: "Yamato yo" to "Amerika yo" no moto de*, Tokyo: Shinsensha.
—— (1988a) "'Chairudohuddo'" no tama," in Nakahodo Masanori and Tsunori Setsuko (eds), *Ikemiyagi Sekihō sakuhinshū*, Naha: Niraisha: 191–203.
—— (1988b) *Iha Getsujō: Ryūkyū no bungei fukkō o yume mita netsujōka*, Tokyo: Riburopōto.

—— (1988c) *Shima uta no Shōwa shi: Okinawa bungaku no ryōbun*, Tokyo: Gaifusha.
—— (1990a) "Okinawa gendai shōsetsu shi: Haisen kara fukki made," in Okinawa bungaku zenshū henshū īnkai (eds), *Okinawa bungaku zenshū*, Vol. VII, Tokyo: Kokusho kankōkai: 344–60.
—— (1990b) *Ryūsho tankyū*, Tokyo: Shinsensha.
—— (1991a) *Okinawa no bungaku 1927–45*, Naha: Okinawa taimususha.
—— (1991b) "Okinawa kindai shōsetsu no dōtei," in Okinawa bungaku zenshū henshū īnkai (eds), *Okinawa kindai bungei sakuhinshū, Shin Okinawa bungaku bessatsu*: 395–403.
—— (1993) "Okinawa kindai shōsetsu no shōten," *Senryō to bungaku*, 91: 265–82.
—— (1994) *Shinseinen-tachi no bungaku*, Naha: Niraisha.
Nakahodo Masanori and Tsunori Setsuko (eds) (1988) *Ikemiyagi Sekihō sakuhinshū*, Naha: Niraisha.
Nakamura Yashu (1990) *Kami to mura*, Tokyo: Fukurosha.
Nakasone, Ronald (ed.) (2002) *Okinawan Diaspora*, Honolulu, Hawaii: University of Hawai'i Press.
Nakazato Isao (1987) "'Yaponeshia ron' to Okinawa," *Shin Okinawa bungaku* 71 (spring): 20.
Napier, Susan (2006) "Matter Out of Place: Carnival, Containment, and Cultural Recovery in Miyazaki's Spirited Away," *Journal of Japanese Studies* 32 (2): 287–310.
Nelson, Christopher T. (2003) "*Nuchi nu Sūji*: Comedy and Everyday Life in Postwar Okinawa," in Glen D. Hooks and Richard Siddle (eds), *Japan and Okinawa*, London and New York: RoutledgeCurzon: 208–24.
Nietzsche, Fredrich (1974) "On Reading and Writing," in *Thus Spoke Zarathustra*, trans. Thomas Common, New York: Gordon Press.
Nishizato Kikō (1981) *Ronshū: Okinawa kindai shi-Okinawa sabetsu to wa nani ka*, Naha: Okinawa jiji shuppan.
Nozato Yō (2007) *Iyashi no shima, Okinawa no shinjitsu*, Tokyo: Sofutobanku shinsho.
Ōe Kenzaburō (1981) *Okinawa keiken*, Dōjidai ronshū 4, Tokyo: Iwanami shoten.
Oguma Eiji (1998) *Nihonjin no kyōkai*, Tokyo: Shinyōsha.
Okamoto Keitoku (ed.) (1969) "Sengo Okinawa bungaku no isshiten," *Okinawa bunka* 29 (2): 15–25.
—— (1972) "Sengo Okinawa bungaku," *Chūō kōron* (6): 192–209.
—— (1977a) "Okinawa sengo bungaku no shuppatsu: Sono shichō to jōkyō," *Shin Okinawa bungaku* 35: 30.
—— (1977b) "Sengo bungaku no tenkai," *Shin Okinawa bungaku* 35: 31–2.
—— (1978) "Ōshiro Tatsuhiro no bungaku to shisō: 'Ryūdai bungaku' to no kakawari no naka de," *Aoi umi* 69 (1): 182–9.
—— (1979) "Okinawasen senki ni tsuite: Sono shoki kiroku o chūshin ni," *Ryūkyū daigaku kiyo*, 23 (1): 1–25.
—— (1981a) *Gendai Okinawa bungaku to shisō*, Naha: Okinawa taimususha.
—— (1981b) *Okinawa bungaku no chihei*, Tokyo: San'ichi shobō.
—— (1990) "*Yaponeshia ron" no rinkaku: Shimao Toshio no manazashi*, Naha: Okinawa taimususha.
—— (1993a) "Kakuteru pātī ron," in *Senryō to bungaku*, Tokyo: Orijin shuppan sentā: 283–94.
—— (1993b) "Okinawa kindai shōsetsushi: seiritsuki," in *Okinawa bungaku zenshū* henshū īnkai (eds), *Okinawa bungaku zenshū*, Vol. VI, Tokyo: Kokusho kankōkai: 384–90.

—— (1995a) "Okinawa sengo shōsetsu no naka no Amerika," in Yoshihiko Teruya and Yamazato Katsunori (eds), *Sengo Okinawa to Amerika: Ibunka sesshoku no gojūnen*, Naha: Okinawa taimususha: 231–51.
—— (1995b) "Sengo o yomu: Shōsetsu 'Kamishima': Ōshiro Tatsuhiro," *Ryūkyū shinpō*, June 29: 3.
—— (1996) *Gendai bungaku ni miru Okinawa no jigazō*, Tokyo: Kōbunken.
—— (2000) *Okinawa bungaku no jōkei*, Naha: Niraisha.
Okamoto Keitoku and Takahashi Toshio (eds) (2003) *Okinawa bungakusen: Nihon no bungaku no eiji kara no koe*, Tokyo: Bensei shuppan.
Okamoto Tarō (1964) *Wasurerareta Nihon: Okinawa bunka ron*, Tokyo: Chūō kōron bunko.
Okaya Koji (1981) *Shima no seishinshi*, Tokyo: Shisakusha.
Okinawa bungaku fōramu jikō īnkai (eds) (1997) *Okinawa bungaku fōramu: Okinawa: dochaku kara fuhen e: tabunkashugi jidai no hyōgen no kanōsei*, Hōkokusho, Naha: Ryūkyū daigaku.
Okinawa bungaku henshū īnkai (eds) (1990) *Okinawa bungaku zenshū*, 20 vols (projected), Tokyo: Kokusho kankōkai.
Okinawa daihyakka jiten kankō jimu kyoku (eds) (1983) *Okinawa daihyakka jiten*, 4 vols, Naha: Okinawa taimususha.
Ikezawa Natsuki (ed.) (1992) *Okinawa iroiro jiten*, Tokyo: Shinchōsha.
Ōno Takayuki (2000) *Okinawa Times*, December 25.
O'Shea-Meddour, Wendy (1999) "The Seduction of the Sirens: Derrida and Woman," *Textual Practice* 13 (3): 465–86.
Oshino Takeshi (1993) "Nantō Orientarizumu e no teikō: Hirotsu Kazuo no 'sanbun seishin'," *Nihon kindai bungaku* 49 (October): 27–38.
Ōshiro Tatsuhiro (1968) *Panarinusuma gensō*, Tokyo: Kadokawa bunko.
—— (1973) "Okinawa no kindai bungaku to sabetsu: 'Okuma Junsa' to 'Horobiyuku Ryūkyū onna no shuki' o megutte," *Aoi umi* 26 (fall): 88–99.
—— (1974) *Kamishima*, Tokyo: Nihon hōsō shuppan kyōkai.
—— (1987) *Taisoku no enerugī: Ajia no naka no Okinawa*, Tokyo: Ningen sensho.
—— (1989) "The Cocktail Party," in *Okinawa: Two Postwar Novellas*, trans. Steve Rabson, Berkeley, Calif.: Institute of East Asian Studies, University of California: 35–80.
—— (1990a) "Kame no kōbaka," in Okinawa bungaku zenshū henshū īnkai (eds), *Okinawa bungaku zenshū*, Vol. VII, Tokyo: Kokusho kankōkai: 221–56.
—— (1990b) "Okinawa de Nihonjin ni naru koto: Kokoro no jidenfū ni," in Okinawa bungaku zenshū henshū īnkai (eds), *Okinawa bungaku zenshū*, Vol. XVIII, Tokyo: Kokusho kankōkai: 31–60.
—— (1990c) *Okinawa engeki no miryoku*, Naha: Okinawa taimususha.
—— (1993a) "Okinawa bungaku no genzai," in *Okinawa tanpen shōsetsushū: "Ryūkyū shinpō tanpen shōsetsu shō" jushō sakuhin*, Naha: Ryūkyū Shinpōsha: 1–16.
—— (1993b) *Ryūkyū no kisetsu ni*, Tokyo: Yomiuri shinbunsha.
—— (1994) *Hāfu taimu Okinawa*, Naha: Niraisha.
—— (1997) *Kōgen o motomete*, Naha: Okinawa taimusha.
—— (2000) "Turtleback Tombs," in Michael Molasky and Steve Rabson (eds), *Southern Exposure: Modern Japanese Literature from Okinawa*, Honolulu, Hawaii: University of Hawai'i Press: 113–54.
—— (2002) *Ōshiro Tatsuhiro zenshū*, ed. Kuroko Kazuo, Ōno Takayuki, Nakahodo Masanori, Tatematsu Wahei, 13 vols, Tokyo: Bensei shuppan.

Ōshiro Tatsuhiro, Nakahodo Masanori, Shima Tsuyoshi et al. (1998) "Okinawa bungaku to hōgen katsuyō ni tsuite," Roundtable discussion, *Urasoe bungei*, 4 (3): 9–47.
Ōta Masahide (1969) *Yopparai Nihonjin: Nihon no Okinawa ishiki*, Tokyo: Saimaru shuppankai.
Ōta Ryōhaku (2006) *Chosakushū*, 4 vols, Naha: Bōdāinku.
Ota, Yoshinobu (1991) "Cultural Authenticity as Entropic Metanarrative: A Case from Ryukyuan Studies," *Central Issues in Anthropology* 9 (April): 87–95.
Ōyama Chōjō (1997) *Okinawa dokuritsu sengen: Yamato wa kaeru beki "sokoku" de wa nakatta*, Tokyo: Gendai shorin.
Palumbo-Liu, David (ed.) (1995) *The Ethnic Canon: Histories, Institutions, and Interventions*, Minneapolis, Minn.: University of Minnesota Press.
Peattie, Mark (1984) *The Japanese Colonial Empire, 1895–1945*, Princeton, NJ: Princeton University Press.
Polan, Dana (1986) "Translator's Introduction," in Gilles Deleuze and Félix Guattari, *Kafka: Toward a Minor Literature*, London and Minneapolis, Minn.: University of Minnesota Press: xxii–xxix.
Rabson, Steve (1989) "Introduction and Afterword," in Ōshiro Tatsuhiro and Higashi Mineo, *Okinawa: Two Postwar Novellas*, Berkeley, Calif.: Institute for East Asian Studies: 1–32, 121–35.
Ranajit Guha (ed.) (1989) *Subaltern Studies VI*, Delhi: Oxford University Press.
Rivikin, Julie, and Michael Ryan (eds) (1998) *Literary Theory: An Anthology*, Oxford: Blackwell Publishing.
Roberson, James (2003) "Uchinaa Pop: Place and Identity in Contemporary Okinawan Popular Music," in Laura Hein and Mark Selden (eds), *Islands of Discontent*, Lanham, Md.: Rowman & Littlefield: 192–227.
Rushdie, Salman (1982) "The Empire Writes Back with a Vengeance," *The Times*, July 3: 8.
Saegusa Kazuko (2001) "Okinawa no kakitetachi: 'Shin Okinawa bungaku-shō' no senkō o tsūjite," *Yurīka* 8: 130.
Sakihara, Mitsugu (1987) *A Brief History of Early Okinawa Based on the Omoro Sōshi*, Tokyo: Honpo shoseki shuppan.
Sakiyama Tami (1994) *Kurikaeshi gaeshi*, Tokyo: Sunagoya shobō.
—— (1996) *Nantō shōkei*, Tokyo: Sunagoya shobō.
—— (1999) *Muiani yuraiki*, Tokyo: Sunagoya shobō.
—— (2000) "'Shōsetsu' no genjō kara," *Kēshi kajī* 27: 22–33.
—— (2001) *Okinawa Times*, November 25.
—— (2002) "'Shimakotoba' de kachāshī," in Imafuku Ryūta (ed.), *'Watashi' no tankyū*, Tokyo: Iwanami shoten: 157–80.
—— (2003a) "Fūsuitan," in Okamoto Keitoku and Takahashi Toshio (eds), *Okinawa bungakusen: Nihon no bungaku no eiji kara no koe*, Tokyo: Bensei shuppan: 384–9.
—— (2003b) "Iyashi no shima: gensō to nashonarizumu," (interview) *Yuibutsu kenkyū kyōkai*, 8 (October): 8–40.
—— (2003c) *Kotoba no umareru basho*, Tokyo: Sunagoya shobō.
—— (2003d) "'Okinawa' to 'watakushi' no bungaku no aida," in Okamoto Keitoku and Takahashi Toshio (eds), *Okinawa bungakusen: Nihon no bungaku no eiji kara no koe*, Tokyo: Bensei shuppan: 400–1.
—— (2003e) *Yurateiku yuriteiku*, Tokyo: Kōdansha.

Satohara Akira (1991) *Ryūkyū-ko no bungaku: Ōshiro Tatsuhiro no sekai*, Tokyo: Hōsei daigaku shuppan kyokukan.
Sekine Kenji (1987) "Ryūkyū-ko no naka no 'Yaponeshia ron,'" *Shin Okinawa bungaku* 71 (spring): 40–6.
—— (1993) *Tekisuto toshite no Ryūkyū-ko*, Ginowan: Roman shobō.
Serafim, Leon Angelo (1984) "Shodon: The Prehistory of a Northern Ryukyuan Dialect of Japanese," Ph.D. dissertation, Yale University.
Sered, Susan (1999) *Women of the Sacred Groves: Divine Priestesses of Okinawa*, Oxford: Oxford University Press.
Shaply, Thomas (1995) "Child's Rape Echoes Rape of Okinawa Itself," *Seattle Post-Intelligencer*, November 14: 9.
Shiga Naoya (1976) *A Dark Night's Passing*, trans. Edwin McClellan, New York: Kodansha.
Shima Tsuyoshi (1990) "Hataraku jikan to hatarakanai jikan: Ōshiro Tatsuhiro shi no tanpen shōsetsu kara," in Okinawa bungaku zenshū henshū īnkai (eds), *Okinawa bungaku zenshū*, Vol. XVII, Tokyo: Kokusho kankōkai: 294–305.
—— (2000) "Bones," in Michael Molasky and Steve Rabson (eds), *Southern Exposure: Modern Japanese Literature from Okinawa*, Honolulu, Hawaii: University of Hawai'i Press: 156–71.
Shimao Toshio (1985) *"The Sting of Death" and Other Stories*, trans. Kathryn Sparling, Ann Arbor, Mich.: Center for Japanese Studies, University of Michigan.
—— (1990a) "Kawa nite," in Okinawa bungaku zenshū henshū īnkai (eds), *Okinawa bungaku zenshū*, Vol. VII, Tokyo: Kokusho kankōkai: 120–31.
—— (1990b) "Yaponeshia to Ryūkyū-ko," in Okinawa bungaku zenshū henshū īnkai (eds), *Okinawa bungaku zenshū*, Vol. XVIII, Tokyo: Kokusho kankōkai: 264–312.
—— (1992) *Ryūkyū-ko no shiten kara*, Tokyo: Asahi bunko.
Shimota, Seiji (1982) *Watashi no sengo shisōshi*, Tokyo: Mizuchi shobō.
—— (1972) "Okinawa hōgen to Nihongo," *Bungaku* 40 (4): 59–64.
Shinjō Ikuo (1998) "Kuwadate toshite no shōnen," *Shinchō* 95 (8): 181–7.
—— (2003) *Okinawa bungaku to iu kuwadate*, Tokyo: Inpakuto shuppankai.
—— (2005) "Okinawa bungakuron no (fu)kanōsei: Okinawa bungaku fōramu," *Nihon Tōyō bunkaron* 11 (3): 49–78.
Shinmura Izuru (ed.) (1998) *Kōjien*, 5th edn, Tokyo: Iwanami shoten.
Shu Keisoku (2001) "Medoruma Shun no shōsetsu ni okeru Okinawa to 'shintai' no seijigaku," Ph.D. dissertation Nagoya University.
Siddle, Richard (1996) *Race, Resistance, and the Ainu of Japan*, London: Routledge.
—— (1998) "Colonialism and Identity in Okinawa before 1945," *Japanese Studies*, 18 (2): 117–33.
Smits, Gregory (1999) *Visions of Ryukyu: Identity and Ideology in Early-Modern Thought and Politics*, Honolulu, Hawaii: University of Hawai'i Press.
—— (2006) "The Politics of Culture in Early Twentieth Century Okinawa," in Joseph Kreiner (ed.), *Japaneseness versus Ryukyuanism*, Bonn: Bier'sche Verlagsanstalt: 59–70.
Spivak, Gayatri Chakravorty (1988) "Can the Subaltern Speak?" in Cary Nelson and Lawrence Grosssberg (eds), *Marxism and the Interpretation of Culture*, Urbana, Ill.: University of Illinois Press: 217–316.
Spurr, David (2003) *The Rhetoric of Empire: Colonial Discourse in Journalism, Travel Writing, and Imperial Administration*, Durham, NC and London: Duke University Press.

Steger, Brigitte (1994) "From Impurity to Hygiene: The Role of Midwives in the Modernisation of Japan," *Japan Forum* 6 (2): 175–88.
Suzuki Tomoyuki (2001) "Gūwateki akui: Medoruma Shun to Okinawa sen no kioku," *Shakai shirin*, 48 (1): 1–52.
—— (2002) "Hōi no tenkō: Sakiyama Tami *Suijō ōkan* ni okeru kioku no kūkan kōsei," *Shakai shirin*, 48 (3–4): 1–56.
Szeman, Imre (2001) "Who's Afraid of National Allegory? Jameson, Literary Criticism, Globalization," *South Atlantic Quarterly* 100 (3): 803–27.
Taira, Kōji (1997) "Troubled National Identity: The Ryukyuans/Okinawans," in Michael Weiner (ed.), *Japan's Minorities: The Illusion of Homogeneity*, London and New York: Routledge: 141–77.
Takara, Ben (1990) "Ryūkyū-ko no shisō no kanōsei to fukanōsei," in Okinawa bungaku zenshū henshū īnkai (eds), *Okinawa bungaku zenshū*, Vol. XVIII, Tokyo: Kokusho kankōkai: 371–80.
—— (1990) "Ryūkyūneshia/hitori dokuritsu sengen," in Okinawa bungaku zenshū henshū īnkai (eds), *Okinawa bungaku zenshū*, Vol. XVIII, Tokyo: Kokusho kankōkai: 332–6.
—— (1995) *Hatsugen: Okinawa no sengo gojūnen*, Naha: Hirugisha.
Takara Kurayoshi (1990) "'Panarinusuma gensō," in Okinawa bungaku zenshū henshū īnkai (eds), *Okinawa bungaku zenshū*, Vol. XVII, Tokyo: Kokusho kankōkai: 331–3.
Takeuchi Mitsuhiro (2000) "Bunka no mado," *Rekishi hyōron* 7 (603): 60.
Tanaka Yasuhiro (1999) "'Okinawa mondai' to 'Okinawa no mondai," in Jōkyō shuppan henshūbu (eds), *Okinawa o yomu*, Tokyo: Jōkyō shuppan: 198–203.
Thiong'o, Ngũgĩ wa (1995) "The Language of African Literature," in Bill Ashcroft, Gareth Griffiths, and Helen Tiffin (eds), *The Post-Colonial Studies Reader*, London and New York: Routledge: 285–90.
Tomiyama Ichirō (1990) *Kindai Nihon shakai to Okinawajin*, Tokyo: Nihon keizai hyōronsha.
—— (1995) *Senjō no kioku*, Tokyo: Nihon keizai hyōronsha.
—— (2000) "'Spy': Mobilization and Identity in Wartime Okinawa," *Japanese Civilization in the Modern World XVI Nation-State and Empire*, Senri Ethnological Studies, 51, Osaka: National Museum of Ethnology: 121–32.
—— (2002) *Bōryoku no yokan: Iha Fuyū ni okeru kiki mondai*, Tokyo: Iwanami shoten.
—— (2005) "Colonialism and the Sciences of the Tropical Zone: The Academic Analysis of Difference in 'the Island Peoples'," in Naoki Sakai, Brett de Bary, and Iyotani Toshio (eds), *Deconstructing Nationality*, Cornell East Asia Series 124, Ithaca, NY: Cornell University Press: 41–60.
Torrance, Richard (1994) *The Fiction of Tokuda Shūsei and the Emergence of Japan's New Middle Class*, London and Seattle, Wash.: London: University of Washington Press.
—— (1996) "Literacy and Modern Literature in the Izumo Region, 1880–1930," *Journal of Japanese Studies* 22 (2): 327–62.
Treat, John Whittier (1994) "Beheaded Emperors and the Absent Figure in Contemporary Japanese Literature," *PMLA* 109 (1): 100–15.
—— (1995) *Writing Ground Zero: Japanese Literature and the Atomic Bomb*, Chicago, Ill.: University of Chicago Press.
Tsubouchi Shōyō (1983) *Shōsetsu shinzui*, trans. Nanette Twine, Queensland: Queensland University Press.

Tsurumi, Patricia E. (1977) *Japanese Colonial Education in Taiwan, 1895–1945*, Cambridge, Mass.: Harvard University Press.
Tsushima Katsuyoshi (1990) *Shimao Toshio ron: Nichijōteki hinichijōteki no bungaku*, Osaka: Kaifūsha.
Uemura Tadao (ed.) (2002) *Okinawa no kioku/Nihon no rekishi*, Tokyo: Miraisha.
Urashima Etsuko (2003) "Okinawa Base Dooms Dugong," *Znet*. Online. Available HTTP: < http://www.zmag.org/content/showarticle.cfm?ItemID=2988 > (accessed 15 September 2007).
Urata Giwa (1992) *Kindai Okinawa to "minami,"* Ginowan: Roman shobō.
Urata Yoshikazu (1990) "Okinawa kindai/gendai bungaku kenkyū gaikan," in Okinawa bungaku zenshū henshū īnkai (eds), *Okinawa bungaku zenshū*, Vol. XX, Tokyo: Kokusho kankōkai: 329–36.
Vlastos, Stephen (ed.) (1998) *Mirror of Modernity: Invented Traditions of Modern Japan*, Berkeley, Calif.: University of California Press.
Wald, Alan (1992) "The Subaltern Speaks," *Monthly Review* 43 (11): 17–29.
Walker, Alice (1982) *The Color Purple*, New York: Washington Square.
Watanabe, Akio (1970) *The Okinawa Problem: A Chapter in Japan–U.S. Relations*, Melbourne: Melbourne University Press.
Weiner, Michael (ed.) (1997) *Japan's Minorities: The Illusion of Homogeneity*, London and New York: Routledge.
Wigen, Kären (1996) "Politics and Piety in Japanese Native-Place Studies: The Rhetoric of Solidarity in Shinano," *Positions: East Asia Critique*, 4 (3): 491–517.
Yamagusuku Seichū (1990) "Kosenshō," in Okinawa bungaku zenshū henshū īnkai (eds), *Okinawa bungaku zenshū*, Vol. VI, Tokyo: Kokusho kankōkai: 31–40.
—— (1991) "Ishigantō," *Okinawa kindai bungei sakuhinshū: shin Okinawa bungaku bessatsu*: 33–9.
—— (1993a) "Kunenbo," in Okinawa bungaku zenshū henshū īnkai (eds), *Okinawa bungaku zenshū*, Vol. VI, Tokyo: Kokusho kankōkai: 17–30.
—— (1993b) "Tsuruoka to iu otoko," in Okinawa bungaku zenshū henshū īnkai (eds), *Okinawa bungaku zenshū*, Vol. VI, Tokyo: Kokusho kankōkai: 6–16.
Yamazato Katsunori (1996) "Minami no zawameki, tasha no manazashi," *Kanazawa daigaku hyōron* 25: 56–64.
Yogi Seishō (1993a) "Tenmatsu," in Okinawa bungaku zenshū henshū īnkai (eds), *Okinawa bungaku zenshū*, Vol. VI, Tokyo: Kokusho kankōkai: 210–44.
—— (1993b) "Yōju," in Okinawa bungaku zenshū henshū īnkai (eds), *Okinawa bungaku zenshū*, Vol. VI, Tokyo: Kokusho kankōkai: 181–209.
Yonaha Keiko (1992) "'Shōfu'sei no kaidoku," *Tōyō Eiwa jogakuin tankidaigaku kenkyū kiyō*, 3: 1–14.
Yonetani, Julia (2000) "Ambiguous Traces and the Politics of Sameness: Placing Okinawa in Meiji Japan," *Japanese Studies* 20 (1): 15–31.
—— (2003) "Future 'Assets,' but at What Price? The Okinawan Initiative Debate," in Laura Hein and Mark Selden (eds), *Islands of Discontent*, Lanham, Md.: Rowman & Littlefield: 243–72.
Yoshimoto Takaaki (1989a) "Nantō ron," *Bungei* (fall): 245–65.
—— (1989b) "'Nantō ron' to Okinawa," *Shin Okinawa bungaku* 79: 16–100.
Zabilka, Gladys (1973) *Customs and Culture of Okinawa*, Tokyo: Charles E. Tuttle.
Zabus, Chantal (1991) *The African Palimpest: Indigenization of Language in the West African Europhone Novel*, Amsterdam and Atlanta, Ga.: Rodopi Press.

Index

Achebe, Chinua; writing style 68–69
Ahmad, Aijaz; Third World Theory 13–14; 184
Akutagawa Prize; *Child of Okinawa* (*Okinawa no shōnen*) (Higashi) 125; *The Cocktail Party* (*Kakuteru pātī*) (Ōshiro) 100; "Droplets" (*Suiteki*) (Medoruma) 130; *Pig's Revenge* (*Buta no mukui*) (Matayoshi) 126
allochronism 45
Anderson, Benedict 15; 45
Angst, Linda 144
Aono, Suekichi; dialect eradication debate 66
Arakaki, Mitoko 46; 91; 199; Arakawa, Akira; on new currency 180
art exhibitions; role of 117
Asahi News 90
Asō, Tarō 183

"The Banyan" (*Yojū*) (Yogi) 75–80
Battle of Okinawa (1945); textbook controversy 14–15
Bhabha, Homi K.; on subaltern identity 52; 54
Bhadra, Gautam; on subaltern identity 54
"The Birth of Life" (*Seikatsu no tanjō*) (Miyagi) 84–87
"Bones" (*Hone*) (Shima) 125
Brandt, Kim; on nationalism 66

"The Catch" (*Shīku*) (Ōe) 136–37
Child of Okinawa (*Okinawa no shōnen*) (Higashi) 125
Chinen, Seishin; use of language 132
Christy, Alan S.; on Okinawan identity 45; 118; on Yanagita 120–21
"Chronicle of a School of Fish" (*Gyogunki*) (Medoruma) 133–37
class divides 58–59
The Cocktail Party (*Kakuteru pātī*) (Ōshiro) 100–104
colonization 3–6
community; creating with language 196
Conversations in Okinawa (*Okinawa taiwa*) 20–21; *22*
Crescent Moon (*Chinzetzu yumiharizuki*) (Bakin) 116

Daniels, Patsy J. 213
A Dark Night's Passing (*Anya kōro*) (Shiga) 163
"Day of Shame" 124
Deleuze, Gilles; concept of minor literature 11; 172; 176–78; 182; on nomadic writing style 166–67; on subaltern identity 53
Dhomhnaill, Nuala Ní 198
dialect; eradication debate 64–69; 197–98; Higashi's use of 126; history 188; island language 12; 212; issue of 11–12; and language education 7; reemergence of 132; Takeuchi on 209; "Turtleback Tombs" (*Kamekōbaka*) (Ōshiro) 99; *see also* language
discrimination; "House of Peoples" (*Jinruikan*) exhibit 6; 23; Kushi's treatment of 71; theme of 180; *see also* inclusion
Dodd, Stephen 10
Dower, John; on "Day of Shame" 124
"Droplets" (*Suiteki*) (Medoruma) 141–48; *143*
DuBois, W. E. B. 4; 60–61

exhibitions; role of 117

Fabian, Johannes 45
Fanon, Frantz 187
"Fantasy Island" (*Panarinusuma gensō*) (Ōshiro) 108–14
Faulkner, William 14
female authors; postreversion period 128–29; *see also* Kushi, Fusako; Sakiyama, Tami
feminization of the islands 118
Field, Norma; criticism of "Turtleback Tombs" (*Kamekōbaka*) (Ōshiro) 93
Fifth Domestic Exposition for the Promotion of Industry (Osaka 1903) 6; 23
Foucault, Michel; on subaltern identity 53
Fujiki, Hayato; on militarization 51

Gabriel, Philip 207
Gerow, Aaron 9
Gima, Susumu; dialect eradication debate 67
"The Ginnemu Mansion" (*Ginnemu yashiki*) (Matayoshi) 126
Goldschmidt, Richard 44–45
Guattari, Félix; concept of minor literature 11; 172; 176–78; 182; on nomadic writing style 166–67
Guha, Ranajit; on subaltern identity 52

Hagiwara, Sakutarō; dialect eradication debate 66
Hartman, Geoffrey; on modernity 145; on public memory 142–44
Hassan, Ihab; *The Okinawa Literary Forum* (Naha 1996) 130
"healing islands" discourse 160–61
Heaney, Seamus; writing style 68
Higashi, Mineo; *Child of Okinawa* (*Okinawa no shōnen*) 125; influence on Sakiyama 159
Hino, Keizō; criticism of "Droplets" (*Suiteki*) 144; *The Okinawa Literary Forum* (Naha 1996) 130
Hirotsu, Kazuo; *The Wandering Ryukyuan* (*Samayoeru Ryūkyūjin*) 43–44; 55–62
history; theme of 180
"House of Peoples" (*Jinruikan*) exhibit 6; 23
Howell, David; on the Ainu 71
humanism 42

identity; silent characters 62; subaltern identity 52–55; theme of 181–82; visible markers of 59–61; weakness of 45
Iha, Fuyū 21
Iha, Getsujō; criticism of "Mandarin Oranges" (*Kunenbo*) 38–39; influence of 7–8; 32
Ikemiyagi, Sekihō; "Officer Ukuma" (*Ukuma Junsa*) 46–47; 47; use of language 180; writing style 67
imperial subjectification; effect of 15
inclusion; desire for 45; use of standard language 64; *see also* discrimination
"IndoYaponesia" (Yamada) 115
Ishigantō 189
Ishikawa, Takuboku 27
island language 12; 212; *see also* dialect
island life 118; 186; *see also* local color
Island of the Gods (*Kamishima*) (Ōshiro) 104–8
Ivy, Marilyn 208
Iwanami Press 9

Jameson, Fredric; Third World Theory 13–14
Japanese verse (*waka*) 25

Kafka, Franz; "The Metamorphosis" 166–67
Kano, Masanao 23
Kawabata, Yasunari; influence on Yogi 80
Kawamura, Minato; criticism of "Droplets" (*Suiteki*)148
Keene, Donald; on Hirotsu, Kazuo 55; on *Snow Country* (Kawabata) 1
Kuniyoshi, Shintetsu; criticism of *The Wandering Ryukyuan* (*Samayoeru Ryūkyūjin*) 56
Kuroi, Senji; criticism of "Droplets" (*Suiteki*)144–45
Kuroko, Kazuo; criticism of "Peace Street" (*Heiwa dōri*) (Medoruma) 138
Kushi, Fusako; "Memoirs of a Declining Ryukyuan Woman" (*Horobiyuku Ryūkyūjo no shuki*) 69–75; 70; use of language 180
Kyushu Art Festival Literary Prize (*Kyūshū geijutsusai bungakushō*) 128

"The Landscape of Language" ("Kotoba no fūkei") (Sakiyama) 174

language; creating community with 196; dual structure 25; eradication debate 197; island language 12; 212; new literary language 24–25; *see also* dialect; local color
language education; *Conversations in Okinawa (Okinawa taiwa)* 20–21; *22*; dialect eradication debate 64–69; encouragement of 131–32; and nationalism 180
Lebra, William P.; definition of *nirai kanai* 211; description of Okinawans 196; turtleback tombs 202
literary forms; emergence of 25–27
literary prizes; Akutagawa Prize 100; 125–26; 130; Kyushu Art Festival Literary Prize (*Kyūshū geijutsusai bungakushō*) 128; 131; *Okinawa Times* 127; *Ryukyu News* 127
Lloyd, David 10
local color; desire for 18; meaning of 17; in speech 65; use of 10

MacKenzie, John 59–60
"A Man Named Tsuruoka" (*Tsuruoka to iu otoko*) (Yamagusuku) 28–30
"Mandarin Oranges" (*Kunenbo*) (Yamagusuku) 34–41
Marukawa, Tetsushi; criticism of "Passage across the Sea" (*Suijō ōkan*) (Sakiyama) 161; on Sakiyama 173
Matayoshi, Eiki; critical attention 131; *Pig's Revenge* (*Buta no mukui*) 126; "The Ginnemu Mansion" (*Ginnemu yashiki*)126; "The Wild Boar that George Shot" (*Jōji ga shasatsu shita inoshishi*) 126–27
Medoruma, Shun; "Chronicle of a School of Fish" (*Gyogunki*) 133–37; "Droplets" (*Suiteki*) 141–48; *143*; early years 131–33; on identity 181–82; literary prizes 128; Molasky on 132; Nakahodo on 142; "Peace Street" (*Heiwa dōri to nazukerareta machi wo aruku*) 137–41; So on 131; "Spirit Recalling" (*Mabuigumi*) 148–52; Suzuki on 145; Takeuchi on 209; "Tree of Butterflies" (*Gunchō no ki*) 152–57; writing style 8
Memmi, Albert; on nature of master-slave relations 50
"Memoirs of a Declining Ryukyuan Woman" (*Horobiyuku Ryūkyūjo no shuki*) (Kushi) 69–75; *70*

Index 231

"The Metamorphosis" (Kafka) 166–67
Miki, Takeshi; on Yaponesia 115
militarization; Fujiki on 51
military conscription 23
military presence 13–14; 183–84
minority fiction 11; Okinawan fiction as 10–11
Mitchell, Timothy; on art exhibitions 117
Miyagi, Sō; "The Birth of Life" (*Seikatsu not tanjō*) 84–87; use of language 180; writing style 67
modernity; Hartman on 145
Molasky, Michael; criticism of *Child of Okinawa* (*Okinawa no shōnen*) (Higashi) 125; on Medoruma 132
Molino, Michael; on Heaney 68
Montague, John; *The Okinawa Literary Forum* (Naha 1996) 130
Movement for Freedom and People's Rights (*jiyū minken undō*) 23
Murai, Osamu; on the feminization of the islands 118; on Yanagita 121; 192
Mushakōji, Saneatsu 42
mute characters 62

Nagadō, Eikichi 129
Nakahodo, Masanori; establishment of Okinawan literature 19; on Medoruma 142
Nakamatsu, Yashu; criticism of "Droplets" (*Suiteki*) 148
Nakamura, Murao; dialect eradication debate 66
national allegory theory 11–13; 61–62
national language policies. *See* language education
National Spiritual Mobilization Campaign; "Standard Language Enforcement Movement" 65
nationalism 65–66; 115–16; 180; *see also* standard language
nature; and nostalgia 87–88
new currency; Arakawa on 180
New Okinawa Literature (*Shin Okinawa bungaku*) 92; *94*; 129–30
New Sensationalist School (*Shinkankakuha*) 63
new style poetry (*shintaishi*) 26
newspapers; postwar literary climate 90–91
Nobori, Shomu; on local color 33
Noma, Seiji 27
nomadic writing style 166–67

nostalgia; "Memoirs of a Declining Ryukyuan Woman" (*Horobiyuku Ryūkyūjo no shuki*) (Kushi) 69–75; 70; and nature 87–88; "The Banyan" (*Yōju*) (Yogi) 74–75; "The Birth of Life" (*Seikatsu no tanjō*) (Miyagi) 84–87; "The Particulars" (*Tenmatsu*) (Yogi) 80–84

Ōe, Kenzaburō; reversion movement 124; "The Catch" (*Shīku*) 136–37
"Officer Ukuma" (*Ukuma Junsa*) (Ikemiyagi) 43–44; 46–54; 47
Okamoto, Keitoku; dialect eradication debate 67; dual structure of language 25; on effect of imperial subjectification 15; on Okinawan literature 16; 19; 159; postreversion period 130
Okinawa; colonization 3–6; impressions of 118; military presence 13; "Okinawa problem" 4–6; 183; postwar literary climate 90–91; prefecture status 5; 124–25; Taishō era 44–45
Okinawa Bureau of Education; "Standard Language Enforcement Movement" 65–66
"Okinawa Initiative" 153
Okinawa Prefecture Student Association (*Okinawa kenjin gakusei kai*); criticism of "Memoirs of a Declining Ryukyuan Woman" (*Horobiyuku Ryūkyūjo no shuki*) (Kushi) 69
Okinawa Times; literary prizes 127
Okinawa Youth Alliance; response to *The Wandering Ryukyuan* (*Samayoeru Ryūkyūjin*) 55
The Okinawa Literary Forum (Naha 1996) 130
Okinesia 116
Ōno, Takayuki; criticism of "Rocking and Rolling" (*Yurateiku yuriteiku*) 212
Origin (Genten) coffee shop *173*
"The Origin of Muiani" (*Muiani yuraiki*) (Sakiyama) 173–78
Orikuchi, Shinobu 44
Ōshiro, Tatsuhiro; Akutagawa Prize 100; ambition of 7–8; career of 91–92; 202; *The Cocktail Party* (*Kakuteru pātī*) 100–104; criticism of "Memoirs of a Declining Ryukyuan Woman" (*Horobiyuku Ryūkyūjo no shuki*) (Kushi) 74; "Fantasy Island" (*Panarinusuma gensō*)108–14; *Island of the Gods* (*Kamishima*) 104–8; "Turtleback Tombs" (*Kamekōbaka*) 92–99
Ōta, Masahide 13; 191
Ōta, Ryōhaku 91

"The Particulars" (*Tenmatsu*) (Yogi) 80–84
"Parting" (*Danen*) (Wakazō) 26–27
"Passage across the Sea" (*Suijō ōkan*) (Sakiyama) 131; 160–67
Peace Street (Heiwa dōri) modern day description 210
"Peace Street" (*Heiwa dōri to nazukerareta machi o aruku*) (Medoruma) 137–41
"people-centrism" (*minponshugi*) 42
Philomela, transformation of 18
Pig's Revenge (*Buta no mukui*) (Matayoshi) 126; 130
poetry 188; new style (*shintaishi*) 26; Ryukyuan verse (*ryūka*) 25; 188
postreversion period 124–31; postwar literary climate 90–91; poverty 43–45
power; balance of 101–2
Prefectural Peace Memorial Museum 152–53
prefecture status of Okinawa 5; 124–25
prizes; Akutagawa Prize 100; 125–26; 130; Kyushu Art Festival Literary Prize (*Kyūshū geijutsusai bungakushō*) 128; 131; *Okinawa Times* 127; *Ryukyu News* 127
prose fiction; emergence of 26
public memory; Hartman on 142–44

regional literature 9–10
reversion movement 124
revival of arts (*bungei fukkō*) 33
Roberson, James 209
"Rocking and Rolling" (*Yurateiku yuriteiku*) (Sakiyama) 174; 212; 215
rural life 43–45; 81–83
Rushdie, Salman; writing style 68
Ryudai Literature (*Ryūdai bungaku*) 92
Ryukyu 4–6; 19–20; 81–83; 187; *Ryukyu News*; literary prizes 127
Ryukyuan verse (*ryūka*) 25; 188
Ryukyunesia 116

Saegusa, Kazuko; criticism of women authors 128–29
Sai, Yōichi; film version of *Pig's Revenge* 130

Sakiyama, Tami; critical attention 131; Higashi's influence 159; on identity 181–82; Marukawa on 173; Origin (Genten) coffee shop *173*; "The Origin of Muiani" (*Muiani yuraiki*) 173–78; "Passage across the Sea" (*Suijō ōkan*) 131; 160–67; "Rocking and Rolling" (*Yurateiku yuriteiku*) 174; 212; 215; "A Tale between Wind and Water" (*Fūsuitan*) 167–73; "The Landscape of Language" ("Kotoba no fūkei") 174; Tsushima on 172; use of language 8–9; 15–16; "A Wild Dance with Island Words" ('Shimakotoba' de kachāshī) 166–67; "Writing the Island" ("Shima o kaku to iu koto") 165
San Francisco Peace Treaty (1951) 124
Satohara, Akira; criticism of "Turtleback Tombs" (*Kamekōbaka*) (Ōshiro) 99
Sekine, Kenji; on Yaponesia 115
Serizawa, Shunsuke; on Shimao 119
Shiga, Naoya; *A Dark Night's Passing* (*Anya kōro*) 163
Shima, Tsuyoshi; "Bones" (*Hone*) 125
Shimao, Toshio; cultural representation 8; *Theory of Yaponesia* (*Yaponeshia ron*) 114–23; use of local color 33; on Yaponesia 192
Shinjō, Ikuo; criticism of "The Origin of Muiani" (*Muiani yuraiki*) (Sakiyama) 176; criticism of "A Tale between Wind and Water" (*Fūsuitan*) (Sakiyama) 171
silent characters 62
Smits, Gregory; on village life 186
Snow Country (*Yukiguni*) (Kawabata) 1
So, Kyonshiku; on Medoruma 131
social injustice 74
"Song of Philomela" 18
"Spirit Recalling" (*Mabuigumi*) (Medoruma) 148–52
Spivak, Gayatri Chakravorty; on subaltern identity 52–53
standard language; desire for inclusion 64; encouragement of 131–32; prewar use 63–64; "Standard Language Enforcement Movement" 65; writers' response to 67–69; *see also* language education
"Standard Language Enforcement Movement" 65

"Stone Talisman" (*Ishigantō*) (Yamagusuku) 30–32
student strike 24
subaltern identity 52–55; 59–61; 194
subjectification; effect of 15
Sugiyama, Heisuke; dialect eradication debate 66
suicide 203–4
Suzuki, Tomoyuki; criticism of "Passage across the Sea" (*Suijō ōkan*) (Sakiyama) 161; on Medoruma 145

Takara, Ben; on Yaponesia 115
Takara, Kurayoshi; criticism of "Fantasy Island" (*Panarinusuma gensō*) (Ōshiro) 113
Takeuchi, Mitsuhiro; on Medoruma 209
Takizawa, Bakin 116
"A Tale between Wind and Water" (*Fūsuitan*) (Sakiyama) 167–73
textbook controversy 14–15
Theory of Yaponesia (*Yaponeshia ron*) (Shimao) 114–23
Third World Theory 13–14; 61–62; 183–84
Tolstoy, Leo 42
Tomiyama, Ichirō 211
Treat, John Whittier 12
"Tree of Butterflies" (*Gunchō no ki*) (Medoruma) 152–57
Tsubouchi, Shōyō 19
Tsushima, Katsuyoshi; on Yaponesia 115
Tsushima, Yūko; on Sakiyama 172
turtleback tombs; current numbers 202
"Turtleback Tombs" (*Kamekōbaka*) (Ōshiro) 92–99

Uesugi 187
United States Civil Administration of the Ryukyus (USCAR) 90; 92; 201
Uozumi, Setsuro; criticism of "Stone Talisman" (*Ishigantō*) 32
Uruma News 90
U.S. military presence 13–14
Ushi; name of 190

village life 43–45; 81–83; 186

Wakazō ("Parting") 26–27
The Wandering Ryukyuan (*Samayoeru Ryūkyūjin*) (Hirotsu) 43–44; 55–56

"The Wild Boar that George Shot" (*Jōji ga shasatsu shita inoshishi*) (Matayoshi) 126–27
"A Wild Dance with Island Words" ('Shimakotoba' de kachāshī) (Sakiyama) 166–67
women authors; postreversion period 128–29; *see also* Kushi, Fusako; Sakiyama, Tami
writing, as a profession 28
"Writing the Island" (*Shima o kaku to iu koto*) (Sakiyama) 165

Yamada, Munechika 115
Yamagusuku, Seichū; "A Man Named Tsuruoka" (*Tsuruoka to iu otoko*) 28–30; career of 40; criticism of 38–39; early career 27–28; "Mandarin Oranges" (*Kunenbo*) 34–41; "Stone Talisman" (*Ishigantō*) 30–32; surname 186; use of language 180; writing style 67
Yanagi, Muneyoshi; dialect eradication debate 64–69
Yanagita, Kunio; Christy on 120–21; dialect eradication debate 66; Murai on 192; religious convictions 197; on the Taishō era 44
Yaponesia; invention of 114–16; 205; Shimao on 192
Yasuda, Yojūrō; dialect eradication debate 66
Yeats, William Butler; influence of 33
Yogi, Seishō; influence of Kawabata 80; in postwar newspapers 91; "The Banyan" (*Yōju*) 75–80; "The Particulars" (*Tenmatsu*) 80–84; use of language 180; writing style 67
Yonaha, Keiko; criticism of Nagadō 129
Yonetani, Julia 124–25; 153
Yosano, Akiko 28
Yosano, Tekkan 26
Yoshimoto, Takaaki 115
Yoshino, Sakuzō; idea of "people-centrism" (*minponshugi*) 42
yuta; role of 200